Using
Technology
to Unlock
Musical
Creativity

USING
TECHNOLOGY
TO UNLOCK
MUSICAL
CREATIVITY

SCOTT WATSON

OXFORD
UNIVERSITY PRESS

OXFORD
UNIVERSITY PRESS

Oxford University Press, Inc., publishes works that further
Oxford University's objective of excellence
in research, scholarship, and education.

Oxford   New York
Auckland   Cape Town   Dar es Salaam   Hong Kong   Karachi
Kuala Lumpur   Madrid   Melbourne   Mexico City   Nairobi
New Delhi   Shanghai   Taipei   Toronto

With offices in
Argentina   Austria   Brazil   Chile   Czech Republic   France   Greece
Guatemala   Hungary   Italy   Japan   Poland   Portugal   Singapore
South Korea   Switzerland   Thailand   Turkey   Ukraine   Vietnam

Published by Oxford University Press, Inc.
198 Madison Avenue, New York, New York 10016

www.oup.com

Oxford is a registered trademark of Oxford University Press.

Library of Congress Cataloging-in-Publication Data
Watson, Scott, 1962–
Using technology to unlock musical creativity / Scott Watson.
     p.   cm.
Includes bibliographical references and index.
ISBN 978-0-19-974276-9 (alk. paper) — ISBN 978-0-19-974277-6 (alk. paper)
1. Music—Instruction and study—Technological innovations. 2. Music and technology. I. Title.
MT1.W39 2011
780.7—dc22   2010034071

Web examples (marked in text with) are available online at www.oup.com/us/musicalcreativity
Access with username Music1 and password Book5983
For more information on Oxford Web Music, visit www.oxfordwebmusic.com

PREFACE

MY INTEREST IN USING TECHNOLOGY in a creativity-based approach to music learning developed over many years. Early in my teaching career, I tended to fall back on pedagogical models I experienced when I was a student. These generally did not incorporate creative activity. This is fairly common among all young teachers, and frankly I absorbed some great stuff along the way since I had many fine music teachers. As a composer, however, I have been interested in creativity for some time. I just didn't see the connection at first between what motivated and facilitated my creativity and my work with students.

It was the concurrence of three things that moved me in the direction of incorporating principles of creativity-based learning. First, I observed that my students—with or without my urging—were naturally creative. Many beginning band students would bring in songs they had written using the first few notes presented in their method book. Their eyes would light up when I helped them typeset their music with notation software, showing them how the software can playback what they had written. One sixth-grade flute student brought me in a self-made CD, recorded and produced with multitrack software at home, titled *Vicki's Greatest Hits*. A middle-school tuba player wrote a song about ocean pollution for a social studies project; all he needed from me was a little help producing it using GarageBand. A colleague from a neighboring town established a popular after-school "recording club" and the tunes they were producing were surprisingly well done. And on and on. Just look online at sites like YouTube if you want to see for yourself the types of creativity, especially musical, that kids engage in all the time without the urging or formal guidance of their teachers. It is truly amazing.

Second, I began to recognize the allure and power for music education of the technology tools I was using to create music myself. I dove head first into using Finale music notation software in my composing, fascinated by its many useful features. I swelled with pride when I presented a professional-looking score to a client, even more so when I heard the work's premiere. The time it took to learn the program was a small price for all that. Did I resent the hours I spent producing music with Digital Performer for a project? Actually . . . *no*. I remember years ago working on incidental music for a play being produced in the Philadelphia area. I had to write and produce about 45 minutes of music in only about three weeks. Working in my office, I would look at the clock and realize that I had spent three hours perfecting a 30-second cue! I thoroughly enjoyed the work, even when it got tedious, knowing the pride I would feel when others heard my music. Of course, my wife would always bring me back to earth with remarks such as, "You spent all night on that?" Eventually I realized that my students would respond to creative activity, using these and other technology tools, in the same enthusiastic way.

The third factor that moved me toward using creative projects in my music teaching was simply the professional confidence and openness to risk taking that comes from experience. When you lead students in creative activities, at least at first, you feel like you are a trapeze artist flying without a net. There are many reasons for this, including the fact that there are not a lot of models to follow and that teachers are unsure how to assess a student's creative output (both of which are addressed in this book). When I first decided to have my high school Music Production class produce a holiday CD (write the arrangements; record, program, and mix the tracks; and market the finished product), it was a little scary. I had no idea if they could actually pull it off! I had seen a couple colleagues around the country do something similar, though, and the results were great. But would my kids come through and put forth the effort required to produce a CD of which we could be proud (or at least not embarrass me)? I set off with my students on a month-long adventure that has now become a much-anticipated annual event for the class. After teaching and proving myself for some time in the same school district, I could stop worrying so much about failure and take the educational chances necessary for creativity-based learning.

Some wonderfully expressive musical creations by my students as a result of this shift are included as examples in this book and on the companion website (www.oup.com/us/musicalcreativity). I hope you will take the time to examine these as they serve a valuable role in bringing life to the main tenets of the book.

Seeing the natural creative bent of so many students, realizing the allure and power of music technology tools, and gaining the confidence to try some new approaches in my teaching have led me to some of the most rewarding teaching moments in my career thus far. Of all the reasons you will read in this book for employing creative projects that feature technology, the one that drives me most is the satisfying reaction I see in the eyes of my students when engaged in such activity.

ACKNOWLEDGMENTS

BACK IN 1999 when I was wrapping up my doctoral degree in composition, having just written as my dissertation project an almost 20-minute *Concerto for Trumpet and Orchestra* and an accompanying 60-page "monograph" to explain the work, I remember telling my wife, Kim, "That was one of the hardest things I've ever had to do." Having spent the last year assembling this book on a technology-centered, creativity-based approach to music learning, I now have one more thing to add to that list. I never could have completed either task without the help and support of many special people.

I would like to thank Oxford University Press for believing in this project, and my editor, Norman Hirschy, for his guidance and advocacy. I appreciate my primary employer over the last quarter-century, the Parkland School District (Allentown, PA), for providing an environment in which I could grow, and take risks, as an educator. Many administrators and colleagues have been both encouraging and instructive. I appreciate the university music programs and their directors, who have given me the opportunity to teach courses to in-service and pre-service music teachers, developing and sharing many of the ideas in this book (Villanova University, George Pinchock; Central Connecticut State University, Drs. Pam Perry and Charles Menoche; and Philadelphia Biblical University, Dr. Paul Isensee). TI:ME (Technology for Music Educators) has played a prominent role in opening my eyes to the possibilities for using technology with students. I am indebted to, and value the friendship of, inspiring music teachers such as TI:ME's founder and former president, Dr. Thomas Rudolph, current President, Amy Burns, and Vice President, Dr. James Frankel. Other professional colleagues who have so generously shared their work products, anecdotes, web materials, and advice used in this book include Brian Balmages (composer and editor, FJH Publications), Nancy Beitler (Southern Lehigh Middle School, Coopersburg, PA), Dr. Rick Dammers (Rowan University, NJ), Barbara Freedman (Greenwich High School, CT), Jill Crissy-Kemmerer (Parkland School District, PA), Dr. Sandi McLeod (Vermont MIDI Project), Dr. Joseph Pisano (Grove City College, PA), Wayne Splettstoeszer (Torrington High School,

CT), Vietta Taylor (Springhurst Elementary School, NY), and Travis Weller (Mercer Area Middle-Senior High School, PA). I have been greatly influenced by, and am grateful for, my friend and composition teacher at Temple University, Dr. Maurice Wright. Maurice, a witty, talented composer of contemporary art music, is also a pioneer in creative multimedia works and online music instruction; he has left a lasting impression.

I could never have conceived to write this book, or done so convincingly, without the help of dozens of current and former students whose creative output—in their parlance—"blows me away." Thanks to each for allowing me to share examples of their wonderful musical creativity in this book and on the companion website. I wish there was room for even more.

Finally, my greatest thanks go to my family—my wife, Kim, my son, Ben, and my daughter, Abby—who for hours upon hours during the past year sacrificed doing without their husband and father in order to give me the time to plan and execute this book. Each possesses a unique creativity—both musical and otherwise—around which I love to be, so the sacrifice was mutual. I am truly blessed.

CONTENTS

x

ABOUT THE COMPANION WEBSITE

A COMPANION WEBSITE has been created for this book. The URL for the site is:

www.oup.com/us/musicalcreativity

Here you will find easy links to all the major web resources mentioned, files to support various lesson plans, and sound and movie clip examples of most of the projects described in the book (marked through by this symbol), created by actual students. Reading about the creative projects detailed in this book is only the beginning. For the "whole story" I encourage you to take the time to check out these wonderful student sample files, which give life to the book's written descriptions. The creative output of students themselves makes the case for using creative projects in music education better than any rationale I can provide. Access with username Music1 and password Book5983.

PART I

PHILOSOPHICAL AND PEDAGOGICAL UNDERPINNINGS

CHAPTER 1
TECHNOLOGY, MUSICAL CREATIVITY, AND THIS BOOK

INTRODUCTION

IT HAS NEVER BEEN EASIER or more fun for your students to compose, improvise, arrange, and produce music-related projects. Why? Because of developments in music technology. In the last several decades, with the advent of personal computing, electronic musical instruments, the MIDI (musical instrument digital interface) software and hardware protocol, the evolution of the Internet, and an explosion of niche software authoring, among other things, teachers and their students in music classes and ensembles have more tools at their disposal than ever for expressing musical creativity. What's more, two trends have brought these great technology resources within the reach of music educators who might not have otherwise been able to take advantage of them. First, program designers have been making the technical side of the technology more and more invisible so users can get at the creative side more easily, without distraction. Second, more and more freeware, shareware, open source, and web applications (online programs) are being created and offered at little or no cost. Indeed, whereas music educators once had to purchase software or, at best, download freeware or shareware applications for music notation and multi-track recording, today they can find web-based applications to accomplish these tasks at no cost anywhere they can get online. Add to that the rise of online resellers dealing in discounted and/or used music gear and you will find that the cost of technology is less of an obstacle than ever.

Leading students in meaningful creative activities must go beyond simply providing helpful technology tools or even offering instruction in using those tools. Thousands have a working knowledge of computer music notation software, such as Finale and Sibelius, or music production programs, such as Pro-Tools. Does that make them all composers or music producers? In one sense, yes, and in another sense, no. Some would say that only a handful of these "operators" write or produce music artistically. Others could point to the subjective nature of art and to how vocational training is rarely the goal of music education anyway. Regardless, creative musical activities provide the perfect environment for grooming the kinds of aesthetic sensibilities that should accompany technical knowledge in our music students at all levels.

ABOUT THIS BOOK

In this book I share with you a pedagogical approach, many project ideas and technology tools, and some assessment tools that can help foster musical creativity. Some of the project ideas include podcasts, song arrangements, student-produced CDs, improvisation activities, notated compositions that cannot miss, and much more. On the one hand, the technology is integral to the approach I present. On the other hand, it is not about the technology itself as much as using it to draw out, assemble, and document students' creative ideas.

Audience

The primary focus of this book is classroom and elective music (general music, music theory, music production, etc.) at all levels, where creative activities and projects can be used to accomplish curricular goals now being met more conventionally. Music teachers looking for solid reasons to move toward developing the use of technology in their programs will find what they are looking for here. These teachers can begin using some of the technology tools and curricular ideas presented almost immediately since the technology is so accessible—at little or no cost and intuitively easy to use. Those less at home using music technology may want to first try just one or two of the many lesson ideas presented in this book. On the other hand, this book has much for teachers looking for fresh ways to use the technology tools they already have. These teachers might want to get more from their students using various music technologies, or perhaps just want to explore an alternative, creativity-based approach. Perhaps you are one of the growing numbers of music educators turning to a creativity-based approach in some small or more comprehensive way. Most of the lessons stand alone and can be inserted into an existing curriculum, and chapter 17 puts forth a complete course curriculum as a model. This book can also help pre-service music educators frame their own approach to music teaching and the role creativity might play in the learning process.

Despite the book's main focus, it has applications for instrumental and choral music teachers as well. Obviously band, chorus, and orchestra directors are primarily preoccupied with ensemble rehearsals, sectional lessons, and the administrative chores that constitute so many hours of their teaching week. Even still, there may be times when the demands of an upcoming performance are not so pressing during which these educators might engage their students in a creative activity that helps accomplish one or more of the MENC (National Association for Music Education) National Standards for Music Education not normally addressed. In early January, right after the winter concerts but before preparations for the spring concert have begun, students could work on composing variations to a theme . . . and then perform them. Students participating in a summer band program might get to choose electives in which they improvise or compose as well. If nothing else, often even band, chorus, and orchestra directors find themselves teaching an elective music course or leading an independent study for which the ideas in this book can be valuable.

Adaptability

The creative projects presented in part II of this book are extremely flexible and adaptable depending on grade level, available technology, and the experience, comfort, and confidence with technology of the teacher and students. For instance, an activity that uses loops[1] as building blocks for a lesson on form and arranging with elementary-age students might involve the teacher facilitating his or her class using a single computer at the front of the class. With the teacher's help, students select loops that complement one another and arrange them vertically (texture) and horizontally (form, such as A–B–A). After making up movements to correspond with the loops they have chosen, they perform the movements as they hear the loops play back. Students in a middle-school general class, working alone, might use a web-based multitrack music production application[2] in their school's computer lab (and home) to create loop arrangements that demonstrate some aspect of musical form or texture. Students in a high school elective music class might work in pairs using the program GarageBand in a small music technology lab or computer cluster, export their finished work as MP3 audio files, and then post these to a class wiki[3] for feedback. As you can see, even this one loop arranging lesson idea has many possibilities to make it suitable for almost any teaching scenario.

For most of the project ideas presented in this book, all one needs is familiarity with using a personal computer; for some very effective lesson plans and projects, no specialized software or hardware knowledge is needed at all. It is my hope that, as you read, you will discover some great project ideas that you can borrow either "right out of the box" or with just a little tweaking for your teaching situation. Adding creativity to your pedagogical repertoire, facilitated by some appealing technology tools, will allow both you and your students to see a different facet of your musical selves.

1. *Loops* are short, musical gestures whose repetition is facilitated by music production software. Most loops involve recordings (audio) or sequences (MIDI performance data) of rhythm instruments (percussion, bass, guitar, etc.) performing some groove element. The tempo and pitch (if applicable) of loops may be easily adjusted using the host music production software.

2. *Web-based applications*, part of a new Internet paradigm often referred to as Web 2.0 or cloud computing, are programs that run on the World Wide Web via a user's browser and are often free and easy/intuitive to use.

3. A *wiki* is a website that allows multiple users to create pages easily (with no specialized web design skill), contribute and update content, and interact by posting to a discussion area.

EIGHT PRINCIPLES FOR UNLOCKING MUSICAL CREATIVITY

A set of eight teacher-tested principals for successfully drawing out student creativity constitutes the heart of this book. These principles work well for shepherding students along in the process of composing, arranging, and producing music and music-related projects. Presented and fully explained in chapters 3–10, these principles are as follows:

1. Allow students to share themselves.
2. Offer compelling examples to imitate and inspire.
3. Employ parameters and limitations that remove distractions and help students focus.
4. Remove parameters and limitations that stifle creativity and lead to contrived expression.
5. Facilitate improvisation.
6. Engage in coaching interaction.
7. Foster opportunities for feedback and critique.
8. Employ performance and recital.

This book presents many lesson plans that illustrate effective ways to implement these principles. You will find that the Eight Principles offer a wide variety of application for music teachers delivering curriculum at all levels—none are strategies for only elementary or only secondary music instruction. Some of the principles need detailed explanation along with examples in order to really understand how they make a difference. Others are pretty straightforward, though even these can be mined for their rich pedagogical resources.

The principles are distinct in that they are aimed at unlocking, releasing, and shepherding the creativity I believe is inside most every student but yet, for a variety of reasons, may be hard to draw out. By incorporating these principles into the creative lesson plans or projects presented here, or those of your own, I am confident you will experience a higher level of student and teacher motivation and reward. I also believe you will be impressed by the creative products turned out by your students of any age or level.

Drawn from Experience

These principles were developed over many years using technology for creative content generation in K–12 teaching. Having worked with students on creative projects for some time now, in a variety of music teaching scenarios at every level from elementary through university, I have had the opportunity to try many methods aimed at drawing forth students' creativity. Some of these approaches surprised even me in their resounding success, while others failed to yield the effect I imagined and had to be refined or discarded. I have also had the benefit of knowing many creative colleagues teaching music with technology at schools all over the United States whose work (teaching and writing) has informed and inspired me.

Supported in Writing and Research on Creativity

Despite their pragmatic and practical development, my Eight Principles are addressed and supported by writing and emerging research on creativity as well. One well-thought-out book that presents a thorough approach to teaching composition—a major area of musical creativity—is Michele Kaschub and Janice Smith's *Minds on Music*.[4] So many of Kaschub and Smith's conclusions match up with my own teaching experience.

Another book that addresses creativity strongly as a component of its overall approach to music education is Jackie Wiggins's *Teaching for Musical Understanding*. Positing that students' "concepts of music are constructed through experiences with music"—that is, *doing* music—Wiggins advocates performing, listening to, and *creating* music as a means of developing a "richer, denser, and more interconnected" understanding of music.[5] I especially like Wiggins's description of teaching music through problem solving. Her discussion of this approach with reference to composition leads her to many of the issues highlighted in my Eight Principles.

Perhaps so few have tackled the topic of composition, let alone other types of creativity, comprehensively in music education is because of its subjective nature. There is a body of research in musical creativity—some more substantial, but some limited in scope—waiting to be digested and presented in books such as Kaschub and Smith's. Of those resources that do deal with a creativity-based approach to music education, however, few if any focus specifically on using technology.

Looking more broadly at models and resources for teaching creativity in general education, one finds excellent guides, such as Robert Sternberg and Wendy Williams's *How to Develop Student Creativity*.[6] Although not written specifically for *musical* creativity, I have found many excellent applications for

4. Michele Kaschub and Janice Smith, *Minds on Music* (Lanham, MD: Rowman and Littlefield Education in partnership with MENC, 2009).

5. Jackie Wiggins, *Teaching for Musical Understanding* (New York: McGraw-Hill, 2001), 26–27. Wiggins develops and describes applications for this *constructivist* view of music education throughout her book.

6. Robert J. Sternberg and Wendy M. Williams, *How to Develop Student Creativity* (Alexandria, VA: Association for Supervision and Curriculum Development, 1996). Although Sternberg and Williams address academic creativity rather than musical creativity, many of their findings have applications for music making.

teaching music among the book's tenets and strategies. I hope we see more writing—from both practical and research perspectives—in this area as more stakeholders in music education discover its worth.

Other Themes of the Book

Along with the presentation of the Eight Principles for Unlocking Musical Creativity, some of the major themes of this book include the following:

1. Delivering a philosophical and pedagogical underpinning for engaging in creative projects with students.
2. Discussing many effective technology-centered, creative projects for use in various music education scenarios (general/classroom music, elective music classes, instrumental/choral music).
3. Description for using several core music technologies (waveform editing, multitrack recording, notation, and instructional software, and more) to design and complete creative projects in support of curricular goals and the MENC National Standards for Music Education.
4. Discussing and modeling effective assessment tools for use with student creative projects.

Creative Projects Support the MENC National Standards for Music Education

The lessons in part II are linked to the MENC national standards and demonstrate how creative projects using technology are well suited to support these standards.[7] For the purposes of reference, the MENC National Standards for Music Education are as follows:

1. Singing, alone and with others, a varied repertoire of music.
2. Performing on instruments, alone and with others, a varied repertoire of music.
3. Improvising melodies, variations, and accompaniments.
4. Composing and arranging music within specified guidelines.
5. Reading and notating music.
6. Listening to, analyzing, and describing music.

7. See MENC's website: http://www.menc.org/resources/view/national-standards-for-music-education.

7. Evaluating music and music performances.

8. Understanding relationships between music, the other arts, and disciplines outside the arts.

9. Understanding music in relation to history and culture.

Standards 1 and 2 deal with performing music; principle 8 urges that creative projects be shared with an audience in all manner of ways. Standards 3 and 4 deal with improvising, composing, and arranging music; principles 3–6 address many aspects of the act of creating via improvisation, arranging, composition, and producing music and music-related content. Music reading and writing, addressed in standard 5, are often part of both creating and performing projects. Standards 6 and 7, which deal with students reacting to music and musical performances, are addressed in principle 7, where feedback and criticism are key. Finally, many of the creative projects described in part II of this book involve making connections both in and out of music, the crux of standards 8 and 9. For instance, a podcast might share information about an assigned composer or a favorite performing artist in words and sound clips. The "New Clothes for an Old Tune" project from chapter 14 involves examining the advent of music synthesis in Wendy Carlos's recording *Switched-On Bach*, as well as merging traditional (Baroque or Classical) and contemporary popular music elements. One of the video-scoring project ideas involves creating a soundtrack to a series of visual art images (such as selected French Impressionist paintings).

A TWO-PRONGED APPROACH

The two parts of this book mirror a two-pronged approach to the topic of using technology to unlock musical creativity.

Pedagogical and Philosophical Foundation

The first prong, rooted in the set of Eight Principles mentioned above, is pedagogical and philosophical. This part of the book describes an educational philosophy and a methodology or pedagogical style. The philosophical premise is that there is value in having students produce music-based creative content in music courses similar to the way that there is value in having students write creatively in language arts courses. Just as language arts teachers routinely supplement teaching reading with creative writing (stories, essays, poems, etc.), so should music teachers supplement learning *about* music with both kinds of music *making*: performing *and creating*. Veteran music teacher and music education technology specialist Dr. Thomas Rudolph reveals that his teaching has become more project oriented over the years:

I realize that when students work on individual or group projects, they tend to put more of themselves into it than if they are passively listening to me, even if I am giving my best lecture. I use projects to engage students and give them an opportunity to perform, rather than sit back and listen or react. While I include listening in almost every lesson, it is not the primary focus. I would rather students put their own stamp on their own work.[8]

Composing, a high form of integrated learning that we should work to develop with our students, is the most obvious form of musical creativity. As you will see, musical creativity can encompass much more than just composing. Improvisation, discussed in chapter 7, is a form of creative musical expression in its own right but also figures largely in the compositional process. Standards 3 and 4 of the MENC National Standards for Music Education emphasize both:

Standard 3: *Improvising* melodies, variations, and accompaniments.
Standard 4: *Composing* and *arranging* music within specified guidelines.

Classroom music courses such as general music, music theory, and music production should include a balanced presentation of musical concepts and application of those ideas in making music (performing and creating).

Practical Usefulness of Music Technology

In the second prong, I hope to demonstrate practical ways that today's music technology can be a dynamic aid in unlocking the authentic musical creativity inside every student. In part II of the book, I provide almost 30 detailed example lesson plans to show how technology can be a vital key to unlocking creativity from within music students of all backgrounds. It certainly was for me.

Every student is both blessed and limited by their musical experience. I began studying trumpet in the fourth grade, took private lessons from the sixth grade on, and ended up a trumpet major while pursuing my music education degree as an undergraduate. I began piano only in the spring of my high school senior year (basically to prepare for my college entrance audition), and yet because of this late start I am much better at pop/jazz improvisation on keyboard than on trumpet (I am also much worse at traditional piano reading). Some students, for instance, those who have had years of piano or flute lessons, may be ready to dive right into composing melodies or entire multipart pieces with notation software. But even these may be limited by their experience. A pop/folk guitarist unable to read music may be much more at home with song writing than an accomplished clarinetist who can read music. Guitarists, however, working

8. John Kuzmich, "A Conversation With Tom Rudolph, Music Teacher Technologist," *School Band and Orchestra Magazine* (June 2009).

from a simple chord chart with lyrics, may need to make audio recordings to fully capture the essence of what they have written. We can use technology to help unlock the creativity inside both the novice and the experienced musician. For example, simple recording software is easy to learn, and in no time students can use it to do things such as import audio, create sound clips, record their performances and improvisations, and edit and apply DSP (digital signal processing) effects. The same technology allows for differentiated instruction and application. Using recording software in well-designed creative projects allows the stronger musicians to soar while the novices still have a great time working with basic features.

This book moves from describing the Eight Principles for Unlocking Musical Creativity with students to a deepened understanding of and appreciation for these principles via a discussion of how they are applied in creative projects drawn from actual assignments used with K–12 music students. All of the projects use music technology in some way, and all support one or more of the MENC National Standards for Music Education, especially but by no means exclusively standards 3 and 4 (improvising and composing/arranging music). Some of the technology is even free! In addition to the plans and projects detailed in this book, there are a number of great resources published traditionally or online for conducting creativity-based projects that incorporate technology. We will take a look at those as well in the beginning of part II.

You may want to skip part I and jump right in trying out some of the many lessons in part II; I have developed and taught many of these activities and projects over and over, and a few others come from colleagues I admire. I know you will find using them (as is, or adapted for your level) worthwhile even without the preliminary philosophical and pedagogical explanations and examples. Nonetheless, I consider the application of the Eight Principles for Unlocking Musical Creativity to be part of why I and many colleagues and our students, have found doing these creative music projects so satisfying and rewarding.

SPECIFIC VERSUS GENERAL APPROACH TO TECHNOLOGY

In the closing chapter of the thought-provoking book *The World in Six Songs*, Daniel Levitin posits that of all the technological advances related to music made from ancient times to the present, two stand out as the most important: (1) music notation, and (2) recording. He reasonably defends these choices by pointing out that *music notation* "allowed for musical works to be preserved, shared, and remembered" and that *recording* "fundamentally transformed the way that people thought about performances."[9] Of course, music notation technology

---

9. Daniel J. Levitin, *The World in Six Songs* (New York: Plume, Penguin Group, 2008), 281–82. The fundamental change regarding recorded performances involves the idea of capturing and sharing a single, authoritative version of a song for everyone.

12

has been evolving for centuries, and with each release of a new version of computer programs such as Finale or Sibelius we are reminded that it continues to do so. Audio recording, though developed much later in history than music notation, is also ever-changing, having transformed itself from the analog to the digital domain. Certainly music notation and recording figure very largely as areas of music technology, and in fact, three entire chapters in this book deal specifically with music notation and various kinds of recording technology.

Any time an author ventures to highlight the use of technology in a book, he or she runs the danger of making the book almost immediately obsolete. Technology by definition is always changing. The premise of this book is that *music teachers, using a certain methodology and technology tools, can draw out authentic musical creativity from students of all levels of experience and, in the process, deliver meaningful music education.* Fortunately, none of this depends on a specific product. Still, to illustrate what I am putting forward, I must speak about specific software and hardware items. The challenge, of course, is to write in a way that offers helpful but not overly dated information to the reader.

One approach I have taken to soften the effect of what I call "technology spoiling" is to focus on the *conceptual* and the *generic* when discussing hardware and software tools. For instance, an activity or project that uses recording does not necessarily require that a specific microphone, audio program, or recording device be mentioned. Furthermore, detailed step-by-step instructions for using specific recording devices—the domain of a product user manual or video tutorial—is not the purpose of this book. Most important here is what teachers and their students can do with a recording device, how the device is introduced and integrated into a music lesson. One of the principal aims of this book is to demonstrate how various technologies can be placed in the service of creativity-based music learning. As it turns out, most of the lesson and project ideas detailed in part II of this book require only an entry-level knowledge of the technology (software and hardware) mentioned for both teacher and student.

At times, however, it will make sense to mention a particular technology item by name. For instance, there are dozens of digital audio workstation (DAW)[10] applications out there, but only one of the entry-level DAWs is so ubiquitous that it is recognized by name: GarageBand. At times I will refer to programs such as this by name, as place holders, in lieu of a clumsy list of other similar applications. I also occasionally discuss certain technologies with some degree

10. The term *digital audio workstation*, or DAW, refers to a single software application that allows for many aspects of multipart music production, including, most notably, audio and MIDI recording, editing, and mixing; applying digital signal processing effects; and use of audio and MIDI loops. It is assumed that a DAW system has accompanying hardware for translating an audio signal from the analog domain (voice sung into a microphone, guitar output from a patch cord, etc.) into the digital domain. This sort of analog-to-digital converter might be as uncomplicated as a simple USB ("plug-and-play") microphone or as sophisticated as a Firewire audio interface with inputs for multiple XLR (typical microphone) and 1/4-inch phone (typical guitar, synth keyboard) plugs.

of specificity to illustrate a concept more clearly. When it was introduced, there was nothing quite like Apple's GarageBand. Now there are several entry-level DAWs. All of these computer applications (that is, "programs") possess the ability to record on multiple tracks, for instance, and to incorporate loops. When discussing the ways an activity might be delivered, it will be helpful to give examples referring to specific GarageBand features or functions, assuming that the reader will understand that other entry-level DAWs have analogous features and functions.

REFLECTION ACTIVITY

Reflection activities are given at the close of each chapter to allow the reader to pause and reflect on what has been presented and to consider how this information might affect his or her own teaching.

1. Now that you have read about the premise of this book, take a few moments to think about or even jot down some of the things you might do (pre-service teachers) or are already doing (in-service teachers) in your teaching to unlock students' creativity.

2. How could or does technology figure in the activity you list above?

3. What, if any, are some of the challenges of engaging in these types of creative projects that concern you?

CHAPTER 2
THOUGHTS ON CREATIVITY

VALUE OF CREATIVE THINKING

SINCE VERY FEW IF ANY of our students will go on to be professional composers or music producers, is there value in spending more than a small amount
of time engaging them creatively? Maybe that question can be answered with
another: Is there value in teaching children to write prose in language arts class,
to investigating nature with science experiments, or to working out abstract
equations in algebra class when they may not go forth to be career writers, sci-
entists, or mathematicians? Obviously the answer is an emphatic *yes*. We must
give music students some experience with musical creativity if we are to provide
them with a balanced musical experience representative of the diversity of musical activity.

Creativity-based learning also makes sense in a larger way. According to
Daniel Pink, author of *A Whole New Mind: Why Right-Brainers Will Rule the
Future*,[1] we have passed through the Agricultural Age to the Industrial Age and
even the Informational Age and are entering the Conceptual Age, where creativity offers workers and businesses a competitive advantage.

Creative Problem Solving in Education

All music educators, and really educators in general, do not have to look too far
to find a compelling rationale to support the worth of creative work. Let's look
at some of the nonmusical creative tasks tackled by music teachers all the time.
Creating a lesson schedule for fourth- and fifth-grade students is a chore the
elementary instrumental teachers in my department undertake each fall to start
the year. The goal is to schedule several hundred band or strings students into
30-minute, "pull-out" lesson groups of like (or at least similar) instruments. On
average, we can schedule 10 lessons per day. So far, so good. The challenge, at
least with our district's scheduling policies, is to schedule these lessons around

1. Daniel H. Pink, *A Whole New Mind: Why Right-Brainers Will Rule the Future* (New York: Penguin
Group, 2005), 48–51.

all the special area classes (art, general music, physical education, library, and computer lab) for each grade. With me so far? Then if a student receives either gifted/high potential or learning support instruction, we are to avoid pulling them for lessons when they receive those services as well. Wait, there's more! We are to avoid holding lessons during each grade's math block (an hour each day) and when certain students receive accelerated (above their grade level) math instruction. There are even more obstacles, but I will not bore you with the details. The point is that building our elementary instrumental schedules each year really is an art that takes a tremendous amount of organization, resolve, and even relational politicking. In other words, it takes a tremendous amount of *creativity*!

Then there are the creative approaches to working with special needs students. I have attended some professional development training and read a book or two on the topic, but as an undergraduate I received no instruction at all in working with special learners. Although I sometimes feel unprepared to meet their needs, I nonetheless teach special needs students each year. I have had to arrive at solutions—creative solutions—for helping them learn to play their instruments in my bands. Investigation (that is, conversations with their parents, aides, and classroom teachers) and trial and error have led me to some *creative* solutions, including playing back accompaniment files at much slower speeds than the performance tempos (via software that slows an audio file without lowering its pitch), rewriting and simplifying parts using notation software, color coding notes and/or rhythms, enlarging music, teaching rhythms by rote using various word phrases as "handles," and writing finger numbers on instrument keys with a bright permanent marker.

Note that the above examples do not include the type of overtly creative tasks undertaken all the time by music educators such as accompanying a chorus, designing a marching band drill, arranging music for an ensemble, or directing a musical drama. The scheduling and special needs examples are typical and demonstrate how creative *problem solving* is part of the daily routine for music teachers (and all educators). Author Robert Franken hits on this key component of creative persons:

> In order to be creative, you need to be able to view things in new ways or from a different perspective. Among other things, you need to be able to generate new possibilities or new alternatives. . . . The ability to generate alternatives or to see things uniquely does not occur by chance; it is linked to other, more fundamental qualities of thinking, such as flexibility, tolerance of ambiguity or unpredictability, and the enjoyment of things heretofore unknown.[2]

---

2. Robert E. Franken, *Human Motivation*, 3rd ed. (Belmont, CA: Brooks/Cole Publishing, 1994), 394.

A Valued Trait in Many Fields

Business leaders realize that some of the greatest and most profitable inventions or developments have occurred because of individuals or companies using a creative approach. I love the story of how lithography, the process by which books, music, and art were reproduced for about half of the nineteenth century, was invented by Alois Senefelder in 1796. Lithography involves drawing or printing on a special limestone with a greasy ink or crayon pen. Because grease repels water, each stone can then be treated and washed with a number of chemicals before paper is finally applied to it in a lithographic press to make a print. Senefelder was a playwright who had a problem: he could not afford to reproduce the plays he was writing. Apparently he had had a modestly successful play or two early in his career but was having trouble gaining traction with later works and was broke. He developed, and later patented, the process of lithography all to make it cheaper for him to reproduce his scripts. At first it seems unlikely that a playwright might devise such a technical solution, but should it surprise us that a creative writer arrives at a creative solution to his problem?

Another similar example of legendary creativity in the business world involves the development of photocopier technology. Chester Carlson, a patent attorney for an electronics firm in New York, was so frustrated by the difficulty and expense of copying documents that in 1938 he worked out a method of transferring images from one piece of paper to another using static electricity. His creative solution, something no one else had imagined, revitalized a stagnant photography paper company that eventually changed its name to Xerox. (Meanwhile its less visionary Rochester, New York, neighbor—Eastman-Kodak—considered this new direction insignificant!) Incidentally, years later in 1970, when Xerox was awash with profits and interested in how computers might figure in their future, they established the storied Palo Alto Research Center (PARC) in California. Work at PARC included developments that would appear in the first generation of graphic-user-interface personal computers. Xerox, however, never acted on the potential of this research. It would take another creative visionary, Steve Jobs, to refine and implement them into the first Apple Macintosh computers.

One of my favorite creativity-in-business examples is the long and arduous formation of the computer animation company Pixar. One would never know that Pixar, which seems to churn out one blockbuster movie after another, took almost 30 years to become the company it is today. The idea for the company was formed primarily in the mind of Ed Catmull, an early computer programmer who had the dream of creating completely computer-animated feature films long before the technology to do so was in place. Beginning ostensibly with work on medical imaging equipment, but with his dream always in mind, Catmull moved across the country and back from one parent company to another.

Along the way, he teamed up with animator John Lasseter and computer entrepreneur Steve Jobs and for years unsuccessfully pursued a partnership with animation behemoth Disney in the hopes of breakout commercial success. Eventually that partnership occurred, and in the end, Pixar outperformed even Disney.[3]

VALUE OF CREATIVITY-BASED LEARNING

A Human Impulse

In describing how music has shaped human evolution, Daniel Levitin's *The World in Six Songs*, mentioned in chapter 1, essentially makes another case for creativity-based learning:

> Our drive to create art is so powerful that we find ways to do it under the greatest hardships. In the concentration camps of Germany during World War II, many prisoners spontaneously wrote poetry, composed songs, and painted—activities that, according to Viktor Frankl, gave meaning to the lives of those miserably interred there. Frankl and others have noted that such creativity under exceptional circumstances is not typically the result of a conscious decision on the part of a person to improve his outlook or his life through art. To the contrary, it presents itself as an almost biological need, as essential a drive as that for eating and sleeping—indeed, many artists, absorbed in their work, temporarily forget all about eating and sleeping.
>
> We create because we cannot stop ourselves from doing so. Because our brains were made that way. Because evolution and natural selection favored those brains that had a creative impulse, one that could be turned toward the service of finding shelter or food when others were unable to find it; toward enticing mates to procreate and care for children amid competition for mates. Creative brains indicated cognitive and emotional flexibility, the kind that could come in useful on the hunt or during interpersonal or intertribal conflicts.[4]

A creativity-based approach to teaching music (or anything) makes sense because of the way our brains are wired. We have a need to create. Not taking advantage of our students' creative impulse in our approach to teaching is to overlook an effective source of motivation and mode of learning.

---

3. This story is told in a captivating way by David A. Price in his book *The Pixar Touch: The Making of a Company* (New York: Random House, 2008).

4. Daniel J. Levitin, *The World in Six Songs*, 18.

Music Composition

As I pointed out in the opening of this book, another reason to consider one type of creative activity—composition—with music students is that it is another mode of musical activity by which students can experience and learn about music. The analogy between teaching language arts and music is apt. Language arts teachers employ many modes of learning, including creative writing. Music learning is incomplete if students do not engage in at least some creating. Michele Kaschub and Janice Smith offer a thorough rationale for why every child should have the opportunity to study and engage in composition in school, including that it "develops a way of knowing that complements understandings gained through other direct experiences of music" and "invites the child to draw together the full breadth of his or her musical knowledge." They also point out that "composition employs a range of technologies" that aid in the transmission and preservation of musical ideas and ready students for the "next musical evolution."[5]

More Than Composition

Aside from composing, arranging, and improvisation, however, many other areas of the music curriculum can be made more enjoyable when creativity is involved. Imagine if you were given class time to either (1) research and write a brief biography of a composer or (2) use software to create a brief podcast, with music clips, sound effects, and recorded narration, about a composer. Both the traditional report and the more dynamic podcast can address MENC national standards 8 (understanding relationships between music, the other arts, and disciplines outside the arts) and 9 (understanding music in relation to history and culture). If you were the student, which would you be more enthused about sharing with your peers and/or parents when finished? Would you be more excited to read your paper for the class and show it to your parents, or do you think you would be more jazzed up to preview your podcast for the class and have mom and dad visit your music class's website to hear it online? This speaks to the area of motivating students, an advantage you will find that creative activities have over more conventional modes of learning.

Enhanced Learning

A case can also be made that creativity-based projects enhance learning. Creative work often involves active learning. When students compose, just as when they perform music on an instrument, they are doing more than memorizing where certain pitches are on the staff or how many beats a certain duration receives. To compose a variation on a theme, or improvise using the blues scale—

5. Kaschub and Smith, *Minds on Music*, 4–5, 11.

activities you will see are especially effective using technology in two of the lesson plans in part II—allows for an understanding of music on a deep level. The "best tool for finding out whether or not students understand a particular musical concept," says Dr. Jackie Wiggins of Oakland University, "is a creative assignment."[6]

In chapter 17 ("Curriculum Integration"), in a discussion of what I call *meta-projects*, you will see that a synthesis of creative activity can lead to even deeper aesthetic experiences in the same way that creative elements such as music, drama, dance, visual art (costuming, set design), and more (lighting, sound) come together in a large-scale art form such as opera. An example of one such meta-project, discussed in chapter 17, is an original operetta in four acts, titled *The Digestive System*. A student performance of this collaborative class composition, with an original libretto that tells the story of digesting food from the point of view of the parts of the digestive system, can be viewed at the Web site that accompanies this book. The four movements are "The Mouth" (**Web Ex. 2.1**), "Eh Soffa Guess" (**Web Ex. 2.2**), "The Stomach" (**Web Ex. 2.3**), and "The Intestines" (**Web Ex. 2.4**).

Another meta-project example, also detailed in chapter 17, involves transforming a high school elective music class into a student-run music production company to produce a holiday CD sold to benefit a charity. From the music arranging, song writing, performing, and recording, to the album cover art and lyric writing, to the marketing and sales of the CD, many interdisciplinary aspects are addressed. You can hear a brief podcast giving an overview of such a project at the companion website (**Web Ex 2.5**).

Advantages for the student that I observe in my first-hand experience teaching with creative musical projects include increased motivation to produce and improve, acceptance of more independence and responsibility in learning, and longer term retention of content. Years later, students may not necessarily remember that the chord built on the fourth scale degree is called the subdominant, but they will treasure fondly the song they wrote and performed as a class. Advantages for me as a teacher of creative musical activities include finding the time spent with students to be more enjoyable, perhaps because my role moves naturally to that of coach and facilitator (discussed in chapter 8). I also enjoy the opportunities for personal artistic expression when modeling musical creativity.

FEW MODELS FOR CREATIVITY-BASED MUSIC LEARNING

Music teachers tend to teach the way they themselves were taught. Traditional modes of music teaching focus on performing music (singing or playing alone

---

6. Wiggins, *Teaching for Musical Understanding*, 110.

or with others) and factual knowledge about music (a half note is two beats in 4/4 time, the dates of the Renaissance were 1400–1650, etc.). More recently, and especially with the adoption of the MENC National Standards for Music Education, teachers and teacher educators are incorporating music creation into their curriculum. Where this is happening, music technology is right there playing a key role. This should not be surprising since these technology tools have become indispensible to music makers outside the world of education. Where composers once pressed pencil to manuscript paper, many who write music today turn to music notation software at some point in their process. Still others—including amateurs working on remixes and mashups[7] as well as singer-songwriters signed to major record labels—employ digital audio workstations (DAWs) such as GarageBand or ProTools.

More and more resources are being written that offer instruction for using specific types of software applications and other technology products in music education, or provide curricular materials (grade or course specific lesson plans) that incorporate these items. Many other resources, including detailed lesson plans, are available online. Part II of this book includes a survey of all of these.

WHAT DO WE MEAN BY CREATIVITY?

The title of this book is *Using Technology to Unlock Musical Creativity*. The term *creativity* is used in many ways. A typical dictionary definition goes something like this:

> Creativity (noun): the use of the imagination or original ideas, especially in the production of an artistic work.

As we look at ways to foster creativity in music students, the two main parts of this definition will come into play. For instance, "use of the imagination or original ideas" focuses on students identifying and developing musical ideas that are inside them or having personal creative reactions to musical stimuli that they encounter. A student, especially one without traditional musical training, might have great musical ideas and sensibilities but be limited in expressing them. That is where technology comes in to aid students in expressing what they genuinely are imagining.

One must be careful, however, about the word "original." Some would equate being *different* with being *original*, but for our purposes being *different* does not necessarily equal being *creative*. Here is what I mean. Many great composers learned their art by modeling and imitating others, at least at first. I find much

---

7. *Remixes* and *mashups* are essentially creative arrangements that reassemble sectional elements of music recordings (called *stems*), possibly combined with new rhythmic material (that is, loops).

value and usefulness in this tradition. A great strategy for unlocking creativity in students involves examining models—the creations of others—to investigate some aspect of how music works, followed by some exercise applying the technique studied. Certainly these academic exercises will be somewhat derivative, but as you will see, they will also be creative. As students create in this way, they build a vocabulary of compositional devices and add to their own intuitive ideas about such things as songwriting, composing, and arranging. The more students practice creating in this way, and the more techniques they experience, the more they will discover how to create their own techniques and eventually begin to establish their own compositional voice.

In contrast, I have observed students engaging in fun, but not necessarily useful, activity when working on a creative project. Imagine a composition assignment undertaken with notation software in which students are exploring the concepts of repetition and variation. Like most music notation applications, students can click pitches of various rhythms onto a staff. If, while working on this project, a youngster begins randomly clicking 32nd and 64th notes wildly all over the staff, resulting in a spastic sonic explosion when played back, I would posit that he or she was very original but not necessarily creative. In truth, I observe this wacky approach all the time when leading students through projects using music notation software for the first time. Each time I observe the results of such erratic, sometimes mischievous, compositional behavior, I have a hard time holding back laughter. In the end, however, my goal is to build up and onto a students' aesthetic sensibilities through experience. The random clicking of a mouse could be evidence that the student has very little experience creating (and also that he or she recognizes the potential for fun with music software). Sharing in the joke, but then returning them to the project at hand, gives these students the experience they need to develop a creative vocabulary.

The second part of the above definition, "in the production of an artistic work," is crucial. Projects give students the chance to engage in a wide variety of components to creativity such as contemplating a theme, improvising, pruning and developing ideas, establishing form, getting feedback from teacher and peers, collaborating with others, and presenting or performing what has been created. A *project-based* approach is ideal for fostering creativity in students. For some, being creative is simply being unusual or different. But for our purposes, being creative must involve *the act* of creation—producing something.

Creativity and Problem Solving

Composing is creative problem solving (or better, creative "solution finding"). When a composer gets a commission, there are often many specific parameters that must be incorporated into the work. The requirements of a commission describe the problem, and then the composer sets about finding an artistically pleasing solution. Robert Sternberg and Wendy Williams encourage teachers to share how they and others have dealt with obstacles during creative endeavors: "Creative people always encounter obstacles. It's the nature of the enterprise. . . . Describe obstacles that you, friends, and famous people have faced while trying to be creative; otherwise your students may think that obstacles confront only them."[8]

Creative work often involves taking into consideration all the guidelines, limitations, and even obstacles presented by a project, then finding ways to make things work in an aesthetically pleasing way. This is reflected in Franken's definition of creativity: "Creativity is defined as the tendency to generate or recognize ideas, alternatives, or possibilities that may be useful in solving problems, communicating with others, and entertaining ourselves and others."[9] Wiggins puts in succinctly: "By the nature of creative processes, students engaged in creating are solving musical problems. When composing or arranging, they are planning and evaluating solutions ahead of time—before the premiere performance of the work. When improvising, they are solving problems instantaneously as they perform."[10]

Years ago I was commissioned by a high school to compose music to commemorate the opening of a new arts wing. The piece, for combined concert band and chorus, had to incorporate the tune and lyrics for the school's alma mater. Fortunately the tune was the English folk song, "Drink to Me Only With Thine Eyes," which offered many possibilities. Communications with the directors helped me focus on other things I would need to take into account. I had to consider the overall difficulty of the piece as well as specific writing for better and weaker players. Smaller sections would need ample doubling. The band had a large, excellent percussion section, so many parts had to be devised. Length was a consideration: we were aiming for about five minutes so that it would not be too hard to learn and rehearse. In the end, all these project parameters led me to write a work of which I am very proud, one that I would not have written were it not for the requirements of the commission.[11] A more thorough discussion of the way parameters and limitations actually enhance the creative process is taken up in chapter 5.

Music technology allows for many noncomposition creative activities, each of which present their own challenges requiring solutions. Recently, for instance, my students were working on producing a 30-second commercial (to advertise the sale of another project, a holiday CD). They had to make many creative decisions dealing with things such as the script for the voice-over (funny, factual, sentimental, etc.), what microphone to use for recording the voice (each mic has its own tone), selecting and editing background music (How many

8. Sternberg and Williams, *How to Develop Student Creativity*, 30–31.

9. Franken, *Human Motivation*, 396.

10. Wiggins, *Teaching for Musical Understanding*, 58.

11. The commission resulted in my *Fantasy On An Old English Air* for concert band (Shawnee Press).

sound clips? Which ones?), and deciding what text, pictures, and other graphics should be incorporated as the "spot" is produced with video editing software.

SYSTEMIC CHALLENGES

Conventional academic structures often stifle creativity. Asserting that creativity is as important in education as literacy, author and speaker Sir Ken Robinson feels all students have talents that are squandered by the educational system.[12] Ultimately, creative work is applied learning that requires demonstration in practice rather than theory. Worksheets in which blanks are filled in with one-and-only-one correct answer are useful only when serving a greater goal. For instance, you might want to use a notes page when reviewing necessary factual information: software features and tools, the various kinds of cables and cable connection, and so forth. Instead, creative work—smaller activities and larger projects—constitutes the bulk of classwork. Creative projects call on students to make connections within and between various disciplines, to find workable solutions in the face of parameters, and to rely on both knowledge and intuition.

This kind of reminds me of the story of how John Chowning, at the time a young Stanford music professor, discovered FM (or frequency modulation) music synthesis. Frequency modulation involves embedding characteristics of one waveform into a second waveform—basically, extreme vibrato. This process allows for very complex sounds to be synthesized efficiently. I had always assumed that Chowning was an electrical engineer or math wizard with some music background. As it turns out, Chowning was a percussionist in the military during the Korean War, went to college on the GI Bill and studied composition, followed by more composition study with Nadia Boulanger in Paris, and then finally wound up at Stanford for graduate school. While in Paris, he was exposed to electronic music (such as Boulez, Berio, and Stockhausen). At the same time he was fascinated by an article in *Science* by Max Matthews (a researcher at Bell Labs) that claimed any sound that could be conceived could be synthesized on a computer.

Back at Stanford, Chowning took a computer programming class, read articles on computers and computer music, picked the minds of students of various disciplines hanging out at the computer center, and even contacted Max Matthews at Bell Labs. Although Chowning took a beginning algebra class at Stanford—the first math class he had taken since high school—he found he learned more from his own self-imposed curriculum in pursuit of what was still a rather undefined goal: "I built up an incidental education. If there was

12. "Ken Robinson says schools kill creativity," TED Talk filmed February 23, 2006, at the TED 2006 Conference, Monterey, CA (www.ted.com/talks/lang/eng/ken_robinson_says_schools_kill_creativity.html). TED (Technology, Entertainment, Design) is a nonprofit devoted to "ideas worth spreading" and features renowned experts and thinkers in various fields at a number of conferences around the world, as well as on their Web site, www.ted.com.

23

something I wanted to know, I would ask the same question of all these people, until I could finally get an answer in a way I could understand it. That's how I learned physics and acoustics."[13] The ability to program various parameters of sound in computer code eventually led to a breakthrough for Chowning during the 1960s, but it appears his lifelong musical training, at least as much as his later math and computer realizations, enabled him to see things others had missed. "Music is a symbolic art," he says. "A painter gets the sensory feedback immediately, but musicians are used to writing things on paper and hearing them later. . . . It might be why music was the first of the arts to make so much artistic use of the computer."[14] It also appears that the unconventional curriculum he pursued, motivated by curiosity and compositional yearnings and facilitated by the free exchange of ideas among departments at Stanford, served him better than would have more traditional and isolated courses. Eventually, Stanford licensed the patent for frequency modulation to the Yamaha Corporation, where Chowning helped develop the first commercially available FM synthesizer, the Yamaha DX7. For many years, this was Stanford's most lucrative patent, generating more income than other departments' patents in electronics, computer science, and biotechnology.

WRAP-UP

Each of us has a creative impulse that is hardwired and part of our humanness. Just as the language arts teacher uses a balanced approach that includes reading and creative writing, so too should music teachers consider an approach more representative of the full spectrum of musical activity by including musical creation as well as factual learning and performance. When you think about the traits that contribute to success in any field, creativity (along with others such as tenacity and hard work) is among those at the top of the list. Certainly it is advantageous to include at least some opportunities for creativity-based projects across the music curriculum. Creative projects in music class should be aimed at allowing for genuine, authentic expression, rather than contrived, academic expression. Music technology employed well can aid greatly in achieving this goal. Analyzing and imitating models is part of the process of building a creative vocabulary and finding one's creative voice. Engaging students in creative projects has many educational benefits, including being ideally suited to teaching musical topics often not addressed in conventional music learning scenarios.

In the next eight chapters, you will learn some effective principles that—when built into the delivery of creative musical activities and projects—make for very satisfying and rewarding aesthetic and educational experiences.

13. Paul Lehrman, "A Talk With John Chowning," *Mix Magazine Online* (Feb. 1, 2005). Available: mixonline.com/mag/audio_talk_john_chowning/.
14. Lehrman, "A Talk With John Chowning."

REFLECTION ACTIVITY

1. This chapter put forward the assertion that creativity is a human impulse and that all individuals have a need to express themselves creatively. Many, however, view individuals as either basically *creative* or *uncreative*, often assigning such labels as *right-brained* or *left-brained*. Consider this apparent conflict and think of ways that both positions are reasonable, particularly in light of the description of creativity presented here (that is, the use of the imagination or original ideas, especially in the production of an artistic work).

2. Many traditional music programs emphasize performance and factual knowledge. When you were in school, did you experience any creativity-based learning? If so, how (if at all) was technology used? If you are a music teacher now, to what degree do you incorporate creative activities and projects that use technology into your curriculum?

CHAPTER 3
PRINCIPLE 1: ALLOW STUDENTS TO SHARE THEMSELVES

WHAT THEY LIKE AND WHO THEY ARE

MOST KIDS SIMPLY LOVE to tell others, especially their teacher, about themselves. One way they can do this is by sharing what they like in music. Allowing students to share their passion for music, or a certain kind of music, can be a great motivator. For many students, the music they listen to contributes to their sense of identity, how they view themselves and want to be viewed by others.

My Favorite Things Podcast

In my high school music production class, I teach a project called "My Favorite Things Podcast" in which students create an audio podcast to tell about some kind of music they like. If you don't know what a podcast is, don't fret. A podcast is a lot like talk radio, where a host talks about virtually any topic. If the topic is music, the host may share sound clips to amplify the topic. For this project, students artfully string together several short audio clips of their favorite artist (or band, or composer, etc.) and then record a simple voice-over narration to provide a little background and explain what they find so compelling about the music they are presenting. Today's music technology makes creating the clips and recording the voice-overs very easy. Topics put forward for this project by past students have varied wildly and include favorite solo artists and bands, or favorite composers—you would be surprised at the music your students listen to and admire.

One of my favorites was called "A Tribute to the Newmans." This podcast by high schooler Julian S. tapped his love of film music, and particularly music by the Newman dynasty of Hollywood film composers (Alfred, his sons Thomas and David, and their cousin, Randy). The podcast begins with the 20th Century Fox theme and includes short clips of music from the film *Scent of a Woman* (score by Thomas Newman), the song "Dayton Ohio, 1903" (by Randy Newman), and the film *The Egyptian* (score by Alfred Newman). Julian narrates, introducing each clip with modest explanations, yet I learned much from the podcast about Julian's musical sensibilities. No prodding at all was required to get Julian and his classmates to prepare this project, which gave them the opportunity to share something of themselves.

Julian's podcast is on the book's website (**Web Ex. 3.1**); I hope you will give it a listen. You will find detailed lesson plans for both creating the kinds of musical clips used in a podcast in chapter 13 and for the "My Favorite Things Podcast" activity itself in chapter 14. Also of interest for projects such as this, which almost always involve using protected music, is a discussion of copyright considerations in chapter 18.

Sharing Favorite Sounds

Another way I take advantage of students' desire to share themselves is to allow them to explore sounds on a keyboard synthesizer and then to share with me and the class which ones they liked best. What makes this an act of sharing themselves is that it is the students who, through investigation and audition, have discovered and selected the sounds. When we do this activity, which I call "My Favorite Sounds," I notice the way kids feel a sense of ownership of the fun, attractive, or interesting sounds that they discover. I believe this is a smaller, but similar, instance of the dynamic described above whereby youngsters develop a sense of identity from their music.

Of course, like so much in teaching, I have other motives with this activity. I also use the "My Favorite Sounds" activity (described in detail in chapter 12) to teach students some basic keyboard operations, such as how to select sounds and use the volume slider, pitch bend, and modulation wheels. I also use it to instigate improvisation (described in chapter 7). All of that, however, becomes secondary to auditioning sounds and selecting the ones students like best. In a music technology or keyboard lab setting, I show the class briefly how to call up and audition the sounds. Then I give them most of the class period to find sounds they like.

If you are worried about losing kids' focus as they work independently or in pairs, then you probably have not heard the incredible sounds made by today's hardware and software instruments. In fact, the kids usually work industriously, absorbed by the amazing timbres they are experiencing inside the world of their headphones. At the end of class, I have as many as possible share their favorite sound. If they are able, I ask students to play a musical gesture as they demonstrate the sound they picked. Students with keyboard background can play music they have committed to memory, maybe something from their piano lessons or just a small tune they picked up along the way. Others in band or orchestra are often clever enough to figure out a phrase they have performed on their instrument. Some just improvise a one- or two-note rhythmic groove. Others simply hold a key down and allow the sound to speak for itself. For some synthesizer sounds that evolve over time, this is not as plain or boring as you might think. There is never enough time to get to everyone who wants to share.

Titles Are Creative Expressions

There are smaller scale opportunities to share oneself as well. I have noticed that one of the favorite tasks of young composers is naming their works. Why? Because this allows them to share something of themselves, something creative they have conceived. Sometimes I have students think of a descriptive title *first*, before writing programmatically. Other times, we assign the title *after* writing the piece. Students both young and old conceive some of the most intriguing titles! And they love sharing these with the class and me. They really want me to hear whatever clever, silly, funny, or beautiful titles they have created, so you can bet I make time for them to share them.

Several fourth-grade band lesson compositions have fairly innocuous titles, like the pleasant, triadic "A Spring Day" or the repetitious work "The Clock." Others have titles so striking I can think of them right off the top of my head. On the first day of our elementary band camp last year, the students and I were startled by a mouse running across the floor of the band room! We decided he would be our mascot; one of the students named him "Bojangles." During the elective composition class, one of the trombonists wrote a minor, scary sounding duet for himself and piano, called "Bojangle's Scurry." Titles of other camp works include those that reveal kids' love of animals ("The Jumping Gerbil," "The Pig in the Tree," "Norm the Rabbit"), interest in epic things ("March of the Devastators," "Quest for Peace"), zaniness ("The Crazed Pretzel"), age-appropriate interests ("Toy Cars," "I Like Pie"), and clever wit ("Dumb Bob Silly Pants"). I believe one of the rewards of composing with notation software for students is seeing their title in a professional-looking manner, typeset at the top of their new piece. Chapter 15 includes several lesson plans for teaching composition with notation software.

ONE'S SELF IN ONE'S MUSIC

All creating is sharing something of one's self. "Creating music where none previously existed is a powerful act of self," posit Michele Kaschub and Janice Smith, "but one that children naturally exercise. Just as children who hear others tell stories usually begin to create stories of their own, children who hear music are eager to create their own songs."[1] The examples given above, sharing one's favorite music, sounds, and personalized titles, however, do not require much specialized musical skill. Eventually, as students gain comfort and confidence in organizing notes (and other more sophisticated forms of music making), they will want to share their melodic phrases, works-in-progress, and complete compositions. It is not long after students begin instrument study in school (fourth grade in the district in which I teach) that they begin to impro-

1. Kaschub and Smith, *Minds on Music*, 6.

vise their own melodic phrases. Not only are they anxious to share their new-found talents and creations, but some even do so with homemade manuscript (made by meticulously drawing groups of five roughly parallel lines on which their notes are penciled).

When I introduce these kids to simple-to-use technology for typesetting their musical ideas,[2] many react as if I have invited them to enter an exclusive, musical inner sanctum. These kids have found a previously unavailable means of expressing themselves through music. When they come to their next band lesson with a newly composed melody—no matter how rudimentary or aesthetically plain—they are anxious to share it: "Can I play it for you, Dr. Watson?" or "Can we all try this song I wrote?" Of course, I am also likely to hear, "What do you think of it, Dr. Watson?" The topic of offering feedback is addressed in chapter 8 (as part of "coaching") and chapter 9 (as students reflect and critique). Needless to say, I want to foster further exploration of my students' creativity, so I try to be encouraging with my words. As I share in my students' enthusiasm for creating, this is not hard at all.

Do not let the normal, hormonal occurrences of adolescence fool you. Middle schoolers may say they do not want to share because their social stakes are higher. They may have experienced unkind words given simply in jest, or actually to hurt, and are therefore more fearful of rejection. While more sensitivity is required to create an atmosphere of safety and acceptance, still even these students have a desire to be known and to be accepted.

Many analogies can be drawn between *creating* artistically and *procreating* biologically.[3] Like parents, composers often view the music they have created with a sense of ownership or custody. Composers invest much effort in forming and shaping their music, which in some ways is a reflection of them. Just as parents want nothing bad to happen to their kids, you will usually meet with some sort of resistance when you ask composers to consider cutting part of compositions they have written. Young composers are especially bad at self-editing. Both parents and composers feel pride inside when their children or compositions receive praise and applause.

WRAP-UP

Just as you will never have to beg a parent to show you recent photos of their children or to relate all the wonderful things their kids have been up to (even if they are just mundane things), you can usually count on students wanting to share something of their aesthetic selves—the sounds and music they like, and

2. As of this writing, two of the best of these in terms of price, ease of use, and accessibility are Noteflight (a free, online music notation application, www.noteflight.com) and Finale NotePad (a low-cost, entry-level version of the professional music notation software Finale).

3. With more than 200 cantatas and 20 children, J.S. Bach was both a prolific composer and father!

the music they have created—with you and others. Acknowledge this as you plan for and teach music lessons, and you will be tapping into an integral component of the creative process. Today's technology tools—electronic musical instruments and music production and notation software, for instance—make this easy to do so.

REFLECTION ACTIVITY

1. Have you ever been excited to share something of yourself with a class or colleague(s), either as a student or a teacher? Describe the experience.

2. Have you ever had the chance to share a composition that you have written with others? For whom and why did you write the music? Did you use music notation software? What was the venue for sharing your music?

3. Describe your feelings about sharing the music. Were you excited, anxious, scared? If this was a bad experience, try to analyze what went wrong without resorting to overly simplistic generalities (such as "I'm just not a creative person").

4. What are the implications of the existence and popularity of social networking sites, blogs, and the like for the premise of this chapter?

CHAPTER 4
PRINCIPLE 2: OFFER COMPELLING EXAMPLES TO IMITATE AND INSPIRE

WHENEVER I INTRODUCE A CREATIVE PROJECT to students, I share the best examples from previous classes. This gives kids a vision for what can be achieved by others like themselves. Robert Sternberg and Wendy Williams explain that the "main limitation on what students *can* do is what they think they *cannot* do. All students have the capacity to be creators and to experience the joy associated with making something new, but first you must give them a strong base for creativity."[1] A good peer example can be the start of such a base.

Is it unrealistic to feature *exemplary* models of student creativity with your classes? After all, the *average* student typically will not produce such results. I know as a band director, it is the sound of the exemplary player that I hold up as a model. Such examples, played in person by a student or on a recording, present an aural goal the kids in band can aspire to imitate. Imagine asking a student trumpeter with mediocre tone to play for the band with the introduction, "Now listen to Bobby and try to sound at least that good. His tone is a little weak and his attacks are fuzzy because he's still struggling with correct tonguing, but that's the most many of you can hope for." The average student instrumentalist recognizes the giftedness of exemplary model players and hopefully responds by improving. There is much to be gained by *every* participant in a performing ensemble, but the goal is to move each forward in terms of where they are on the spectrum of instrumental proficiency. In the same manner, the average classroom music student should be able to appreciate the outstanding creations of a handful of exceptional composers alongside of whom they sit. Nonetheless, my premise and belief is that *all* students benefit from creativity-based learning as they move forward in their ability to work and express themselves aesthetically. Listening to and examining excellent models is a key part of the groundwork that should be laid before students launch into creating.

From time to time, I create a model project myself. While I prefer to use a student example, I might need to do this, for instance, when I am introducing a new project idea for the first time just to "get the ball rolling." There certainly is

---

1. Sternberg and Williams, *How to Develop Student Creativity*, 8.

value in demonstrating that "those who teach . . ." really *can do*. Sternberg and Williams point out that even beyond specific project examples, all a teacher's creative activities have a positive influence:

> The most powerful way to develop creativity in your students is to be a role model. Children develop creativity not when you tell them to, but when you show them. The teachers you most remember from your school days are not those who crammed the most content into their lectures. The teachers you remember are those whose thoughts and actions served as your role model. . . . When teaching for creativity, the first rule is to remember that students follow what you do, not what you say. You can't simply talk the talk and expect results, you have to walk the walk.[2]

Michele Kaschub and Janice Smith concur: "Teachers who are active composers within the community can model all manner of compositional behaviors. As students watch their teachers seek an initial idea or work through a challenging musical transition, they are able to identify processes that they then can use in their own work."[3] As I share in chapter 8, all teachers can let their students in on these processes by helping to identify them in good music and then appropriately apply them to student work via coaching.

USING A COMPELLING EXAMPLE

I do a unit with my high school music production class called "New Clothes for an Old Tune." The project (described in detail in chapter 14) is based loosely on the seminal album *Switched-On Bach*, in which keyboardist Wendy Carlos performed music by Johann Sebastian Bach on an instrument only recently invented by New York engineer Robert Moog, making the name Moog almost synonymous with the term synthesizer. When it comes to performing older music on new instruments, *Switched-On Bach* is the granddaddy of them all. In addition to making the musical world sit up and take note of the synthesizer, it also made possible the conception of other neo-Baroque, synthesizer-based compositions such as "Baroque Hoedown," the theme music heard at Disneyland and Disney World for the Electric Light Parade for many years.

For the "New Clothes for an Old Tune" project, I have class members produce a contemporary rendering of a short Baroque or Classical keyboard piece (or a self-contained section of one), such as J.S. Bach's "Musette in D major" (from the *Notebook of Anna Magdalena Bach*) or C.P.E. Bach's "Solfeggietto."

2. Sternberg and Williams, *How to Develop Student Creativity*, 7–8.
3. Kaschub and Smith, *Minds on Music*, 105.

These variants of the *Switched-On Bach* tracks are fun to create and are facilitated by the MIDI sequencer and looping features of an entry-level digital audio workstation like Apple's GarageBand.[4] The notes of the original keyboard piece are assigned to be played back by instruments such as synthesizer or electric guitar, which give it a fresh sound. Students then populate other tracks of the multitrack environment with drum and bass loops, a task the application makes fairly easy. Other arranging chores are accomplished by applying basic editing operations (cut, copy, paste) creatively. There are great ways to employ technology so that even nonkeyboard players, or those who do not read music, can easily get the notes for their Baroque or Classical keyboard piece into the multitrack software for this project (such as importing a MIDI file, discussed in the lesson in chapter 14).

I begin this project with carefully selected listening. First we listen to some tracks from the original *Switched-On Bach* album. We also take time to listen to and discuss examples that demonstrate the fusion of art music and popular music, a component of the project. I like to share a track such as "Deck the Halls" by Chip Davis from his first Mannheim Steamroller holiday album, *Christmas* (American Gramaphone, 1990), as well as a cover[5] of the Disney "Baroque Hoedown" mentioned above but by the eclectically influenced Indie-pop band, They Might Be Giants (*Moog: Original Film Soundtrack*, Hollywood Records, 2004). These are but two of many great examples one might use.

I also take time to play for the kids an excellent example by a student in a previous class. One of my favorite "New Clothes for an Old Tune" student projects was a setting of C.P.E. Bach's "Solfeggietto" crafted by Allison H. You can hear Alli's setting of "Solfeggietto" on the book's website (**Web Ex. 4.1**). Allison pretty much preserves every note of the original keyboard piece while adding exciting rhythm-and-blues drum and bass loops. The strength of her setting, though, is the orchestration. Applying deftly a principle I teach called "layering" (explained more in the chapter 14 lesson "Loops and Layering"), we hear instrument timbres fly in and out of the arrangement. All the while the keyboard part, assigned alternatively to piano and rock organ, is the thread that holds it all together. I love Alli's piece; while many students have created fine "New Clothes for an Old Tune" projects over the years, I always think sharing hers sets the bar high for this particular project. I hope you will take time to listen to it and perhaps be inspired to teach the "New Clothes for an Old Tune" lesson yourself.

---

4. Right now, GarageBand is the most notable of these entry-level digital audio workstations (or DAWs), but several other software manufacturers have produced competing applications, including MixCraft by Acoustica, Sequel by Steinberg (the makers of Cubase), and Music Creator by Cakewalk.

5. A *cover* is a performance of an existing song by a new artist. The cover may employ the same or a very similar arrangement of the song, or it may approach the song in an altered, even strikingly different, way with a unique, new arrangement.

STUDENT EXAMPLES BRING CREATIVE GOALS WITHIN REACH

Creative activities like the "New Clothes for an Old Tune" project can be a little daunting to some students. Some students may not see themselves as especially creative, plus the task before them may seem ambiguous and hard to conceive. For these reasons, it is very important to share exemplary projects created by other students. Hearing what a fellow student can do, perhaps even someone known by your class, brings everything into the realm of possibility. Hearing or seeing what a successful finished project sounds and/or looks like can remove uneasy feelings about the task that lies ahead. A fine peer example can do the same as the music of a professional artist. Compelling examples can open up students' ears to new musical possibilities beyond their own limited sonic experience—they can inspire.

I hope you will indulge me a story from my own experience that further demonstrates the power of *example* to inspire. When I was a young teen, my parents allowed me to attend a summer band camp at the College of William and Mary in Williamsburg, Virginia. Each week of the program, the camp concert band would present a concert on the green in front of the iconic Wren Building at the entrance to the college grounds. Working on the concert repertoire in sectional and full band rehearsals made up the bulk of the daily schedule, but we also had a daily class in music theory. Knowing that later in life I chose to pursue both a masters and a doctoral degree in composition, you would probably think that I enjoyed the camp's music theory class. To be honest, I do not remember a thing about music theory at camp! But here is one of my most vivid memories. There was a young man, a trumpeter named James Hosay, who was sort of the star of the camp. Not only was he an excellent high school trumpeter, but he was a composer as well. We rehearsed and performed one of his works with the band one summer, and it left an indelible impression on me. A real, live person—and someone only a year or two older than me—could compose music. I was inspired. I went home and banged away at the family piano, an old clunker, and began my life as a composer. It was a compelling example, not music theory lessons, that moved me to create music by whatever means I could.[6]

TECHNOLOGY'S ROLE IN CONVEYING EXAMPLES

Technology figures prominently in the *creation* of all the lessons in this book, but it can also aid the music educator in *delivering* the compelling examples he or she has chosen to present. To demonstrate the wide variety of modes and means useful for presenting examples, let's just take the case of sharing Allison H.'s "Solfeg-

---

6. By the way, James Hosay went on to become staff arranger for the U.S. Army Band and continues a very successful career as a widely published composer.

gietto" in preparation for the "New Clothes for an Old Tune" project. First, the audio file could be played from any source connected to amplified speakers: an iPod or other MP3 player, a desktop or laptop computer using some media player (iTunes, Windows Media Player, etc.), or even a conventional CD player (assuming the track has been burned to a CD-R).[7] Students could also monitor the example with headphones, with the audio coming from a media player on a student workstation, or from a teacher's playback device (computer, CD player, etc.) through a lab audio management system (such as Korg's GEC3[8]).

Since the arrangement was created with GarageBand, you could use a computer video projector or an interactive whiteboard (such as a SMART Board)[9] to share the *look* as well as the *sound* of the project with students. Perhaps it would be helpful to have the example posted online where students could listen to it as part of a homework assignment. Right now, wikis are one of the easiest ways to do this. Literally in minutes you could create a page on your course wiki for the project and then upload and insert the MP3 audio example.

If you want to annotate the playback of the file with audio commentary, you could make a podcast using software such as Audacity or GarageBand. To add visual support, such as slides that indicate formal sections, PowerPoint (Microsoft) or Keynote (Apple) could be used in two ways. Either record the voice-over narration and drop the MP3 audio into the slide show, or export the slides as graphics (for example, JPEG) and import them, along with the MP3 audio, into a movie program such as iMovie. You could also import the slide images and MP3 audio into a program such as GarageBand and save as a video podcast.

Say you want to have viewers see the song playback in GarageBand, with audio and/or video commentary before/during/after playback, and be able to save all of this as a movie that you can post online. You can do that, too, with screen capture software. Screen capture programs video record whatever is happening on a computer's screen while audio recording whatever is coming from the computer's sound system and/or a microphone.[10] Once these examples are

---

7. A *CD-R* is a (one-time) recordable compact disk.

8. The *GEC3* (Korg Group Education Controller 3) is an audio routing system used in music labs. Settings on the unit allow students, with headphones, to monitor sound from their own computer and synth keyboards as well as those of the teacher. Sound from auxiliary inputs can be sent through the system, and sound from within the system can be sent to external speakers for all to hear in the room. Other system features include teacher-student and student-student communication using headset microphones, and the ability to configure student work groups so they hear only their own computers and keyboards and not those of others. In my opinion, this is the best system for music lab management in terms of function and durability.

9. Projectors transfer the video (that is, VGA, or video graphics array) output of a computer to a mounted or freestanding screen. The computer's audio output needs to be amplified as well. An interactive whiteboard (such as SMART Board) not only projects an enlarged image of a computer display onto a whiteboard but also allows the user to directly interact with the image, just as he or she would with a mouse on a computer.

10. Some screen capture programs are ScreenFlow and Jing. ScreenFlow (by Telestream) also allows for the recording of video from a built-in camera and audio from connected microphones. Other useful features include the ability to zoom in, add text, and highlight various things on the screen. Jing (by TechSmith) is freeware.

posted online, it is very convenient to direct absent students to a class wiki or website to see what they have missed. I hope you get the idea: Technology offers *many* great ways for sharing examples with your students.

WRAP-UP

Listening to exemplary models by other students and compelling works by professional artists helps prepare students for what they will need to do in a project. More important, though, it charges up their imagination. It has been said that "education is not the filling of a pail, but the lighting of a fire."[11] Educator and writer William Arthur Ward affirms this: "The mediocre teacher tells. The good teacher explains. The superior teacher demonstrates. The great teacher inspires." The examples of creative excellence you put before your students could make all the difference.

REFLECTION ACTIVITY

1. This chapter advocates sharing excellent example works with students *before* asking them to create a similar project of their own. What are the pedagogical pros and cons of sharing with students excellent, compelling projects created by other students or the teacher?

2. A lot of technology for sharing examples of creative content was mentioned in this chapter. With which of these items do you have experience, as a student, teacher, or individual? Describe any items for which you have either a strong positive or negative opinion.

---

11. This quote is usually attributed to the twentieth-century Irish poet William Butler Yeats.

CHAPTER 5
PRINCIPLE 3: EMPLOY PARAMETERS AND LIMITATIONS THAT REMOVE DISTRACTIONS AND HELP STUDENTS FOCUS

STRAVINSKY'S FAMOUS PARADOX

WHILE YOU MIGHT THINK that rules would always restrict creativity, I have found that well-thought-out guidelines actually foster it. One of my favorite twentieth-century composers, Igor Stravinsky, actually spoke to the subject of the benefits of parameters when composing in a series of lectures he gave during the 1939–40 academic year at Harvard University:

> What delivers me from the anguish into which an unrestricted freedom plunges me is the fact that I am always able to turn immediately to the concrete things that are here in question . . . in art as in everything else, one can build only upon a resisting foundation: whatever constantly gives way to pressure, constantly renders movement impossible. My freedom thus consists in my moving about within the narrow frame that I have assigned myself for each one of my undertakings.
>
> I shall go even further: my freedom will be so much the greater and more meaningful the more narrowly I limit my field of action and the more I surround myself with obstacles. Whatever diminishes constraint, diminishes strength. The more constraints one imposes, the more one frees one's self . . . and the arbitrariness of the constraint serves only to obtain precision of execution.[1]

As a composer writing in the first half of the twentieth century—a period when many conventions of musical composition were being discarded for more progressive approaches—I am sure Stravinsky was very cognizant of the pros and cons of having rules in place when writing. And yet, examining his music reveals self-imposed constraints that focus his ideas and give it cohesiveness. A

---

1. Igor Stravinsky, *Poetics of Music in the Form of Six Lessons* (Cambridge, MA: Harvard University Press, 1970), 65–66. Stravinsky's *Poetics* was first delivered in French as part of the Charles Eliot Norton lecture series during the 1939–40 academic year at Harvard University. A widely quoted English translation was produced in 1947.

case in point is the opening (the first "tableau" or scene) to Stravinsky's ballet *Petroushka*. Considering the extremely chromatic music being composed by his twentieth-century contemporaries, Stravinsky greatly limits the number of pitches he uses in this magical, but harmonically static, passage of music. In fact, the controlled collection of notes and the way they unfold incrementally, with repetitive rhythmic ostinato, foreshadow the minimalist movement.[2] Yet the piece sounds fresh and modern, building from a pastoral dream state and then moving forward purposefully to more weighty statements.

The implications for facilitating student creativity of the approach proffered by Stravinsky are enormous. Recall that in the last chapter I mentioned that composing (really, any creative activity) may seem daunting to some students who do not see themselves as especially "creative." One way to unlock the creativity that I believe is inside everyone is to *more narrowly define the task*. This limits the number of choices so that students (1) are not dizzied by the many paths they theoretically might go down (what Stravinsky calls the "anguish" of "unrestricted freedom") and (2) can concentrate their creative energies on a few areas where there is latitude. The second of my Eight Principles for Unlocking Musical Creativity (see chapter 1), dealing with compelling examples that serve as models, speaks to helping students understand the goal of their creative efforts, what a finished product "looks like." This third principle deals with eliminating distractions from the sometimes overwhelming number of creative choices that could be made in order that students might better enjoy the well-defined area in which they may exercise more freedom. All of this allows them to move forward with their work, gaining artistic confidence as they experience this progress.

HOW TO APPLY THIS PRINCIPLE

The "Pedal Point Duet" composition lesson described in detail in chapter 15 is an excellent example of a successful student composition project that has fairly strict, well-defined parameters, but which usually yields great music. *Pedal point* has roots in the drone used in medieval and ancient times, but is so-named because of a technique often used when writing for organ. The "pedal point" is a single, sustained note played on one of the organ's foot pedals while the organist plays other, usually faster moving material on the keyboard manual(s) with his hands. At times the pedal point may be a note that is part of one of the chords played by the organist's hands. Other chords might *not* include that pedal note, so then it becomes nonharmonic. Musicians who are not organists generally

---

2. Early minimalist composers such as Terry Riley or Steve Reich, or later minimalists such as Philip Glass or John Adams, present a limited number of pitches at first, usually in a hypnotic rhythmic figuration, and then introduce additional pitch and rhythmic material gradually, in a controlled and disciplined manner, causing the piece to unfold slowly.

first encounter pedal point as a type of nonchord tone when they study harmony. Because the technique is so easy to apply and because it yields such great results, many composers have employed pedal point in a wide variety of styles of music.

One obvious parameter of the "Pedal Point Duet" project is that it must be for two instruments. Since I use this activity during our summer elementary band and strings camp, I keep things simple by requiring that they be two of the *same* instrument (two clarinets, two alto saxophones, etc.). Another parameter or limitation is that the bottom part of the duet must remain on the first tone of the scale employed (that is, the tonic, referred to as "Do" in solfège); this will be the pedal point. There are other parameters as well. The top part must start and end on "Do." The top part should follow a melodic contour, preferably one of those we have seen and discussed in other melodies we have examined. Although we use a simple notation program to create the music,[3] the composer must be able to perform all the music he or she writes. In fact, the goal is to perform the duets (as per principle 8, which deals with performance and recital), some in a demonstration concert at the end of camp.

All these guidelines and limitations focus the students' efforts on being creative with the parameters they are allowed to manipulate. Since the kids generally have little experience with the notation software, some of my energy is spent on reviewing features of the tool (Finale NotePad, Noteflight.com, etc.). Most of the time, however, I discuss with the students pertinent compositional considerations: When might they consider repeating an idea?, Are there too many competing thematic ideas in such a short space?, Would using silence here and there help them achieve what they want?, When should the top part use the same or different rhythm as the bottom part? And on and on. Students can use features of the notation program to easily effect change in each of these areas and then audition the changes via software playback. Despite the confines of the project, there are many great lessons about composing that can be taught and learned.

Parameters Helping Beginning Student Composers ("Pedal Point Duet")

Students at every level who work on this project almost always turn out great pieces, a fact I credit at least partially to the good set of parameters in place. "A Day at the Park," by fourth-grader Rebecca L., is an example of one of the duet projects composed during our district's summer elementary band and strings camp (**Fig. 5.1** and **Web Ex. 5.1**). While following the basic guidelines for the project, she used repetition well to convey her main idea. There is still enough

3. I have used Finale NotePad but now use Noteflight.com so students can continue to work on their projects and other music of their choosing at home, at no cost.

A Day at the Park

Rebecca L.

► **FIG. 5.1**

Pedal Point Duet example composed by an elementary school student: *A Day at the Park*, by Rebecca L. Used with Permission.

variety, however, to make the short piece interesting. Rebecca finds ways to have the two parts interact, such as the brief back-and-forth mimicking in measures 3 and 9, and where she breaks the pedal in favor of harmonic thirds in measures 8 and 10. Note that I favor the term "parameter" over the more inflexible "rule." Parameters are used to free the artistic spirit and foster forward motion on a creative project. If a student is making good progress, as Rebecca was, and has time and interest in beginning to explore the boundaries of the projects' parameters, then by all means take that impulse where it leads. That, by the way, is an aesthetic journey most composers make. One of the toughest decisions I have to make as teacher is how long to allow my students to dwell on a project. Dwelling allows more time for revisions and additions, but moving on allows students to have other experiences and learn new lessons. If Rebecca would have been given another session (approximately 40 minutes), she might have added more articulations or further developed one of her melodic gestures.

Parameters Helping Older Student Composers ("Pedal Point Duet")

Some adjustments I make when working with older, more experienced composers include allowing more flexibility with pedal point (that is, letting students "break" the pedal to give other material to the bottom part, moving the pedal to the top part, or even using more than one pedal) and encouraging longer works (via a second formal section). One of my all-time favorite student examples was created by Noam F., a high school junior. His piece, cryptically titled "asdfjkl;" (the keys on a computer keyboard's middle row of letters), is simply beautiful (**Fig. 5.2**). In fact, *it is the piece's simplicity* that makes it so

▶ **FIG. 5.2**

Pedal Point Duet example composed by a high school student: *asdfjkl;*, by Noam F. Used with Permission.

41

asdfjkl;

Noam F.

beautiful. A recording of Noam's piece is on the book's website (**Web Ex. 5.2**); I urge you to take the time to listen to it. As with Rebecca's piece above, Noam stayed within the basic guidelines of the project but still found ways to write unique and effective music. Note the balanced, *da capo* form (consisting of equal 16-measure sections) in this more highly developed work. The pedal shifts from the lower instrument (clarinet) in part 1 to the upper instrument (flute) in part 2. The hauntingly beautiful melody, based on a black-key minor scale, is thematically tight and features an ascending sequence to set up the return of the first section.

DEVISING PARAMETERS FOR CREATIVE PROJECTS

Criteria for devising good parameters for the creative projects you undertake with students can best be conveyed by providing more examples. Successful parameters may be very comprehensive, as with the "Pedal Point Duet" lesson. They may also be very negligible, such as insisting that students use only two fingers to trigger two percussion sounds[4] on a synth keyboard for a percussion improvisation. Think of the way an elementary classroom music teacher removes any Orff instrument keys (bars) he or she does not want students to play. Creative projects can similarly insist that students use a limited set of notes on an electronic keyboard: using only black keys suggests a pentatonic scale or E-minor blues, and using only white keys suggests C major or an impressionistic, pandiatonic sound.

Effective rules can even be arbitrary. For instance, a project must be exactly 30 seconds in length, or employ exactly 100 notes—no more, no less. When devising the parameters for a creative project for the first time, I usually work through the activity myself to understand where kids might need boundaries or guidelines. I also draw on my own experience as a composer and musician. A deadline itself is a parameter and—at least in my experience—one that motivates students toward completion more than almost any other. I remember when I was on sabbatical to complete my doctoral dissertation, a concerto for trumpet and orchestra, and the idea of forcing myself to compose in a very limited time frame actually helped me write. I had sketched the entire first and last movements but was experiencing writer's block with the slow, middle movement. My teacher and adviser, Maurice Wright, recommended that I find a morning that suited me, sit at the piano, and write the entire movement in a day. I did exactly that, and years later I am still proud of the music I wrote.[5]

---

4. In addition to the many tonal instrument sounds that can be chosen, most keyboard synthesizers have one or more "drum kits" in which each key of the keyboard triggers a different percussion sound. Low C is a bass drum, low D is a snare drum, and so on (see **Fig. 7.2**).

5. My doctoral dissertation project was *Concerto for Trumpet and Orchestra*, premiered October 2001 at the Academy of Music, Philadelphia, PA, by the Temple University Symphony Orchestra, Luis Biava, conductor, with Terell Stafford as soloist. The second movement is the one I sketched in a day.

Sometimes limitations, such as deadlines, are simply pragmatic. Because students like the "My Favorite Things Podcast" activity so much, they always ask if it would be OK if they use *more* than three sound clips, or if their clips can be *longer* than 30 seconds. Since it is important to me that we not spend more than a week on this activity (there are so many other experiences I want to move on to) and that we listen to and briefly discuss each finished podcast, I have to insist that they adhere to my criteria. Compositional considerations can lead to parameters you might want to institute. With what musical elements am I most interested in having my students work? With what challenges do I want them to wrestle? What obstacles can I help them avoid? In the end, trial and error are key when devising parameters: Repeat and build on what has been successful; tweak, revise, or eliminate that which has not. This is where the idea of comfort with risk taking mentioned in chapter 1 comes in handy.

WHOSE PARAMETERS AND LIMITATIONS?

Interestingly, Michele Kaschub and Janice Smith cite the Stravinsky quote I used at the start of this chapter but draw a significantly different conclusion: Noting that Stravinsky created the limitations and boundaries he used *for himself*, they feel it is important that student composers *themselves* be the ones to impose constraints. Nonetheless, they point out that views "on the roles of freedom and constraint within task design remain split"[6] and note that some researchers suggest that limitations could make compositional tasks more approachable for students. It is important to understand that the principle of employing parameters, limitations, and tools needs to be applied in concert with the other principles presented here. Overemphasizing "rules" can lead to contrived, unauthentic writing and is the focus of the next chapter. Even a well-conceived project, without the coaching interaction described in chapter 8, can leave students floundering. Kaschub and Smith conclude: "Finding the appropriate balance of freedoms and constraints for each composer is important since it will allow task structures to fulfill their role in supporting compositional growth."[7]

Robert Sternberg and Wendy Williams recommend student ownership of creative decisions as they define and redefine problems and tasks: "Encourage creative thinking by having students choose their own topics for papers or presentations, choose their own ways of solving problems, and sometimes choose again if they discover that their selection was a mistake."[8] Still, teachers must be a safety net, suggesting (or even insisting on) limits to the scope of goals students

---

6. Kaschub and Smith, *Minds on Music*, 56.

7. Kaschub and Smith, *Minds on Music*, 56.

8. Sternberg and Williams, *How to Develop Student Creativity*, 16.

44

have chosen that are beyond their reach. Such limitations are especially valuable when class time or student ability is limited.

PARAMETERS AND LIMITATIONS HELP STUDENTS DISCOVER NEW POSSIBILITIES

As Noam's class reflected about their experience working on the Pedal Point Duet (as per Principle 7, which deals with offering feedback), he remarked to me that at first he thought the parameters I imposed would actually limit his ability to be creative. Later, when the project was complete, he saw that the parameters and limitations actually allowed him to write interesting music he otherwise would not have been led to create. He liked where the process led him. Another student, Sam P., had a similar experience: Dissatisfied with using a public-domain Hanukkah song for our music production class's holiday CD project, Sam wanted to have fun writing his own. I was concerned that he not push the envelope too far with lyrics that might offend. I insisted that he use no "swear words" and receive approval for the lyrics from his rabbi. Note the use of the word "k'vell" in verse 2 (see **sidebar**): "So spin your dreidel, and drink your wine / It's gonna be one k'vell of a night." In Sam's original version it was going to "be one *hell* of a night." Being a good sport (and because I made him), Sam went back to the drawing board and substituted the Yiddish word "k'vell," which means "to be delighted, bursting with pride." The final version of the lyrics he crafted was funnier not in spite of the constraints, but *because* of them. Needless to say, I was very proud of Sam.

"This CD Needed a Hanukkah Song"

Words and Music by Sam P.

VERSE 1
Well I'm the only Jew in Music Production,
It's time that I set things right.
Not a good song was written before 1923
About the "Festival of Lights."
So I'm done with this public domain,
I'm gonna go ahead and keep playin'.
I'm not saying it's wrong
All I'm saying is that this CD needs a Hanukkah song!

REFRAIN
Yeah, this is my Hanukkah song.
I thought this CD needed one.

'Cuz by the time your done with your Christmas shopping
Hanukkah will already be done.

VERSE 2

Well we've got latkas, we've got the menorah
We've got eight crazy nights.
We've got Judah and the Maccabees,
We don't waste any time hanging lights.
So spin your dreidel, and drink your wine;
It's gonna be one k'vell of a night.
This year's celebration will be the best by far.
Oh yeah, yeah, yeah.

REFRAIN

[RAP]
Latkas, oil, light the menorah
Come get together, we'll all do the Horah.
We don't fast this ain't no Yom Kippur-a,
So its time to spit some crazy verses from the Torah:

[SUNG]
Baruch atah adonai
Eloheinu melech ha'olam
Asher kidishanu b'mitzvotav
L'hadlich ner shel . . .
Hanukkah!

REFRAIN

I hope you will listen to Sam's song, sung by himself and his friend Britany, at the companion website for this book (**Web Ex. 5.3**).

WRAP-UP

Many students favor engaging in creative projects over more traditional approaches. Those who do not are often simply stressed about the unknown: What am I supposed to do? How do I get started? What are the steps I need to take? Some of the uneasiness that causes students to freeze up when asked to be creative can be ameliorated by employing good models and good parameters. Once students become involved in the project at hand, the stress about the unknown begins to melt away. This is even more true when students experience the process again in subsequent creative activities. Well-crafted parameters define the task ahead, create a comfort level that helps break the creative ice, and provide the forward motion many kids need to be productive and creative.

REFLECTION ACTIVITY

1. Have you ever been in a situation where constraints or guidelines forced you to create something you otherwise would not have?

2. As stated in this chapter, "the roles of freedom and constraint within task design remain split." There are those who believe that any limitations placed on a project should emanate from the student, without interference from the teacher. Others believe that stronger music can be fashioned, and important lessons learned, via teacher-imposed limitations, instruction, and suggestions regarding the work. What are your thoughts?

CHAPTER 6
PRINCIPLE 4: REMOVE PARAMETERS AND LIMITATIONS THAT STIFLE CREATIVITY AND LEAD TO CONTRIVED EXPRESSION

CHAPTER 5 DISCUSSED LIMITATIONS in the form of project parameters and guidelines as positives aimed at freeing students to move forward creatively. Obviously there is a connection between that principle and this one. Principle 4 is something like the inverse of principle 3 but largely involves employing certain technologies that facilitate creative expression to remove students' musical limitations. It is here that technology shines most brightly, particularly for those with little conventional music training, sometimes called "nontraditional music students." The term *nontraditional music* (or *NTM*) *student* was coined by music education technology researchers Dr. David B. Williams (Illinois State University, IL) and Dr. Rick Dammers (Rowan University, NJ).[1] In a nutshell, NTM students are the approximately 80% of high schoolers that have received little or no conventional music performance training and therefore are disenfranchised from traditional school music department ensembles such as band, chorus, or orchestra. Despite their limited or alternative musical background, many NTM students thrive in elective music courses that emphasize creativity and technology.

While not as apparent as with NTM students, even those with conventional music training—such as those in band, orchestra, or chorus—have musical limitations connected to their experience. This chapter, and this book, offers ideas for using technology to help these move forward as well, in terms of expressing and refining musical ideas.

REMOVING BARRIERS TO CREATIVE EXPRESSION WITH TECHNOLOGY

Imagine the many barriers to musical creativity that were removed when Apple introduced GarageBand in 2004. Apple opened the realm of multitrack recording to millions through GarageBand's attractive, approachable user interface, simple audio and MIDI recording features, and especially by including hundreds

---

1. See their website, Music Creativity Through Technology, at www.musiccreativity.org.

of loops that adapt easily to the key and tempo of a project. Indeed, Dr. David B. Williams (Professor Emeritus, Illinois State University) remarked that the release of GarageBand

> was as significant for music education as the release of the first Macintosh computers in 1984 with Professional Composer notation software along with personal laser printers and Postscript printing of music notation. Both events helped to democratize a music process previously reserved for the professional: the former, music publishing, the most recent, music composition. GarageBand and similar music technology tools empowered anyone, young and old, to create music using their ear as their guide, by shaping their expression through easy manipulation of high quality loops, audio snippets, sounds samples, along with adding the creative potential through live recording with USB keyboards, mics, guitars, and other devices.[2]

Examples of Technology that Removes Limitations

Limitations faced by NTM students can include little or no ability to read or write conventional music notation and modest music performance facility. Limitations of students conversant with music notation, who have some proficiency on an instrument, often include lack of comfort improvising or performing popular music. Regardless of background, most music students have little experience developing and organizing musical materials for a larger work.

There are many examples of great music software and hardware that can be used with students to remove these and other limitations to creative musical expression. I mention a few examples here to demonstrate the principle of this chapter; in most cases I list specific products for clarity. Most of these are discussed in more detail in part II, in the chapter that corresponds with their specific technology category.

Keyboard Synthesizer

As teachers of beginning band and orchestra students know well, producing a pleasing tone on an instrument takes years. Yet quality sounds of interest can be initiated by the touch of a finger, or even triggered by sequencing software, on a keyboard synth by students without that experience. While composers might prefer to have an excellent, live player perform their music, in most cases this is not possible within school music classes. Plus, keyboard synths offer many unique sounds not produced by acoustic instruments. Keyboard synths (and software instruments) break the barrier to quality sounds in a big way.

---

2. David B. Williams, Music Creativity Through Technology (www.musiccreativity.org).

Loop-Based Composing and Arranging Program: GarageBand et al.

I have already mentioned GarageBand, which serves to represent many other programs like it, many times in this book. These loop-based tools allow students to work with prefabricated cells of musical material, choosing and arranging them vertically and horizontally to construct a wide variety of musical content. The software allows students to deal with issues that occupy the minds of traditional composers and arrangers: timbre, texture, form, tempo, and much more.

Most software that facilitates looping also allows for multitrack MIDI and audio recording. Welcome additions to the Mac OSX and Windows loop-based recording programs are several newer online applications for multitrack looping.[3]

Music Notation Software

Chapter 15 ("Creativity With Computer Music Notation Applications") details many ways that music notation software can be employed in creative music endeavors. Here, let me focus on one limitation that the software removes: aural feedback. When performers translate a composition from the page into a sonic happening, the composer receives invaluable feedback. I remember many times when I was coming up as a composer, before music notation software was widely available, hearing a reading of something I had written and thinking, "That's just what I'd imagined," or "Wow! I had no idea it would sound that way." Music notation software gives immediate, if somewhat flawed, feedback to the young composer that is so important. I say "flawed" because the synthesized or sampled sounds are not "real" and because the software can play back with ease even very difficult, unidiomatic passages. I cannot tell you how many times I have had to point out to students that what they have written is nearly impossible for live players to perform.

And yet, I believe this single aspect of music notation software is responsible for developing far more composers of music of all kinds in our age than at any other time. It would be great to have a laboratory ensemble to perform what we write as soon as we write it. This ensemble's numerous performances of our music at all stages as it comes to mind and is notated would help us make corrections, revisions, and refinements, leading to a polished final version. While this may be theoretical for most, removing the limitation of immediate aural feedback is one service that music notation software provides for our students.

Musical Creativity Software: Band-in-a-Box

Band-in-a-Box (manufactured by PG Music), which runs on both Windows and Mac OS computers, makes intelligent decisions for the user about the notes

---

3. Two multitrack web applications that support looping at this time are Myna (aviary.com) and Soundation (www.soundation.com). There are others.

generated and played by combo instruments (keyboard, bass, guitar, drums, etc.) given the chords a user types in. For many years students have been using the program to craft all sorts of musical creations with little or no keyboard or other performance skill involved. Students type in chords (C, C7, Csus4, etc.), select a style (light rock, blues shuffle, etc.), and adjust a variety of other settings as desired, and the software intelligently renders a combo performance of the music. These creations might be the accompaniment to a rap, or perhaps an improvised vocal or instrumental melody, each of which can be recorded into a solo audio track in Band-in-a-Box if desired. Another approach that spurs student creativity involves importing a MIDI file[4] of an existing melody, say, "Yankee Doodle," into a MIDI-capable program. Thousands of tunes can be downloaded for free from the Internet in MIDI file format for play in programs such as Band-in-a-Box (or GarageBand, etc.). Using the melody as the basis for a song arrangement or set of variations, students' imaginations can run wild auditioning and responding to the many wonderful styles and loops at their disposal. Students might begin a project with a rock sound in mind, only to be won over by exotic, world percussion loops, morphing their work into something completely different. Likewise, new musical possibilities form when the notes of a traditional melody are assigned to an attractive synthesizer sound.

Musical Creativity Software: Groovy Music and Making Music

While Band-in-a-Box and GarageBand are well suited to remove musical limitations of students in older elementary grades and higher, other software takes a similarly unconventional approaches for even younger students. The Groovy Music suite of software programs (made by Sibelius)[5] provides kids a fun alternative to traditional notation or multitrack recording. With Groovy Shapes, aimed at young elementary ages, an avatar-like character walks a path filled with colorful shapes placed there by the student. Different shapes trigger various timbres and existing or newly created melodic loops.

Composer Morton Subotnik, a pioneer of electronic music, has authored six software titles and an accompanying website all aimed at helping young children create music in ways accessible to them. On Subotnik's Creating Music website (www.creatingmusic.com), for instance, a musical "Sketch Pad" allows students to draw different colored blocks representing sounds of different in-

---

4. MIDI files are digital records of performance data including key number (such as key 60 = middle C), note on and off timing, velocity (how hard the key was pressed), patch (sound), and much more. The analogy is often made to a player piano roll: the roll describes the performance but needs the piano to play it (the way a MIDI file needs a software or hardware instrument).

5. There are three programs in the Groovy Music series: Groovy Shapes (ages five and up), Groovy Music Jungle (ages seven and up), and Groovy Music City (ages nine and up). The programs include music lessons and tutorials as well as their creative component.

struments on a blank canvas. The longer the block, the longer the duration of a note, and the higher the block on the canvas, the higher the pitch of the note. Tools labeled with intuitive icons allow the user to perform common composer operations (such as duplicate, invert, reverse) on the material. Students can play back the music they create on the canvas by pressing a Play button. The Sketch Pad, with even more fun and intuitive composer features, is a component of two of Subotnik's software programs, Making Music and Making (More) Music (Viva Media, distributed by Alfred Publishing).

Pattern Sequencer: iNudge

A great example of a genre of creative music software that removes limitations is the pattern sequencer. Pattern sequencers trigger sounds according to selections made by the user along a horizontal (time) and vertical (pitch, volume, timbre, etc.) matrix grid; the pattern can loop to create a groove. If the grid is 16 × 16, the sound of a steady beat would result if the first, fifth, ninth, and thirteenth horizontal positions were chosen. Students can approach musical creation very analytically or very intuitively based on the physical location of a box in a grid. **Fig. 6.1** shows a 16 × 16 matrix pattern sequencer grid in which the melodic contour generally ascends until near the end, where it descends. The only "rest," where no sound is triggered, is about halfway through.

iNudge (inudge.net) is one of several online pattern sequencing tools I discovered on the web. Like many web applications, it's free, and like most software

51

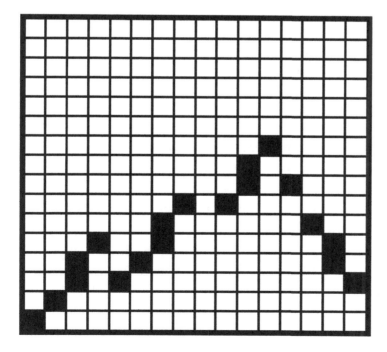

▶ **FIG. 6.1**
16 × 16 Matrix pattern sequencer grid. Graphic by Scott Watson.

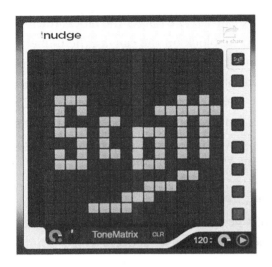

▶ **FIG. 6.2**

The "sound of my name" in a matrix pattern sequencer grid. Screen shot graphic by Scott Watson.

pattern sequencers, it's easy to use.[6] Pattern sequencers are great tools for getting kids to approach musical creation in a new way; even nonmusical ideas for note generation—such as "drawing" one's own name on the sequence grid—produce musically interesting results (**Fig. 6.2** and **Web Ex. 6.1**).

Hybrid Pattern Sequencer/Loop-Based Composing Software: O-Generator

O-Generator (by O-Music Ltd.) is software that combines features of pattern sequencing with loop-based recording in a novel and attractive graphic interface. The program is laid out in concentric circles, where each circle represents a category of sounds the user can choose, such as drum sounds (bass drum, tom-tom, etc.), guitar sounds (chord, strum gesture, etc.), or cymbal sounds (closed hi-hat, ride cymbal, etc.). These events are triggered in clockwise order, with one full circuit representing a measure. New, successive measures can be programmed, based on existing ones or with brand new content, to complete a song file. Song files can be exported as audio files for further use in programs such as Audacity or GarageBand.

Hybrid Auto-Accompaniment/Recording Software: Songsmith

Songsmith (manufactured by Microsoft Research) automatically generates a chordal accompaniment to a recorded vocal performance. Users select a musical style, or "groove," if you will, such as "50's rock," as well as a tempo. After pressing the record button, a two-measure count-off sounds, and the user sings freely—whatever he or she likes—along with the drum beat provided (to keep the timing true). When done, Songsmith analyzes the vocal recording and creates a chordal accompaniment, in the chosen style, based on the notes that have

---

6. Some pattern sequencers, such as those on a hardware drum machine or those built into the virtual music studio program Reason, can be sophisticated and complex.

been sung. What's more, each of the chords of this auto-generated accompaniment has a drop-down menu for selecting any other chord choices the user wants to try. Online videos of Songsmith creations demonstrate the potential for uneven or unexpected results, yet it is definitely worth checking out for Windows users.

Digital Audio Workstation Software: GarageBand et al.

Too many times, students' musical experiences conspire with the parameters of a creative activity to limit their ability to draw forth ideas as they have conceived them. Nontraditional music students might be very comfortable strumming chords on a guitar but cannot tell you the rhythm or exact notes they are strumming. Traditionally trained music students might be able to perform a syncopated rhythm but would be uncomfortable improvising on their major instrument in a popular idiom.

One technology tool that might help both NTM and traditionally trained music students is an entry-level digital audio workstation (DAW) like GarageBand, or any of its more sophisticated relatives (ProTools, Cubase, SONAR, Digital Performer, Logic, etc.). The guitarist can record his or her strumming right into an audio track, documenting the music as it is truly felt. The accomplished flutist can enter the notes of a composed melody, one note at a time, with a pencil tool.[7] Very young students can improvise rhythms far more intricate and complex than what they could notate, but set up a microphone and hit the record button on whatever recording software or hardware device you have, and you can capture that authentic expression.

STRUCTURAL PROBLEMS

Sometimes the structure of an activity—criteria and guidelines—contributes to stifled, contrived musical expression. Many years back when I taught seventh- and eighth-grade general music, I used to assign a percussion trio composition project. The kids worked in cooperative learning groups and were given blank percussion trio manuscript. One of the lesson parameters dealt with the size and makeup of the performing forces: They had to write for three different small percussion instruments. Another parameter dictated that students write in 4/4 time using basic rhythms: whole notes, half notes, quarter notes, and maybe even eighth-note pairs.

As kids worked in their groups around the room—improvising and interacting together—I remember hearing the coolest, complex, syncopated rhythms.

---

7. There are MIDI controllers available for string players (both violin family and guitars), wind players, and percussionists, but they are not very prevalent in K–12 music due to their expense and the time required to become fluent with the technology. A MIDI wind controller, which looks like a space-age, high-tech recorder, allows the player to use a fingering system similar to that of a flute or saxophone to play notes into a GarageBand MIDI track.

These rhythms were the authentic music I should have been most concerned with developing for the project. But the wonderful syncopations the kids were tapping, patting, clapping, stomping, and even vocally popping did not fit into the limitations I forced onto the project. Unwisely, I insisted that students simplify their rhythms if they could not notate what they were clapping. I discovered that if you tell eighth graders that they must write a percussion trio in 4/4 time, using only whole, half, and quarter notes—or rhythms that they can accurately notate—you are likely to get some dreadfully uninspired music!

Contrived expression is what you get when all the projects begin to sound more or less the same, with the sound of one unremarkable trio blurring into the next. When that happens, you probably have some stifling procedures that need to be removed.

Getting at Students' Authentic Creative Expression

The backward approach to the percussion trio composition assignment described above is an innocent mistake made by many music educators. **I was operating on the false assumption that the starting place for good composing is facility with and understanding of the rules of music notation.** Now I see that is like saying that good storytelling begins with the ability to write or type. Of course, many cultures have vibrant storytelling traditions even where literacy is not prevalent. Instead, I should have allowed students to begin creating from within, from the rhythms they seemed to intuitively and naturally produce. **Authentic expression is the communication of the true creative ideas inside the student.**

So where did the cool rhythms come from that I heard the students patting and clapping? How might I have tapped into that wellspring of rhythmic creativity for the project more effectively? Most kids are listening all the time to rhythmically active, syncopated popular and folk music; they tap, pat, clap, and stomp rhythms that emerge from this music without even thinking about it. Despite their experience and comfort with these rhythms, unless they have had years of traditional music performance training, they may not know how to document with standard music notation what they can so naturally perform. A little pedagogical tweaking, with the use of one technology tool or another, could greatly transform the percussion trio composition lesson mentioned above. As should be obvious, improvisation—both individual and collaborative—plays a big part in the sort of authentic expression described here. Since improvisation (principle 5) is discussed thoroughly in the next chapter ("Facilitate Improvisation"), I address here the way technology tools can remove the creative limitation that might be imposed on students who are uninterested in simple rhythms and/or uncomfortable with standard music notation. Depending upon what you determine is most important, there are many options.

Example: Dealing With the Limitations of Conventional Music Notation

The opening of this chapter demonstrates the great power for technology to remove limitations for students, especially students with limited experience with music notation.

Working With a Conventionally Notated Score

If you really want students to have an interaction with standard music notation with the rhythm project described above, have them record their rhythm—perhaps a one- or two-measure ostinato—into either a notation program or a multitrack MIDI recording program that offers a "notation view."[8] They could do this by tapping their rhythm on the key(s) of a MIDI keyboard (synthesizer or controller)[9] or pad of a MIDI drum trigger device, connected to a computer running the software.[10] The program transcribes the performance into on-screen notation for the student to examine, analyze, discuss, edit, and revise. If you set up the program so the kids hear a solid metronome click while recording, and so any minor rhythmic errors played are automatically adjusted (called quantizing),[11] you are likely to get some good results. Each member of the trio group could share the same keyboard (different keys = different drum sounds) and perform his or her MIDI-triggered drum part simultaneously with the others as they record. Both music notation and multitrack recording software allow students the option of recording one part at a time as well, in a "track-over-track" fashion. After the first student records his or her rhythm, the second student records in a new staff or track while hearing—and interacting with—the first recording. The same for the third student, and so on.

I have witnessed problems similar to those described with the percussion trio composition project with other composition activities that allow for tonal

---

8. Notes played into GarageBand may be viewed as rectangular bars of varying length (duration) on a grid or as conventional notes on a staff.

9. Use a MIDI-capable keyboard without onboard sounds that allows note data to be played or entered into MIDI programs (such as GarageBand and Finale). Typically, controllers depend on the software being used to produce the instrument sounds desired. Keyboard controllers come in different sizes (25-key, 49-key, etc.) and with various other features (limited onboard sounds, built-in audio interface, tap pads for triggering drum sounds, etc.), which affect cost. See chapter 12.

10. Thankfully at this time it is far more prevalent for the MIDI interface to be built into the keyboard (synthesizer or controller), requiring only a USB cable to connect it to a computer (see **Appendix 1**). When MIDI was developed around 1984, an external interface box translated performance data flowing back and forth between a synth keyboard and a computer running music software. A serial cable connected the box to the computer; specialized MIDI cables went from the box to the keyboard's MIDI "in" and "out" ports. While the benefits of MIDI were wonderful (arguably revolutionary), many found negotiating this configuration daunting.

11. *Quantizing* is the rounding of rhythms to the lowest subdivision of the beat. For instance, if you set the quantizing value to a sixteenth note, any rhythm played into the software that is smaller will be rounded to the nearest sixteenth note. In other words, play a 32nd note ahead of the beat and the software will "fix it" so it sounds as if you did not enter early.

55

components. For an eighth-grade composition project, for instance, students write songs with keyboard accompaniments they can play "by ear" but cannot notate. Here again, the authentic music students hear and create is limited, or impeded, if we force them to notate it traditionally. Michele Kaschub and Janice Smith suggest that the teachers themselves may decide to transcribe the students' musical inventions into standard notation if they feel comfortable with this sort of task.[12] This takes time and removes the students from part of the process, but it is a valid approach.

Other Ways to Document a Musical Performance

If seeing and working with conventional music notation are not important for this particular project, you do not necessarily need to use software that transcribes the rhythms the kids play, or a controller to enter those rhythms into the software. Instead, you could employ any number of audio recording methods to capture three actual percussion instruments (hand drums, wood block, triangle, etc.). Most kids would love to experiment with and incorporate into the project the cool sounds of a synth keyboard or electronic drum pad as well, if available. The options for making an audio recording are many, including using a handheld digital recording device or software on a computer in the room.[13] As in the scenario above, the players could record their performances all at once (together) or one at a time (track over track). You will need a set of headphones if you record one player at a time; the player being recorded wears the headphones to monitor and sync with the previously recorded part.[14] A great advantage of any of the digital recording schemes described above is that the "takes" (recordings) can be played back for evaluation and, if desired, edited. Kids love listening to their excellent and not-so-excellent attempts. An initial recording can easily be updated to include new phrases or sections created during subsequent class meetings. In the end, the recordings may serve only to remind students what they have composed in order to prepare for a culminating, live performance. A fairly complex percussion piece can be assembled from shorter recordings using multitrack recording software.[15] More complex *textures* are

12. Kaschub and Smith, *Minds on Music*, 85–86. In their scenario "Ms. Jones Plans a Project on Creating a School Song," the authors explain, "Because Ms. Jones had a good ear and a strong theory background, she felt she could transcribe whatever the children created into standard notation."

13. Many handheld devices have built-in microphones. If you decide on a computer/software recording scheme, you could use the computer's built-in microphone, or one of the fine, inexpensive, and simple-to-use USB microphones available, or a standard microphone connected to an audio interface via a conventional XLR microphone cable. See chapter 13.

14. For various reasons (timing, interaction, etc.), you will want the previously recorded part to play back as the next player records new material. Without headphones, the microphone will record both the live performer and the playback of the previously recorded part.

15. The "shorter recordings" can be "takes" recorded with a handheld recording device, audio recording software, or both. Audio recorded with a handheld device is usually dumped onto a computer via a USB cable or jack, or a media card.

achieved when the recordings are layered *vertically* in multiple tracks; more sophisticated *forms* are achieved when components are arranged *horizontally*.

Suggestions for Avoiding Project Parameters That Stifle Creativity

It is somewhat hard to know exactly which parameters or limitations stifle, rather than foster, creativity without *trial and error*. One thing is for sure: When you have imposed such strictures on an otherwise creative student, you will know it. Be open to revising plans that do not seem to be working as expected. The following are suggestions for removing structural limitations to creative activity guidelines:

1. **Do not try to do too much.** When I took undergraduate courses in teaching methods, my professors stressed thorough planning, suggesting we have extra activities ready just in case we wound up with spare time at the end of a class. Since then, I can count on one hand the number of times that has happened! Far more often I run out of time and do not get to everything I thought I would. Students can loose momentum or get overwhelmed if there are too many elements to a project. Instead, try breaking up a complex creative project into several activities of smaller scope.

2. **Allow kids to be part of the solution.** As educators we often feel we need to have everything worked out in advance for our kids. While I surely do not advocate being unprepared, it is entirely appropriate that students take ownership in the problem solving that accompanies creative endeavors as they grow in maturity and experience. When discussing their music technology students at Kennard-Dale High School in Fawn Grove, Pennsylvania, father-son teachers Carl and Matt Barr share, "It's not like we try to solve everything for them up front." Instead, the Barrs allow students to encounter challenges and find solutions using the tools at their disposal.

3. **Emphasize the artistic over the technical.** If I have an hour to work with kids composing with notation software, I would rather err on the side of spending too much time discussing musical considerations (repetition, form, harmonic rhythm, etc.) than how to use the program. When working with any multipart music production program, I think it is more important to focus on the music you will be creating than the way the program works. Ultimately, if the students are motivated musically, they will discover the techniques they need to accomplish their musical goals. Barbara Freedman, a gifted colleague who teaches electronic music at Greenwich High School in Greenwich, Connecticut, wisely likes to say, "Teach music, and the technology will follow."

4. Give students space to create. Some things are hard to do in front of other people. I believe this is often the case with authentic creativity. If students are never given time to explore, experiment, and improvise, they probably will not discover musical gestures about which they feel enthusiasm and ownership. Sometimes this happens better for students working alone, but other times a group, collaborative dynamic sparks creativity.

IMPLICATIONS FOR LEARNERS WITH SPECIAL NEEDS

The principle of removing limitations to authentic creativity has implications for all students, including those with special needs. The same technology tools that allow an NTM student to create with musical elements such as pitch, rhythm, and timbre hold similar benefits for the special learner as well. Many MIDI recording programs show notes as different-length rectangular bars placed at various vertical and horizontal positions on a grid (**Fig. 6.3**). When I first began working with software sequencers, I found this view of music to be awkward for me. After working in that environment for a little while, and witnessing how quickly most NTM students feel comfortable with it, I realized the benefits of using alternative approaches to organizing sound. The same is true for youngsters that have not formally studied an instrument but can arrange shapes that correspond to sounds and short musical gestures (loops) as easily as they can finger paint. Technology can bring sophisticated decision making into reach for students with even modest music background.

Novel Music Hardware Solutions

Some technology tools, because of their unconventional approach to music making, inspire musical creation that otherwise would never have been imagined by the student. Such is the Kaossilator (manufactured by Korg; **Fig. 6.4**), a

▶ **FIG. 6.3**
Two views of "Yankee Doodle" in Garage-Band: graphic grid (top) and notation (bottom). Graphic created by Scott Watson.

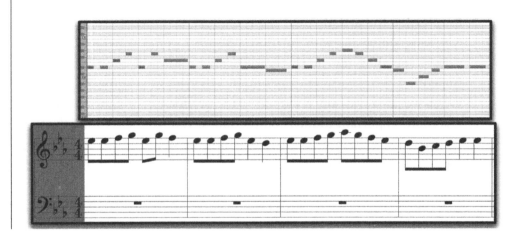

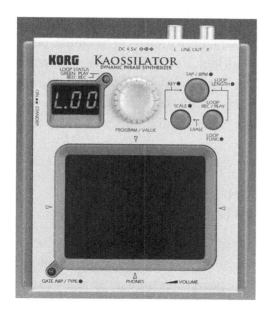

► **FIG. 6.4**
Kaossilator "Dynamic Phrase Synthesizer" (by Korg). Graphic provided by Korg USA. Used with permission.

handheld synthesizer that levels the playing field between students with and without traditional musical (instrumental or vocal) training. This device allows students to improvise and record gestures on a touch pad, which are translated into patterns of various scales and timbres depending on a number of intuitive variables. Each new pattern can be layered on top of previous patterns for complex textures. Kaossilator creations can be recorded via the audio output jacks. Because the Kaossilator calls on such radically different paradigms of sound organization, it is hard to know whether to call it an instrument or music production hardware. One thing is certain: Creative technology tools such as this prompt students to create in new and interesting ways. Barbara Freedman, who leads a large electronic music program at Greenwich High School in Greenwich, Connecticut, employs Kaossilators to enable students of all musical backgrounds to create and perform collaboratively. You can see a brief video of some of her students performing with Kaossilators and other technology at the companion website (**Web Ex. 6.2**).

Soundbeam (manufactured by Soundbeam Project)[16]—a product that senses movement and converts it into sound—has been shown to hold benefits for students (and older adults) with more significant limitations. Originally conceived for triggering musical events (loops, ambient textures, tones, etc.) and changes (events and timbres, pitches, volume, etc.) to movements by dancers, this product has been found to be valuable "assistive technology" by those working with individuals with a variety of special needs. Soundbeam responds to pronounced, dancelike motions or even very subtle, nuances gestures. Soundbeam

16. Soundbeam is distributed in the United States by SoundTree. I encourage readers to check out the fascinating videos of children and adults with special needs using Soundbeam at their website (www.soundbeam.co.uk).

delivers a sense of agency and creative control to youngsters and adults with or without mental or physical limitations and has much potential for music therapists or music educators looking for alternative means of musical creativity and expression. Since there are no widely acknowledged "rules" for performing or creating with technology tools such as the Soundbeam or Kaossilator, students may feel freer to explore and improvise (an aspect addressed in the next chapter).

EXAMINING CONCEPTUAL AND AESTHETIC LIMITATIONS

For many of us, the biggest limitation to creativity deals with our concept of music. As Robert Sternberg and Wendy Williams observe, "We all have assumptions. . . . Creative people question those assumptions and eventually lead others to do the same."[17] The more broad our answer to the question "What is music?" the more open are we to experiences with electronic sounds, soundscape/collage-type compositions, aleatoric elements, graphically notated scores that use symbols rather than notes on a staff, and other unconventional musical formats. Since this sort of "limitation" is primarily one of experience, I highly recommend engaging students in listening to, examining, and discussing musically provocative examples, such as those from the electronic art music, minimalist, or serial music traditions. Audio recordings of some of these pieces may be somewhat hard to locate, but it may surprise you to learn how often one can find examples of all of these types of progressive music in film scores.[18] Several years ago I played a track by legendary computer music composer (and Princeton University professor) Paul Lansky for students in a high school music theory class. The piece, "Idle Chatter Junior," features severely edited spoken word recordings used in a percussive way, along with other MIDI/synthesizer elements. The students enjoyed hearing the track, discussing the concept of creating music from speech, and broadening the discussion to include other nontraditional approaches they had observed in popular and alternative music. After class I overheard several students outside my lab discussing the class. One of them said, "I can't believe Dr. Watson even knows who Paul Lansky is!" Intrigued, I joined the group and asked about their remark. It turns out that the English alternative rock band Radiohead admired Lansky and "sampled" one of his ear-

---

17. Sternberg and Williams, *How to Develop Student Creativity*, 11.

18. For instance, the soundtrack to the 1980 Stanley Kubrick thriller, *The Shining*, includes music by Béla Bartók (*Music for Strings, Percussion and Celeste*, third movement), Krzysztof Penderecki, György Ligeti, and Wendy Carlos, among others. An earlier Kubrick film, *A Clockwork Orange* (1971), featured music by synthesizer artist Wendy Carlos (better known for her album *Switched-On Bach*). Less disturbing films that incorporated "progressive" music include *Chariots of Fire* (1981; music by new-age composer Vangelis) up to more recent films such as *The Illusionist* (2006; music by minimalist Philip Glass). It is hard to find a film made recently that does not incorporate at least some synthesized sound.

lier works in one of their popular songs.[19] These Radiohead fans had stumbled upon one of many examples of how experimental art music has contributed to popular/commercial music. Chapter 13 includes a lesson for creating electronic art music with digital audio recording software, accompanied by a selected discography of music to consider for listening examples.

WRAP-UP

As I mentioned in the opening to this book, risk taking is a big part of delivering your curriculum via creative projects. While we attempt to thoroughly think through the steps and stages of a unit beforehand, we must be willing to give new ideas a try, to reflect with discernment and candor on what worked well and what did not, to make revisions as necessary, and then move on. Sometimes when complications and problems outweigh the anticipated benefits of a lesson or project, "moving on" means jettisoning it altogether. More often than not, a great lesson idea falls flat because of parameters or limitations that stifle. If you are excited about a lesson idea, chances are your students will be, too. If, after working through the lesson, things look different, maybe the project idea is sound but limitations need to be removed. Consider how one of the technology tools at your disposal might do this.

REFLECTION ACTIVITY

1. Describe *authentic creativity*, as opposed to stifled or contrived expression.

2. What are some ways technology can foster free, genuine expression from less experienced musicians?

3. What are some ways that technology itself might prove to be a distraction to students engaged in creative musical activity? How can this sort of distraction be minimized or avoided?

19. The song was "Idioteque" from their 2000 album *Kid A* (Capitol). Radiohead sampled several seconds from Lansky's "Mild und Leise," an early tape piece from 1973. The four chords in this excerpt become the signature chord progression for the entire song.

61

CHAPTER 7
PRINCIPLE 5: FACILITATE IMPROVISATION

THE KEY ROLE OF IMPROVISATION

THE REGULAR SCHOOL DAY IS OVER, and most kids have cleared out of the building. I stay after school to help a few of my music production students with some tracking sessions for a class project. I walk into the music technology lab to find a student seated at one of our keyboard synths, apparently lost in creative reverie. The music he is playing is simple, yet intriguing. I do not recognize it. "Hey, what are you up to?" I ask. "Nothing," the student replies, "just fooling around." He's improvising. "Fooling around" seems apropos for several reasons. I can hear the stop and start of an experimenter; he is not playing an existing piece of music. Instead, he's auditioning various notes and chords and keyboard figurations in search of music that is slowly forming in his imagination. The process, what Michele Kaschub and Janice Smith call "thinking *in* music," as opposed to "thinking *about* music,"[1] is a little ambiguous, but it can be very satisfying.

Many composers turn to improvisation like this as a starting point, the creative spark, for generating material for a piece. When a composer feels a certain gesture, phrase, or passage improvised is worth preserving, he or she documents it for use later. Even experienced composers with strong aural skills enjoy the tactile interaction with an instrument as they play and "feel" for ideas that inspire. There are times when improvising at the keyboard that I unintentionally hit certain keys but yet find the sound to be very interesting and possibly useful for a future piece. I call these occurrences "musical penicillin" after the legendary accidental discovery in 1928 of the life-saving antibiotic by Scottish research scientist Alexander Fleming. Once "discovered," these ideas can be recorded in a sketchbook or developed immediately as part of a composition. Improvisation opens the door for musical discovery.

Employing rhythmic or melodic improvisation might be useful for developing an initial theme for a melodic composition. Instrumental music students

---

1. Kaschub and Smith, *Minds on Music*, 21. Kaschub and Smith consider this sort of "fooling around" to be part of a precomposition process they call "exploration." As a composer, I view improvisation broadly to include this very informal tinkering.

could use their instruments (in school or at home) to experiment with melodic gestures, settling on a favorite as the basis for beginning the melody. Students composing in groups in a general music class might each improvise a rhythmic pattern, with the teacher transcribing them, and then vote on the pattern they would like to use to start the piece.

Improvisation is also an active way to participate in music as we hear it. Although some improvisation is very free, much improvisation calls for participants to know in advance something about the music's plan and to respond according. Very few students will have enough familiarity with an instrument and/or harmonic theory to be able to improvise in the way you might at first be thinking, like when a jazz musician follows chord changes. But as was noted in chapter 7 when discussing the percussion trio composition, rhythmic improvisation comes more naturally to most students and can be exploited.

TECHNOLOGY AND PEDAGOGY FACILITATING IMPROVISATION

Some great music technology, both hardware and software, can be used to break students free from their inhibitions to achieve spontaneous, "in the moment" creativity and to document these improvisations for further use. The attractiveness of synthesized or sampled sound, for instance, or the comfort of a certain interface (drum pad, pitch bend wheel, etc.) invites experimentation with expression. In addition to the technology, we rely on pedagogical principles (modeling, coaching, employing carefully chosen parameters) to create an environment in which students—especially those with limited formal music training—can succeed in improvising.

Favorite Sounds Redux

One very simple but effective activity I do with students involves adding a small layer of improvisation on top of the "My Favorite Sounds" lesson mentioned in chapter 3 (and described in detail in chapter 12). This activity can be adapted to almost any level; I have done it with older elementary, high school, and university students. I give my kids a predetermined amount of time to explore and audition the many attractive sounds on a keyboard synthesizer, noting a few of their favorites—students love exploring the sounds so much that they hate when I tell them the time is up! After a time, I require that each student play one of these "favorite sounds" for the class using a melodic or rhythmic phrase they have developed. Most will be able to perform some kind of demonstration of their favorite sound, even if it's just a one- or two-note rhythmic pattern. The sounds are so attractive, they often inspire students to invent melodies, chords, or rhythms. As they explore the sounds, students devise these short rhythmic or melodic gestures or phrases by improvising. To ensure that each student comes up with a decent example of their favorite sound to show off to the class, I incorporates principle 2 (offering compelling examples) and principle 6 (coaching). This means that (1) I first demonstrate a few of my favorite sounds to the class by improvising short, easy gestures, and (2) once the students begin working, I try to coach students that seem uncomfortable with the task. For instance, to demonstrate how just two notes can create an interesting groove, I usually play a two-note version of the bassline for the George Benson tune "On Broadway" (**Fig. 7.1**).

There are many other "tricks" that can effectively get students to open up and create with the sounds on a synth keyboard. If your keyboard has pitch bend and modulation wheels (or levers, etc.), encourage kids to experiment with those and—if they like—incorporate them into their improvisation. You could tap into principle 3 (employing parameters) by suggesting to students that they stick to either all white keys (pandiatonic) or all black keys (pentatonic). Use of a drone or pedal point can also lead to improvisation inspiration. You can differentiate the task for stronger musicians, too. Students who have studied piano or a band instrument can usually figure out or recall melodies. I encourage these to improvise idiomatically for whatever instrument they select. If they choose a slapped bass sound, maybe they can figure out a funk gesture in the bass range; if they choose a piano sound, perhaps something arpeggiated; if they choose a folk guitar sound, they can consider how to approximate strumming. The possibilities are endless.

In the end, I believe something about the attractiveness of the technology itself encourages kids to be creative. All the keys, buttons, sliders, and wheels invite tactile learners; all the evocative sounds engage auditory learners. Visual learners like exploring the display and/or a listing of sounds I sometimes hand out as a guide. At times, I add a cognitive layer on top of the creative task by asking students to choose a favorite sound in several categories of timbre (woodwind, brass, percussion, strings, guitar, bass, keyboard, sound effect, etc.). What's more, students who engage in this activity get great practice with the basic operations of a keyboard without even realizing it. I always look forward to hearing what students have created through improvisation at the conclusion of the "My Favorite Sounds" activity. Anyone who has explored the sounds of a good synth keyboard knows there is a connection between timbre and the musical imagination. The same sort of activity can be done using the wonderful software instrument sounds in GarageBand. An added advantage with Garage-Band is that the student's sound demonstration can be recorded for playback if desired rather than performed live. The "My Favorite Sounds" activity only re-

▶ **FIG. 7.1**

Simple bass line based on George Benson's, "On Broadway." Graphic created by Scott Watson.

quires a short demonstration of a keyboard sound students find attractive, but the exercise often leads to longer, more involved creations.

Music Technology and Rhythmic Improvisation

With MIDI synthesizers, the term *drum kit* refers to a mapping of different percussion sounds to each of the keys of the keyboard. Press a low C and get a bass drum, a D above that triggers a snare drum, the F-sharp above that is a hi-hat, and so on (see **Fig. 7.2**). Some keyboard controllers include a set of drum trigger pads to which drum sounds (onboard or software sounds) can be assigned. Stand-alone trigger pads, such as Korg's nanoPAD (**Fig. 7.3**), do this as well.

Some improvisation activities I have used involve improvising with drum sounds on a synth keyboard drum kit. These activities include (1) choosing several drum sounds, (2) performing rock drum set patterns, (3) improvising a short "drum fill" at the end of a phrase, (4) creating a drum improvisation with a partner, and (5) accompanying a story with sound effects. In the "drum fill" activity, students are assigned and taught one of several parts to a rock drum beat (e.g., snare drum, bass drum, ride cymbal) to be performed with appropriate music technology (a MIDI drum kit on a synth keyboard, software drum

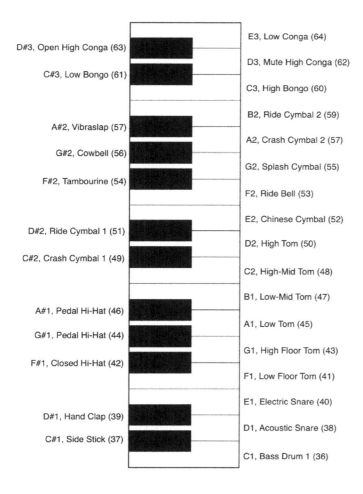

Key	Sound
D#3	Open High Conga (63)
C#3	Low Bongo (61)
A#2	Vibraslap (57)
G#2	Cowbell (56)
F#2	Tambourine (54)
D#2	Ride Cymbal 1 (51)
C#2	Crash Cymbal 1 (49)
A#1	Pedal Hi-Hat (46)
G#1	Pedal Hi-Hat (44)
F#1	Closed Hi-Hat (42)
D#1	Hand Clap (39)
C#1	Side Stick (37)

Key	Sound
E3	Low Conga (64)
D3	Mute High Conga (62)
C3	High Bongo (60)
B2	Ride Cymbal 2 (59)
A2	Crash Cymbal 2 (57)
G2	Splash Cymbal (55)
F2	Ride Bell (53)
E2	Chinese Cymbal (52)
D2	High Tom (50)
C2	High-Mid Tom (48)
B1	Low-Mid Tom (47)
A1	Low Tom (45)
G1	High Floor Tom (43)
F1	Low Floor Tom (41)
E1	Electric Snare (40)
D1	Acoustic Snare (38)
C1	Bass Drum 1 (36)

▶ **FIG. 7.2**

A portion of the General MIDI Standard Drum Kit keyboard assignments. Graphic created by Scott Watson.

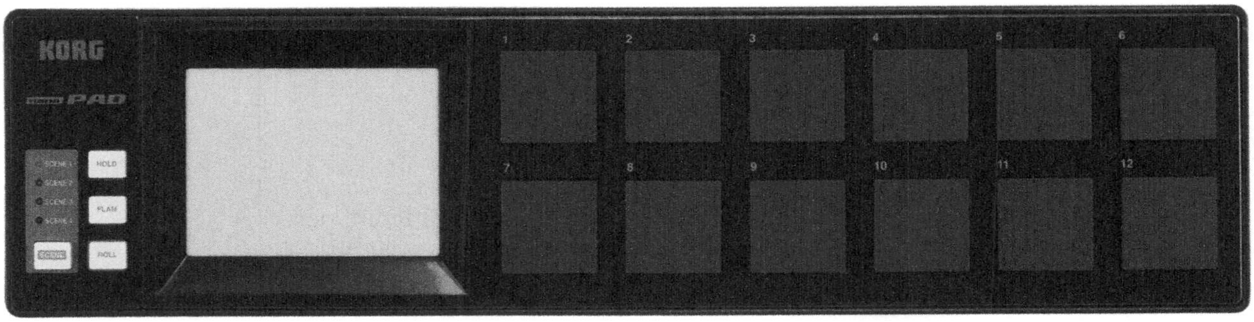

▶ **FIG. 7.3**

Korg's nanoPAD can be programmed to trigger software drum sounds. Graphic provided by Korg USA. Used with permission.

sounds triggered by QWERTY keys, an electronic drum pad, etc.). The class performs the rock drum beat for three measures as an ostinato, but leaves the fourth measure open (resting) for solo drum fills. This framework allows students to take turns improvising a one-measure fill on any instrument sound(s) available to them. The one-measure solo is pretty nonthreatening; most students will participate without urging. Some will no doubt desire a longer solo. That is just one more adaptation you may consider. Other variations to this incredibly adaptable lesson include changing the style (such as from rock to jazz swing), combining acoustic percussion instruments, having pairs of soloists play duet fills, and having students create their own multipart percussion ostinatos. These lessons, based on ideas from veteran music teacher and music technology specialist Dr. Tom Rudolph,[2] are detailed in chapter 12 ("Creativity With Keyboards").

Rhythmic improvisation can be paired with more formally composed music. Each year I assign a brief modal composition project to my high school AP music theory class. In presenting this first composition project of the school year, I explain the parameters they must follow (which include length, mode choice, and following one of three composition models: a hymn, a wind or string instrumental etude, or a piano "song") and share a few examples from previous years. I offer them the choice of using notation software for the project, but since it is so early in the year I do not require it. I do require that they, or another student they secure, perform the finished piece (principle 8 deals with employing performance and recital). A few years back, Julia W. wrote a great piece for solo violin in fulfillment of this assignment that another class member agreed to perform. After hearing her piece in class, which had the air of a rustic, Renaissance dance, the other students and I agreed that it needed

2. Dr. Thomas Rudolph is Director of Music for the Haverford School District in Pennsylvania, where he teaches middle-school general and instrumental music. He is a pioneer in the use of music technology in general music keyboard and computer labs at Haverford and with his music education technology workshops and courses for teachers. He is a founder and former president of the organization TI:ME (Technology for Music Education). The chapter 12 drum improvisation lessons are based on activities I have seen Tom use when teaching the TI:ME course "Basic Skills in Music Technology: Electronic Instruments, MIDI Sequencing, and Notation" (TI:ME 1A).

some percussion. We borrowed a conga drum from the band room and had the violinist perform Julia's etude while another student improvised on the drum. We made an in-class audio recording of these performances; here, the technology was used *to capture* the improvisation. Adding an improvised drum part to an already composed student project often transforms the piece into something even more effective and compelling. You can hear the class recording of Julia's piece, "Dorian Mode," at the book's website (**Web Ex. 7.1**).

ADVANTAGES OF UNCONVENTIONAL INSTRUMENTS

It is worth noting that several of the technology tools mentioned in chapter 6 (such as Kaossilator and Soundbeam) could be mentioned again here as examples of technology that facilitates improvisation. Performing on these relatively new, unconventional, technology-driven devices is so unlike that of any orchestral instrument that the advantage or disadvantage of traditional musical training is negligible, and students feel free to improvise with them. These instruments remind me of the Theremin, invented as a classical instrument but best known for its use in 1950s space sci-fi movie scores to suggest aliens.[3] Even today, about 100 years after its creation by Russian inventor Leon Theremin, only a handful of concert artists in the world perform on the instrument. As with all technology, one must weigh the costs of using these devices against their benefits. Adopting certain tools may not be warranted if the devices carry a high per unit price tag, will be used only by a small fraction of students, and require a lot of additional training to learn.[4] On the other hand, their cost may be justified if you are looking to engage special needs students in creative musical expression.

The QWERTY keyboard on a desktop or laptop computer is a ubiquitous input device that can be used to improvise musically. While its use in this way is unconventional, it certainly is an interface that is very familiar to students. *QWERTY* refers to the six consecutive letters in the top left row of alphabet keys on the computer keyboard. The term is often used when making a distinction between it and the synth (piano) keyboard. Programs such as GarageBand and Band-in-a-Box allow for sounds to be triggered from a QWERTY keyboard, turning the computer keyboard into an instrument. Band-in-a-Box links the keys of the QWERTY keyboard to an attractive, fun-to-play virtual drum set emulation (**Fig. 7.4**). Be sure to check out the "Band-in-a-Box Drum Window Improvisation" lesson in chapter 16.

---

3. Many people would say the best-known use of the Theremin is in the Beach Boys hit "Good Vibrations." Actually, the instrument used was the Electro-Theremin, developed by Bob Whitsell in 1958 for Paul Tanner to play on the Beach Boys recording (for this reason, it is also know as the Tannerin). In live performances of "Good Vibrations," however, the Beach Boys used a Moog ribbon controller.

4. These are exactly the factors that have kept MIDI woodwind, brass, and guitar controllers from being more widely adopted by school music programs.

▶ **FIG. 7.4**

Students can trigger various percussion sounds from Band-in-a-Box's Drum Window using the computer's QWERTY keys. Graphic created by Scott Watson.

Imagine assigning different sounds or loops to each key of a computer's QWERTY keyboard. Then imagine students pressing those keys to trigger, in real time, the corresponding sounds or loops. This scenario is fairly easy to configure using programs such as GarageBand, SOund BOard (The Music Interactive), and Alphabet Soup (Oz Music Code). Computer keys can trigger drum loops, synth drones, various percussion instrument sounds, a hand clap, a sneeze, or pretty much anything a student wants to record. The audio files may be any sound you create or record yourself, or sounds or loops already on your computer. GarageBand and Alphabet Soup do this simply with a graphic emulation of the QWERTY keyboard; users drag and drop any audio file on their hard drive onto the key to which they want it assigned. SOund BOard involves just a bit more (storing the audio file in a specific folder and then listing it in a text document). Individuals, small groups, or entire classes or ensembles (such as laptop orchestra) can then call on these sounds in interactive improvisation. Recording original sounds and calling on them in improvisations are things students of almost any grade level or musical experience will enjoy. Be sure to examine the lesson "GarageBand Key Sounds" in chapter 14.

MELODIC AND HARMONIC IMPROVISATION

You will notice that in sharing examples of creative improvisation so far, I have not mentioned the "J word": jazz. I believe a lot of music teachers shy away from incorporating improvisation into their teaching because they associate the practice with jazz or rock performance alone. As we have seen, improvisation encompasses many things. Nonetheless, there are some very effective ways to encourage improvisation in jazz, blues, and other popular music genres, especially with the help of technology. A great approach is to limit the note choices. This accomplishes two things: (1) as per principle 3, students will be able to focus more if there are less notes from which to choose, and (2) as compelling melodic ideas are created with only a handful of notes, and used effectively via repetition, students will experience the compositional "truth" that sometimes less is more. A note collection many educators have used with keyboards for teaching blues improvisation is the black-key pentatonic scale. The notes of this collection align nicely with five of the notes of the E-flat blues scale (1, ♭3, 4, 5, ♭7). Of course, there is a difference between running up and down the black-key pentatonic scale and playing aesthetically pleasing ideas with that scale. What makes improvised blues or jazz solos interesting are the same sorts of things that make well-composed music interesting: limiting the number of themes, controlled repetition and variation of the themes and phrases, and so forth. Once students feel safe using the notes of the black-key pentatonic scale, you can begin to inform their melodic ideas via listening examples and coaching.[5] The "Blues Keyboard Improvisation" lesson in chapter 12 shares ideas for using the black-key pentatonic scale for blues improvisation with keyboards, as well as variations that work well with programs such as GarageBand and Band-in-a-Box.

Since Band-in-a-Box (manufactured by PG Music) was introduced about two decades ago, instrumental music teachers have recognized the potential of this intelligent accompaniment software to reinforce improvisation. Type in chords and other information (style, tempo, number of repeats, etc.) as desired, hit the play button, and a virtual jazz combo plays back what has been entered. Band-in-a-Box has many other useful features, such as the ability to generate a solo in the style of famous jazz artists that can be printed out to examine or play.[6] Band-in-a-Box also makes accessible the harmonic aspect of music creation for all music students. While not strictly improvisation, Band-in-a-Box facilitates something similar in the area of harmonic exploration by allowing students to type in and audition various chords.

---

5. For other note collections, I have placed small red-dot stickers (available at most stationary stores) on certain white keys of the synth keyboards in my lab to highlight the notes from which I wanted students to choose for improvisations.

6. You could also print the bass part that Band-in-a-Box generates to demonstrate "walking bass" to your jazz band bass player, or the keyboard or guitar part to demonstrate "comping" to changes (chordal accompaniment). The manufacturer of Finale music notation software (MakeMusic) has licensed Band-in-a-Box's intelligent accompaniment technology and incorporated it into a "plug-in" called Band-in-a-Box Auto Harmonizer. This plug-in analyzes a melody and its accompanying chord changes and can generate some nice-sounding instrumental parts.

RISK TAKING AND MISTAKES

Nobel-winning scientist, author, and peace activist Linus Pauling once said, "The best way to have a good idea is to have lots of ideas." Improvisation offers students the opportunity to try out many ideas in the form of notes and musical gestures. Some (perhaps many) of these may at first sound wrong, like mistakes. Although they might not make it into the final version of a work, these attempts are vital to the process. Sternberg and Williams explain, "Anyone who generates many ideas is going to have some poor ideas and make mistakes. Did you know that baseball's king of home runs, Babe Ruth, also held the strike-out record?"[7]

WRAP-UP

Improvisation is a type of creative expression in its own right but can also serve as a gateway to composing. Software and hardware tools can stimulate, guide, and help document improvisation efforts as ends unto themselves or as part of the process of building larger creative structures. Examples of technology that facilitates improvisation include both simple and more specialized interfaces. Sounds can be intuitively triggered from the keys of a QWERTY keyboard, the keys of a MIDI synth or controller keyboard, a MIDI synth drum pad, or more exotic devices such as Korg's Kaossilator. As the technology itself invites musical exploration, improvisation "happens." Other times, an environment can be created pedagogically where improvisation is fostered and the technology is there to capture it for students to play back, edit, save as is, or incorporate into something larger.

REFLECTION ACTIVITY

1. How can one's experience learning an instrument affect one's comfort improvising?

2. Consider and discuss how some technology inspires improvisation while other technology removes barriers to documenting it.

3. Can a student be too inexperienced to improvise? What are some technology tools and solutions that make it possible and fun for even inexperienced musicians to employ improvisation as a part of the precomposition process?

4. This chapter includes exploration and experimentation under the umbrella of improvisation. Describe the process of moving from this sort of precompositional "fooling around" to the beginnings of building a composition.

5. What effect might improvising with a partner or collaborator have?

7. Sternberg and Williams, *How to Develop Student Creativity*, 30.

CHAPTER 8
PRINCIPLE 6: ENGAGE IN COACHING INTERACTION

COACHING IS THE KEY!

I LOVE REACTING TO students' emerging efforts as they begin to assemble their ideas in fulfillment of a project. In their varied feats of creativity I see many of the same situations that all composers and arrangers must think about, such as the use of repetition, contrasting ideas, and timbre (instrument choice or orchestration, if you will). Other types of creative projects—podcasts, movies, web pages, multimedia slideshows, and so on—have conventions of their own to address. One of the most efficient ways to address particular issues with your students, who tend to work at varying levels of comfort and proficiency, is via one-on-one or small-group interactions built into instructional time. I call this "coaching." The topic of coaching with regard to creative projects is huge. I employ coaching because I really enjoy this particular aspect of creative music teaching. But more important, I find that coaching makes a big difference in the level of student understanding and (as should come as no surprise) the quality of creative output. When I am consulting with a colleague who is experiencing some difficulty in carrying out a creative project with their students, I can usually trace it back to a problem with, or the lack of, coaching.

The relative length of this chapter speaks to both the importance of coaching and the many ways it can be carried out. Although I offer numerous suggestions and provide scenarios for this form of instruction, the goal of this chapter is just to get the ball rolling, to demonstrate the key role coaching plays when shepherding kids in creative musical endeavors.

OTHER MODES OF LEARNING

Before turning to the advantages and methodology of coaching, I want to briefly mention two modes of learning that coaching is meant to complement: large-group instruction and students working independently. The traditional "sage on the stage" teacher will lecture or demonstrate from the front of the room and then give a seatwork or homework assignment that students carry out on their own. While these pedagogical methods are fairly conventional, I do want to mention some important considerations with regard to creative projects that use technology for each.

Large-Group Instruction

Large-group instruction is an important tool for introducing projects, explaining important concepts, relaying factual information, and rehearsing content with students. One of the best ways to deliver technology-centered instruction is via a computer video projector or interactive whiteboard—the overhead projectors and blackboards of the twenty-first century.[1] The whole class can focus together on activities such as viewing slides or movies, demonstrating software features, or having students perform various operations they have learned. Large-group instruction is often a great way to begin and wrap up creative lessons. It is also useful for disseminating information vital to a creative project, or delivering training on some feature of the software being used, before releasing students to work independently.

Students Working Independently (Alone or in Small Groups)

If you are going to engage students in creative work, they will need time *during class* to work on their own (or in small groups). I do not like to compose with people all around me watching and listening; I imagine many students feel the same way when they are creating. Composition and other creative work sometimes require an environment in which students can look inward for ideas and consider options without the inhibitions caused (rationally or not) by others close by. There are several reasons that a big chunk of this independent (or small group) work should be during class time. In class the teacher can watch over students, especially as they start out, and be sure they are on track. Many students have no precedent for engaging in the types of musical creativity featured in the lessons later in this book. Other students might understand the task but simply have a creative block (such as "Where should I go now?"). An ideal environment for creative work in school is one in which students can work on their own (or with a partner or two), exploring ideas for completing the creative task at hand, but still have the safety net of guidance and suggestions from the teacher if needed. Such is the case when a student is working in a computer or

1. It is fairly standard for school districts to provide a personal computer connected to the Internet for their staff. With this music teachers can (1) access many great music education websites, wikis, and blogs, (2) download many freeware music learning applications, and (3) access an increasing number of useful web applications. After that, in my opinion, the most valuable technology item is a computer video projector or interactive whiteboard, which allows you to use these resources as a class. Used projectors, available for a small fraction of their new retail price at online resellers such as eBay and Amazon.com, are more approachable—even on a tight budget—than ever.

keyboard lab, with headphones on, able to workout their ideas by improvising, experimenting, auditioning, and imagining. If your classroom or school does not have a computer lab, music technology lab, keyboard cluster,[2] computer pod,[3] or other area for students to work independently, they may be able to take advantage of new web developments to do this work from home.

The Internet and Increased Access to Music Technology

Time for independent work *in school* is doubly important when a technology-dependent lesson calls for software or hardware that students do not have at home. The web is changing, however, in exciting and helpful ways. Each year we are seeing more and more online music applications for things such as notating, recording, and synthesizing music.

As I write this, for instance, many music educators have begun to incorporate the online notation application Noteflight.com into their curriculum. This free service allows students to establish an account, engage in entry-level music typesetting tasks, and then save, retrieve, or update their work whenever and wherever they are online. Students can begin an assignment in school, go home and work some more, and then return to school the next day to share their progress with the teacher and/or fellow students.[4] What's more, Noteflight allows users to create web links to its files or even embed them into other web pages, blogs, or wikis. Noteflight, like so many others being introduced, has much potential for use in the music curriculum, creative or otherwise (**Fig. 8.1**).

Other musical web applications for sequencing, creating, and arranging loops, audio recording, and more are appearing on the Internet all the time. Many kids love the convenience, privacy, and satisfaction of performing creative musical tasks online at home with these web tools. However, when I employ them I always try to have an in-school option (class time, recess, before school, after school, lunch with the teacher, etc.) since for some students—especially in lower socioeconomic areas—students may not have access to the Internet, the necessary operating system, or even a computer at home.[5]

---

2. A *keyboard cluster* is a limited number of (usually) inexpensive electronic keyboards, with headphones, set up somewhere on the perimeter of the music room where students can take turns working on creative tasks.

3. A *computer pod* is a small group of computers (say, three to five), arranged usually somewhere on the perimeter of a classroom, where students can take turns accomplishing technology-assisted tasks.

4. Because Noteflight.com stores the files online and allows users to make certain "share" settings, your students can collaborate with other students (in your class or even a different school). This year my high school music theory students and I partnered with a colleague and his students in another part of our state for several rewarding interactions using Noteflight.

5. Where I teach, most families have a computer and broadband Internet access. However, some computers running older operating systems do not have current utility applications necessary for many of today's online applications to work. Without a recent version of the Adobe Flash Player, for instance, use of Noteflight is limited.

▶ **FIG. 8.1**

Noteflight (www
.noteflight.com),
a well-conceived,
web-based music
notation application.
Graphic created by
Scott Watson.

74

COACHING IS EFFICIENT AND EFFECTIVE

If you try to lead kids through creative activities using only large-group instruction and individual (or small group) work time, you will find that the most proficient kids do okay while the others flounder, with everyone achieving less than they could. Because of our students' differing musical and technical backgrounds, I have found that coaching (or conferencing) as part of a differentiated instruction approach better serves the creative process for both stronger and weaker students, including especially those with special needs.

Perhaps I gravitate to the pedagogy of coaching because of my instrumental music background. When I first started teaching, my district allowed for only once-per-week, large-group instruction of second-year band students. Addressing everyone's diverse challenges—helping clarinetists to play higher notes (notes "above the break") or snare drummers to learn the various rolls (5-stroke, 9-stroke, etc.) was really tough. Small-group and private instrumental lessons are so effective in conveying, reinforcing, and assessing musical concepts because the teaching can be more easily tailored to the students' needs. The classroom management challenges of coaching interaction are obviously greater for general and elective music courses than for small-group instrumental lessons, but finding ways to offer this sort of focused instruction pays huge dividends in terms of student understanding and work quality.

COACHING CONCERNS

How Do I Find Time for Coaching?

Coaching takes time and planning, but coaching moments do not need to be long or to occur every class meeting. Make time for them regularly along with large-group instruction and student work sessions so you are aware of how students are progressing. Coaching sessions do not need to be lengthy and, in fact, may be very brief. Whether you are coaching individuals as you circulate around a lab, or at the classroom piano while others work at their seats or on the floor, or in front of the class while others observe, you should be able to address issues in a meaningful way in about three to five minutes. While longer coaching sessions are great, they are normally not practical unless you have small, seminar-type classes. If you feel you need longer than five minutes, you should probably adjust the scope of the task for which you are coaching.

Getting Started

One of the most important times to hold brief coaching sessions is near the start of a creative project when students often must make defining choices. Imagine that you are having your fifth graders work in small groups on scoring a 20-second video clip (see chapter 14 for a detailed lesson plan). Some defining choices might include selecting the video clip from a choice of three and spotting the clip for where musical and sound effect elements should occur (notated on a cue sheet). It is unlikely that students need coaching guidance in selecting the video—presumably, all three video clips have been preselected by the teacher to lend themselves to the project's requirements. There are more variables, and possible problems, with the spotting task; the teacher's coaching early on can help students avoid possible pitfalls. Overly eager students might select far more events ("cues") to score than they have time to implement. The more open-ended a project, the more important that defining choices benefit from teacher guidance since students will have to live with these choices as they go forward. Even if a student's initial idea seems unwieldy, perhaps the teacher can help him or her find a way to develop the concept or see other possibilities.

Example: Preparing Sound Clips

Let's look at an example in which students working in a computer lab with audio software are preparing three 30-second sound clips with appropriate fades (that is, fade in, fade out) for a podcast. You might take five to eight minutes to demonstrate the procedure to the entire class (via a projector or interactive whiteboard) and answer any questions, then allow another five to eight minutes for students to work on their own, and then begin circulating around the lab "coaching." Here, this would mean listening to a sound clip, confirming what was done well (correct length, good signal levels, fades inserted correctly, etc.), and offering help where needed. If you see a trend developing—maybe the first three or four students, even after your large-group explanation, still do not understand how to create a fade-in or fade-out—you can break in and address the whole class again to clarify. If the task is simple and well defined, and you keep a disciplined pace, and there are no technical problems, you might get through the entire class before the period is over. Otherwise, use part of a second class period to finish coaching while those with whom you have met move on to another phase of the project, such as creating the other two sound clips, writing the script for the podcast narrator, or recording the narration.

Example: Composing With Notation Software

Let's look at another scenario in which students use notation software to compose short, original B–A–G songs for recorder.[6] During coaching interaction with students, the teacher could use the notation software to address any parameter for melodic writing stressed in the project. *Repetition* is accomplished by copying and pasting; *sequence*, almost as easily by transposing copied fragments; *melodic contour* can be created by dragging notes higher or lower on the staff. After demonstrating suggestions or making changes, the revisions can be reviewed using the software's playback controls. Even better, performances of these songs can be recorded later using waveform audio editing software (such as Audacity) and enhanced with the software's DSP (digital signal processing) effects (reverb, pitch shifting, chorus, flange, etc.).

One of the hallmarks of a well-conceived creative musical activity or project is that its requirements can be fulfilled by students at various levels of musical experience. As Michele Kaschub and Janice Smith observe:

> Students who have had some successful composing experiences may approach a new composing task quite differently from those who are composing for the first time. Those with several years of private instrumental instruction may also approach a composition task differently from students who have never studied an instrument. This is particularly true of pianists and guitarists who have experience in working with more than one line of sound at a time.[7]

When coaching, the teacher meets students where they are and helps move them forward. Keeping the coaching to about five minutes might mean prioritizing and focusing on one aspect that needs the most attention. As I mentioned in chapter 5, it is more about improvement than meeting a certain standard level of sophistication. In the end, everyone's music is stronger for the coaching.

Coaching Helpers

There may be ways to be creative with coaching in your situation. I teach a composition elective in a 26-seat computer lab during our summer elementary instrumental music camp. While I could manage things fairly well by myself, I choose to use about four "camp helpers"—middle- and high-school-age camp alumni—as my assistants. I instruct them in what to look for and how to re-

---

6. Songs using the notes B, A, and G. These notes use the top three holes on the soprano recorder and are usually the first three introduced to beginners.

7. Kaschub and Smith, *Minds on Music*, 65.

spond to the activities we do throughout the week. They feel comfortable with the basics of the software we use and can answer most questions the younger kids have about using it. That means they can field simple questions, such as "How do I enter a rest?" or "How do I delete a mistake?" This saves me lots of time and allows me to move about the lab zeroing in on other, more musical issues with camp participants. When a student's work-in-progress has some issue I want everyone to think about, I open it on the teacher workstation and project it to the screen so I can discuss it with the entire group (with Noteflight, any file set to "share" can be opened by other accounts). During the school year, I have also used student teachers and student observers from several universities in our area in similar ways.

If you are lucky enough to have a lab with a lab controller system, such as the Korg Group Education Controller, you have many possibilities for coaching. In general, lab controller systems steer the audio signal from various sources (student or teacher computer, headset microphone, synthesizer keyboard, auxiliary input) to the headphones of whomever you like. This means a teacher can conference with one student (or a group or students) via the headset (headphones plus microphone) while the rest work on their own.

What Do the Other Students Do While I Am Coaching?

Teacher Comes to Students

If you are in a keyboard, music technology, computer, or other lab, the answer is obvious: While you coach, your students continue to work individually, in pairs, or in whatever other configuration you have in place. One of the reasons this book depends so much on technology to accomplish creative projects is that technology allows kids both in school and at home, to work on their own and at their own level. When kids have headphones on and are at work with technology that offers some sort of feedback (computer or laptop with application, electronic keyboard, etc.), they can be positively occupied. Mobile computer labs—carts with laptops, often with wireless Internet—are available for sign-out at more and more buildings. The availability of even a handful of small, inexpensive electronic keyboards (with headphones, of course) or a small pod of computers opens up opportunities for students to work on their own or in small groups.

The first scenario presented in this chapter, the fifth-grade video-scoring project, would work well in a lab (or with a laptop cart) where all the workstations have GarageBand or some other entry-level digital audio workstation. Be sure you have headphones! Adapting the lesson so that coaching can take place in a classroom where there is only one computer, or just a few computers, takes some creativity. As a class, the teacher might explain the project, share an example of a finished video (with music and sound effects), and show students how to use the program's counter and timeline to mark where important visual

77

events occur. Using a custom cue sheet created by the teacher, which includes a timeline and list of video events (car stops, woman opens door, steps out onto road, etc.), students work in groups around the room discussing things such as where various sound effects should go and what tempo and style of music are suggested by the action onscreen. As the teacher circulates and coaches students, he or she selects a group (or groups) of students who are ready to use the classroom computer (or computers) to begin one phase of the work. This might be to select the tempo and drag in style-appropriate loops, or it might be to locate and drag in sound effects to align with the action onscreen. The teacher continues to circulate and coach the groups working with their cue sheets. As groups finish their seatwork, they either rotate onto the classroom computer(s) or join others who have finished in an extra activity, such as playing a music-related game.

Students Come to Teacher

If you do not have the sorts of technology described above, perhaps your class will work on their own while you take turns conferencing with individual students. That is what I often do when I conference with students in my music theory classes. Since I integrate creative projects into more conventional academic units, I might assign for the class a workbook activity on building or recognizing modes while individuals join me at the piano bench to show me a sketch of the opening phrase of a modal composition we are working on. The podcasting lesson mentioned above could easily be adapted to many technology scenarios. For instance, while one group of students is preparing sound clips at a small pod of computers in the back of the room, the rest could work on writing their narrator scripts at their seats, with selected students recording their voice-over narration one at a time in the hall (or a practice room) using a handheld recorder.

Using the online notation application Noteflight allows students to complete limited, well-defined tasks at home. Students might be asked to create a file from scratch or begin from a template posted by the teacher. As with any software computer music notation program, students can print out their work, show it to the teacher in coaching sessions, and receive comments and score markings for further improvement. Because Noteflight is a web application, students can also email their teacher the URL (web link) for their composition.[8]

Public Coaching

I also enjoy coaching students in front of the class; as I react to individual project work, I can highlight key themes that benefit everyone. Where appropriate, project the student's work on a large screen so the discussion is more meaningful

---

8. For much more on Noteflight, see chapter 15.

to everyone. Ask leading questions about creative gestures, and invite limited input from the class: "Does anyone see evidence of the principle of repetition at work in Samantha's sketch?"[9] Not only can the teacher offer verbal coaching, but he or she can also demonstrate score manipulations and play them back for the student's consideration. (Noteflight users can allow others to make changes to their documents, but Noteflight keeps track of changes so the user can revert to previous versions if desired.) Remember, in this scenario your class is participating as an audience while you coach, rather than working, so adjust your project timetable accordingly.

How Do I Know What to Say When Coaching?

Regardless of the project, when a student shares with me a work-in-progress I normally am aware of literally dozens of things that might be addressed. Perhaps you are worried that when you first look at or listen to a student's creative work you will not know what to say, or what is most important to say. Let me offer some advice that I hope will lay your fear to rest: Coaching is about meeting students where they are, sharing information they are ready to handle, and moving them to the next level of sophistication.

I recommend that teachers look at or listen to a student's (or group's) work, identify one aspect that could be enhanced, and then address that item via questions, suggestions, or further instruction. If the project involves recording, maybe the levels are too "hot," causing distortion, or too weak, making it hard to hear important elements. If the piece has melodic elements, maybe there are too many motives introduced in a short time, causing thematic confusion. If the piece has harmonic elements, maybe there are notes that do not seem to fit into the prevailing harmony, causing an awkward, uncomfortable tonal tension. Perhaps there is rhythmic disunity rather than cohesion, or maybe the piece is too busy and would benefit from less dense activity . . . or even some silence. If the project involves composing or arranging for instruments, real or synthesized, is the writing idiomatic and in appropriate ranges? As music education professionals, we have lots to offer, but we must also exercise restraint. I do not think it is very useful to burden a student with a laundry list of a dozen or more things to work on at once.

Compositional Themes

Nonetheless, I can offer some ideas for specific areas in which to coach musical creativity. These suggestions have curricular ramifications and are based on my belief that young composers have much to learn by studying great music (all styles) and *imitating models*. Johann Sebastian Bach did just this when he studied

---

9. For more on formal and informal feedback, see chapter 9.

and copied by hand the Italian concerti of his contemporary Antonio Vivaldi in order to better understand that genre and synthesize it into his own musical language. An early and important stage for our students involves their studying important *compositional devices* used by others, working with these devices and then synthesizing these external influences with their individual expression. This can best be achieved in a series of lessons that sequentially introduce these devices and then gradually allow students more and more freedom to incorporate (or discard) them as they wish. Over the course of the series, imitation and modeling yield to nurturing personal expression.

I suggest that teachers stick to a limited number of universal themes found in music of lasting worth. In many coaching situations, the teacher is working with the student as if it were a very brief composition or arranging lesson. These "lessons" will be more meaningful if they draw on just a few broad themes, presented to the class again and again. Two such themes I recommend visiting with students, regardless of age, over and over again are (1) *repetition versus contrast* and (2) *compositional narrative*.

Repetition Versus Contrast

I posit early on with my elective music students that processing music has a lot to do with expectations. The listeners' sonic experience—both immediately in the piece to which they are listening, and long-term as they draw on their listening history—informs their expectations. Neuroscientist Daniel Levitin, in his book *This Is Your Brain on Music*, has a lot to say about how expectation and repetition lend meaning to music. Levitin explains, "The thrills, chills, and tears we experience from music are the result of having our expectations artfully manipulated by a skilled composer and the musicians who interpret music." He goes on to describe in detail how sounds begin at the eardrum and are processed, evaluated, and passed from one center of the brain to another. Near the end of this circuit, the frontal lobes access an area of the brain called the "hippocampus and regions of the temporal lobe and ask if there is anything in our memory banks that can help to understand this signal. Have I heard this particular pattern before? If so, when? What does it mean? Is it part of a larger sequence whose meaning is unfolding right now . . . ?"[10]

Therefore, repetition is key in determining how listeners perceive the music they hear. Repetition can be literal, limited (repeating rhythm but not pitches), with alterations, or obscured (such as in inversion). Variation involves alteration, but is related to repetition. When a musical thought resembles something the listener has heard before, or proceeds as expected, the listener is comforted. When something unexpected or new is presented, the listener takes note of the difference, perhaps with amusement, surprise, or even shock. Using music no-

---

10. Daniel J. Levitin, *This Is Your Brain on Music* (New York: Penguin Group, 2006), 130–31.

► **FIG. 8.2**

Lydian-sounding, five-note motif from Aaron Copland's *Third Symphony*, second movement (Allegro molto). Graphic created by Scott Watson.

81

tation and music production software, which allow the user to copy and paste small and large musical passages, makes it easy to employ repetition in compositions and arrangements.

Despite this, so many young composers "waste" musical materials by introducing one new theme or motive after the next, never expanding upon or developing these ideas, creating the musical equivalent of multiple personality disorder. Both the fourth grader and the university composition major can benefit by being economical with their musical thoughts, a hallmark of many a great composer. One of my favorite composers is Aaron Copland. Copland is well known for using his musical motifs efficiently, repeating them and reusing them economically, more so than many of his contemporaries, and certainly more than the relatively "wasteful" Romantic composers of the middle to late nineteenth century whose rhapsodic narratives spawned the term "through-composed." The composer Virgil Thomson was talking about this trait when he said of Copland, "Musically, he knows how to make five cents perform the services of a dollar." Another observer, according to Copland biographer Howard Pollack, put it this way: "Aaron Copland's musical ideas are like pennies shrewdly invested."[11] A good example of all this can be found in the second movement of one of my favorite twentieth-century American compositions, Copland's *Third Symphony*. Most people know this work from the well-known "Fanfare for the Common Man," which appears in the final movement. But the fast second movement (Allegro molto) demonstrates how much music can be spun out of a simple five-note motif. The motif, with its Lydian-sounding raised fourth scale degree (**Fig. 8.2**), occurs more than a dozen times in the opening 30 seconds of the movement. Even more impressive: the first three and a half minutes of the movement are almost entirely derived from this motive. I encourage you to check out the entire symphony, and especially the second movement, but measures 66–82 (**Fig. 8.3**) demonstrate Copland's strong use of repetition (you can hear a recording of this excerpt at the companion website for the book, **Web Ex. 8.1**).

Compositional Narrative

Composers effectively use repetition and contrast to create a narrative that emotionally manipulates the listener. The idea of compositional narrative in-

---

11. Howard Pollack, *Aaron Copland: The Life and Work of an Uncommon Man* (Chicago: University of Illinois Press, 1999), 520.

▶ FIG. 8.3

Copland uses his five-note motif extensively throughout this passage, and the entire movement. Graphic created by Scott Watson.

volves giving one's audience something interesting to follow as a piece unfolds and has many implications. This might mean that rather than having everyone play all the time, the instruments are varied according to a plan, creating a *timbral narrative*. The principle of "layering," first mentioned in chapter 4 and explained more in chapter 14 ("Loops and Layering" lesson) deals with exactly this and can be found in both popular and classical "art" music. Acknowledging the importance of narrative might mean sensing when your listener is ready for something new and introducing contrasting material. Contrasting material is more the opposite of repetition and serves as a foil against which the original material stands out. After moving to some contrasting music, composers often return to the original material, creating an A–B–A formal gesture. We see this formal shape in brief melodies (a–a–b–a), song form (verse/chorus–bridge–verse/chorus), and sonata-allegro form (exposition–development–recapitulation). In this sense, repetition (and its opposite, contrast) is deployed for dramatic reasons, serving the piece's narrative. All good music balances repetition with some contrast and exhibits an interesting narrative. It should not be hard to find things about which you want to provoke thought, constructively criticize, or offer suggestions in the simplest melodies fashioned by elementary-age children to pop-style songs written by teens. Once you get the hang of coaching, your greatest challenge will be limiting the many things you would like to address to the one or two most vital that you have time to address.

Other Compositional Themes

Kaschub and Smith offer a list of "five foundational correlates," five pairs of complementary musical concepts, that could be used by teachers when coaching student composers to provoke thought about their music:[12]

1. **Sound/silence.** Silence sets apart sound; one formal section sounds and then is silent as another takes over; certain instruments sound and then are silent as others continue.

2. **Motion/stasis.** The pace of the music suggests rest or activity, as well as the passage of time, either consecutively (such as a change of tempo or mood) or simultaneously (two layers with different levels of activity).

3. **Unity/variety.** "Commonality provides a foundation for expectation" (with regard to patterns of timbre, notes, rhythms, etc.); the brain can be pleased with, but eventually lose interest in, the familiar; new ideas surprise and excite.

4. **Tension/release.** The listener's predictions about events are confirmed or disproved as the music unfolds; those that frustrate expectations yearn for resolution, which—when it comes—rewards.

5. **Stability/instability.** Music events are compared to their background; regular patterns in a composition, and writing that conforms stylistically, are interpreted as stable; events that standout against the backdrop, or compositions that challenge assumptions, are unstable.

Each of these pairs can provoke discussion with students about their music while suggesting an abundant number of musical choices to consider. Note how the two themes I highlight—repetition/contrast and narrative—hit on many of the same ideas as these five foundational correlates. Kaschub and Smith observe that beginning students "tend to create pieces that reflect the continuum extremes of the principles. They may create pieces that are either highly stable (and quite repetitious) or highly unstable in that they lack any sense of cohesion (no repetition)."[13] Based on my experience with beginning composers of all ages, I heartily agree.

Compositional Devices

Compositional *devices* are not as broadly applied as themes but are still valuable compositional tricks of the trade worth highlighting during coaching sessions. An example of a device is the use of pedal point, which can be observed in great music of many styles over the last several hundred years. This device, which

83

12. Kaschub and Smith, *Minds on Music*, 15–18.
13. Kaschub and Smith, *Minds on Music*, 66.

involves sustaining a single drone tone amidst various melodic and harmonic changes, appears in the dulcimer music of Appalachia, in Celtic pipe music, for most of the "Mars, Bringer of War" movement of Gustav Holst's *The Planets*, throughout the introduction of the Spencer Davis Group's rhythm and blues hit "Gimme Some Lovin'," and during the opening of what I would estimate to be one-fourth of all feature film scores. Furthermore, it is conceptually easy to understand and practically easy to deploy in music. Other examples of compositional devices include the fashioning of an introduction from the closing bars of a composition, or using a phrase extension to wrap up a song. Things like these are very easy to create when students are using notation software to write their music—just copy and paste. Likewise, placing silence just before an important musical event is a very effective way to draw attention to it. With notation software this can be accomplished easily by converting notes to rests with the press of a key. Sometimes when I am coaching students who are stuck, suggesting devices such as those I have mentioned is just what is needed to help propel them—and their music—forward.

TWO COACHING SCENARIOS

In the moments I have to coach students in class, I enjoy applying broad themes to my students' work, pointing out opportunities for students to employ devices presented in class, and sharing pointers I have learned along the way as a fellow composer and creator. These can be very minor or more involved.

Take the case of an elementary-age composer, Anna, whose initial sketch employed all notes and no rests. Chatting with the student, I learned that she was trying to create excitement by her steady stream of notes. After pointing out that sometimes silence sets notes apart in exciting ways, demonstrating what I meant, and giving her time to experiment, her music was both more interesting *and more exciting*. All it took was replacing a few notes with rests.

Ed, a high school rock guitar player, wanted to use piano in a song he is writing. His first sketch looked like a series of root-position whole-note chords in the piano's lower register. I asked him to just write chord changes instead, of the sort he was used to reading with guitar, and we found another student in class who was comfortable with pop keyboard style. The next day the collaborator came into class, having worked with the chord changes at home, and recorded the piano part. Not only was Ed pleased, but the mood set by the keyboard player propelled the song forward as he layered in other elements—MIDI drums and his own bass playing. Ed applied the same approach of collaboration with both a male and female vocalist for his song. Ed's vision and outline for his music, along with the talented input of his collaborators, produced a great song. You can hear Ed's song, "Spend All Night," at the companion website (**Web Ex. 8.2**).

COACHING BY GUEST ARTISTS

While the music teacher is the primary coach, guidance from others can be very helpful and a welcome alternative to the routine. Consider bringing guest artists to your classroom or school to share their unique perspective of the creative process. Guest or visiting artists might be professionals whose talent, stories, and advice can inspire your students. They might also be local semiprofessional and amateur artists with lots to offer. Professional artists can be very exciting to meet and work with but typically require more advance planning and funding (via your school district budget, grants, or fund-raising). Local artists are often happy to volunteer their time, or would be grateful for a modest honorarium, yet still offer a fresh voice to teach and challenge your students. The following scenarios demonstrate a variety of guest artists.

One of the high school science teachers in my school district is a fine jazz saxophonist. He has recorded as a "session" player for several student arrangements and in the process always lends his expertise, sharing suggestions and encouragement. The kids are impressed with his strong musicianship, but they love just as much the way he enjoys making music with them, treating them with respect as creative collaborators.

One of our students has an uncle who plays keyboards for a Grammy-nominated musical artist and who runs his own Nashville recording studio.[14] As soon as I learned about this, I began working on bringing him to meet with my students. It took about a year, but we finally got him to stop by when he was in our town visiting his family. During a special double-period workshop he played for the kids, talked about his career and music making, shared some audio and video projects he was producing, listened to and offered comments on some of my students' music, and took questions. It was a great time.

A few years ago we commissioned film composer Eric Schmidt to write a combined band and strings finale to close our districtwide fifth-grade band and strings concert. We chose Eric because he writes a lot of music for children's animated television shows and films. We scraped together the funds to bring him from his home in California to Pennsylvania to work with our kids in rehearsals and then to conduct his music in several concerts. Eric was good enough, however, to conduct a workshop with my elective music classes while he was with us. The students were mesmerized as he explained his compositional process and shared sketches and finished work. After his group presentation, he sat down with members of my AP music theory class for a more intimate discussion.

I have visited several schools as "composer-in-residence," leading students in technology-based composition activities and writing music for school ensembles

---

14. The keyboardist is Jim Daneker, who plays for Grammy and Dove Award-winning artist Michael W. Smith. His Nashville studio is the Whine Cellar (www.whinecellarstudio.com).

with the input of student performers. However, a guest artist does not need to be a composer to be an outstanding coach. Consider bringing in an excellent instrumentalist or chamber group to perform student works written for them. Students never listen so carefully as when a great player is questioning them about their compositional intent, sharing tips for idiomatic writing, and demonstrating different options on his or her instrument.

Technology-Assisted Virtual Coaching

Sometimes technology can be used to facilitate interaction with a guest artist or mentor. An artist in a different area of the world can be brought right into your class or rehearsal room via a variety of teleconferencing tools. One of the simplest of these is Skype, which allows for two-way voice and video connections at no cost. Some excellent podcasts feature creative musicians speaking about their craft; these can be downloaded from program websites and the iTunes Store. For example, I ran across a February 5, 2008, interview that Terry Gross did on her National Public Radio program *Fresh Air* with singer-songwriter Sheryl Crow. I love playing this interview for my music production class. In the interview, Crow shares that at several points early in her career she chose to "go back to the drawing board" when she was not happy with her music—even when others were ready to produce it. In the end, her disciplined self-editing led to her breakthrough sound in the 1990s. While this mode of delivery does not offer interaction, it does allow for famous artists to influence students as "virtual coaches."

The Vermont MIDI Project (www.vtmidi.org) facilitates coaching interaction between professional composers and student composers from many participating schools. Composing with notation software, students submit their works at various stages of completion to a password-protected site where professional mentors offer them guidance. The "Mentoring Guidelines" posted at the Vermont MIDI Project site are excellent. Although they are aimed at online mentoring, I find they work well for the kind of brief, in-class coaching described in this chapter:

- Consider context/age of students and their assignment.
- Try to ensure that pieces receive responses in a timely manner.
- Offer two or three suggestions without overwhelming young composers.
- Comments should be designed to help a student revise and improve, not to completely redo a piece.
- Encourage development of material with specific suggestions.
- First comments deal with broader issues, and as pieces near "completion" the finer tuning takes place.
- One-to-many mentoring informs whole community—always be aware of larger audience.

- Ask questions to focus thinking.
- Make suggestions in language rather than changing their music for them.
- Use phrases like: "Have you considered" and "I wonder if" rather than being directive.
- Lead students to discover what their piece can be.
- Be sensitive to "letting go" of a piece when the student is ready to move on.
- Too much flowery praise is not useful, nor is it seen to be sincere.
- Humor is entirely appropriate, but sarcasm has no place in the critique process.

Some of the Vermont MIDI Project mentors are university faculty composers. Other educators have established similar relationships with composers from nearby colleges or musical organizations. Music teachers themselves, within or without a school district, can offer valuable guidance and encouragement for one another's students. These connections can be arranged by setting up a wiki. I have done this with a colleague in another part of the state and have found it rewarding to see and react to his students' work. Students post, or link to, their work on the wiki periodically so teachers and other students can provide feedback. Using Noteflight (www.noteflight.com) for composition assignments has really made this sort of partnering fun and easy since it allows notation files to be embedded or linked.

WRAP-UP

Since there are always interruptions to the routine that tend to put you behind schedule, you may be tempted to regard time for coaching as an unnecessary luxury. Field trips, in-school assemblies, snow days and late starts, early dismissals, pep rallies, and special testing are just some of the things that seem to conspire to put you behind schedule. Nonetheless, I urge you to make time for coaching interaction with your students and to resist the urge to skip coaching in order to "stay on schedule." On the other end of the spectrum, however, it is important to find the right balance of offering help to students but not dominating their work time with too much talk.

If you are an instrumental music teacher, you probably value having large group rehearsals, yet a lot of important work no doubt gets done when students receive guidance from you or another in private lessons or small-group (or sectional) lessons. Home practice is crucial as well, and maybe your school even has practice rooms for kids to work out passages on their own at school. Large-group instruction, private or small-group coaching, and individual work time forms a winning combination when having your general and elective music students create. Just as small-group instruction makes all the difference for developing instrumentalists, coaching is a vital pedagogical piece that takes students from their first attempts organizing musical materials to expressing themselves

87

with confidence. Coaching might be accomplished by a teacher leaning over her students' shoulders in a lab, or by a guest coach offering comments on a wiki or via Skype. When leading your students in creative projects, make time for coaching.

REFLECTION ACTIVITY

Two legitimate points of view regarding teaching composition to students in music classes can be compared and contrasted. The student-centered approach to teaching composition, typified by the following quote from Kaschub and Smith is one: "By acknowledging that learning begins with the experiences of the child, teaching composition becomes a process of drawing out what the composer already knows while providing challenges that invite growth." Adherents to this view caution teachers against imposing "preconceived notions of right or wrong,"[15] or their own artistic sensibilities, on the students' creative work.

Another view focuses on introducing a vocabulary of compositional themes, conventions, and devices to be tried, evaluated, and eventually synthesized by the student into their experience. Early works are based on models and may be somewhat derivative, but over time students develop a more personal voice. As far as research is concerned, these two approaches—plus a host of others—have been shown to have a place in the pedagogy of creative musical endeavors, depending upon a number of factors, including the background and experience of both teacher and student.

1. Take time to consider the pros and cons of the two teaching postures mentioned. What do you think would be the substantive differences in the creative output of students groomed as composers under these alternative approaches?

2. How, if at all, should formal university composition study be regarded differently than K–12 school music program composition study?

3. Imagine that students in your class are going to be writing a variation on the tune "Frere Jacques." Describe the different technology and classroom management strategies you might use as you coach students. Base your response on either your current teaching situation or that of a colleague in your district. If you are a preservice teacher, base your response on a music classroom you have observed or experienced recently.

15. Kaschub and Smith, *Minds on Music*, 19.

CHAPTER 9
PRINCIPLE 7: FOSTER OPPORTUNITIES FOR FEEDBACK AND CRITIQUE

THIS PRINCIPLE COULD BE AMPLIFIED to read, "Offer opportunities for and help foster comfort and confidence in offering and receiving feedback and critique." Feedback and criticism can take many forms and can flow from teacher to student or between students. Conversational feedback between a teacher and a student (or small group) is almost always a part of the coaching described in chapter 8 and involves praise, observations, suggestions, and thought-provoking questions. The teacher can also offer more formalized feedback via a rubric or other assessment tool (addressed in chapter 11). However, this chapter deals primarily with teacher modeling, moderating, and guiding students in offering one another useful feedback and criticism during classroom discussions or even more novel, technology-assisted feedback on blogs or wikis.

There is a distinction to be made between feedback offered to students (whether as composers, arrangers, producers, improvisers, etc.) *during the creative process* and criticism of the *final product*. Both deal with the same aesthetic considerations, but one helps the student make decisions and refine while the other is more a final judgment.

BENEFITS OF PEER FEEDBACK AND CRITICISM

While I certainly find it helpful to give kids feedback myself, I work hard to give students the chance to hear one another's work and to offer and receive criticism early on, in the midst of, and near the end of a project. This helps kids know if they are on target with their own work as they compare their approaches and solutions with those of their peers. It also helps train students to listen critically for the sorts of musical features they are supposed to be incorporating in their own work. You have no doubt heard the old adage, "The best way to learn something is to teach it." Similarly, a great way to solidify students' understanding of a musical principle or device is to have them listen for and discuss it in the work of others. I have noticed a reciprocal relationship between students' sensitivity to the use of creative gestures in the work of others and their comfort and confidence with these same features as they create. The ability to articulate insightful musical observations benefits everyone as our students engage in the complementary roles of critic and creator.

Michele Kaschub and Janice Smith recognize the importance of sharing feedback and criticism by peers and teacher as well: "One of the most valuable parts of the community of learners is the availability and frequency of constructive, useful feedback on works in progress. The sharing of partial pieces often leads to teachable moments for the teacher and to valuable suggestions from the other young composers."[1] The Vermont MIDI Project agrees, pointing out that when "reflection and critique are a part of the culture of a classroom, with students critiquing their own and others' work, their ability to listen, analyze and describe music (national standard 6) and to evaluate music and music performances (national standard 7) is enhanced, and this in turn enriches their compositions."[2] Jackie Wiggins points out that feedback in the context of peer collaboration "puts students in the position of having to explain, clarify, or defend their ideas" to one another, causing them to "think things through more carefully."[3]

CREATE A SAFE ENVIRONMENT

You may find that students are reluctant at first to say anything substantial when responding to one another's work. Early in a course when my students and I begin to listen to works-in-progress, I will ask for reactions, comments, or suggestions from peers. Usually only a few volunteer, and those who do offer brief, nonthreatening remarks such as, "it was good" or "pretty neat." In my opinion, this is often because they are afraid of rejection, both from peers and from their teacher—they are afraid to say something their classmates will think is silly or stupid or that I might deem "wrong." For this reason, it is important to create a classroom environment in which students feel "safe" sharing. The teacher's reaction to student comments makes all the difference. Students should be hearing responses to their comments such as:

- "Great observation, James!"
- "Wow, Sharon! You've got very discerning ears."
- "You know, everyone, Samantha makes an excellent point . . ."

Make each student glad, not embarrassed, that he or she opened up and all students will be more likely to participate in the discussion. Even when a student volunteers something off-base, as long as it is given sincerely, I believe a good

---

1. Kaschub and Smith, *Minds on Music*, 90.

2. Anne K. Hamilton, "Reflection and Critique in the Classroom," available at www.vtmidi.org/reflect _critique.html. The Vermont MIDI Project is one of the nation's first and longest running organizations that brings professional composers together with student composers for mentoring. Students compose largely using Sibelius notation software, and selected composers participate in an annual concert with accomplished musicians performing their works.

3. Wiggins, *Teaching for Musical Understanding*, 50.

teacher guide can extract something useful. Let me offer a scenario to demonstrate what I mean.

Repetition is an important aspect of good music, but it can be overdone. Both too little repetition and too much literal repetition are reason for concern. Many music software programs make it easy to replicate a musical gesture and accomplish repetition. In GarageBand a loop "region" is pulled by a handle to make multiple copies for as many measures as desired. In the Groovy Music programs (such as Groovy Shapes, Groovy Jungle, and Groovy City), colorful shapes that represent various musical gestures can be dragged multiple times onto the timeline for a piece. In all computer music notation and DAW (digital audio workstation) programs, measures of music can be copied and pasted for repetition. Imagine Joanna has created a composition with one of these programs but has not used repetition of melodic material even once. Every measure presents new, unrelated material. However, accompanying every measure is a consistent drum set pattern, maybe a rock drum beat. When asked to comment on the music, Bethany contributes, "It's pretty neat, but there's too much repetition. It gets boring after a while." Here, the student might be onto something. It might be uninteresting, but not because there is "too much repetition" (in fact, it is precisely because of the opposite). There are many ways to turn this around while still stroking the student. "Sounds like you liked some things but not some others, Bethany," the teacher might begin. "Me too! Let's make a list of what is repeated so Joanna can consider if she wants to make any changes." The list on the board would include the continuous rock beat, as well as some other elements the teacher might have to draw out of the class such as time signature, dynamics, and instrumentation (assuming the same instruments play the changing melodic gestures). The teacher should also use the discussion to point out, or elicit from the students, that the melodic material keeps changing, exhibiting no repetition at all. The point is that all this reflection and discussion make Joanna's composition stronger.

MODEL REFLECTION AND CRITIQUE

Beyond their inhibitions, many students simply do not know what to say when asked to critique peer efforts. Students seldom listen to or discuss music analytically and therefore, upon hearing something, are not prepared to say anything more specific than whether or not they like it. Despite students' reticence, there really are an infinite number of helpful comments and opinions that could be shared. To compensate for students' lack of experience offering criticism, teachers should demonstrate how to offer appropriate and helpful remarks, modeling for their students the type of comments and vocabulary they would like them to use. If it's quiet the first time I ask for reactions to an example, I often tear through a dozen observations or suggestions, one after the other, just to demonstrate fitting and useful comments.

Some critical observations or comments refer to a musical principle or device at play ("Great restraint, Natasha, in terms of waiting until measure 13 to introduce new material"), some remarks are general and subjective ("I'm sold, Todd; because of the way you've begun this piece, I definitely want to hear more!"), some are questions ("Where are you going with this, Alice?"), and some are suggestions ("I'd like to hear your piece breathe once in a while. Maybe you could employ rests or longer durations at the phrase endings").

When students do begin to open up, they may not know exactly how to say what they want to suggest, and I find myself interpreting for them, explaining the appropriate musical terms for what they have described. Once again, it is possible to do this in an upbeat, encouraging way: "Yes, Elisa! When you talk about the ending using notes from earlier in the piece, that's a 'coda.' In pop music we might call it a 'tag.' Great observation!" Certainly students can be insightful without being overly technical; these are teachable moments. They are learning the language of musical criticism largely by imitating you, just as they learned to speak and build vocabulary by imitation.

PROMPT WITH QUESTIONS

Another way to prompt students to be discerning listeners and to share their thoughts is to ask interesting and provocative questions. Questions can serve a number of pedagogical purposes. In some cases, the teacher might use questions to stimulate discussion about a student work-in-progress played for the class. Alternatively, the teacher may want to steer discussion to a particular aspect of the piece. Many types of questions can generate good student interaction and artistic thought. Here are a few:

1. **General/subjective:** What did you find especially effective or compelling about Theresa's project?
2. **Scenario:** You're a producer for Bling Records and Stephanie brings you this as her demo. What, if anything, would you still need her to work on to "green light" her project?
3. **Technical:** What did you think of the mix levels in Ian's project so far? Mariah's composition is eight measures long; how many measures should she place in each line (system)?
4. **Aesthetic:** Which word better describes Troy's project so far: conventional or novel? If conventional, what would really shake things up?
5. **Musical:** What do you think of Dustin's sense of formal proportion? Does Dustin spend too little, too much, or just the right amount of time on each section of the project? Is there something you wish you could hear more of? How about something you think drags on too long?

I recommend avoiding using terms such as "good" or "bad." Note, instead, the use of terms such as "compelling" and "effective" even when eliciting a subjective impression. Students are welcome to share their opinions, but asking the right questions will keep the conversation focused on craftsmanship and artistic accomplishment rather than taste. Try to elicit comments from every student, but do not make a big deal about those who are reluctant at first; just move on. If you are worried about some students not volunteering, employ a neutral process. For example, (1) ask for reactions from students sequentially as they are seated, or (2) ask the student to the right of the student whose example is being played to comment.

FORMAL TOOLS FOR SHARING CRITICISM

More formal methods for sharing feedback may be employed, especially at the end of a creative activity. Almost every grading rubric I employ has a place for written (or typed) comments. I figure if my students can spend a week or more working on a project, I can devote five minutes sharing my reaction to their work.

Formal peer assessment might be employed as well. I assign to students in my music production class a written critique of a song project they have all completed. Students draw randomly from a hat the name of a classmate whose song production they must review. Once complete, the reviews—written in the voice and style of a music critic for *Rolling Stone* magazine—are read for the whole class. An evaluation form and a checklist that students fill out for one another are other examples of formal assessment tools. While written forms of feedback can be useful, I favor verbal discussions for three reasons:

1. The immediacy of verbal feedback makes it more useful in shaping the recipient's creative decisions. A comment offered and discussed at the start of a class can already be incorporated into a student's project later in that same period.
2. Verbal feedback takes less time. I do not want an inappropriate balance of time spent on applied musical creativity versus written work.
3. Verbal feedback can be "steered" toward useful topics the instructor has planned, as described above.

TECHNOLOGY SUPPORTING FEEDBACK AND CRITICISM

The most obvious technology that aids teachers and students in reacting to student creativity is the technology responsible for representing the work. We often take for granted how programs like Finale and GarageBand offer immediate playback (with varying degrees of realism) so that works at every stage of completion can be shared for reactions. Take the example of a short etude composed with music notation software. Projecting the notation file (or a PDF[4] version of the file) on a large screen allows everyone to see its musical features (melodic and rhythmic repetition, melodic contour, etc.). Playback of the music as it scrolls by offers an aural counterpart to the visual score. Some classes may be listening together to music emanating from large, classroom speakers. In other classes, students may be listening in pairs through headphones connected to a headphone splitter. In yet another school, students may be listening through the headphones of a lab management system that controls sound to and from them.

Some of the same technology that can be employed for coaching may also be used to facilitate student feedback. Student projects of almost any media type (image files, MP3 audio, QuickTime movies, PDF documents, etc.) can be embedded on a class wiki for review or playback. Class members can be asked to leave teacher-moderated comments for their peers about these works using a wiki discussion page. A teacher could also require students to post feedback and criticism on a course blog. The teacher, functioning as "administrator" of the wiki or blog, invites and accepts students to be "members" or "contributors" so they can leave their comments.

The online music notation application Noteflight (Noteflight.com) incorporates several features of social networking sites that might be employed for feedback. For instance, anyone with a Noteflight account can leave comments about a piece if the composer allows. As previously mentioned, Noteflight files can be linked to or embedded in a website, wiki, or blog page as well. Check with the appropriate administrator in your school or district to be sure you are following all necessary procedures when posting student work and comments online. In my district, a "Permission to Post" agreement (see **Fig. 10.1**) must be signed by a parent at the start of the year. Additionally, you may want to avoid posting students' last names or close-up photos.

WRAP-UP

Regardless of how you work it in, be sure to take time to engage students in commenting on each other's creative work. Offering teacher criticism serves the dual purpose of providing helpful feedback to students while modeling appropriate topics and vocabulary. When you make self- and peer-reflection part of the routine, students will grow accustomed to sharing in this way. When students have to teach, they learn their subject in an even deeper way. When students offer criticism, they begin to look with discernment at their own work

---

4. *PDF* refers to Portable Document Format, a ubiquitous file type created by Adobe for electronic exchange of documents. PDF files incorporate text, fonts, images, and layout independent of specific applications, operating systems, and platforms.

as well. The more opportunities we give students to respond, react, and comment on one another's creative work, all the while drawing them out, the better they will get at expressing the elements of our discipline both verbally and in their music. The ultimate goal of all feedback and criticism is to make the students' creative work stronger.

REFLECTION ACTIVITY

1. When I was in college one of my professors told me about a study in which the reactions of American and Japanese students to classroom criticism were recorded. When the American students received criticism they withdrew, remaining quiet and slumping in their chairs. When the Japanese students received criticism, they leaned forward eagerly, retaining a positive demeanor. What are some ways to encourage students to receive feedback and criticism appropriately, even eagerly?

2. What are some considerations and precautions a teacher must make when posting student creative work and comments online on a class blog or wiki?

CHAPTER 10
PRINCIPLE 8: EMPLOY PERFORMANCE AND RECITAL

ONE OF THE BEST WAYS to ensure that students are motivated to work earnestly toward a good *end product* is to include an *end-of-project* sharing element into the plan. The most straightforward application of this principle is an in-class performance or recital of projects. During these presentations students can share the fruits of their labor and feel a sense of celebrity for their creative efforts. The term *recital* connotes a smaller scale time of sharing at the end of a class period. This could be something simple, such as students sharing their favorite synthesizer sounds, or modest activities such as students performing a brief percussion duet improvisation. The term *performance*, on the other hand, connotes a more substantial work such as a live reading of an instrumental duet, the notation software playback of an eight-measure melody, or playback of a completed multitrack song project.

Many projects can and should be performed conventionally, but as you can see, some recitals consist of software, audio, or video file playback. In each case, I am defining performance simply and in a general way: *presenting a creative work for an audience*. This broad definition allows for technology-facilitated dissemination such as posting works on web pages and including them in podcasts. Though not live, these kinds of "playback performances" have much merit, too. Of course, there is a precedent for this in the electronic and computer-generated art music recitals that have been taking place mostly on university campuses since the 1960s. Plus, there is a bonus many students appreciate: you get all the benefits of a public hearing, minus the nerves associated with performing live for others!

BENEFITS OF PERFORMANCE AND RECITAL

So what are those benefits? For one, students are more motivated when they know an audience will hear their work. Seeing something you have conceived come to life in a premiere performance is an artistic "high." A second, related, benefit is that the quality of work tends to be stronger when students understand that a broader audience will hear their creative efforts. Another benefit of recital and performance is acknowledgment and confirmation. When a student performs or plays back his or her project as part of an in-class recital, the rest of the class and I normally acknowledge the effort with applause. Peers are generally supportive, plus they empathize as companions who have also participated in the creative feat. Performances such as these also offer the opportunity for interaction between student creators and their audience. Following the presentation of student works, I normally allow opportunities for praise, feedback, and even questions. These are great times for further confirmation, aesthetic insight and reflection, and even instruction. In-class performance also helps the teacher identify "strengths and weaknesses in the class's musical understanding,"[1] allowing him or her to focus instruction, especially in designing subsequent activities.

In some cases, an end-of-project performance allows a more complete documentation of the work to be made. While an instrumental etude can be documented with notation software, and even realized with synthesizer or sampled sound by the software, a live, human performance with an acoustic instrument better represents the work. An arrangement made using multitrack music production software[2] can be played in class, but compile a CD with each student's arrangement, perhaps with attractive, student-generated artwork on the cover, and students have something more powerful to share with mom, dad, and even the larger school community.

Finally, performance is one of the goals of creativity. In today's parlance, it offers *closure*. Without it, the entire enterprise seems comparatively hollow. Performance has always been an expected and integral part of the learning arc for students who participate in music ensembles. Every band, chorus, or orchestra director understands the powerful motivating influence of an impending concert. In general and elective music classes, deliberate use of performance of student-generated works—for one's own class or an audience beyond the classroom—has not been as prevalent or routine. Including performance and recital into the plan for a creative unit, whether as easygoing moments of sharing or as more formal presentations, can give the music educator one more way to accomplish standard 1 (singing alone and with others) and standard 2 (performing on instruments alone and with others) of the MENC National Standards for Music Education.

INFORMAL SHARING

Mini-recitals at the end of a class can be very informal. If you give your students a class period to find their favorite sounds (such as on a keyboard synthesizer or

1. Alex Ruthmann, "The Composers' Workshop: An Approach to Composing in the Classroom," *Music Educators Journal*, Vol. 93, No. 4 (March 2007): 42.
2. For instance, the "New Clothes for an Old Tune" project described earlier and detailed in chapter 14.

with software such as GarageBand or Band-in-a-Box) and then another period to create a brief melodic or rhythmic gesture to demonstrate one of these sounds, leave some time near the end of the activity for the students to perform what they have devised. A few might not want to share, and I would not push it; that will change as you establish a safe class environment and you gain the confidence of these apprehensive students. If you spend the class period working on blues improvisation with electronic keyboards or some recording software, allow as many kids as you can to play (or play back) their improvisations for one another. If you have kids partner up for part of a period to create a two- to four-measure percussion groove, spend the rest of the class allowing the kids to share the drum pattern they have fashioned.

Even casual performances can raise the bar for students in terms of motivation and quality of work. Providing an audience for your students can be as simple as inviting the class next door or across the hall (and their teacher) in to sit on the floor for a few minutes while your students share what they have been working on.

FORMAL PRESENTATIONS

Performances can be more formal. In chapter 5 I mentioned the "Pedal Point Duet" project I conduct with fourth- and fifth-grade student composers in our elementary summer band and strings camp.[3] The demonstration concert that closes camp features performances by our camp band and string orchestra, plus a sampling of all the camp's elective activities. Because of time, only a couple Pedal Point Duets can be included. When I share this bit of information, there is a noticeable increase in student focus and effort. All the projects are played in class for one another, and since we use Noteflight.com, the projects are available online for all parents to check them out. You may recall that one of the parameters presented and enforced for this project is that students write only music they can perform. For this reason, it's a snap to rehearse the two selected duets in preparation for the demonstration concert. Before, during, and after the demonstration concert, the benefits of performance and recital described above—motivation, quality, acknowledgment, interaction, documenting, and closure—are evident.

Near the end of the year, my music theory students write and perform a collaborative "class song." Students can play the class piano or a synthesizer we have on hand (sometimes just pedal tones or other simple gestures). Others bring in their guitars, flutes, or any other instrument they play. Some play carefully selected mallet or nonpitched percussion instruments. The creative process is based on improvisation and developing small gestures into larger formal sec-

3. A detailed lesson plan for the "Pedal Point Duet" project, which I also do with my high school music theory students, appears in chapter 15.

tions. In the past, either I or a strong student records each day's progress on the board informally, using chord notation and slashes, notating melodic gestures when necessary for traditional players. This serves as a guide/outline when the class resumes composing the song the next day. I serve as coach, moving things forward when we get stuck; the melodic, harmonic, and rhythmic ideas are the students'. The whole project takes about a week, and the song always has a spontaneous, fresh feel to it.

On the day for the final performance, which takes place either in our classroom or on the auditorium stage, we set up a stereo microphone fed to a simple audio-recording application running on a laptop. We rehearse a bit, hit the record button, and voila!—we have documented our efforts. This past year, we reserved the auditorium for our performance and invited a handful of guests to be with us. When we showed up to the auditorium we were surprised to find more than a hundred students there we had not invited—it turned out that a couple study halls were rescheduled to the auditorium that day for some reason. The addition of this unexpected audience turned what was to be a modest *in-class performance* into another especially rewarding way to share a class project with the school community: a *concert demonstration*. I was impressed with my class, which carried on nonplussed and delivered a great reading of their song. I was also heartened and impressed by the kids in the study halls whose courtesy and interest we appreciated as we played and recorded. A recording of one of these Music Theory 2 class songs, enigmatically titled "Snake, Diamond, Moose," is posted at the companion website (**Web Ex. 10.1**).

My AP music theory class also writes a collaborative class project of their choosing at the end of the year. One recent section chose to create a four-movement operetta they called *The Digestive System*. The work, which features an original libretto and music for three singers and small orchestra, is an example of what I call a *meta-project*.[4] Such a special student work, which utilized members of my other music theory class performing in a small orchestra, called for a unique showcase. We decided to invite special guests (faculty and certain language arts classes) to a performance and videotaping of the operetta in one of our large rehearsal rooms near the end of the school year. During the presentation, we introduced the composers and performers and explained each movement to the audience. We performed each of the four short acts (or movements) twice to be sure we got a good "take," and to allow the audience to hear them twice. One student videotaped the reading while another engineered a sound recording. The video and audio were edited into a digital movie as part of a DVD that the class could then view for further reflection at a wrap-up meeting. You can view the four movements of *The Digestive System* at the companion website (**Web Exs. 2.1–2.4**).

---

4. You can read more about leading students through meta-projects in chapter 17 ("Curriculum Integration"), in the section titled "The Meta-project: Putting It All Together."

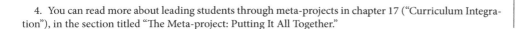

Some music teachers are using the idea of performance to drive a program in an even more comprehensive way, where all courses in a program (not just a course) build student skills that can contribute toward a culminating show. Such is the case with teacher Jamie Knight at Huntington Beach High School in California, where students in his guitar and technology courses (music and media, song writing, recording) present a meta-project at year's end they call the "Really Big Show." It has "dozens of acts, many student producers, three cameras, and hundreds of spectators" and is described as "a massive mix of performance and multimedia created by the students and presented in a flamboyant style reminiscent of American Idol."[5]

Another trend in music education is the "informance," which combines musical performance with demonstration and explanation, usually for parents. Informances may occur in the evening on a traditional stage, or during the school day in the class or rehearsal room. Since informances include the teacher and/or students sharing with the audience, and short musical examples that highlight the work of the class or ensemble, start-to-finish readings of musical selections make up only a portion of them. A colleague of mine staged an evening concert band informance in the cafeteria so the audience could sit around the ensemble rather than in front as they traditionally would in an auditorium.[6] Her informance involved a demonstration of the work the band had been doing on improvisation. This sort of less formal presentation allowed the teacher, through discussion and demonstration, to let the audience in on how the soloist would derive his or her material, what the ensemble would be doing to back up the soloists, and even why improvisation was being taught. The most risky—but rewarding—part of her informance was introducing new improvisational material to the students for the first time at the presentation so those in attendance could see the process from the very beginning. Although this example involves instrumental music, an informance may be the perfect vehicle for sharing students' creative work in general and elective music classes.

NOVEL TECHNOLOGY-ASSISTED PRESENTATIONS

Some less conventional ways to share student work include posting completed projects to a course website, blog, or wiki and releasing a class CD with all (or selected) class projects. A 2005 article for *Education World* by Lorrie Jackson notes some advantages of sharing student work with an online audience in general education classes:

5. Chad Criswell, "The Innovative Path to a 'Really Big Show,'" *Teaching Music*, Vol. 17, No. 1 (August 2009). As of this writing, you can find many video examples of this program by searching YouTube.com for APA CRAD (Academy of Performing Arts, Commercial Recording Arts Department).

6. Nancy Beitler, Southern Lehigh Middle School, Coopersburg, PA. The informance described took place in spring 2010.

Educators know that students write better when they have a real audience —not just a teacher with a red pen. In the past, finding such an audience was a challenge. But with Internet access and some basic software, any student can write for the world to see. Although blogging in schools is still in its infancy, anecdotal evidence suggests that students' interest in, and quantity of, writing increases when their work is published online and—perhaps even more importantly—when it is subject to reader comments.[7]

Indeed, emerging research is demonstrating several advantages of using web technology to improve the quality of writing by students in language arts classes, perhaps because students are aware of the larger audience that will view their work.[8] I have every reason to believe the same dynamic is true for students sharing their creative musical work online.

I feel I have had such good success with the "My Favorite Things Podcast" activity in part because the kids understand I will be posting their work online. The capstone project of my music production class is a three- to four-week activity in which we produce an entire CD of winter/holiday music. The CD is sold to the school community for a worthwhile charity the kids pick themselves. The CD, which includes student-generated cover art and student and faculty performers, is an example of the principle of using performance and recital. However, when the CD is ready to be introduced to the world, we hold other performance/recital events, such as an invitation-only CD release party (with cake and goodies) in class or a school wide coffee house launch event. At the coffee house, guests (which include district administrators, local media, students, faculty, and family) can buy and enjoy hot beverages and baked goods, purchase the CD, hear live performances of selected tracks[9] between playback of tracks from the entire CD, and get information about the charity. If you really want to be hip, you can offer your class's CD for sale at the iTunes Store by using a third-party service, such as TuneCore (www.tunecore.com). TuneCore helps you set up your own independent label, walks you through the process of uploading audio files, tracks your sales, and manages your account, all for a reasonable fee.

Many schools have the ability to broadcast video to televisions in classrooms. Any performances that are video recorded can be replayed over these systems.

---

7. Lorrie Jackson, "Blogging? It's Elementary My Dear Watson!" April 13, 2005, updated November 13, 2008 (http://www.educationworld.com/a_tech/tech/tech217.shtml).

8. Rama Ramaswami, "The Prose of Blogging (and a Few Cons, Too)." November 1, 2008 (http://thejournal .com/articles/2008/11/01/the-prose-of-blogging-and-a-few-cons-too.aspx). The article gives a good overview of several studies that demonstrate how blogging can improve student writing.

9. While some students can pull off an unplugged performance of their track, most create karaoke tracks for a live vocalist or instrumentalist. To do this with multitrack software such as GarageBand, simply save the project under a new name ("Save As"), then mute or delete the recorded vocal or instrumental lead(s), and burn a CD for playback at the event. Alternatively, it could be saved as an MP3 file in an iTunes Playlist to playback on an iPod or other MP3 player.

Simple-to-learn video editing software (such as Apple's iMovie), perhaps with the help of a technology or media paraprofessional, can be used to add things such as titles, transitions, and special effects. Creative products, such as slide-show-style presentations, can be broadcast as well. A colleague of mine used GarageBand to produce classroom raps that spoke out against bullying. Students wrote the raps in cooperative learning groups, chose loops with the help of the teacher, and then rehearsed. Final performances of the raps were audio recorded and embedded in a PowerPoint slide show that showed the words of the rap along with pictures of the students in class. It's a snap to export the entire PowerPoint file in a digital video format such as MPEG[10] to share on television or online.

WHEN PRESENTING PROTECTED CONTENT

Another important and timely topic that arises when you record music for a CD or to post or sell online is that of intellectual property. If you allow your students to record (on a physical CD) or post (online) protected music, you will need to secure a *mechanical license*, based on the number of CDs you will make. Sometimes a copyright holder will waive this fee, so I encourage you to use the Internet to find out who this is (publisher, composer, etc.) and make your request. In many cases, though, you will need to pay the mechanical licensing fee. This is easiest (albeit a bit more expensive) using the Harry Fox Agency (www.harry fox.com). I think it is good for our students to be aware of these intellectual property issues. Today's busy educator has to be pragmatic, as well, so I suggest limiting the use of protected material. For podcasts I require that sound clips be short enough to qualify as fair use (say, 30 seconds or less), and when creating song arrangements I require students use public domain music (anonymous folk songs, baroque and classical keyboard works, public domain Christmas carols, etc.) or original material. A student's creative work—an original composition, an original arrangement of public domain material, an originally produced podcast, or whatever—is *their* intellectual property. Before posting student creative work online, I recommend having a student (if they are of age) and/or their parents (if they are minors) sign a release.[11] In this digital age, with so many teachers using online resources such as wikis that incorporate student contributions, chances are your school district already has a form you can use. If not, consider something like the "Permission to Post" form shown in **Fig. 10.1.** Check with the appropriate building or school administrator to be sure of your district's policies.

---

10. *MPEG* stands for Motion Pictures Expert Group, part of a larger organization responsible for developing audio and video formats used online, for television, and in DVD media.

11. To be clear, the student's creative product is *their* intellectual property regardless of age, but most schools still require the consent of a parent/guardian when posting the school assignment of a minor.

PERMISSION TO POST STUDENT CREATIVE CONTENT ONLINE

Dear Parent/Guardian:

I would like from time to time to post original coursework created by your son/daughter to a course wiki to enhance the educational process of the course, Music Production. Posting student work has many benefits including extra motivation and fostering a sense of pride and accomplishment. Our wiki may be found at:

http://parklandmusic.wikispaces.com

Please indicate below your preference regarding posting below, then sign and return this form. Thank you.

Dr. Scott Watson, watsons@parklandsd.org

❏ I give permission to have original creative content produced by my son/daughter

posted to the PHS Music Production wiki site, and to have this work

acknowledged with their first name.

❏ I give permission to have original creative content produced by my son/daughter

posted to the PHS Music Production wiki site, but I do not wish to have his/her

name appear.

❏ I DO NOT give permission to have original creative content produced by my

son/daughter posted to a PHS Music Production wiki site.

Parent/Guardian Signature _____

Date _____

▶ **FIG. 10.1**
Use a "Permission to Post" form such as this when placing student work on a course website, wiki, or blog. Created by Scott Watson.

WRAP-UP: EMPLOYING PERFORMANCE AND RECITAL

There are many benefits to employing a recital or performance at the close of a creative activity or project. These include an increase in student motivation and quality of work, receiving acknowledgment, facilitating creator-audience interaction, documenting the work more completely, and artistic closure. Informal recitals can consist of students sharing the results of limited creative tasks completed in class, or brief projects that are small in scope. Performances give students the opportunity to share more substantial projects during in-class or more formal presentations. For our purposes, performance is defined as *presenting a creative work for an audience* to allow for technology-facilitated sharing. Examples of this include in-class playback of projects created with notation or digital audio workstation software, posting of works on class wikis, or including recordings of works on physical CDs or in podcasts. Advantages of these sorts of "playback performances" include the benefits of public performance, without the stress or need for rehearsal. Be mindful of copyright considerations when student projects incorporate protected music. Larger projects, for which students invest more time and energy, warrant unique performance opportunities. These may require making special arrangements and devoting at least some time to rehearsing, but they also yield greater rewards. Consider video or audio recording these larger, end-of-project performances to enjoy and reflect upon later with your class.

WRAP-UP: EIGHT PRINCIPLES FOR UNLOCKING MUSICAL CREATIVITY

The Eight Principles for Unlocking Musical Creativity presented in chapters 3–10 support one another in an interconnected way. Just as it is virtually impossible to discuss one principle in these chapters without referring to one or more of the others, teachers will find that it is easy to incorporate many, even all, of the principles when they lead students through creative activities and projects such as those detailed in part II of this book. Principles such as allow students to share themselves (principle 1), offer compelling examples (principle 2), and facilitate improvisation (principle 5) can be used to get the creative juices flowing, especially at the start of a project. Principles such as employing parameters and limitations that help (principle 3) and remove parameters and limitations that stifle (principle 4) help teachers conceive successful creative experiences for their students while giving students clear steps to make forward motion as they work. Principles such as include coaching interaction (principle 6) and foster opportunities for feedback and critique (principle 7) provide training, instruction, and feedback. As these are implemented at intervals throughout a unit, they not only strengthen student work but also make students better composers, arrangers, and producers. Principle 8, employ performance and recital 8, supports many of the others. Students can share themselves when they perform or play back their work. Past performances of excellent projects, if recorded, become current compelling examples to imitate. Improvisation in class might necessitate performing for the teacher, a fellow student or two, or the whole class. Coaching and feedback are often offered as a reaction to "performances" of works-in-progress. To eschew end-of-project recital or performance seems just as unnatural as rehearsing repertoire for weeks or months but never performing it for an audience.

In his article "The Composers' Workshop: An Approach to Composing in the Classroom," Alex Ruthmann describes a composition-based class for middle schoolers that he designed to be delivered in a computer lab. Prominent features of this successful class include the use of exemplars (by both established artists and students), sharing works-in-progress to receive peer feedback, breakout instruction tailored to the needs of individuals or small groups (which he calls "minilessons"), "conferring sessions," and in-class sharing of final works. These features, which work especially well in a technological setting (such as a computer lab), certainly have their analog in some of the Eight Principles: "compelling examples," "opportunities for feedback and critique," "coaching," and "performance and recital."

Notice that none of the Eight Principles are necessarily technology dependent, and yet also note that in virtually every example cited *technology figures prominently*. In part II of this book, I share information on curricular materials for creative projects that incorporate (even depend upon) technology. I highlight many excellent published and online resources, but I also offer 29 favorite lessons that feature musical creativity. These lessons, representing various categories of music technology you might have (or hope to have), have worked well for me and my students as well as many colleagues who have used them. There are about as many possibilities for using technology creatively as there are creative teachers. In this sense, the lessons I offer are merely a springboard to get you started. I am sure once you discover the potential for teaching music via creative projects assisted by today's technology tools, you will discover and develop many lessons, activities, and projects of your own, perhaps even better suited to your situation. I urge you to incorporate the Eight Principles into all the creative teaching you do to help you get the most from your students.

REFLECTION ACTIVITY

1. How does the incorporation of technology serve to broaden our definition of performance? What are some advantages and disadvantages of technology-assisted performances?

2. Discuss any connection you see between principle 1, sharing oneself, and principle 8, employing performance and recital.

3. Choose a technology-dependent creative musical project idea and address how each of the Eight Principles for Unlocking Musical Creativity may be appropriately implemented. The project can be one mentioned in chapters 3–10, one you currently do with students, or one you have observed or experienced in a music class recently.

PART II

CURRICULAR MATERIALS

CHAPTER 11
TWO PATHS

CARROLL RINEHART, AN EARLY PIONEER in the movement to integrate creativity into music education, wrote in 2002, "It is no exaggeration to say that the teaching of composition within the context of general music is undergoing a dramatic transformation. Attention has been focused on composition as a result of its explicit inclusion among the National Standards for Music Education."[1] Indeed, music educators now more than ever are finding fun and effective ways to engage their students in composing, arranging, improvising, and other creative activities using increasingly ubiquitous and user-friendly technology tools. Teachers who have caught this technology-fueled "bug" and feel the need to ramp up the type and number of creative activities in the courses they teach have many choices for proceeding, but two main paths emerge: (1) using prepared curricular materials and (2) creating self-made or "custom" curricular materials.

In this chapter I share some examples, listed according to various categories, of prepared curricular resources. We will also look at the idea of creating your own lesson plans, offering some suggestions and a template for doing so. The next five chapters contain almost 30 lesson plans, each incorporating technology to draw out and develop musical creativity, that serve as examples. This chapter closes with some thoughts on an important curricular topic, assessing the creative work of students in music courses.

PREPARED CURRICULAR MATERIALS

Prepared curricular materials include traditionally published books and workbooks (sometimes supplemented by CD-ROM and/or Internet resources) as well as Internet websites containing lesson plans, project ideas, and other related material.

---

1. Carroll Rinehart, ed., *Composing and Arranging: Standard 4 Benchmarks* (Reston, VA: MENC, 2002), 2.

Published Materials

As more and more schools have acquired general technology (computers, Internet access, etc.) and music technology (MIDI keyboards, music software, etc.), more publications incorporating music technology have appeared. The number of music educators who have attained a level of comfort and confidence with music technology also seems to be increasing. These teachers, both young and old, are seeking to integrate these tools. Some valuable resources—great collections of lesson plans for using technology to teach various aspects of the music curriculum, and several books about such an approach—are described below. This book is really an example of both: the chapters that follow present many ready-to-use lesson plans, and much of part I discusses both the philosophy and pedagogy of using technology in creative music teaching. Let me also highlight some other publications.

Books and Workbooks

Besides this book, the following are examples of traditionally published books or workbooks of great value for teaching musical creativity with technology:

1. *Composing Music With Notation*, Book 1, from Alfred's Music Tech Series, by Floyd Richmond, Tom Rudolph, Lee Whitmore, and Stefani Langol (2007), workbook with CD. This and the following two entries are from Alfred Publishing's Music Tech Series, a collection of sequential lessons that introduce musical concepts and the technology necessary to create with them in a well-thought-out manner. The lessons are detailed enough that a less experienced teacher can follow the plans, yet flexible enough that teachers working in a number of courses and grade levels can adapt them for appropriate use.

   In this particular book, music notation elements are introduced along with composing and arranging concepts. Although the book is technology driven, I really appreciate that students begin their music notation experience rather conventionally: The book begins with students copying by hand the French folk tune "Are You Sleeping" ("Frere Jacques"). As this first unit progresses, students learn to typeset the tune, copy and paste it into other staves to create a round, add dynamic and tempo markings, and orchestrate the round by altering instrument choices (see **Web Ex. 11.1,** a video that demonstrates part of Unit 1 from the book). I love the way these lessons can be adapted to different grade and expertise levels. I have used or adapted the lessons with success with elementary, high school, and university students, but I think the "sweet spot" for this book is middle school (the book's target audience is grades 4–12). These lessons are meant to be done in a music technology or computer lab, or even with laptop computers in class. Be sure students have headphones.

A CD-ROM with activity files accompanies each of the workbooks in this series. (For this particular book, Finale, NotePad, Sibelius, and MIDI files that can be used with any notation software are included.) This allows students who miss a class to catch up quickly. All of the Music Tech Series workbooks are "consumable" (that is, they are used and written in by particular students and then need to be replaced for subsequent students/courses). Certainly the recurring cost is a concern, but there are advantages to students having their own books, including the ability for them to work independently, at their own pace. There is a comprehensive teacher's manual that includes pages for all three workbooks accompanied by detailed lesson ideas.

2. *Sequencing and Music Production*, Book 1, from Alfred's Music Tech Series, by Stefani Langol, Lee Whitmore, Tom Rudolph, and Floyd Richmond (2007), workbook with CD. The well-paced activities in this beginning-level workbook introduce students to digital music composition and recording. The lessons are meant to be carried out in a music technology lab equipped with MIDI controllers (keyboards) and music production software capable of audio and MIDI recording and editing. Similarly configured laptops would work well in a classroom setting, too. Musical concepts are presented in a way that does not depend on students reading conventional music notation, so nontraditional music students can experience authentic musical creativity. For instance, in a Unit 2 activity shown in **Fig. 11.1,** students record (one track at a time) the bass drum, snare drum, and cymbal parts of a rock drum beat. Note that suggested rhythms for each are indicated using a pattern/grid approach rather than a musical score.

3. *Playing Keyboard*, Book 1, from Alfred's Music Tech Series, by Tom Rudolph, Lee Whitmore, Stefani Langol, and Floyd Richmond (2007), workbook with CD. *Playing Keyboard* is designed for the beginning piano student who is learning the piano in a group lab setting. Designed for grades 5–9, it can be used for an elective or general music class as long as there is access to piano keyboards of some type. Although this is primarily a resource for teaching keyboard performance, I include it here because (a) several activities include creative expression by allowing students to choose sounds or improvise to some degree, and (b) students learn their way around an electronic keyboard.

4. *Teaching Music With Technology*, 2nd edition, by Thomas Rudolph (2004), book with companion CD-ROM. This is perhaps the most comprehensive and practical book on the subject of integrating technology

▶ **FIG. 11.1**
following page
Alfred's Music Tech Series: *Sequencing and Music Production,* Book 1, pages 32–33. Alfred's Music Tech Series: *Sequencing and Music Production,* Book 1, by Floyd Richmond, Tom Rudolph, Lee Whitmore, Stefani Langol (Van Nuys: Alfred Publishing Co., 2007). Used with permission.

■ Activity: Creating a Song – Part 1
Recording a Rock Drum Beat (Groove) using Loop Record

Create a rock-drum groove to a song using loop record.

1. Launch your MIDI/Digital Audio software.

2. From the <u>File</u> menu, choose <u>Open</u>.

3. From the companion CD-ROM, open the Sequencing Unit 2 folder.

4. Open the file: *looprecord.mid*

5. Click <u>play</u> and listen to the song from beginning to end. The song is 12 measures in length. Pay close attention to the bass drum rhythm pattern on track 9. The bass drum is playing on beats 1 and 3. Click <u>stop</u>, then <u>rewind</u> or <u>move to beginning</u> when you are finished listening. Note that track 9 is set to channel 10 and has been assigned to GM sound standard drum kit.

		Measure 1								Measure 2							
Beat	1	+	2	+	3	+	4	+	1	+	2	+	3	+	4	+
Bass Drum	●				●				●				●			

6. Click once on track 10 to select it. To complete the simple rock-drum groove you will use loop record to add the snare drum and the ride cymbal on track 10, channel 10. Track 10 has already been assigned to GM sound standard drum kit.

7. Locate the snare drum and the ride cymbal sounds on your MIDI keyboard. These sounds are located to the left of middle C on your MIDI keyboard.

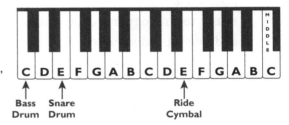

8. Enable loop recording on your MIDI/Digital Audio software. Refer to the "Basic Steps for Loop Recording" below. Set the beginning loop point to measure 1 and the ending loop point to the beginning of measure 5. The range of your measures for loop recording should include measures 1–4.

Basic Steps for Loop Recording

1. Enable loop recording by clicking once on your MIDI/Digital Audio software's loop (or cycle) button.

2. Set the beginning and ending loop measures. For example, if you want to start loop recording at measure 1, set the beginning point to measure 1. If you want to stop loop recording at the end of measure 4, set the ending point to the beginning of measure 5. Starting at the beginning of measure 1 and ending at the beginning of measure 5 will allow you to loop record four complete measures.

   NOTE: Follow the instructions provided by your teacher or refer to the help menu in your MIDI/Digital Audio software for specifics on turning on loop record and setting beginning and ending loop points.

3. Arm the track (click the record button on the track) you would like to use for loop recording. If you are using GM drums, make sure the track you are using is set to channel 10.

4. Click the record button on the transport control. Record your first part on the first pass. Record your second part on the second pass. Continue this process for as many times as needed.

5. Click stop on the transport control to stop recording.

Tips for Loop Recording

1. You can let a pass go by in between each part you record. This will give you time to prepare between each part.

2. If you make a mistake while recording, use the keyboard shortcut ctrl-Z (on a PC) or ⌘-Z (on a Mac) to undo the recording. This will undo what you just recorded. On the next pass, you can re-record your music.

9. Enable the metronome on your MIDI/Digital Audio software. Set your metronome to a comfortable recording speed, such as 80 bpm.

10. Review the snare drum and ride cymbal part you will be recording.

Beat	Measure 1								Measure 2							
	1	+	2	+	3	+	4	+	1	+	2	+	3	+	4	+
Ride Cymbal	●		●		●		●		●		●		●		●	
Snare Drum			●				●				●				●	
Bass Drum	●				●				●				●			

11. Click record. For the first pass, record four measures of the snare drum rhythm. The snare drum occurs on beats 2 and 4 of every measure. The bass drum is already recorded on beats 1 and 3.

Beat	Measure 1								Measure 2							
	1	+	2	+	3	+	4	+	1	+	2	+	3	+	4	+
Snare Drum			●				●				●				●	

12. Once the song cursor reaches the end of measure 4, it will jump back to the beginning of measure 1. Let one pass go by. When the song cursor jumps back to measure 1 again, begin recording four measures of the ride-cymbal rhythm.

Beat	Measure 1								Measure 2							
	1	+	2	+	3	+	4	+	1	+	2	+	3	+	4	+
Ride Cymbal	●		●		●		●		●		●		●		●	

13. When you are done recording, click stop. Click rewind or move to beginning, then click play to listen to your performance.

14. Are all the parts of the rock-drum groove in sync? If not, you will need to quantize the rhythm track you just recorded.

15. Quantize the rhythm track you just recorded. Refer to the "Basic Steps for Quantizing a Track" to the right. Set the quantize resolution to a quarter note.

16. Click play to listen to the result.

17. Copy and paste the simple rock groove you just recorded on track 10 to complete the drum track:

    a. Click on track 10 to select it.
    b. From the Edit menu, select Copy.
    c. Move the song cursor to measure 5.
    d. From the Edit menu, select Paste to paste a copy of the four-measure drum groove at measure 5.
    e. Move the song cursor to measure 9.
    f. From the Edit menu, select Paste to paste a copy of the four-measure drum groove at measure 9 to complete all 12 measures of the drum track.

18. Save your song. Be sure to give it a new name by using the Save As command from the File menu. Name your song [your name] looprecord.mid.

19. Share your song with your classmates.

What is Quantizing?

Sometimes, the rhythmic timing of a recorded performance does not quite match up with the steady beat provided by the metronome. The way to fix rhythmic inaccuracies is to use a feature called quantization. Quantization allows you to adjust rhythms that are out of sync with the metronome by aligning the recorded performance to a rhythmic grid. The rhythmic grid can be set to any of the basic rhythmic values (whole, half, quarter, eighth, sixteenth notes) in addition to smaller rhythmic values.

Most MIDI/Digital Audio software will allow you to quantize a whole track, a section of a track, or individual notes. It's best to quantize to the smallest rhythmic value contained in a recorded performance. For example, since the rhythm patterns you recorded for this activity contain quarter notes, it would be best to set the quantization value (also known as resolution) to a quarter note.

Basic Steps for Quantizing a Track

1. Select the track or tracks you want to quantize by clicking on them with the mouse.

2. Every sequencing/digital audio software program accesses the quantization feature in different ways. Follow the instructions provided by your teacher, or refer to the Help menu in your MIDI/Digital Audio software to locate your MIDI/Digital Audio software's quantization tool.

3. Select the appropriate quantization value which should be a quarter note for this drum pattern. The recorded material on the track you selected will align to the rhythmic value you selected.

113

114

into the music curriculum. General explanations and "teaching strategies" are provided for major music technology categories (such as electronic instruments, instructional software, notation software, MIDI-sequencing software, digital audio, practice and accompaniment software, multimedia, and Internet applications). The "teaching strategies" are brief, one-sentence ideas for lessons and activities, some of them involving student creativity. Rudolph expands or comments on these to varying degrees in his text. For instance, in the MIDI-sequencing chapter we find "Teaching Strategy 100: Students create radio commercials using sequencing software." Rudolph shares that a colleague of his "asks his middle school general music classes to create original radio commercials. Students work collaboratively in groups. They create the idea, write the copy (words), compose the music, and then they record the spoken part of the commercial using a MIDI sequencer" (p. 220). Dozens of such ideas can inspire you to design the specifics of rewarding creative activities for your students. The companion CD-ROM includes complete plans and files necessary for some of the lessons.

5. *Technology Integration in the Elementary Music Classroom*, by Amy Burns (2008). This book for teachers of music students in grades K–6 includes about a dozen detailed lesson plans that center on using music technology to deliver general music content. A companion website hosts files related to the lessons (www.ti-me.org/TIEMC). Part II of Burns's book includes lesson plans that emphasize composing and creating music. In the lesson "Reinforcing Crescendo and Decrescendo with Sibelius's Groovy Jungle," students in grades 1–3 using the software Groovy Jungle are presented with the opening of a composition: an "A" section. Working as a class (led by the teacher), the students create a contrasting "B" section. In Groovy Jungle, colorful objects (such as trees and butterflies) represent different rhythmic and melodic loops, so developing the "B" section is fun and easy for young students. Finally, students determine the dynamic levels of the contrasting sections. Dynamics are as easy to program as other elements, in this case by choosing colors associated with levels of loudness on a spectral wheel.

6. Making Music with GarageBand and Mixcraft, by Robin Hodson, James Frankel, Michael Fein, and Richard McCready (2011). While the opening chapters of this book introduce the core features of these two popular entry-level DAWs, subsequent chapters introduce creative projects (a dozen for each program) that allow students to employ recording, composing, and producing music. A companion

DVD includes additional tutorials and exercises to augment chapter content.

7. *Technology Guide for Music Educators*, edited by Scott Watson (2006). The main purpose of this guide, written by teachers for teachers, is to describe and recommend specific software and hardware solutions for music educators according to six key areas of technology: electronic musical instruments, music production, music notation software, technology-assisted learning, multimedia, and productivity tools/ classroom and lab management. Nonetheless, every chapter has specific teaching suggestions and ideas. Some of these involve creative lessons and projects.

8. *Technology Strategies for Music Education*, 2nd edition, by Tom Rudolph, Floyd Richmond, David Mash, Peter Webster, William I. Bauer, and Kim Walls, edited by Floyd Richmond (2005). Compared to the others above, this book is more of an outline of how technology can be used in music education. It does, however, include dozens of "one-line lesson plan ideas" in every area of music technology and for each of the MENC National Standards for Music Education (including more than a dozen for standards 3 and 4). You will have to flesh out the ideas yourself.

Internet Resources

Music educators interested in technology solutions for incorporating creative projects in their music curriculum can turn to a limited number of established institutions/organizations and a growing number of independent music teachers who post lesson plans and other course materials online that may be helpful. Here are some examples of those I have found to be of valuable to in-service K–12 music teachers.[2]

Institution/Organization Websites

1. TI:ME—Technology for Music Education (www.ti-me.org). TI:ME is a nonprofit organization whose mission is to assist music educators in applying technology to improve teaching and learning in music. As leaders in the field of K–12 music education technology, TI:ME's website contains a host of useful information and features for both visitors and members. Members have access to a database of more than 600 lesson plans, searchable by technology area (electronic instruments,

---

2. Because of the ephemeral nature of websites, blogs, and wikis, some listed here will likely move or disappear to be replaced by others. Regardless, they serve as examples of how the Internet is a valuable source of curricular materials for music technology-driven creative lessons.

115

notation, music production, multimedia, Internet, etc.) or MENC national standard. The quality of the lessons, like the level of teaching and technology experience of the TI:ME members who submitted them, is varied: Some are quite good, others include good ideas in need of some tweaking, but some are weak.

2. SoundTree Lesson Plans (www.soundtree.com/lesson-plans). SoundTree, the educational division of Korg USA, hosts at its website a repository of dozens of excellent lesson plans that incorporate music technology. Since the lessons come from the body of work of the highly regarded music teachers recruited to post them, they are evenly excellent. One of several I really like by teacher Mike Fein (Haverford School District, PA), called "Rearranging a Song in 2-Track Stereo Digital Audio Software," involves students analyzing the form of a pop song and then using waveform audio editing software tools (cut, copy, paste, etc.) to rearrange the song. This lesson could be accomplished with a wide range of software: from the freeware, cross-platform Audacity, to Apple's GarageBand, to a pro-level digital audio workstation (DAW) such as ProTools.

3. Connect With Music (www.connectwithmusic.org). Created with a grant from the National Association of Music Merchants, this site focuses on interdisciplinary lesson plans that utilize multimedia, music, and technology and boasts 30 free lessons to augment language arts, mathematics, and science instruction at the middle-school level. One lesson I really like is "Probability and Chance Music," by Jim Frankel and Katy O'Malley, in which students learn about "theoretical and experimental probabilities by rolling a set of dice and recording the results." This lesson, like all those at the site, is accompanied by useful links and downloadable handouts. One of the handouts converts numbers rolled on the dice to pentatonic scale pitches and rhythms to be used with notation software for students to create their own "chance" music.

Music Educator Websites

Many of the authors of the above resources are in-service teachers themselves and have an online presence for their programs or specific courses. They post this content mainly to centralize information (directions, rubrics, etc.) and course files for themselves and their students. In keeping their websites, blogs, and wikis public, they generously make their material available to all who visit. It makes sense that those teachers comfortable with music technology also take advantage of the power of the website for organizing and disseminating materials. At some sites you will find a complete semester's worth of lessons; with so many good lessons from which to choose, your biggest problem could be deciding which to use. Here are examples of some of the great places on the Internet where music educators have posted resources for creative projects that incorporate technology. These examples are only a fraction of all the great teacher sites created by tech-savvy music educators:

1. Scott Watson (parklandmusic.wikispaces.com). At this wiki, established for students in some of the elective music courses I teach at Parkland High School (Allentown, PA), you will find online resources for a complete high school music production and advanced placement music theory curricula. Many of the lessons detailed later in this book are based upon the activities and projects found here, which I have used and refined over and over.

2. Karen Garrett (www.musictechteacher.com). Karen Garrett teaches elementary general and instrumental music in Birmingham, Alabama, and has created a site rich with information, activities, lessons, useful links, and much more pertaining to music education technology. Click on the "Lessons" link for several dozen complete lesson plans. All are great, and some involve generating creative musical content.

3. Wayne Splettstoeszer (www.thsmusic.net/tech.htm). Wayne teaches high school band and music technology at Torrington High School (Torrington, CT) and is well known around the country for the lesson plans and other resources he has been posting at this site for more than a decade. Look around the Torrington site and you will get lost in all the great ideas Wayne has stored there, including complete lesson plans for entire courses, and other miscellaneous lessons. One emphasis of Wayne's work has been getting the most out of free, low-cost, and even older technology.

4. Elementary Music/Music Technology Blog (musicroomburns.net). This is the elementary music and music technology blog of Amy Burns. In addition to her tenure as an elementary classroom teacher at Far Hills Country Day School (Far Hills, NJ), Burns is a highly regarded music education author and presenter who emphasizes using technology with elementary-age music students. At the blog, click on the "Lesson Plans" category along the side for several dozen ideas. These are not formal lesson plans, but rather posts highlighting various lesson ideas and music activities.

5. MusicTechTips (musictechtips.com). Katie Wardrobe is a music education technology trainer in Melbourne, Australia. At her blog she posts music technology news, products reviews, step-by-step tutorials, and suggestions for using technology in creative projects.

Adapting Materials for Use With Technology

Some great collections of lessons have addressed composing and arranging apart from the role technology can play. Lesson plans from these resources can be easily adapted to include software or hardware at your disposal. As teachers

117

become familiar with the features and operation of various music software and hardware, they will see the potential for bringing new life to many fine creative lessons not explicitly written for use with music technology. Here are a few examples:

1. *Composing and Arranging: Standard 4 Benchmarks*, edited by Carroll Rinehart (2002). This volume is organized in three sections according to grade level: K–4, 5–8, and 9–12. Each section offers several examples of "Assessment Tasks" (summary descriptions of project lessons) with corresponding descriptions of "responses" (example products by students in fulfillment of these projects). The examples in the grades 9–12 section include lessons for ensemble classes (band, chorus) as well as general electives.

2. *Music by Kids for Kids: Blueprints for Creativity: A Composing Curriculum* (Saint Paul, MN: American Composers Forum, 2007). Written by composer and educator Janika Vandervelde (Perpich Center for Arts Education, Golden Valley, MN), this series of units is aimed at teaching composition in general music classes in middle school through high school. It was designed to be used with music notation software. The units, arranged in each of five topical and sequential units (counterpoint, melody, rhythm, harmony, and musical architecture), are ostensibly for beginning composers, but they assume students possess a solid foundation with standard music notation (notes and rhythms) and call on them to employ a variety of computer music notation techniques early on. Be prepared to offer lots of software coaching unless you teach a small, seminar-type class.

SELF-MADE CUSTOM CURRICULAR MATERIALS

The creation of custom curricular materials has been a necessity for some music educators due to the rate at which development occurs in the world of technology. When GarageBand was introduced in 2004, for example, many music teachers—including myself—immediately saw the potential for making composition and arranging accessible and fun for their students. Some may even have attended a presentation or workshop at a professional conference or elsewhere exposing them to ideas for using GarageBand with their students. Rather than wait for a book of GarageBand lesson plans or a published GarageBand curriculum, many of us devised our own lesson plans to accomplish elements of our particular curriculum while allowing us to capitalize on the program's appeal and effectiveness. Right now the same thing is happening with Noteflight.com (founded in 2008 and released in version 1.0 in 2009), the free online music notation tool, and other technology.

118

Teacher-generated, custom lesson plans are also a response to the limited number of music technology curricular resources developed by publishers, especially those that tackle topics as underexplored as musical creativity. Access to music technology is increasing, along with the emphasis most school districts place on technology in education, so the tide may be changing. Still, until technology tools become more a staple of general music classes, rather than for use in specialized, less common music technology electives, conventionally published curricular resources will probably remain just one "piece of the puzzle."

Finally, I find that music teachers drawn to technology are generally somewhat creative, so it makes sense that they would be at ease creating their own lessons for using the technology they find so appealing.

About the Example Lessons

The lessons in the five chapters that follow serve many purposes. First, they demonstrate how the Eight Principles for Unlocking Musical Creativity may be applied in actual activities. Each of the lessons was created for, and has been taught with, the pedagogical posture detailed in the Eight Principles. Many, if not all, of the Eight Principles are explicitly included or implicitly suggested in the lesson procedures. As a reminder, these are the Eight Principles for Unlocking Musical Creativity:

1. Allow students to share themselves.
2. Offer compelling examples to imitate and inspire.
3. Employ parameters and limitations that remove distractions and help students focus.
4. Remove parameters and limitations that stifle creativity and lead to contrived expression.
5. Facilitate improvisation.
6. Engage in coaching interaction.
7. Foster opportunities for feedback and critique.
8. Employ performance and recital.

Second, these example lessons are models that pre-service and in-service music teachers can use for creating their own custom lesson plans. I hope they provide inspiration for hundreds more great lessons that can be used to teach musical concepts while drawing out authentic creativity in students. The template used for each example lesson presented follows a fairly standard format:

119

Title: Title goes here.

Audience: Lists the grade level and, where appropriate, the type of music class (general, instrumental, choral) for which the lesson is intended.

Objective: What is the purpose of this lesson? What should students expect to learn and experience in this lesson?

Materials/Equipment: Lists both software and hardware, as well as anything else, required to do this lesson with students.

Duration: How many minutes and/or sessions are required to deliver this lesson?

Prior Knowledge and Skills: Does this lesson build on knowledge previously taught? What foundational skills, if any, do students need in order to participate fully and benefit from this lesson?

Procedure:

1. Step one goes here.
2. Step two goes here, and so forth.

Adaptations: Suggestions for, and examples of, ways this lesson might be adapted for different grade levels, musical or technology expertise, or different teaching scenarios.

Feedback/Evaluation: Opportunities for student reaction and comments, as well as discussion that adds meaning to the activity. Also, what means of assessment will be employed to know if the objectives have been reached? How will the efforts of students in the activity be honored?

Extension/Follow-up: Includes ideas for furthering the learning that occurred in the lesson, possibly in follow-up lessons. Also includes ideas for differentiated instruction to stimulate students for whom the lesson comes easy and/or who finish early.

National Standards Addressed: Listing of the MENC National Standards for Music Education addressed in the lesson:

1. Singing, alone and with others, a varied repertoire of music.
2. Performing on instruments, alone and with others, a varied repertoire of music.
3. Improvising melodies, harmonies, and accompaniments.
4. Composing and arranging music within specified guidelines.
5. Reading and notating music.
6. Listening to, analyzing, and describing music.
7. Evaluating music and music performances.
8. Understanding relationships between music, the other arts, and disciplines outside the arts.
9. Understanding music in relation to history and culture.

The example lesson plans in chapters 12–16 are annotated with detailed explanations and additional pedagogical commentary.

Third, the lessons demonstrate ways to unlock or draw out musical creativity using five broad categories of music technology tools:

1. Keyboards (chapter 12)

2. Sound recording applications (chapter 13)

3. Multitrack music production applications (chapter 14)

4. Music notation applications (chapter 15)

5. Instructional software and other music applications (chapter 16)

Each of these technology categories is described in the openings of chapters 12–16, but suffice it to say that they are broadly defined. A lesson that can be accomplished with Finale or Sibelius, the leading professional music notation applications, can also be accomplished with a much less costly, "entry-level" notation program, or even a free, online music notation tool. Many of the same lessons that might use a professional-level DAW program (ProTools, Logic, SONAR, Digital Performer, etc.) can also be accomplished with an entry-level DAW such as GarageBand or even the freeware digital audio program Audacity.

Fourth, the example lessons provide music educators interested in creativity-based activities a ready-made, teacher-tested collection of lessons from which to choose. These lessons demonstrate the theme of this book: using technology to unlock musical creativity in students. The specific lessons were chosen for inclusion here because of their effectiveness from the standpoint of student motivation, productivity, and learning. As has been noted, the lessons are adaptable. If you are a middle school music teacher and like a particular lesson but see that its audience is listed as high school, don't discount it. Almost every lesson, with some adjustments, can work well at the elementary, intermediate, or high school level (and beyond).

THOUGHTS ON ASSESSING MUSICAL CREATIVITY

Assessment in education is broadly defined as gathering information about, and appraising, what students know and can do in an attempt to improve student learning. A wide variety of assessment tools can be employed, including tests and quizzes, portfolios, performance evaluations, student self-evaluations, peer assessments, and teacher observation. Many of the more informal assessment approaches are discussed in chapter 8 on coaching and chapter 9 on offering/receiving feedback. In the process of coaching, peer evaluation, and self-evaluation, students take in valuable information (both praise and critique) to increase their understanding and strengthen their creative output.

Here I want to present some thoughts on formal assessment tools such as rubrics or listings of project criteria ("task lists"). A well-crafted rubric or other assessment tool should inform and even challenge. A rubric is a scoring tool that lists the criteria for an assignment, along with a rating scale for each of the criteria. The higher on the rating scale, the more points awarded. Rubrics allow teachers a vehicle for awarding credit to students for doing clearly defined tasks that are vital to a project, most of which can be objectively evaluated. The rubric for the "My Favorite Things Podcast" activity (described in chapter 14) contains examples of criteria with a corresponding rating scale for each (**Fig. 11.2,** which can be downloaded at the companion website as **Web Ex. 14.2**). Note the three generic headings: "Misses Expectations," "Meets Expectations," and "Exceeds Expectations." Some thought must be devoted to describing the characteristics for each rating category (such as Theme/Title, Sound Clips, Narration, Production Quality, Timing), but once it is created, a rubric streamlines the grading process and offers students concrete feedback.

Assessment tools allow students to be made aware of the grading criteria for a project as they venture into it. One of the easiest and best ways to do this is to provide them with the assessment tool you will use, as part of the introduction to the project. Formal assessment tools also provide final feedback to students at the close of a project. Their value for educators includes things such as simplifying the grading process, providing a rationale for at least a part of the student's grade, making clear to students and their parents what was expected and why the student received the grade he or she did.

The Goal of Assessment

Assessing student musical creativity is tricky business. Devising the right assessment tool depends on the purpose for engaging students in creative work. Where the goal is fostering the most sophisticated art, only a small number of the most gifted students will rate highly. Instead, creative projects should be used as vehicles to demonstrate understanding of musical concepts (texture, form, harmony, etc.) or technical skills (copying music, adding dynamics/ articulation markings, applying DSP [digital signal processing] effects, automating volume levels on a track, etc.). Choosing a creativity-based learning approach with students serves primarily to motivate them while adding meaning for them to their learning tasks. Though we encourage and shepherd students toward attaining a certain level of aesthetic achievement as part of coaching, that should not be *emphasized* in a formal assessment tool.

Grade level is an important consideration. For the youngest composers, Michele Kaschub and Janice Smith recommend praising and crediting participation "regardless of technical mastery. . . . With beginners, it is attempting the process that is most important. Simply creating something is an accom-

MY FAVORITE THINGS PODCAST

Name: _____

Episode Name _____   Grade _____

	Misses Expectations (0–5)	Meets Expectations (6–10)	Exceeds Expectations (11–15)	
Theme/Title	Your theme is somewhat "free-wheeling" and un-unified. The relationship between your title and theme is unclear.	The relationship between your audio clips is somewhat evident. Your title refers in some way to your theme.	Your episode makes clear the relationship between your audio clips, and the title conveys this.	
Sound Clips	Only 1 sound clip, or sound clips not prepared correctly (length, fades, conflict with voice).	Only 2 sound clips, each 15–30 secs. in length. Fade in/out used where clips do not start/end cleanly. Volume levels mostly appropriate.	You have 3 sound clips, each 15–30 secs. in length. Fade in/out used where clips do not start/end cleanly. Volume levels work well.	
Narration	Little care devoted to preparing and recording voice-overs. Hard to follow narration. Poor research.	Voice-overs are adequate, with good research, but there are some distractions due to poor script-writing, improvisation, or enunciation.	Voice-overs are well conceived (written and researched script and/or appropriate improvisation); spoken clearly.	
Production Quality	Sloppy recording; poor signal for voice-overs. Levels uneven.	Some unevenness in sound levels (clips, voice-overs). Perhaps some distortion, noise in signal, or levels too low.	Audio levels of clips and voice-overs matches. Signal is clean.	
Timing	Your podcast is less than 0:45.	Your podcast is 0:46–1:00.	Your podcast is 1:01–1:30 or more.	
Total Score [75]				

Comments:

▶ **FIG. 11.2**
Grading rubric for the "My Favorite Things" podcast activity. Created by Scott Watson.

plishment."[3] Older elementary-age children can also be expected to demonstrate musical and technical concepts in their creative work and can be credited for following directions about implementing these as well. The majority of a middle-school-age student's grade should be based on accomplishing clearly defined creative and technical tasks proficiently. For older junior high and high school projects, a minor portion of a student's grade might be for evidence of aesthetic thought. While a bit harder to discuss in concrete terms, things such as changes in dynamic and timbre or the judicious use of silence, melodic variation, or dissonance are very much a part of the creative process.

Building Appropriate, Effective Grading Rubrics

Creating rubrics for assessing creative projects can be a challenge, but here are some guidelines and suggestions for crafting an effective tool for drawing out students' best efforts.

Clear Criteria

Rubrics for creative projects should primarily include categories that rate easily measurable items, but might also include one or two less concrete elements that sometimes must be addressed. Examples of easily measurable items include length (in time or measures), number of tracks, number of expressive markings, number of sounds/sound clips, or using a certain collection of notes. Examples of less concrete elements include choosing loops that complement one another, timing synchronization (such as lining up with click track or loops), creating a contrasting theme, writing music you can perform, or following a certain melodic contour.

Sometimes, rather than a rubric, with its rows and columns, it seems more appropriate to evaluate a creative project according to a listing of project criteria. For these, I often use a linear, arrow-type rating scale to assign a score for the various elements of the project (**Fig. 11.3**). Note that the scale begins at "6" and goes up to "10." This is in keeping with Kaschub and Smith's idea that just the act of participation in a creative activity deserves credit.[4] I use this scale even with high school students. If I believe a student has made a good-faith effort to engage in the activity, I award an "8," "9," or "10." If they at least went through the motions, I never give lower than the "6" at the bottom of the scale. An example of a project criteria assessment that uses this type of scale is the one I use to grade the "New Clothes for an Old Tune" project (**Fig. 11.4**) described in chapter 14.

▶ **FIG. 11.3**

An arrow scale such as this can be used on an assessment tool to rate components of a creative project. Created by Scott Watson.

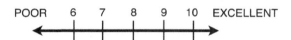

POOR   6   7   8   9   10   EXCELLENT

3. Kaschub and Smith, *Minds on Music*, 91–92.

4. Kaschub and Smith, *Minds on Music*, 91–92. The authors write, "With beginners, it is attempting the process that is most important. Simply creating something is an accomplishment."

NEW CLOTHES FOR AN OLD TUNE—Grading Rubric

Name: _____

Project (Song): _____

Category					Score
TIMING [20 POINTS]:	**20–30 Seconds [11–13 points]**	**30–44 Seconds [14–16 points]**	**45–59 Seconds [17–19 points]**	**60+ Seconds [20 points]**	
DEPTH OF PRODUCTION [10 POINTS]: You may use as many tracks as you have time to implement well. I suggest between 5 and 10 tracks. POOR 6 7 8 9 10 EXCELLENT					
LAYERING [20 POINTS]: Your project should exhibit evidence of thoughtful layering (the timbral narrative): introducing various synth or live instrument sounds, doubling melodic/harmonic elements for resonance, or emphasizing form. POOR 6 7 8 9 10 EXCELLENT					×2
TECHNIQUE [20 POINTS]: Good signal levels, smooth edits, good timing (if any real-time recording). POOR 6 7 8 9 10 EXCELLENT					×2
AESTHETIC STATEMENT [10 POINTS]: This is our subjective reaction to your artistic statement. Have you given new life and interest to the piece you used? Or, is it just a mechanical setting? POOR 6 7 8 9 10 EXCELLENT					
Total Score [80 possible]					

Comments:

125

▶ **FIG. 11.4**

Grading Rubric for the "New Clothes for an Old Tune" project. Created by Scott Watson.

126

Rubrics Calculate but Rarely Motivate

Although rubrics play a vital role in demonstrating to students what is expected, I believe other aspects of creative projects, factors beyond the rubric, are more responsible for inspiring and encouraging students to be their creative best. Think of the rubric as a grade calculator. For motivating students, look to the inspiring examples you will share, the encouragement that coaching can deliver, the peer comments and critique students know they will be receiving, the joy of collaborating with others, or the anticipation of your end-of-project performance.

A clear listing of the project criteria, however, can remove ambiguity about what is necessary and what will be graded. As Carroll Rinehart recommends, "Students should regard assessment as a useful tool rather than as a source of fear or anxiety. They should use it as a means of furthering learning and as a means of measuring their own progress."[5] In this way, rubrics and other assessment tools offer a level of confidence that can free the student to be creative and take chances within established boundaries. The task sheet for the "My Favorite Sounds" activity is designed to assess students as they audition and search for different instrument sounds on a synthesizer keyboard or software sounds (such as those in GarageBand) triggered by a keyboard controller. This assessment tool is meant to give forward motion to a project that is so fun that students can easily get sidetracked (**Fig. 11.5,** available for download from the companion website as **Web Ex 12.3**). For the final task of this activity, "Improvise/compose a brief example of an attractive sound you've found," I would award full (or close to full) credit, as well as verbal praise, for almost any demonstration of the student's sound. Again, the idea is to reward participation in a creative endeavor and build trust and comfort in sharing.

Small, but Important, Aesthetic Component

For creative projects with students in middle and high school, it is entirely appropriate that some aspect(s) of the assessment be subjective in nature. This leaves room in the rubric to inspire and honor students for efforts in the affective domain. Including categories such as "Aesthetic Statement" or "Production Creativity" allows for the introduction of the idea of client-oriented taste, so much a part of the artistic/musical world beyond the classroom. Nonetheless, this should be a small part of the total credit awarded for a creative project, in my opinion no more than 10–15% of the grade.

Your Comments Mean So Much

Since these projects are decidedly aesthetic in nature, always leave a place at the bottom of the rubric or other evaluation tool for comments. For smaller activities

5. Rinehart, *Composing and Arranging*, viii.

FAVORITE SOUNDS ACTIVITY

Name: _____

Section: _____   Date: _____

You'll be assigned points for accomplishing several tasks related to discovery of instrument timbres on a synth keyboard or from *GarageBand*.

Task	Points

1. What are your favorite sounds in these categories?
 	
 • Piano/Keyboard sounds _____ [3]
 	
 • Bass sounds _____ [3]
 	
 • Instrument you might use for a solo/lead:
 	
  Category: _____ [2]
 	
  Name: _____ [3]	

2. The favorite sound of all that I found today was called _____ [3] and was in the category _____ [2]. I would describe this sound as (one or two adjective descriptors) _____ _____. [4]	
3. Improvise/compose a brief example of an attractive sound you've found. Some ideas of how to share include an excerpt from a piano piece you know, a short melody you know (or can read or figure out), a two- or three-pitch repeated "groove," or a one- or two-measure rhythmic pattern. Play your brief example using a keyboard controller or the QWERTY keyboard with GarageBand's Musical Typing feature. [20]	
Total Points [40 possible]	

▶ **FIG. 11.5**
Task Sheet for the "Favorite Sounds" activity. Created by Scott Watson.

and project, I leave anything from a few words to a few sentences. For larger projects, I usually write my students a paragraph or two in response to their piece. I think if a project is worth students spending a week or more creating and refining, then it's worth me spending five or ten minutes sharing my thoughts and comments about their creative work.

Recognizing that you have taken the trouble to thoughtfully respond to their work, students will be more receptive to criticism you might offer. Since students should have received coaching and other instructive feedback along the way, most of your comments should be positive. We've all heard the saying, "You can attract more flies with honey than vinegar." Your positive comments will reinforce the content you value going forward. Taking the time to bless a student with a good word about their project will also build the trust necessary for creativity to flourish. If your students' works are anything like mine, you will not have to work hard to find things to praise.

Recently I wrote a comment on an evaluation of a brief, 20- to 30-second performance by a student in one of my classes. My remarks were brief, something like, "You have a lovely voice. Thank you for sharing your gift with us!" When I handed out the evaluations, I noticed the student beaming as she showed the comment to some of her friends. More substantial feedback should be offered for more substantial project work. The **sidebar** presents an example of the comments I gave my student Ed B. for work on his song "Spend All Night" (**Web Ex. 8.2,** highlighted when discussing coaching in chapter 8).

128

The introduction sets the perfect mood—mellow piano, then synth, then the opening vocals by Carlos, and then Jess. Frankly, I could have stood to hear just that combination and groove for a while more before going on to the techno-arpeggiated feel you introduce next; but I did not mind that change.

I like so many things about the track:

- Beautiful vocals: so glad you brought Carlos and Jess into the project. I also liked the effects used on the vocals.
- Your approach to percussion—just what's needed, never more!
- I like the way the song ends with just the vocals hanging out there, dissolving onto thin air.

There are a few times when the words are a bit obscured, but I do appreciate all the time you spent working on levels, signal, etc.

A very pretty ballad . . . with lyrics in the tradition of some old standards such as "Let It Snow," and "Baby It's Cold Outside." If you do not know the lyrics to these songs, I suggest you check them out for literary devices they use, as you do, to convey the theme.

For better or worse, teachers are busier than ever taking care of administrative and organizational chores that often cause them to have less energy for instructional tasks like making the types of comments described here. Find the time to write thoughtful, even heartfelt, remarks on formal student assessments and you will set yourself apart from many of the other teachers your students encounter. Your comments send an important message: "What you created in my class *really matters* to me."

Resources for Developing Assessment Tools

A number of excellent Internet sites offer suggestions for building rubrics either specifically for music courses, or more generically for any subject. Although these are not necessarily geared toward creative tasks, or those using technology, the sites offer many good ideas and features. Here are two examples of sites on the Internet that can help with developing assessment tools:

1. Music Assessment Website (www.music.miami.edu/assessment). This comprehensive website, developed by Edward P. Asmus (music education professor at the University of Miami), is packed with information, resources, and links for understanding and developing assessment tools for music courses.

2. Rubistar (rubistar.4teachers.org). The stated purpose of this online tool is to "create rubrics for your project-based learning activities." What could be more perfect for creative musical projects? I really like the site and have used its rubric generator for several projects, but I always need to make modifications. The "My Favorite Things Podcast" rubric, for instance, was made with Rubistar and then modified. Fortunately, Rubistar allows users to save and download their rubrics in a number of formats. The most useful of these for modifying is Microsoft Excel format, but others include PDF and even HTML (possibly useful if you want to post a rubric to a course website). Rubistar allows users to save rubrics permanently at their site as well. Rubistar is one of many useful tools at the 4Teachers.org website, which promotes integrating technology into the classroom.[6]

MURPHY'S LAW AND TECHNOLOGY

There are so many great reasons for using technology with music students, especially to allow them to authentically express themselves. Using technology with your students, however, is not without its problems. Murphy's law states that if something can go wrong, it will. While you and your students might enjoy some technology—whether it be a software program running on a single computer or the interaction between all the facets of a music technology lab— "hassle-free" for months, inevitably various problems crop up. These problems can be distractions at the very least and, at their worst, stop work dead in its tracks. Sometimes a student, or even the teacher, causes this to happen by clicking where they should not or changing software settings or hardware cabling.

6. 4Teachers.org is a project of ALTEC (Advanced Learning Technologies) at the University of Kansas Center for Research on Learning.

Sometimes there seems to be no apparent explanation other than that a file is "corrupt" (a euphemism for "this file no longer works and I have no idea why"). Teachers experienced with technology can often troubleshoot the problem and make the required fix.[7] Those with a lower comfort level for fiddling with settings and connections will need to call in school or district technology staff to help. Either way, technical setbacks have implications for designing and assessing creative learning activities.

Saving Student Work

One of the major benefits of students using technology in creative work, according to music teacher Matt Barr (Kennard-Dale High School, PA), is the way it allows them to "hold onto their work" from session to session. Since many of the lessons in the chapters that follow use software, I urge you to discuss with the students how important it is to save their work often. Teaching them to use a quick keyboard shortcut for saving (Windows: control-S, Mac: command-S) and reminding them from time to time can save everyone a lot of frustration. File management is another area that must be addressed when students in several classes are all using the same computer. Perhaps your school provides students with "home directories" on a network where they can save their work. Maybe individual student folders will be created on each computer for saving work; in this case, specific students will need to be assigned to specific computers in each class. Older students may bring to school their own means of backing up files (such as portable [USB flash] drives or CD-Rs on which files may be burned).

Online music applications such as Noteflight.com make file management easy. In the free version, students have their own account and save their work to Noteflight's servers. Whenever and wherever students log in, they can work with their saved files or create new ones.

Build Margin Into Your Plans

Teachers need to build a safety margin of time into their lesson plans. If nothing goes wrong during a unit, the additional time can be spent refining projects or engaging in postproject reflection. But if something does happen, the class can still stay on schedule. Teachers must be aware of this in terms of assessing technology-dependent creative work, too. On the day of an in-class recital of projects, I have had students raise their hands and say, "Dr. Watson, I can't find my

---

7. Most technology glitches are ones I have seen again and again. When I do encounter something new, I can almost always find a solution by typing a brief description of the problem into an Internet search engine and then following the resulting links to a product user group or manufacturer support page. Remember, there are millions of users out there, so it is likely that others have already found solutions to your technology problems.

file. I know it was here yesterday," or "Honest, Dr. Watson, when I finished work on this last class, my drum parts were finished. Now there's nothing there." Whether they forgot to save their work or another student accidentally deleted it, this student is now behind and accommodations need to be made to either recover what is missing or credit the work even though it is missing. For the former, perhaps the student can be grouped with another (or others) for the remainder of the activity. Alternatively, that student might be able to catch up on his missing work as others perform or playback their projects. For the later, if you have been coaching the student along the way, you know what had been accomplished and can assign a score based on that.

REFLECTION ACTIVITY

1. Take some time to peruse at least one of the prepared curricular materials listed above—either one of the conventional publications available to you or one of the Internet resources. Also consider examining a prepared curricular resource introduced via personal investigation, a colleague, or your instructor. Choose one lesson plan or project you liked to share, describing its strengths and how it may need to be adapted for various scenarios (such as your current teaching assignment or one in which you hope to find yourself).

2. What are some good reasons for creating self-made, custom curricular materials for creative musical activities that incorporate technology?

3. This chapter provided many ideas on creating effective, useful rubrics (or other assessment tool) to award credit for student efforts on a creative project. Several rubric creation resources were cited as well. Construct a rubric (or other assessment tool) for one of the projects in this workbook (either one for a project that does not already have a rubric, or one *different* than the rubric provided). Use a program such as Microsoft Word or Excel, an online rubric generator, or some combination to craft your rubric.

CHAPTER 12
CREATIVITY WITH KEYBOARDS

ALL ABOUT KEYBOARDS

KEYBOARDS HAVE BECOME the electronic musical instrument most identified with music education technology and can be used in a host of wonderful learning and artistic scenarios in school music programs.

Easily Produced, Attractive Sounds

Keyboards allow students to initiate sounds easily, with the press of a key. In a stand-alone setup, students can work with hundreds of built-in sounds; as part of a MIDI workstation,[1] students can trigger even more software sounds. Some of these sounds approximate acoustic instruments such as piano, trumpet, or violin; others imitate electronic instruments such as electric guitar, fretless bass, or rock organ; still others produce synthesizer lead and pad[2] sounds, as well as other novel sounds (such as sound effects). One set or bank of sounds that is advantageous to have on a keyboard is the General MIDI (GM) sound set. This set of 128 sounds allows students to reliably call up certain instrument sounds (manually or by software message) by standardized "patch" or program numbers (#1 is always a grand piano, #33 is always an acoustic bass, #76 is always a pan flute, etc.). **Fig. 12.1,** also available as a PDF download on the companion website (**Web Ex. 12.1**), shows the General MIDI sound set. An instrument's own proprietary (that is, unique to the manufacturer) sounds are usually higher quality and more intriguing than GM sounds but do not have equivalents on other keyboards or for use by music software. Keyboards, which allow kids to explore and initiate compelling sounds of all kinds with the touch of a key, bring the timbral aspect of musical creativity within reach for students with little or no instrumental experience.

---

1. A basic *MIDI workstation* consists of a computer, a keyboard (synth or controller) for inputting musical data, and some means of monitoring sound (headphones, speakers, etc.). See **Appendix 1** for a detailed description and configuration information.

2. A *synth lead sound* usually plays a melodic role in a music production, similar to a lead electric guitar. A *synth pad* usually plays a warm, atmospheric background role.

GENERAL MIDI SOUNDS

1–8 Piano		33–40 Bass		65–72 Reed		97–104 Synth Effects	
1	Acoustic Grand	33	Acoustic Bass	65	Soprano Sax	97	Rain
2	Bright Acoustic	34	Electric Bass (finger)	66	Alto Sax	98	Soundtrack
3	Electric Grand	35	Electric Bass (pick)	67	Tenor Sax	99	Crystal
4	Honky Tonk	36	Fretless Bass	68	Baritone Sax	100	Atmosphere
5	Electric Piano 1	37	Slap Bass 1	69	Oboe	101	Brightness
6	Electric Piano 2	38	Slap Bass 2	70	English Horn	102	Goblins
7	Harpsichord	39	Synth Bass 1	71	Bassoon	103	Echoes
8	Clav	40	Synth Bass 2	72	Clarinet	104	Sci-Fi
9–16 Chromatic Percussion		**41–48 Strings**		**73–80 Pipe**		**105–112 Ethnic**	
9	Celesta	41	Violin	73	Piccolo	105	Sitar
10	Glockenspiel	42	Viola	74	Flute	106	Banjo
11	Music Box	43	Cello	75	Recorder	107	Shamisen
12	Vibraphone	44	Contrabass	76	Pan Flute	108	Koto
13	Marimba	45	Tremolo Strings	77	Blown Bottle	109	Kalimba
14	Xylophone	46	Pizzicato Strings	78	Shakuhachi	110	Bagpipe
15	Tubular Bells	47	Orchestral Harp	79	Whistle	111	Fiddle
16	Dulcimer	48	Timpani	80	Ocarina	112	Shanai
17–24 Organ		**49–56 Ensemble**		**81–88 Synth Lead**		**113–120 Percussive**	
17	Drawbar Organ	49	String Ensemble 1	81	Square	113	Tinkle Bell
18	Percussive Organ	50	String Ensemble 2	82	Sawtooth	114	Agogo
19	Rock Organ	51	Synth Strings 1	83	Calliope	115	Steel Drums
20	Church Organ	52	Synth Strings 2	84	Chiff	116	Woodblock
21	Reed Organ	53	Choir Aahs	85	Charang	117	Taiko Drum
22	Accordion	54	Voice Oohs	86	Voice	118	Melodic Tom
23	Harmonica	55	Synth Voice	87	Fifths	119	Synth Drum
24	Tango Accordion	56	Orchestra Hit	88	Bass Lead	120	Reverse Cymbal
25–32 Guitar		**57–64 Brass**		**89–96 Synth Pad**		**121–128 Sound Effects**	
25	Acoustic Guitar (nylon)	57	Trumpet	89	New Age	121	Guitar Fret Noise
26	Acoustic Guitar (steel)	58	Trombone	90	Warm	122	Breath Noise
27	Electric Guitar (jazz)	59	Tuba	91	Polysynth	123	Seashore
28	Electric Guitar (clean)	60	Muted Trumpet	92	Choir	124	Bird Tweet
29	Electric Guitar (muted)	61	French Horn	93	Bowed	125	Telephone Ring
30	Overdriven Guitar	62	Brass Section	94	Metallic	126	Helicopter
31	Distortion Guitar	63	Synth Brass 1	95	Halo	127	Applause
32	Guitar Harmonics	64	Synth Brass 2	96	Sweep	128	Gunshot

133

▶ **FIG. 12.1**

The basic General MIDI sound set. Created by Scott Watson.

Most keyboard "patches" or programs map a particular sound across the entire range of the keyboard. *Drum kits*, on the other hand, are keyboard programs that assign a *different* percussion sound to each key of the keyboard. In this way a student might trigger a bass drum by pressing one key and a snare drum by pressing another. The map of the GM standard drum kit shown in **Fig. 7.2** is also available as a PDF download from the book's companion website (**Web Ex. 12.2**).

Powerful Music Input Device

A keyboard is a powerful input device for a MIDI workstation, allowing students to record notes, rhythms, and other performance data into music production, notation, and other music software. The following are examples of some keyboard features that affect the type and scope of performance data that can be input:

1. **Keys.** It is common for electronic keyboards used as part of a computer music workstation to have 61 keys (five octaves). A Transpose button (or buttons) allows the user to access notes above or below the keyboard's physical range. Other options include 76 and 88 keys, which are nice for performing but more costly. More portable keyboard controllers may come with as few as 25 keys (two octaves).

   The keys on most electronic instruments are similar to the lighter, plastic keys on an organ. These are fine for most music education applications, but because they offer little resistance when being pressed, some pianists find them unsatisfying to play. In response to this, some keyboards (especially digital pianos) have semiweighted or weighted keys to approximate the feel of a piano.

   Some electronic instruments have miniature keys. Full-size keys are recommended for instruments that will be used in performance; however, mini keys may be perfect for a set of inexpensive keyboards used in the elementary classroom or for smaller, more portable keyboard controllers (such as those one might use with laptops).

2. **Expression Controls.** Items such as a pitch bend wheel (or lever) and a modulation wheel (or lever) allow the user to add expression to sounds. These controls make possible instrumental gestures such as bends, scoops, falls, and increasing the intensity of vibrato so common with electric guitar, synth leads, and jazz/rock organ.

3. **Pedals.** Better keyboards and controllers have *sustain pedal* and *volume pedal* jacks. Less expensive keyboard sustain pedals are essentially a box-shaped switch; better pedals look and work just like that of a piano. Some students might appreciate having a sustain pedal to press while playing keyboard. A volume pedal, which works like a car's gas pedal, is less common in labs but can come in handy for live performance.

4. **Velocity Sensitivity.** Better keyboards measure how hard (quickly) or soft (slowly) a key was struck and respond accordingly. Dynamics on instruments that are not velocity sensitive are limited to adjusting the volume slider (an awkward movement during performance) or using a volume pedal.

Tonal Collections Suggested by Arrangement of Keys

The white- and black-key arrangement of the keyboard lends itself to several easy-to-learn tonal schemes that facilitate improvisation and creative expression even by novices. Students can improvise using notes from any of several collections of "white only" or "black only" pitches, each with their own resting tone.

1. **C Major Pandiatonic.** *Pandiatonicism* is a term created to describe a compositional technique used in some of the more populist twentieth-century concert art music by composers such as Aaron Copland and Igor Stravinsky. With pandiatonicism, the notes of a diatonic scale are used, but not with concern for conventional melodic or harmonic considerations. In other words, students can engage in a white-key-only improvisational free-for-all! Nonetheless, the resting tone is C. Whether the students improvise melodically or harmonically, their overall piece should gravitate around the tone C, most likely beginning and ending there.

2. **A Minor Pandiatonic.** This is a minor-sounding version of item 1 whose resting tone is A. Whether the students improvise melodically or harmonically, their overall piece should gravitate around the tone A, most likely beginning and ending there.

3. **G-flat Major Pentatonic.** This is a major-sounding black-key improvisational free-for-all. Any black key works well, but G-flat is the resting tone. Whether the students improvise melodically or harmonically, their overall piece should gravitate around the tone G-flat, most likely beginning and ending there.

4. **E-flat Minor Pentatonic.** This is a minor-sounding version of item 3, with E-flat as the resting tone and the overall piece gravitating around the tone E-flat, most likely beginning and ending there. This collection of notes works great against an E-flat 12-bar blues chord progression.

I have even used small, red dot stickers (the kind you might buy at stationary stores to use as price tags) to highlight other note collections (such as G pentatonic) just as one might remove keys/bars of an Orff instrument to limit the note choices.

Other Electronic Instruments

Other electronic instruments, such as electric guitars, synthesizer drum pads and drum sets, and nonkeyboard MIDI controllers (wind instrument, guitar, violin, etc.) may be used by students for creative musical activities in music

135

courses. While these instruments facilitate creative expression with certain (especially older) students, there are reasons they are not as ubiquitous in the realm of music technology. Although guitars can be used for participation in the musical creativity activities presented in this book (improvisation, multi-track arranging, etc.), they require a performance skill that only a handful (albeit a notable handful) of middle and high school students possess. Synth drum pads are far more accessible to all students in music class, even those without percussion experience. A majority of students have natural rhythmic sensibilities that allow them to be expressive triggering drum sounds from a drum pad. These instruments focus on triggering nontonal sounds. A synth drum set (such as V-Drums by Roland), while a great music production tool to have, shares this timbral limitation. Add to that the fact that they may not be as easy for a novice to operate, and that they can be costly, and one can see why they are not widely used in schools. MIDI wind and guitar controllers are meant to trigger all manner of sounds, but likewise require specialized performance training and can be costly.

Types of Keyboards

Keyboard technology is constantly changing, with manufacturers always working to improve the quality of their sounds and function of their instruments. Keeping in mind that it is hard to definitively group keyboards by type, one could categorize keyboards according to their primary features and functions. Note that if the keyboard is to be used in a computer music workstation, it will need either a built-in USB MIDI interface or MIDI IN/OUT ports. A built-in USB MIDI interface is preferred and requires only a standard USB cable to connect the keyboard to the computer. Most recent keyboards (of all types) come with this and therefore can be used as a "controller" (see below). Only the least inexpensive, "toy" keyboards lack some sort of MIDI connectivity and should be avoided since this greatly limits how they can be employed. Older keyboards with MIDI IN/OUT (and THRU) ports require an external MIDI interface, MIDI cables (one "IN" and one "OUT"), and a serial (that is, USB) cable. Obviously this configuration is more complicated. See **Appendix 1** for details on configuring a keyboard as part of a general-purpose music workstation.

1. **Entry-Level, Portable Keyboard.** These tend to be the most affordable, consumer-quality keyboards with a decent amount of on-board sounds. These keyboards are portable, usually have built-in (though not high quality) speakers, optional battery power, and ample (though lower quality) sounds, and may include an auto-accompaniment function.

2. **MIDI Controller.** Keyboard controllers have no, or a limited number of, on-board sounds. The main purpose of a controller keyboard is to enter performance data (notes, rhythms, etc.) into music software

(GarageBand, Finale, Sibelius, etc.) for playback by virtual instruments. Controllers are also used in live performance to trigger software or hardware (such as a sound module) instruments. Controllers come in all sizes from the Korg nanoKEY with its 25 miniature keys (**Fig. 12.2**), to the M-Audio Sono 88 with its 88 full-sized, semiweighted keys. Some MIDI controllers also contain an audio interface for connecting an XLR microphone or a 1/4-inch cable for an instrument such as electric guitar.

3. **Digital Piano.** The main draw here is a high-quality piano sound triggered by keys that feel like real piano keys. One would assume these are used mostly in performance situations in music education (accompanying classroom singing or choir rehearsal/performance, jazz band keyboards, etc.), but they can also serve as a controller in a MIDI workstation. Most digital pianos offer limited additional sounds (electric piano, organ, clav, strings, etc.) and may come with built-in speakers and a furniture-style stand.

4. **Synthesizer.** Here, sound is the key. Synthesizers use different sound topologies (that is, methods for building sounds) to produce a plethora of classic and unique synth sounds. Sound-generating elements (oscillators, filters, envelope generators, etc.) combine to create audio waveforms; knobs and sliders are often included for altering some aspects of the sounds. Sound sets vary widely from approximations of conventional orchestral instruments, to popular electronic instruments, to synthesizer basics (such as "leads" and "pads"), to original—sometimes very creative and bizarre—sounds. An arpeggiator and the ability to layer sounds are examples of features that extend the use of the keyboard's sounds.

5. **Keyboard Workstation.** These are multifunction keyboards that include a wide variety of synthesized and sampled sounds, a built-in multitrack MIDI (and sometimes audio) recorder, DSP (digital signal processing) effects, and more. Many workstations include an audio interface for connecting an XLR microphone or a 1/4- or 1/8-inch cable for instruments such as electric guitar or bass.

▶ **FIG. 12.2**

Korg's nanoKEY, an extremely portable and inexpensive USB controller keyboard, can be used to trigger software instruments. Graphic provided by Korg USA. Used with permission.

137

Note that some keyboards combine features/functions of several categories. For instance, a professional-level keyboard workstation might come with high-quality on-board speakers. While some keyboards are dedicated "controllers," any keyboard with MIDI connectivity can serve as one. A high-end synth keyboard usually includes a great sampled piano sound; if it has 88 weighted keys, it can serve as a digital piano.

Sound Monitoring

One of the most vitally important aspects of using keyboards in music education is how the sound of the keyboard—or the sounds it, as controller, triggers—will be monitored. When a keyboard's sound is amplified by built-in speakers or an external amplifier, the student playing the keyboard and everyone else can hear it. If you are in a classroom or lab with a bunch, or even just several, keyboards this would be chaotic. There are several good options for students monitoring their sound as they work.

Headphones

The cheapest and most technically simple method for monitoring a keyboard's on-board sounds is to use a pair of stereo headphones. Almost every keyboard has either a 1/4-inch or 1/8-inch headphone jack. I personally would not purchase one without this. If your headphones have a different-size plug, you can buy a very inexpensive adapter plug at any retail electronics store. Some keyboards have two headphone jacks, which facilitate students working and monitoring sound in pairs. If this option is desired but the keyboard only has one headphone jack, you can purchase an inexpensive headphone splitter.

Lab Monitoring System

On the other end of the price and function spectrum is a lab monitoring system, such as the Korg General Education Controller (GEC). These systems are meant for keyboard or computer music workstation labs and consist of a teacher module, student workstation interface box, headphones (some with microphones), and various cables. Audio from the student computers and keyboards (and possibly headphone mics) is routed via cables through the student interface boxes to the teacher module. The teacher can send audio from his or her computer and keyboard (and possibly headphone mic) into the system as well. All of this enables the teacher to monitor and route audio in almost any way. Whereas with headphones the student can only monitor sound from their keyboard (on-board sounds) or their computer (software sounds), a lab monitoring system allows for both.

The most common configuration with a lab monitoring system involves students hearing audio from their own workstation, with the teacher listening in to check on how things are going. Ideally, the teacher module is connected to a stereo sound system (or powered speakers). If so, the teacher's workstation (computer and keyboard), or any student's, can be heard out in the room without headphones. This is very helpful when the teacher is demonstrating for students, or when the teacher wants to share and discuss a student's work with the entire class. Examples of other helpful configurations include setting up "groups" of selected students to hear one another and work together, and a "lecture" mode that mutes the sound from student workstations so that only the teacher's audio (and possibly voice via the headphone mic) is heard.

Powered Speakers

A third possibility for monitoring keyboard sound involves a combination of powered monitor speakers with headphones. This is a compromise between using headphones only and a lab monitoring system, both in function and in cost. Be sure to get powered monitor speakers that include several audio inputs and a headphone jack, because (1) this will enable you to route audio from the student's keyboard and computer into them, and (2) this will allow the student to hear all of this in their headphones rather than out in the room. If you want the student to share, simply unplug the headphones from the monitor speakers for everyone to hear.

EXAMPLE LESSONS

The pages that follow present several lessons that feature the use of keyboards in creative musical activities and projects. Several were discussed in part I of this book when illustrating how to implement the Eight Principles for Unlocking Musical Creativity. I hope you will see many ways to bring the Eight Principles into your teaching of these lessons. Unless otherwise indicated, all the lessons are ones I have developed and used in my own teaching at various levels.

139

LESSON TITLE: FAVORITE SOUNDS

Audience: Grades 4–12, general and elective music classes.

Objective: At the conclusion of this lesson, students should have a good grasp of the concept of instrumental timbre, be able to perform basic keyboard synth operations such as changing programs ("patches") and adjusting volume, and be able to demonstrate a sound they find appealing in a creative way. This could be a rhythmic or tonal improvisation (alone or with a partner), a brief melodic gesture that uses the sound idiomatically (such as a trumpet patch playing "Taps" or a short fanfare), or a phrase or longer section from some existing music the student knows (something student remembers or figures out from band, piano lessons, guitar lessons, etc.).

Materials/Equipment: Synth keyboard with amplification; ideally students work primarily with headphones. Also may be accomplished using a keyboard controller triggering softsynth (GarageBand, etc.) sounds. You may want to use a handout such as a General MIDI sound set (**Fig. 12.1**), available as a download from the companion website (**Web Ex. 12.1**), or a form on which to record sounds explored and chosen.

Duration: Depending on the number of students, this should take between 40 and 80 minutes (one to two class periods).

Prior Knowledge and Skills: No special skills or prior knowledge is necessary, but familiarity with the notes of a keyboard will enhance the activity for the student.

Procedure:

1. Demonstrate for the students how to do the following basic operations on the keyboards they will use: power on, volume, bank and/or patch change (if appropriate), pitch bend and/or modulation wheel (if applicable), and sustain pedal (if applicable). Practice with the class.

2. Demonstrate the sound of several "patches" (programs, sounds) by playing them for students. Ideas for thoughtful interaction include asking students to guess the sound demonstrated and asking students which sounds seem most/least successfully synthesized.

3. Allow students time to explore the sounds in a bank. Ideas for thoughtful interaction include having students choose their favorite sounds in a category (for example, families of instruments: keyboard, bass, lead, etc.). After giving some time to investigate and audition sounds, ask for volunteers to share the sounds they liked best (play a single note). Discuss with students which sounds would be good in various musical settings (use as a solo instrument, as a background instrument, evoking different style periods, etc.).

4. Improvisation/performance. Have each student prepare a brief demonstration of a favorite sound to play for the rest of the class. This could

be an excerpt from a piano piece the student knows, a short melody they figure out, a two- or three-pitch groove (such as the example in **Fig. 7.1**), or a two- or four-measure ostinato or other rhythmic pattern. If using a keyboard controller to trigger software sounds in a recording program such as GarageBand, you could have students record their examples to playback instead of having them demonstrate them "live."

Adaptations: You may want or need to have two students share a keyboard (some keyboards have two headphone jacks, or you could use a headphone splitter) and collaborate. The pair would explore and/or share their findings together and then improvise their demonstration of a favorite patch as a duet team. If there are only a handful of keyboards available, for instance, in a pod at the back of the room, students could be rotated onto the keyboards while the teacher leads the majority of the class in a related activity.

Some schools have laptops that can be signed out for use in class. This lesson would work nicely with GarageBand sounds running Mac OS laptops triggered by small controller keyboards such as the Korg nanoKEY. GarageBand instruments are organized in categories (pianos and keyboards, guitars, bass, horns, etc.), which are helpful for student exploration. If no controller keyboards are available, you could do this lesson with GarageBand's virtual keyboard (a screen version of a piano keyboard) or using the computer's QWERTY keys with GarageBand's "Musical Typing"[3] (**Fig. 12.3**).

Feedback/Evaluation: After each student's example, ask the class for feedback. You will probably have to model this for the class a few times before they open up with good comments. I use each sound shared as a chance to

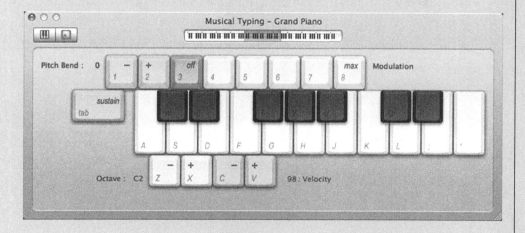

▶ **FIG. 12.3**
GarageBand's Musical Typing window. Created by Scott Watson.

3. GarageBand's "Musical Typing" allows software instruments to be triggered by the computer's QWERTY keys. Although it takes a little getting used to, it allows for polyphony, octave transposition, and such expressive techniques as pitch bend, modulation, and sustain.

instigate a discussion about timbre and sound synthesis. With older students, if someone shares a percussive sound we can talk about *envelope* (attack, decay, sustain, release) and its importance in sound synthesis. A student might notice that electronic instruments such as electric bass or synth pads sound more convincing than wind instruments. Here, we can talk about *synthesis topologies* (the different "recipes" for synthesizing and sampling sound that yield various levels of effectiveness or realism).

If you want this to be a graded activity, you could simply award credit for participation. Alternatively you might employ a "task sheet," such as **Fig. 11.5** (available for download from the companion website, **Web Ex. 12.3**) that awards credit for certain basic criteria for this activity.

Extension/Follow-up: Students really seem to enjoy exploring all the various sounds on a synthesizer. Some keyboards (or software instrument libraries) have hundreds, if not thousands, of sounds. If some students finish early, they will enjoy having extra time to explore and audition additional sounds. No doubt there are benefits to repeating this activity either as is or with some variation.

National Standards Addressed: Each of the following standards is addressed to some degree in this lesson:

- **Standard 2,** Performing on instruments, alone and with others, a varied repertoire of music
- **Standard 3,** Improvising melodies, harmonies, and accompaniments
- **Standard 4,** Composing and arranging music within specified guidelines
- **Standard 5** (optional), Reading and notating music
- **Standard 6,** Listening to, analyzing, and describing music
- **Standard 7** (optional), Evaluating music and music performances

LESSON TITLE: PERCUSSION SOUNDS IMPROVISATION

Audience: Grades 4–12, general and elective music classes.

Objective: At the conclusion of this lesson, students will be able to perform a basic rock beat (using quarter and eighth notes/rests), as well as improvise a short drum "fill" solo.

Materials/Equipment: Synth keyboard with amplification. At first, students work with headphones (either alone or in pairs with a headphone splitter). For the conclusion of the lesson, students need their percussion sounds to be heard along with others in the class. This lesson may also be accomplished using a keyboard controller triggering a softsynth (GarageBand, etc.) drum kit.

You may want to write the easy or regular rock beat score (**Figs. 12.4** and **12.5**, respectively) on the board or project it to a screen (or interactive whiteboard) for students to read as they play. Student's parts of the rock beat may also be taught by rote.

Duration: 30–45 minutes (about one class period).

Prior Knowledge and Skills: No special skills or prior knowledge is necessary, other than the ability to operate the keyboard.

Procedure:

1. Have students find the keys for some basic percussion instruments. Ask them to locate a snare drum, bass drum, and a cymbal sound (ride, hi-hat, etc.) and check. You may want to provide (as a handout) or project on a screen the GM standard drum kit map (**Fig. 7.2, Web Ex. 12.2**); however, allowing students to discover sounds on their own can be a successful part of the lesson. Be sure to have them locate sounds for bass drum, snare drum, ride cymbal, and hi-hat and/or cowbell.

2. Divide the class into four or five groups—bass drums, snare drums, ride cymbals, and hi-hats and/or cowbells. Teach students to perform their part to a basic rock beat from notation (on the board, overhead, projection screen, etc.) or by rote and practice as an ostinato.

3. Now have the class perform the rock beat together for three measures in a row but resting on the fourth measure. Teach this pattern as a four-measure repeated cycle. Choose different student soloists to fill

▶ **FIG. 12.4**

Easy Rock Beat score. Created by Scott Watson.

▶ **FIG. 12.5**

Rock Beat score. Created by Scott Watson.

every fourth measure with a solo drum fill when class drops out.[4] If needed, allow students a few minutes to work out material for their solo. Some parameters that may help foster attractive solo material include using only one or two percussion sounds, and performing only with index finger tips (as if drum sticks).

Adaptations: Certainly two students can share a 61-key (or larger) keyboard using a headphone splitter. If you do not have enough keyboards, augment keyboard-triggered percussion sounds with any hand percussion instruments (hand drum, tambourine, cowbell, etc.) available. Have students take turns rotating onto the keyboards to participate and take a drum fill solo.

This lesson would work nicely with GarageBand sounds triggered by small controller keyboards such as the Korg nanoKEY (**Fig. 12.2**). Have students select one of the GarageBand drum kits (Pop Kit, Techno Kit, etc.). If no controller keyboards are available, you could do this lesson using the computer's QWERTY keys with GarageBand's "Musical Typing" (**Fig. 12.3**).

Feedback/Evaluation: Perform repeating pattern of three measures ostinato beat (class), one measure improvisation (solo), rotating each student into the solo spot. Assign participation grade for accurately performing the Rock Beat and for taking a solo. Consider recording the class and playing it back for discussion.

Extension/Follow-up: Select one or more stronger students to add a tonal element, such as a repeated bass or synth gesture, to the beat pattern as the class performs.

Teach students different pop or other music beat patterns, such as jazz/swing, hip hop, march rhythm, or blues shuffle. Use the new beat pattern in the same way to feature student drum fill soloists.

Create with the students a drum part to a CD track (or excerpt from a CD track prepared with audio editing software).

Have students work in pairs or groups of three to develop a percussion improvisation with some basic formal scheme—such as arch (A–B–A) or rondo (A–B–A–C–A–B–A)—and elements of improvised and predetermined notes.

---

4. The idea for assigning solo fills at the end of each phrase/cycle comes from Dr. Tom Rudolph (Haverford School District, PA). It is a great ice-breaker for those reluctant to improvise.

National Standards Addressed: Each of the following standards is addressed to some degree in this lesson:

- **Standard 2,** Performing on instruments, alone and with others, a varied repertoire of music.
- **Standard 3,** Improvising melodies, harmonies, and accompaniments.
- **Standard 4** (optional), Composing and arranging music within specified guidelines.
- **Standard 5** (optional), Reading and notating music.
- **Standard 6,** Listening to, analyzing, and describing music.
- **Standard 7** (optional), Evaluating music and music performances.

LESSON TITLE: BLUES KEYBOARD IMPROVISATION

Audience: Grades 4–12, general and elective music classes.

Objective: Students will use the notes of the black-key pentatonic scale to perform an improvisation over an E-flat, 12-bar blues accompaniment track.

Materials/Equipment: Synth keyboard with amplification and a recorded accompaniment track that repeats the E-flat, 12-bar blues chord changes (listen to, and/or download, **Web Ex. 12.4** from the companion website) played through a classroom sound system. At first students work with headphones, but for the conclusion of the lesson students need to be heard along with the accompaniment track.

Duration: 45 minutes (or approximately one class period).

Prior Knowledge and Skills: No special skills or prior knowledge is necessary, other than the ability to operate the keyboard, but familiarity with the notes of a keyboard will enhance the activity for the student.

Procedure:

1. Show students the black key pentatonic collection of notes, emphasizing E-flat as a resting tone or tonic (**Fig. 12.6**).
2. Demonstrate for the students how improvisation using this collection works well with an E-flat, 12-bar blues accompaniment. Use the recording posted at the companion website (**Web Ex. 12.4**) or one you create with a program such as Band-in-a-Box or GarageBand.
3. Give students time to select a synth sound they would like to use and to experiment and improvise with the black-key pentatonic scale. Short, three- to five-note melodic motives work well for getting kids started with improvisation. Against the accompaniment track, do some call-and-response (such as trading measures) with the kids to show how effective melodic ideas can be very simple: play one- or two-measure, brief blues "licks" using a minimum of notes and see if kids can echo/imitate you. **Fig. 12.7** shows some very simple, yet pleasing, call-and-response blues licks developed and used by Dr. Tom Rudolph (Haverford School District, PA) when working with students

▶ **FIG. 12.6**

A keyboard's black keys work beautifully when improvising to an E-flat blues accompaniment. Created by Scott Watson.

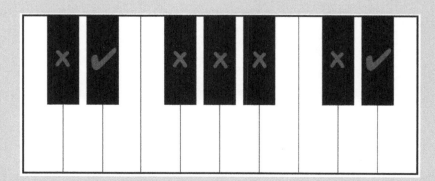

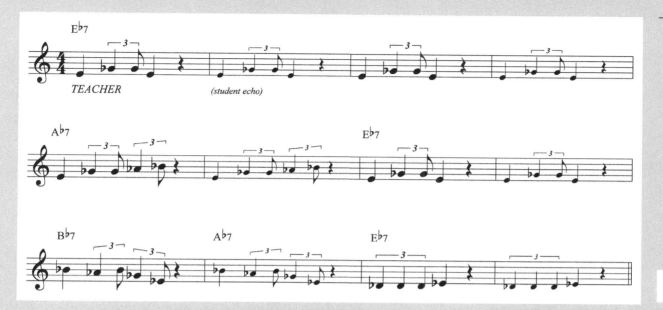

147

on blues improvisation.[5] It is not essential that students exactly parrot you; what is important is the experience developing short melodic gestures.

4. Play the accompaniment track and allow students to try out their own ideas for solos.

5. Invite students to take a chorus (once through the E-flat, 12-bar blues progression) soloing for the class.

Adaptations: This lesson is valuable even if there is only one keyboard (with amplification) on which students take turns improvising in front of the class. If you have several keyboards, allow some students to improvise with those while the rest of the class plays rhythm instruments along with the accompaniment track. Orff mallet instruments, with the appropriate bars removed, may also be used for improvising to the E-flat blues accompaniment. Blues scales could also be written out for students in class willing to try improvising with their band or string instruments.

In place of the E-flat, 12-bar blues track that can be downloaded from the book's companion website, you could create your own accompaniment using Band-in-the-Box, GarageBand, or some other music production software.

Feedback/Evaluation: Record students' improvisations; award credit for participation. If you want to assign a grade, assign additional credit for repeating a rhythmic and/or melodic motive at least once.

Offer students the chance to comment on one another's instrument choice and solo content.

 FIG. 12.7
Short "licks" like these can jump start motive-based blues improvisation. Blues phrases developed by Dr. Tom Rudolph. Used with permission.

5. Thomas Rudolph, "Improvising the Blues in the Keyboard Lab." Available at the Lesson Plans area of SoundTree.com.

Extension/Follow-up: Demonstrate how to use pitch bend and modulation controls and encourage students to employ these in their improvisation to be more expressive.

If multitrack music production software is available, consider having students record their improvisations along to the E-flat, 12-bar blues track. In GarageBand, for instance, drop the accompaniment audio file into one track and set up a second track for the student to choose an instrument sound and record his or her blues improvisation.

Really, this lesson can be adapted to explore improvisation using any of the note collections outlined in the introduction to this chapter (such as C major pandiatonic, A minor pandiatonic, G-flat major pentatonic, E-flat minor pentatonic).

National Standards Addressed: Each of the following standards is addressed to some degree in this lesson:

- **Standard 2,** Performing on instruments, alone and with others, a varied repertoire of music.
- **Standard 3** (optional), Improvising melodies, harmonies, and accompaniments.
- **Standard 6** (optional), Listening to, analyzing, and describing music.
- **Standard 7** (optional), Evaluating music and music performances.

LESSON TITLE: SOUND EFFECTS STORY OR POEM

Audience: Grades 3–12, general and elective music classes.

Objective: Students will become familiar with the sound effect sounds on a synth keyboard by composing a sound effects soundtrack to underscore a short, descriptive story they write, tailored to the sounds employed.

Materials/Equipment: Synth keyboard with amplification. At first, students work with headphones (either alone or in pairs with a headphone splitter). For the conclusion of the lesson, students need their sound effect (SFX) sounds to be heard as a story is read to the class. This lesson may also be accomplished using a keyboard controller triggering one of the softsynth (GarageBand, etc.) sound effect kits.

Students will need a text editor or writing pad and pencil on which to write their brief story or poem, and later add indications for sound cues.

Duration: 135 minutes (or approximately three class periods).

Prior Knowledge and Skills: No special skills or prior knowledge is necessary, other than the ability to operate the keyboard, but familiarity with the notes of a keyboard will enhance the activity for the student.

Procedure:

1. The General MIDI sound set includes some sound effects, but many keyboards have one or more additional sound effects kits (a variety of sound effects mapped to each key of a keyboard). Have students explore the SFX and other imaginative sounds on the keyboard you are using. Ask for volunteers to share an evocative sound they found.

2. Form groups and assign roles. Group roles should include a reader, a recorder, and two or more "Foley artists" (sound effect performers). If desired, a "director" may be appointed as well to coordinate everything.

3. Allow students time to choose approximately six sound effect sounds (or other intriguing sounds) they like. It is best if you assign a specific number of sounds for the activity. Have the recorder note which sound effects were chosen, including the program number (and bank, if appropriate) so they can be recalled easily.

4. The students should discuss the sounds chosen for dramatic possibilities and then write a story or poem around the sounds, developing dramatic moments that correspond with each sound effect. This activity works well with Halloween topics. One of the students should type or write the brief story or poem as the group creates it, aiming for no more than one or two paragraphs. *Important:* Leave ample spacing between lines of text to indicate the moment when the sound effects should occur.

149

5. Have students notate above the words of the story or poem where and what sound effects are played. Consider having students devise a symbol or small picture for each sound effect cue.

6. Using the "score" (text plus SFX symbols) created by the students, have groups practice their sound effect stories and then perform for the class.

Adaptations: In a lab with a sound management system, configure groups of three, four, or five students to work together. Certainly two students ("Foley artists") can share a 61-key (or larger) keyboard using a headphone splitter. If you do not have enough keyboards, augment keyboard triggered sound effects with live "Foley" sounds produced from objects you provide (or that students bring in).

This lesson would work nicely with GarageBand sounds on laptops triggered by small controller keyboards such as the Korg nanoKEY (**Fig. 12.2**). Have students select one of the GarageBand sound effect kits (Comedy Noises, Nature Sounds, etc.). If no controller keyboards are available, you could do this lesson by using GarageBand's "Musical Typing" feature with the computer's QWERTY keys. For a description of how to assign different, or custom, SFXs to the QWERTY keys, see the "GarageBand Key Sounds" lesson at the end of chapter 14.

Feedback/Evaluation: A good assessment tool should award credit for (1) crafting a story that alludes to and employs all the SFX (or other) cues chosen, (2) creating a clean copy of the story with indications for when the SFX cues occur, and (3) performing the story with appropriately timed cues.

Extension/Follow-up: See the "Scoring a Children's Poem" activity in chapter 14.

National Standards Addressed: Each of the following standards is addressed to some degree in this lesson:

- **Standard 3** (optional), Improvising melodies, harmonies, and accompaniments.
- **Standard 4** (optional), Composing and arranging music within specified guidelines.
- **Standard 5** (optional), Reading and notating music.
- **Standard 6** (optional), Listening to, analyzing, and describing music.
- **Standard 7** (optional), Evaluating music and music performances.
- **Standard 8,** Understanding relationships between music, the other arts, and disciplines outside the arts.

REFLECTION ACTIVITY

Consider how synth keyboards might be put to use by you and your students in creative projects in your teaching assignment.

1. In-service teachers: Describe a lesson/project presented in this chapter that you think would work well in your teaching assignment. Alternatively, describe a lesson/activity you already do that incorporates ideas presented in this chapter.

2. Pre-service teachers: Describe how you could use or adapt a lesson/project idea presented in this chapter in the type of music teaching assignment you hope to do.

3. Describe a lesson/project idea not in this chapter, but which comes to mind after examining the ideas presented in this chapter. How might the Eight Principles for Unlocking Musical Creativity enhance the activity? Which of the MENC national standards would be addressed?

CHAPTER 13
CREATIVITY WITH SOUND RECORDING APPLICATIONS

OVERVIEW

SOUND RECORDING HARDWARE AND SOFTWARE can be used to allow students to capture, organize, edit, and alter sonic events for creative projects, the sort of activity suggested by composer Edgard Varèse's provocative definition of music as "organized sound."[1] When Varèse said this, he made a distinction between being a composer of traditional music and a "worker in rhythms, frequencies and intensities." At the advent of the electronic music era, he and like-minded others were imagining a sonic palette of instrumental tone clusters, unusual percussive sounds, prepared piano, and recorded and synthesized sounds. Today's technology certainly makes it easy to work with those sorts of sonic materials in the electronic art music tradition, but it also invites students to organize and arrange drum, bass, and guitar loops and excerpts from already recorded music (sometimes called "samples"). Whether developing an electronic art music sound collage work, or a pop music remix or mashup, audio recording software is the perfect tool. Digital audio recording tools are also valuable for documenting classroom and more formal student performances.

In this chapter, we will look at the idea of using basic, single-part recording and editing for all of these purposes. The term *sound recording* technically includes multitrack recording, too, and all the things mentioned here could be accomplished with any multitrack recording software (GarageBand, Cakewalk Home Studio, etc). Limiting our discussion in this chapter to single-part sound recording applications allows us to focus on some of the characteristics of waveform audio recording and editing. Plus, sometimes multitrack recording offers more power and complexity than is required or even desired. In this chapter we will also examine some common recording schemes such as using a handheld digital audio recorder, a plug-and-play USB microphone with audio recording software, and a conventional microphone running through an audio interface into audio recording software.

---

1. From a lecture given at Yale University in 1962, reprinted in Edgard Varèse and Chou Wen-chung, "The Liberation of Sound," *Perspectives of New Music*, Vol. 5, No. 1 (Autumn–Winter 1966), 17–18.

Equipment that might be employed for recording includes handheld digital audio recorders, computers for running audio recording software, a variety of microphones (those with and without built-in audio interfaces), audio interfaces, and accessories (cables, microphone stands, pop filters, etc.). While these are just a small portion of all the hardware one might use in the classroom, music tech lab, home studio, or fully outfitted, professional studio, they do allow for a wide variety of possibilities in music education.

A FEW WORDS ABOUT DIGITAL AUDIO

I have deliberately avoided being overly technical in this book, choosing instead to focus on how to use technology to open the flow of creative musical ideas with students. Since personal computers are so ubiquitous in our society, and since the technology tools I enjoy using most with kids are designed intuitively and easy to learn, this has not been hard. On the other hand, depending on the type course you are teaching or the type of students in it, you might appreciate having (and possibly sharing with students) some background regarding digital audio. You will find this, described in as short and simple a fashion as possible, in **Appendix 2.** For now, I want to introduce a few helpful terms and concepts you are bound to encounter with digital audio applications.

The Concept of Digital Audio

Digital audio involves describing a signal (i.e. the physical sound pressure fluctuations of an acoustic source such as a flute or human voice, or the voltage changes of an electronic source such as an electric guitar) as data. The data is stored, edited, processed, and eventually fed back to a playback system to hear. Digital audio data is, at the most basic level, a series of numbers. The numbers describe the amplitude—or strength—of the signal instant by instant, many tens of thousands of times per second. A *waveform* results by smoothly connecting this series of amplitude data points, called samples, with a single continuous line that tracks the signal.

The Waveform

A waveform is a graphic representation, or picture, that describes sound.[2] Often you will hear the term "waveform editor" used with reference to digital audio programs. If you zoom into the waveform far enough, you will see the crests and troughs that represent the compressions and rarefactions[3] of the fluctuating

2. A waveform is the result of connecting with a continuous line points along an x-y axis where x (horizontal) = time and y (vertical) = amplitude. Some waveform audio programs allow the user to see these sample points as "dots" when zoomed in enough.

3. When an object vibrates it causes an alternating bunching up (*compression*) and expansion (*rarefaction*) of the air molecules around it.

sound wave. The higher the crests (and lower the troughs), the greater the amplitude of the audio signal, and the stronger (louder) the sound. For higher frequency (pitch) sounds, the crests of the waveform will appear closer to one another. The sine wave is the simplest type of sound wave. Recorded music is typically much more complex, resulting in a correspondingly much more complex waveform appearance. When zoomed out, the individual crests and troughs of a waveform are not discerned. Instead, the waveform shape reflects the amplitude (volume) of the signal in a general way.

Tracks Versus Channels

An audio track is a separate area on the recording medium where data for an audio signal is stored. Multitrack audio software arranges tracks vertically, one on top of another, in a "track" window; horizontally, the timing of all tracks is synchronized, shown as real time (say, seconds) or musically organized in measures/beats. A single audio track may have one or two channels. A single monaural (mono) channel can record the signal from a single microphone or guitar cable. Two channels, one left and one right, are needed to create a stereo image. A track with two channels is needed to record the signal from two separate microphones into a single stereo track. Some "stereo microphones" really have two microphones built into the mic housing, but the recorded waveform shows two, concurrent layers (stereo right and left) in a single track.

Advantages of Digital Audio

Because digital audio devices and software store sound as data, the data can be manipulated easily, cheaply, and in many ways. In the old days a sound engineer would take a razor to a piece of magnetic tape to make a (literal) "cut." Now that cut is made with the click of a mouse along the waveform display of an audio program such as Audacity. As the user does this, the software notes what part of the data stream it should ignore.[4] To increase the volume (gain) of a signal, a simple mathematical operation that adds a constant number to the amplitude values is applied by the software, making everything louder.

The same is true, though conceptually more complex, of sound effects such as reverb, chorus, flange, distortion, and pitch or tempo shifting. Since all these operations are accomplished in the digital (data) realm, they are known collectively as *digital signal processing* (DSP). To employ these sorts of effects without software DSP "plug-ins," one would need more costly, external hardware effects units.

---

4. The software would place a marker at the beginning and end of the "cut" and just skip from the first marker to the second. This type of "nondestructive" editing allows the user to restore the cut material if desired.

CAPTURING STUDENT PERFORMANCES, AND RECORDING IN GENERAL

Most of this chapter, including all the lesson plans, deals with using sound recording hardware and software in creative activities with students. However, the idea of performance was stressed as principle 8 of the Eight Principles for Unlocking Musical Creativity. Recording in-class and more formal performances is a valuable way to document what your students have accomplished. Once made, a digital recording can be played back in class for enjoyment and celebration by students; burned onto a CD or posted on the Internet for parents and others to enjoy; used for reflection, criticism, and assessment by both students and teacher; and saved as part of a digital portfolio. Having a digital recording of student projects allows the best to be played as examples when you teach that lesson with the next group of students (principle 2). These are just some of the possibilities.

When my students complete a composition activity, especially collaborative class projects, I normally require a live, in-class performance of the finished product. The students rehearse each piece briefly in class, and then we record them. I believe that knowledge of the impending recording causes the students to take seriously their completion of the assignment. The recording allows us to sit back and enjoy listening to the final results at the conclusion of a unit and makes possible several modes of digital dissemination (burn on a CD, post to a blog or wiki, attach to an email, etc.) if desired.

The Sound Check

Several types of audio recording are described below. All of them involve capturing a sound source and converting it into the digital domain. Regardless of the source, success largely depends on capturing the signal at an appropriately strong level. If the level is too weak, you can boost the output (gain) after the fact, but this operation increases the level of any noise in the signal as well. If the level is too strong the signal will distort. The best way to ensure a good signal level when recording is to check the device or software's VU (volume units) meter during a brief sound check beforehand.

A VU meter graphically shows the signal strength of each channel (stereo left and right). You can affect the input level either by positioning the recording device or microphone relative to the source or by adjusting an input (sometimes called "trim") control. For this brief "sound check," record the performer(s) playing just a few measures of the loudest section of the work. Ideally, the VU meter should register above 50% but not too close to 100%, where "clipping" and distortion occurs.

Handheld Devices

In the 1970s and 1980s, compact audio cassettes overtook the grooved, "long playing" (LP) record as the dominant media for commercial audio recordings. One of several good reasons for this medium to take hold was the availability of reasonably priced, portable cassette recording devices. When the compact disk (CD) overtook the cassette tape in the 1990s, consumers appreciated the dramatic improvements in their sound quality and durability. But it took some time for affordable and portable digital recording devices to appear.

An entire class of small, extremely high-quality handheld digital audio recorders is now available. It is tempting to cite specific manufacturers and models here, but each year these change. These devices can be held in the palm of your hand and have built-in (usually stereo) microphones and built-in and/or removable disk storage for recording a couple hours of audio. A USB jack (or built-in port) allows for dumping audio files onto a computer so they can be opened, edited, and used in a software audio program. Most have a 1/8-inch audio-out/headphone jack and possibly a small, built-in speaker for monitoring what has been recorded. Smart phones (such as Apple's iPhone) and some MP3 music players can also run applications ("apps") for portable recording, using either their built-in microphone or a separate mic purchased as an accessory.

Making classroom recordings does not have to be complicated to get a decent, serviceable result. If you have a handheld recorder, simply place it where it can pick up the sound of all performers as close to equal as possible. Sometimes this is in the center of all the action, and sometimes this is out in front of everyone. Record the performer(s) playing a few measures from the strongest section of the work to check the recording level for distortion; the recorder's VU meter should not peak out. When everyone is ready, record a "take." If there is time, try to get two takes per project. After recording, either play back the recorded performances from the recorder itself or "dump" the audio files from the unit to your computer (for example, via a USB jack, cable, or memory card).

Recording Software on a Computer

You do not have to justify the expense of a personal computer or laptop for digital audio recording: Computers are standard equipment in our schools. Since there are great audio recording programs available for free, you might as well use them on an available computer. While recording with a handheld device is portable and simple, software recording allows for more editing and enhancing options and gives the user on-screen controls, which are easier to see and manipulate. Audacity is one of the most ubiquitous waveform audio recording and editing applications, perhaps because it is free, cross-platform,[5] and simply works so well. Many other free or low-cost programs exist as well.

5. Audacity can run on Windows, Mac, or Linux operating systems.

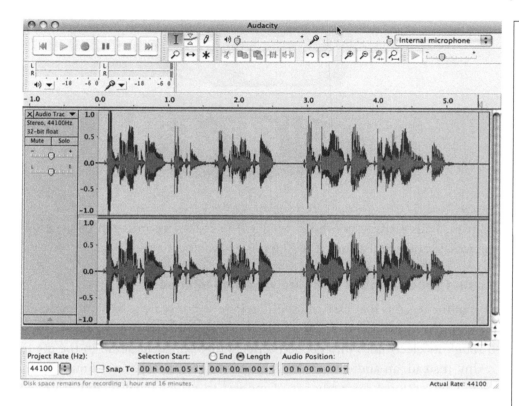

▶ **FIG. 13.1**

Waveform representation of stereo recorded sound shown in Audacity. Created by Scott Watson.

When you are ready to record a complete "take," click the "record" button. When done, click the "stop" button. A waveform representation of the audio recorded will appear on screen in a "track" (**Fig. 13.1**).

Getting Sound Into the Software via Internal Microphone

The simplest and least expensive way to record with a computer and audio recording software is to use the computer's built-in microphone. The results can be decent if you can either get the computer (such as a laptop) near the sound source or have the sound source near the computer.

Getting Sound Into the Software via USB Microphone

A very fine audio signal can be recorded using a USB stereo microphone. Before recording with an external USB mic, confirm that the software recognizes it via the operating system or the software sound preferences. Next, record the performer(s) playing a few measures from the strongest section of the work to check the recording level for distortion; the software's VU meter should not peak out. It is important that the microphone not be too close or too far from the source. When everyone is ready, record a "take." If there is time, try to get two takes per project.

I routinely keep a "no fuss" USB microphone[6] connected to my "teacher" computer at the front of the room—mounted to a conventional microphone

---

6. One such USB microphone at this time is the Snowball by Blue Microphones.

► FIG. 13.2

Male (top) and female (bottom) ends of a typical XLR microphone cable. Created by Scott Watson.

stand—so it is ready to go when I need it. This makes recording in-class performances, lectures, music dictation quizzes, or whatever a snap.

Getting Sound Into the Software via Audio Interfaces

One of the reasons that USB microphones are so convenient is that they do not require a separate audio interface box to convert the analog signal coursing through its electronics into coded numbers that represent audio in the digital realm. Instead, an audio interface is built into the microphone's housing, unseen. Conventional microphones of modest to professional quality normally use an XLR plug (**Fig. 13.2**) and require a separate audio interface device.

Audio interfaces, sometimes called "breakout boxes," receive analog audio from a microphone or electronic instrument (electric guitar, bass, etc.) via XLR and 1/4-inch or 1/8-inch phone jacks, translate the audio signal into a digital data stream, and send this data to your computer via a single (USB or Firewire) cable. Some inexpensive audio interfaces allow for just one or two inputs (such as a microphone or instrument); other more costly units have jacks for eight, ten, or even more inputs. Note that a conventional XLR microphone, the kind that might be mounted on a mic stand for a singer or placed in front of a guitar amp for recording an electric guitar, is *monophonic* and records just one channel of waveform audio. You may need to configure your audio recording software to receive the signal from an XLR mic into a mono track.

Other Considerations

Your audio input might simply be a built-in or USB microphone. It might also be an XLR microphone or the phone jack of an electric guitar (or bass, etc.) routed through an audio interface. Regardless, you will need to configure your audio recording software to receive that source.[7]

Whether you have recorded using a handheld device or with computer audio recording software, you may want to perform a few quick postrecording opera-

---

7. For GarageBand and Audacity, the input source setting can be set in the program's audio preferences.

tions to the best take of each work using a waveform audio editor such as Audacity. For instance, you might want to edit out any dead air or other unwanted parts, apply desired DSP effects such as reverb or normalization, and/or export the recordings in a compressed format (most likely MP3) to reduce file size for use on the web or to email.

DSP Effects

The following are examples of common DSP effects, found even in entry-level audio recording software. For the simplest recordings, or for those that are just beginning to use audio recording software, it is not necessary that any of these be employed. For more creative sound activities, however, or when producing recordings with more creativity and sophistication, these can come in handy.

1. **Normalize.** This procedure raises the level of the highest peak to 0 dB and then raises all other parts of the signal by the same proportion. Normalizing is useful when a signal has been recorded at too low a level or when the volume is inconsistent throughout.

2. **Reverb.** Reverberation is the decaying residual sound that remains after a sound occurs and is created by the sound's multiple reflections off of surfaces in an acoustical space. Adding digital reverb can liven up samples and alter the virtual acoustics of the space within which your digital audio exists, creating anything from subtle room ambience to the rich echo of a large stadium. **Echo** is a DSP effect similar to reverb.

3. **Compression/Gain.** An alternative to normalizing is for students to apply compression to squash the high peaks (reducing the dynamic range of the signal) and then increase the gain to raise the strength of the overall signal. Recorded spoken and sung voice often has compression applied to increase its impact.

4. **Chorus.** This time-based effect makes a single instrument sound like that of a large group. Use this effect plug-in to "fatten up" a signal.

5. **Pitch Correction.** One of the most visible (really, audible) DSP effects used in commercial recording at this time is a plug-in by software manufacturer Antares called Auto-Tune. This plug-in was developed to correct the pitch of out-of-tune notes performed by vocalists; its use by recording engineers is widespread. Other programs incorporate something similar, such as GarageBand's "Enhance Tuning," which accomplishes some of the same things.

6. **Flange.** This effect produces a swooshing sound, originally accomplished by splitting the signal into two identical versions, and then

applying a constantly varying, short delay (usually 2 to 15 milliseconds) to the signal and mixing the altered signal with the original. The name comes from the act of pressing a finger against the flange of a reel-to-reel tape deck's supply reel to slow it down, causing the delayed signal to be out of phase with the original.

7. **Filters.** By eliminating some of the spectral content, you can alter the timbre subtly or greatly. Depending on the software, you may be able to control parameters such as the filter's center frequency and the range (bandwidth) of the area to be attenuated. A high-pass filter, for instance, allows frequencies higher than a set limit to pass freely while attenuating those lower than that limit. Some filters even allow for "filter sweeps," by moving the filtered area over time.

8. **Equalization (EQ).** EQ allows the user to amplify or attenuate various frequency regions, sometimes called "bands" (for example, 100 through 1000 hertz). Multiband EQ allows the user to set the levels for each of the defined bands. A thin vocal sound can be filled out by boosting the bass frequency bands and pulling back a bit the extreme high frequencies.

9. **Pitch Shifting and Time Expansion/Compression.** In the digital domain, unlike analog recording, frequency and playback speed can be edited independently of one another. Therefore, a signal's pitch can be raised or lowered without affecting its length. Likewise, you can shorten or lengthen audio without changing its frequency. A low, scary voice like that of the evil Darth Vader from the Star War films can be manufactured by pitch shifting a recorded voice and adding reverb.

10. **Reverse.** When the audio signal is reversed, interesting sounds can result, such as the reverse cymbal sound that is part of the General MIDI sound set. The plug-in is usually applied by highlighting the area of a waveform you wish to reverse.

Recording Accessories

The following are recording accessories that you may find helpful or necessary when recording as part of your music teaching.

1. **Cables.** As mentioned in previous chapters, conventional microphones normally use XLR cables to connect the microphone to an audio interface. Other common cables include 1/4-inch mono "phone" cables used for electric guitars or keyboards, and 1/8-inch and RCA stereo cables for line-level devices such as a computer's audio output or an MP3 player. Cables come in various lengths to make it from the source to your recording setup.

2. **Microphone Stand.** In almost every recording scenario, you will want the microphone mounted securely on a stand, rather than held by hand. When ordering a microphone stand, think of how it will be used. There are many kinds of stands, such as those that only raise vertically and those that have horizontal arms for placing a microphone near an amplifier or over an open grand piano, for instance.

3. **Pop Filter.** When speaking or singing certain consonants (such as B, P, and T) into a microphone, you may notice annoying explosive bursts of energy—"pops"—in the signal. To diminish or remove these, place a pop filter between the source and the microphone. Pop filters look like a hoop with fabric stretched across it.[8]

4. **Wind Screen.** Sometimes an inexpensive foam cover is all that is required to reduce vocal plosives to an acceptable level, or—as its name implies—remove noise introduced by wind.

5. **Shock Mount.** Suspending a microphone in a shock mount is in many cases unnecessary. If you feel movement may be an issue, a shock mount can stabilize the microphone.

Recording a Class for Missing Students

Classroom recording can help busy teachers avoid having to take time out to catch up absent students on what was missed. When a student is missing from class, just pull out the handheld recorder, hit record, and go about teaching the class. At the end of class, hit the stop button, pop out the device's built-in USB jack, and download the audio to your computer. Now the audio can be posted to a class wiki, placed on the student's lab computer, or burned to a CD to give the student. The same can be done with a "no fuss" USB microphone sent to a computer or laptop running a simple digital audio recording program. The handheld recorder is especially convenient if you are a traveling teacher who changes rooms or even buildings during your work week.

EXAMPLE LESSONS

On the pages that follow are several lessons that feature the use of digital audio recording in creative sound and music activities. The lessons are presented from the perspective of waveform audio recording and editing software, though portable, handheld devices may be incorporated for recording as well. Good waveform recording and editing software such as Audacity is free, and most teachers have at least one computer at their disposal.

161

---

8. Pop filters are relatively inexpensive, plus you or your students could make your own pop filter from household supplies using plans found on the Internet.

As mentioned earlier, all these lessons could be accomplished by audio recording into a single track of any multitrack music production software. In this sense, these lessons serve as a good introduction to digital audio recording and editing in preparation for work with multitrack recording you might be doing with your students later in a course or in a different, more advanced course.

Unless otherwise indicated, all the lessons are ones I have developed and used in my own teaching at various levels.

LESSON TITLE: CREATING A SOUND CLIP TO SHARE

Audience: Grades 5–12.

Objective: As a result of this activity, students will be able to perform basic editing operations such as select, cut, delete, and/or crop ("trim") and be able to create a volume fade in and fade out.

Materials/Equipment: Simple waveform editor (such as Audacity) and a track of prerecorded audio (for example a track from a CD, downloaded from the Internet, or provided by the instructor), and a computer with headphones for listening.

Duration: 45 minutes (about one class period).

Prior Knowledge and Skills: Experience using a computer mouse and keyboard.

Procedure:

1. Share a sound clip with students to demonstrate what they will be doing themselves. Point out the volume fade in at the beginning of the clip and the fade out at the end of the clip.

2. Have students, working alone or in pairs/teams, acquire the audio track with which they will be working.

   a. If using a track from a CD: Insert the CD in the computer's CD drive. Import ("rip") one of the tracks from the CD onto the computer's hard drive and then open it in the audio waveform editor program (such as Audacity).

   b. If using a track already on the computer's hard drive: Locate the file and open it in the audio waveform editor.

   c. Either way, the student will now see the audio as similar waveforms in two parallel channels in a stereo track in the audio program.

3. Have students preview the audio file by pressing the program's play button and listening. They should also try moving the play head[9] to different points in the timeline. Have them select (highlight) approximately 30 seconds for their sound clip. All waveform audio programs allow the user to see time in hours, minutes, and seconds (i.e. 0:00:00; consult your software's documentation to see where).

4. Create the sound clip in one of several ways:

   a. Delete before and after: Select (highlight) everything in the waveform up to where the clip will begin and then delete the selected area. Now select (highlight) everything in the waveform from the point where the clip will end up to the end of the file and then delete

163

---

9. The *play head* is a vertical line that shows where the file will begin playback. The user can drag the play head to a point along the file's timeline or often just double-click along the timeline, to choose the position of the play head. Pressing the space bar is a common short cut for initiating and stopping playback.

164

all of that. What remains is the excerpted sound clip. You may need to move this remaining portion of the waveform back to the beginning of the timeline.

b. Trim (recommended for Audacity): Select (highlight) the approximately 30-second sound clip area of the waveform. Choose "trim" or "crop" from the Edit menu. Only what was selected, the excerpted sound clip, remains.

c. Insert cuts: Place cuts in the waveform at the start and end of the clip. Sometimes this involves placing the play head or insert point at the location and choosing "cut" from the Edit menu. Sometimes this involves using a "cut" tool (usually looks like scissors) and clicking in the waveform. Delete the region of the waveform before and after the cuts.

d. Resize (recommended for GarageBand): Some audio editing programs allow the user to resize a region of the waveform in a track by click-hold-dragging its left or right edges. To create a 30-second clip, just click-hold-drag the left edge to the right, up to where the clip should begin. Then click-hold-drag the right edge to the left, back to where the clip should end. You may need to move the remaining portion of the waveform back to the beginning of the timeline.

5. Apply a *fade in* and *fade out* to the beginning and end of the excerpt in one of several ways:

a. Effect (recommended for Audacity): Select (highlight) about five seconds from the beginning of the waveform. Choose "Fade In" or its equivalent from the appropriate menu (for example, in Audacity, from the Effect menu). Then select about five seconds from the end of the waveform and choose "Fade Out" or its equivalent from the appropriate menu.

b. Automate (recommended for GarageBand): If your audio editing program allows for graphically automating volume changes, use the mouse to click in *break points*—points of articulation connected by an automation line—along the waveform to determine the location and direction of volume changes (Fig. 13.3).

6. Have students play their sound clip for the class, sharing any relevant information they would like about the music.

7. (Optional) Have students export their sound clips as MP3 audio files.

▶ **FIG. 13.3**

GarageBand audio track with volume automation to create a "fade in" and a "fade out." Created by Scott Watson.

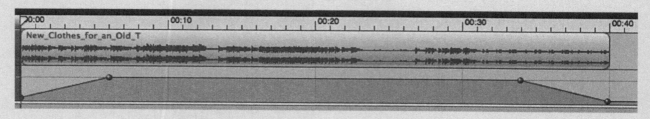

Adaptations: Removing choices is a great way to make this lesson flow more smoothly, especially with younger students. To that end, the teacher may want to prepare in advance a folder of audio tracks to use and copy it to each student's computer.

The teacher might also use this activity to reinforce earlier music learning. For instance, if the class has been discussing song form, assign students to make sound clips of various sections (verse, refrain/chorus, bridge, etc.) of the tracks. If the class has been discussing timbre or instrument families, assign students to make clips featuring various instruments or instrument families in the tracks provided.

Instead of sharing (all) the sound clips in class, older students could be required to post their sound clip to a class wiki.

Evaluation: Award credit for creating a short audio clip according to the following basic criteria: (1) length (approximately 30 seconds) and (2) fades (clip begins and ends with a smooth fade in and fade out). Additionally, you may want to award credit for sharing the clip, either in class or otherwise (posted to a wiki, etc.)

Extensions/Follow-up: Sound clips created for this lesson could be used for the "My Favorite Things Podcast" lesson in chapter 14.

National Standards Addressed: Each of the following standards is addressed to some degree in this lesson:

- **Standard 6,** Listening to, analyzing, and describing music.
- **Standard 7** (optional), Evaluating music and music performances.
- **Standard 8** (optional), Understanding relationships between music, the other arts, and disciplines outside the arts.

LESSON TITLE: DO-RE-MI (OR 1–2–3) EDITING: CUT, COPY, AND PASTE

Audience: Grades 6–12, general and elective music classes.

Objective: As a result of this activity, students will be able to perform basic editing operations such as cut, copy, and paste. They will demonstrate this by rearranging sound events using waveform audio editing software. Students who finish early may have time to experiment with and apply DSP effects as time permits.

Materials/Equipment: Simple waveform editor (such as Audacity) and a track of prerecorded audio (for example a track from a CD, downloaded from the Internet, or provided by the instructor), and a computer with headphones for listening.

Duration: 90 minutes (about two class periods).

Prior Knowledge and Skills: Experience using a computer mouse and keyboard.

Procedure:

1. Option 1: Begin with a prerecorded audio file that contains someone singing the syllables Do, Re, Mi, Fa, Sol (**Web Ex. 13.1**). Option 2: Have students, working alone or in pairs/teams, begin by recording their own file with them singing Do, Re, Mi, Fa, Sol. Either way, be sure the notes/syllables are sung clearly and separately so they may be edited more easily.

2. Demonstrate: Show students how to select (highlight) a portion of the waveform. Show how to cut and copy a selected area. Show how to place the play head along the waveform and paste something that was cut or copied.

3. Have students copy and paste syllables from the audio file so that the file now sounds Do-Do, Re-Re, Mi-Mi, Fa-Fa, Sol-Sol.

4. Next have students cut, copy, and paste syllables to create either the opening phrase from a familiar tune, or their own melodic phrase. The following are tunes they may want to create:

    a. "Mary Had a Little Lamb": Mi-Re-Do-Re-Mi-Mi-Mi
    b. "Jingle Bells": Mi-Mi-Mi, Mi-Mi-Mi, Mi-Sol-Do-Re-Mi
    c. "Ode to Joy": Mi-Mi-Fa-Sol-Sol-Fa-Mi-Re-Do-Do-Re-Mi-Mi-Re-Re

5. Teacher should check student results, playing selected files for class.

6. (Optional) Have students export their final result as an MP3 audio file.

Adaptations: Students who finish early should be shown how to apply some fun DSP effects, such as reverb, echo, pitch shift, vocoder,[10] and so forth.

---

10. Vocoder is a contraction of "voice encoder" and is technique for altering/synthesizing voice that results in a mechanical, "robotic" sound.

This activity provides a musical experience for students with basic wave-form editing. In an elective class with nontraditional music students, such as Digital Audio or Music Production, or with younger students, you may want to have students work with a conceptually simpler audio file. For instance, have students record themselves counting 1, 2, 3, 4, 5 (clearly, separately), or use a prerecorded file with those numbers (**Web Ex. 13.2**). Their task, then, would be to copy/paste numbers so the file sounds 1–1, 2–2, 3–3, 4–4, 5–5. Next have them cut/copy/paste to create a file with their phone number (or a general phone number such as 555–1212). Students who finish early could apply DSP effects.

Feedback/Evaluation: Award credit for successfully completing the first copy/paste task (Do-Do, Re-Re, Mi-Mi, Fa-Fa, Sol-Sol) and the second cut/copy/paste creative task (arranging syllables to form a melodic phrase). Allow students to discuss what they hear when students' works are played for the class (for example, do they like the note choices? Do they hear timing/rhythmic issues?).

Extensions/Follow-up: Consider doing something more complex with spoken word editing. Find a spoken word audio file online (I really like www.archive.org), or have them record something (say, a short poem), to "slice-and-dice" into something that has a whole different meaning.

Once students feel comfortable with recording sonic events, editing them, and applying DSP effects, they are ready for the "Electronic Art Music Sound Collage" lesson that appears later in this chapter.

Finally, if using multitrack software that allows for audio editing and the implementation of loops (such as GarageBand), students can extend the project by syncing the copied syllables with drum (and other) loops.

National Standards Addressed: Each of the following standards is addressed to some degree in this lesson:

- **Standard 1** (optional), Singing, alone and with others, a varied repertoire of music.
- **Standard 4,** Composing and arranging music within specified guidelines.
- **Standard 5** (optional), Reading and notating music.
- **Standard 6** (optional), Listening to, analyzing, and describing music.
- **Standard 7** (optional), Evaluating music and music performances.

LESSON TITLE: SIDE-BY-SIDE SONG COMPARISON

Audience: Grades 6–12, general and elective music classes.

Objective: As a result of this activity, students will strengthen their basic audio editing (cut, copy, paste, move) skills. They will demonstrate this by arranging two audio clips in a track to be played back, one after the other, in as seamless a way as possible. The clips are each to be one complete formal unit of a song (such as a verse or chorus) that make sense following one another. For instance, verse one in clip 1 could be followed by verse two or a chorus in clip 2. The clips could come from two different versions ("covers") of the same song, or any two songs the students feel go well together (even ones that are very different stylistically).

Materials/Equipment: Simple waveform editor (such as Audacity) and tracks of prerecorded audio (for example a track from a CD, downloaded from the Internet, or provided by the instructor), and a computer with headphones for listening.

Duration: 90 minutes (about two class periods).

Prior Knowledge and Skills: Experience using a computer mouse and keyboard. The ability to discern pitch and tempo differences is helpful.

Procedure:

1. Demonstrate: Play for students an example of two song section sound clips spliced together in a continuous audio file (**Web Ex. 13.3**). Discuss if the merging of the two seems natural, pleasing, surprising, and so on. Also discuss the musical differences between the two (style, tempo, pitch/key, instrumentation, etc.).

2. Have students, working alone or in pairs/teams, use waveform audio editing software to create two sound clips, each being a complete formal section of a song (such as verse, chorus). They will have two separate files open (be sure to save each).

3. Select (highlight) the waveform for the entire second sound clip and copy it to the clipboard[11] (Edit menu—Copy). Now turn to the first clip file and place the cursor (insert point) at the point on the waveform right after the first clip. Paste the second clip there (Edit menu—Paste).

4. Audition the result and remove additional portions of either the first or second clip so the two clips blend seamlessly (**Web Ex. 13.3**). Students may need to zoom in to see if the splice is at the right point.

5. Have as many students play their results as time allows; discuss and critique.

6. (Optional) Have students export their final result as an MP3 audio file.

---

11. The *clipboard* is unseen hard drive space available for temporarily copying data to be retrieved when the user selects Paste.

Adaptations: If desired, older students could use software "markers" (labels that can be placed along the timeline) to analyze the form of the songs used in this lesson.

Students that finish early could analyze the tempo and pitch of the two clips—with the help of the teacher if needed—and apply the software effect for changing tempo and/or changing pitch to one or both of the clips so their tempo and/or pitch matches.

To focus on a particular musical comparison, or just to streamline the act of deciding on source music for the two clips, the teacher could decide musical pairings ahead of time and have those sources (CDs, audio files) already copied to the student's computers.

Feedback/Evaluation: When students play their side-by-side audio files, discuss the results as a class. Address things such as how the two clips complement one another, as well as their musical differences (style, tempo, pitch/key, instrumentation, etc.). Award credit for creating two sound clip files, each of which sound just one formal section of the source music. Also award credit for merging the two separate sound clips into one audio file.

Extensions/Follow-up: This activity may be extended by allowing for several formal sections of a song to be spliced together. For instance, given two recorded versions of a song or two different songs—labeled A and B—a student could splice together the following: verse 1 (A), verse 2 (B), chorus (A), chorus (B).

Also, using multitrack music production software and the skills acquired in this activity, students could create remixes (reworking of a song) or mashups (combining elements of different songs). Loops and original recorded material may be incorporated.

National Standards Addressed: Each of the following standards is addressed to some degree in this lesson:

- **Standard 4** (optional), Composing and arranging music within specified guidelines.
- **Standard 6,** Listening to, analyzing, and describing music.
- **Standard 7,** Evaluating music and music performances.
- **Standard 9** (optional), Understanding music in relation to history and culture.

LESSON TITLE: INTRODUCTION TO DIGITAL
SIGNAL PROCESSING

Audience: Grades 6–12, general and elective music classes.

Objective: Students will demonstrate their understanding, and the sonic benefits, of common digital signal processing (DSP) effects as they modify a short, percussive and a sustained, tonal sound.

Materials/Equipment: Simple waveform editor (such as Audacity), microphone (built-in, USB, or with audio interface) or handheld recorder, a computer with headphones for listening, and pencil and scratch paper.

Duration: 90 minutes (about two class periods).

Prior Knowledge and Skills: Experience using a computer mouse and keyboard, and familiarity with the basics of a waveform audio editor.

Procedure:

1. Demonstration: Record for the class a short, percussive sound (single strike of a woodblock, snap of fingers, etc.) and a sustained tonal sound (held clarinet note, sine wave generated by the waveform software, etc.), preferably in the same audio file. Show students the list of DSP effects (or "plug-ins") available with the software being used. Review with students the thumbnail definitions for the 10 DSP effects listed in the introduction to this chapter. Select (highlight) the short, percussive sound and apply one of the DSP effects. Discuss with the students how they think the sound will be altered, play the result, and then discuss the outcome. Do the same with the sustained, tonal sound.

2. Have students, working alone or in pairs/teams, record their own pair of sounds, one short/percussive and one sustained/tonal. Alternatively, students could use two contrasting sounds prepared by the teacher, copied to their computers (or posted for download to a website or wiki).

3. Assign different students (or groups of students) a different one of the 10 DSP effects listed in the introduction to this chapter. Give them time to apply that plug-in to both the short/percussive and the sustained/tonal sounds. After a time (perhaps the first class period), ask for volunteers to demonstrate their assigned effect. Discuss.

4. Give more time for students to apply two or more DSP effects to each sound (perhaps during a second period) and ask for volunteers to share the most surprising and unusual results. Use a horizontal scale like the one in Fig. 13.4, with "SFX" (sound effect) on the far left and "MUSIC" on the far right, to discuss the quality of each student example played.[12] Discuss whether/how these sounds, altered by two or more DSP effects, could be used to produce interesting music.

---

12. Here, I am not implying that sound effects cannot be used musically. Although it would be more correct to have the term "conventional music" opposite "SFX" on this scale, I wanted to keep it simple.

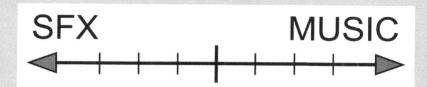

5. (Optional) If time is available, challenge students to cut, copy, and paste the recorded sounds, and apply DSP effects, to create something more music than sound effect.

6. (Optional) Have students export their final result as an MP3 audio file.

171

Adaptations: If available, handheld recorders might be used by students when recording the short and sustained sounds for this project. Since handheld devices are portable, students could visit the band room or other locations in the building to do "field recording."

This lesson could be accomplished with a single, "teacher" computer at the front of a classroom. The teacher would facilitate, selecting students to come to the front to record sounds and apply the various DSP effects. Alternatively, if there is a cluster or pod of computers in the room, students can be rotated back to these computers to work in small groups once the teacher has demonstrated the project for the entire class.

Feedback/Evaluation: Award credit for recording the two sounds, and for successfully applying the assigned DSP effect.

Extensions/Follow-up: To explore more the effect of multiband EQ, import an audio track from a commercial CD and apply various multiband EQ settings to it. This could also be accomplished quite simply with the Apple iTunes program, which includes a very easy-to-understand graphic EQ window that allows users to apply presets based on musical style (classical, jazz, pop, rhythm and blues, etc.) to music it plays.

This lesson is good preparation for the lesson that follows, in which students fashion an electronic art music "sound collage" composition.

National Standards Addressed: Each of the following standards is addressed to some degree in this lesson:

- **Standard 1** (optional), Singing, alone and with others, a varied repertoire of music.
- **Standard 2** (optional), Performing on instruments, alone and with others, a varied repertoire of music.
- **Standard 4** (optional), Composing and arranging music within specified guidelines.

- **Standard 6,** Listening to, analyzing, and describing music.
- **Standard 7,** Evaluating music and music performances.
- **Standard 8,** Understanding relationships between music, the other arts, and disciplines outside the arts.

LESSON TITLE: ELECTRONIC ART MUSIC
SOUND COLLAGE

Audience: Grades 7–12, general or elective music classes.

Objective: As a result of this activity, students will be able to create a work in the electronic art music, "sound collage" tradition that demonstrates the musicality of organized sound. This activity gives students the opportunity to compose music apart from the rules of traditional, Western classical music.

Materials/Equipment: Simple waveform editor (such as Audacity), microphone (built-in, USB, or with audio interface) or handheld recorder, a computer with headphones for listening, and recordings of electronic art music to listen to and discuss.

Duration: 180–225 minutes (four to five class periods).

Prior Knowledge and Skills: Experience using a computer mouse and keyboard, and familiarity with the basics of waveform audio recording and editing, including microphone recording and applying DSP effects.

Procedure:

1. Listen/discuss: Start by engaging students with the mind-broadening aesthetic question "What is music?" Listening to and discussing recordings of tape, synthesizer, and computer music can help students see beyond the sonic experience they have inherited, enlarging their understanding of musical expression (see sidebar, "Electronic/Computer Art Music Suggested Listening"). After listening, discuss terms such as *musique concrète* and found sound, as well as the role electronic art music has played in music in the twentieth and twenty-first centuries.

2. Acquire sounds: Two categories of sound recordings should constitute the raw materials for the work. I recommend students select one or the other, but stronger students could be allowed to use both.

   a. Speech: Students record short spoken word recordings. Examples include answers to a prompt/question (for example, "What's your favorite sport?" or "What comes to mind when you think of rain?"), a brief phrase, or the students working together stating their names. Brief sung, improvised phrases may also be employed.

   b. Sound: Students record found sounds. Students will love the adventure of hunting for good source material. Recording of notes (single or improvised gesture) from simple instruments (such as recorder or ocarina) or voice may also be employed.

3. Transform sounds: A screwdriver tapping a file cabinet or someone biting a stalk of celery can generate sonically interesting events when treated with one or more DSP effects. Speech becomes percussive when consonants are isolated and sustained when vowel sounds are elongated by copying and pasting. All sounds can be transformed by filters

and pitch shifting into content that has interesting tonal contours. Encourage experimentation and the pursuit of interesting timbres.

4. Arrange sounds: Once they acquire their palette of sound source material, students should map out how the composition unfolds in terms of properties such as timbre (sounds, qualities), texture (collage, ambient, event-oriented, beat-oriented), pitch, loudness, and other aspects such as articulation. Encourage both small-scale and large-scale repetition to create cohesiveness to the work and suggest a formal shape. A length of 0:40 to 1:00 should allow for some development of ideas without the students becoming too bogged down.

5. (Optional) Some waveform audio recording and editing software, such as Audacity, allows for multiple tracks of audio. If yours has this feature, allow students to overlap and layer tracks for more interesting textures.

6. Critique: During a project such as this students need some guidance and confirmation that they are on the right track. Set aside some time for student and teacher critique (reactions, praise, suggestions, encouragement). Here are some items that might be addressed:
   a. How well do you feel the instructions were followed?
   b. What are the challenges of making this piece?
   c. Did anything go really well?
   d. What are one or two ways the work-in-progress could be improved?

7. Present: Have students export their final result as an MP3 audio file to play in class, post to the Internet (website, wiki, etc.), burn on a CD, and so forth.

8. Wrap-up. Ask some students to volunteer comments on the following:
   a. Did you enjoy this sort of creating? Why or why not?
   b. If you had to do something like this again, would you do anything differently? If so, what?

Electronic/Computer Art Music Suggested Listening

The following are recordings that were chosen to get kids' attention and provoke stimulating conversations rather than for historical or geographical completeness. Besides the typical sources (such as Amazon.com), you may have to locate some in an area university's music library or online on eBay.

1. *Pioneers of Electronic Music.* Composers Recordings, Inc. (1991). Vladimir Ussachevsky, Otto Leuning, Mario Davidovsky, et al. Includes Leuning's *Fantasy in Space* (1952), featuring tape-manipulated recordings of flute.

2. *Early Modulations: Vintage Volts.* Caipirinha (1999). John Cage, Pierre Schaeffer, Vladimir Ussachevsky, Iannis Xenakis, et al. A great survey of

experimental music of the 1950s thru 1960s. Subotnick's breakout composition, *Silver Apples of the Moon* (1967), features exotic synthesized timbres and dance-inspired rhythms. Max Matthews shows off his voice-synthesis work for Bell Labs in the cute *Bicycle Built for Two.*

3. *Dodge: Any Resemblance Is Purely Coincidental.* New Albion Records (2004). Music of Charles Dodge. Includes *Speech Songs* (settings sketches by poet Mark Strand), which employed brand new speech-synthesis techniques being developed at Bell Labs in New Jersey.

4. *Columbia-Princeton Electronic Music Center 1961–1973.* New World Records (1998). Charles Dodge, et al. Includes representative pieces by many who were attracted to this famed electronic-music facility.

5. *Contes de la Memoire.* empreintes DIGITALes (1996). Music of Jon Appleton, a codesigner of the legendary Synclavier keyboard synthesizer. Includes *Newark Airport Rock* (1969), a random survey of passengers' thoughts about new electronic music. Humorous raw vocal material ("great," "cool," "sucks," and "I prefer music played by musicians without computers") is fused with hip, sequenced electronics.

6. *Maurice Wright: Suite for Piano/Chamber Symphony/Night Watch/ Sonata II.* Composers Recordings, Inc. (1993). Wright's *Chamber Symphony for Piano and Electronic Sound* receives a strong performance from Canadian virtuoso and new-music champion Marc-Andre Hamelin in this two-channel CD adaptation. Wright, another younger generation Columbia composer, showcases the expansive timbral possibilities of computer-generated sound.

7. *Ride.* Bridge (2001). Music of Princeton composer (and Radiohead muse[13]) Paul Lansky. *Ride,* like his 1992 piece *Night Traffic,* uses recorded sounds from the road, with some processed voices, in a trek with changing sonic landscapes. *Idle Chatter Junior* features recorded voices dissected into pieces and organized as music, forming and combined with attractive rhythmic grooves.

8. *Secret Geometry: Music for Piano and Electronic Tape.* Composers Recordings, Inc. (1996). Milton Babbitt, Mario Davidovsky, James Primosch, et al. The first-generation Columbia-Princeton school passes the electroacoustic baton to Primosch (Davidovsky's student), after whose 1993 piece the album is named.

175

13. The Radiohead song "Idioteque" (*Kid A*, Capitol, 2000) features a looping chord progression sample from Lansky's 1973 computer tape piece "Mild und Leise."

Adaptations: Students can work alone or in small groups on every phase of this activity. Students in a group can share artistic decisions while fulfilling particular roles such as engineer (microphone recording), performer (recite speech and/or initiate sounds), editor (perform cut, copy, paste with software), and scribe (documenting the source sounds or spoken words, and the DSP effects used).

This lesson involves audio only, but it would work well with multitrack music production software, such as GarageBand.

Feedback/Evaluation: Create a rubric or task list that awards credit for acquiring three different sounds or spoken gestures, applying a minimum of five different DSP effects, evidence of both small- and large-scale repetition, and achieving a length of at least 40 seconds.

Extensions/Follow-up: Hold a recital of electronic art music, or post compositions to a course website or wiki.

Invite a composer of electronic/computer art music in your area (likely found at a nearby university) to come to your school to share his or her work with your students.

National Standards Addressed: Each of the following standards is addressed to some degree in this lesson:

- **Standard 1** (optional), Singing, alone and with others, a varied repertoire of music.
- **Standard 2** (optional), Performing on instruments, alone and with others, a varied repertoire of music.
- **Standard 3** (optional), Improvising melodies, harmonies, and accompaniments.
- **Standard 4,** Composing and arranging music within specified guidelines.
- **Standard 6,** Listening to, analyzing, and describing music.
- **Standard 7,** Evaluating music and music performances.
- **Standard 8,** Understanding relationships between music, the other arts, and disciplines outside the arts.

REFLECTION ACTIVITY

Consider how waveform audio recording and editing software might be put to use by you and students in creative projects in your teaching assignment.

1. In-service teachers: Describe a lesson/project presented in this chapter that you think would work well in your teaching assignment. Alternatively, describe a lesson/activity you already do that incorporates ideas presented in this chapter.

2. Pre-service teachers: Describe how you could use or adapt a lesson/project idea presented in this chapter in the type of music teaching assignment you hope to do.

3. Describe a lesson/project idea not in this chapter but that comes to mind after examining the ideas presented in this chapter. How might the Eight Principles for Unlocking Musical Creativity enhance the activity? Which of MENC's National Standards for Music Education would be addressed?

177

CHAPTER 14
CREATIVITY WITH MULTITRACK MUSIC PRODUCTION APPLICATIONS

OVERVIEW

IN CHAPTER 13 WE DEALT WITH creative activities using waveform audio, concentrating on software applications that use one track of mono (one channel) or stereo (two channels, left and right) audio. This allowed us to focus a bit on acquiring the signal (microphone recording, using an audio interface, etc.), digital audio theory, waveform audio editing, and digital signal processing. In this chapter we turn to multitrack music production (MMP) software, which includes digital audio workstations (DAWs) such as GarageBand (entry level) or ProTools (professional). MMP software allows the user to record and store more than one concurrent stream of waveform audio or MIDI performance data, called *tracks*. The added capabilities of *MIDI recording and editing*, described below, greatly expands what can be done with audio tracks alone. Modern DAW software also facilitates working with loops, which are usually one- or two-measure audio or MIDI recordings of rhythm instruments (percussion, bass, guitar, etc.), meant to be repeated again and again to create a groove. All the lessons in the last chapter—and so much more—can be accomplished with MMP software's increased capabilities.

The availability of multiple audio and MIDI tracks opens up many possibilities for creative content. Students can modify previously created *MIDI files* to fashion their own arrangements. Audio and MIDI *loops* can be layered (stacked vertically) and arranged by themselves or along with other recorded content to create original compositions, arrangements, and hybrid remixes and mashups. Students can record their own improvisation *in one track* along to a previously recorded accompaniment *in another track*. Students can produce *podcasts* with separate tracks for voice/narrator(s), sound clips, sound effects, and more. MMP software is the perfect tool for students or entire classes to use when writing and producing songs and raps.

Also note that many MMP programs come with built-in software instruments. GarageBand, for instance, comes with more than 100 sampled or synthesized sounds of all kinds, including keyboards (grand piano, electric piano, etc.), guitars and basses (acoustic guitar, electric lead, fretless bass, etc.), wind instruments (flute, alto sax, pop horn section, etc.), orchestral strings, synth pads, drum sets, and much more. Therefore, only a keyboard controller, without on-board sounds, is necessary for MIDI recording and playback. These built-in software instruments might also be used along with a keyboard controller to accomplish the "My Favorite Sounds" lesson in chapter 12.

MIDI Tracks

As described in chapter 13, audio tracks contain the waveform representation of the recorded sound and can be edited and processed. MIDI tracks contain performance data that describe things such as note,[1] duration, and intensity of attack,[2] as well as a host of expressive alterations (volume, pan position, pitch bend, modulation, etc.). Recording MIDI performance data is known as *sequencing*. Performance data can be recorded with a keyboard into a MIDI track (usually to a metronome click) in real time by clicking the software's "record" button. Since MIDI data is not affected by tempo, the tempo can be very slow as you record but full speed as the file is played back. MIDI data can also be "step-recorded" graphically, one note at a time, without regard to time/tempo, using a pencil or paint tool. Other performance data, such as data sent by a pitch bend wheel, modulation wheel, or sustain pedal, are recorded as well.

Another way to acquire MIDI performance data is to import a prepared MIDI file (sometimes called a "standard MIDI file" or SMF) into a MIDI track in the software. Thousands of MIDI files of all types of music are available on the Internet for free download. Also, files from many music programs such as Finale, Sibelius, and Band-in-a-Box can be saved as MIDI files to use in MMP projects. A user already comfortable with one of those applications can create the musical content first, then export it as a MIDI file to use with MMP software. In many cases, importing MIDI files is as simple as dragging and dropping them into the MMP software's track window.

MIDI Graphic Display

Just as a graphic waveform is a typical way for software to display an audio signal, MIDI data is typically displayed in a *graphic editor* as rectangular bars on a grid (**Fig. 14.1**). The vertical aspect of the grid corresponds to pitch; the horizontal aspect of the grid corresponds to time and can be displayed as measures and beats or minutes and seconds. The length of a bar indicates its duration, and its vertical placement indicates pitch. Despite the technical sound of this

1. For notes, MIDI describes the key number (such as middle C on a MIDI keyboard = 60), not the frequency.

2. *Intensity of attack* is note-on velocity, the time it takes for a key on a MIDI keyboard to go from the up (rest) position to the down (played) position. Obviously, the harder the key is hit, the greater its velocity, so velocity data affect dynamics.

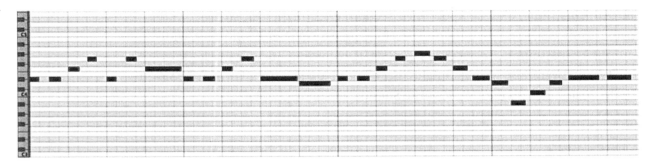

▶ **FIG. 14.1**

Graphic view of MIDI performance data (notes, durations, etc.). Created by Scott Watson.

description, this way of representing music is fairly intuitive. I observe that many nontraditional music students find it makes sense and adapt quickly to working with it. In fact, it is far less arbitrary than conventional music notation!

MIDI Editing

Editing MIDI data graphically is easy and intuitive. Any MIDI data recorded in one track can be selected to be cut (deleted) or copied and pasted to some location within that same track or another track. To change any pitch, move the bar representing that note vertically, either higher or lower on the grid. To change the time at which a note sounds, drag the bar representing it to the left (earlier) or right (later). To adjust a duration, drag the right edge of the bar horizontally either to the left (shortening the note) or right (lengthening the note). All sorts of other performance data (intensity of attack, when sustain pedal was pressed, amount of pitch bend or modulation wheel used, etc.) can be edited as well. These many MIDI editing options bring the ability to work creatively with the materials of music within reach even for nontraditional music students.

Audio and MIDI Configuration

The inputs and outputs of audio and MIDI tracks need to be configured. Luckily, in many cases the software you use—especially when it is an entry-level program, such as GarageBand—will automatically do this for you. Often the default settings are just what you need and require no adjustment. Nonetheless, I want to describe the most common audio and MIDI input configurations briefly.

Audio Configuration

Audio tracks that will be used to record an external signal have to be assigned to an *input* source such as a built-in or USB microphone, or an audio interface that will receive a conventional mic plugged into its XLR port, or an instrument (electric guitar, bass, etc.) plugged into an audio interface's 1/4-inch phone jack.

Audio tracks also have to be assigned an *output* source. In other words, what will convert the digital data that describes the audio signal into the analog sound that comes from a speaker or headphones? The usual and easiest choice in music education scenarios is the built-in output; this is your computer's audio system.[3]

MIDI Configuration

When recording MIDI tracks, the source for receiving performance data—usually a keyboard synthesizer or controller—needs to be connected to the computer via a MIDI interface and assigned to a track. This allows notes played on the keyboard to be recorded as performance data in the MIDI track. This setup is easiest when the keyboard has a built-in USB MIDI interface. In this case, all that is required is a standard USB cable and perhaps a configuration setting in the MIDI software you will be using (see **Appendix 1**). A more complicated setup, rarer today but still encountered, involves an external MIDI interface (see **sidebar**).

Unlike the USB serial data hardware protocol, MIDI only allows for a one-way serial data stream. Therefore, you need two MIDI cables (one for data to flow from the keyboard to the interface, and one for data to flow from the interface to the keyboard). The external interface translates MIDI data back and forth and has a standard USB cable on the "computer side." When a key is struck on a keyboard to enter a note into some MIDI software, here is the data trail: The data flows from the keyboard (via the MIDI OUT jack), into the interface's MIDI IN jack, through the computer (and software used), back to the interface where it leaves via the MIDI OUT jack, and back to the keyboard's MIDI IN jack. Quite a trip!

The computer will also have a utility for describing and selecting MIDI gear connected to it such as the Audio MIDI Setup for Mac OSX or the MIDI Settings area of the Control Panel for Windows. More advanced MIDI software may require a further setting to choose the MIDI input source, such as a drop-down menu in the track.

A MIDI track's output needs to be assigned to an instrument that will be *realizing* (playing) the MIDI data contained in the track. This could be an external keyboard synthesizer, but more and more these days it is an internal software instrument. With the former, the sound is actually coming from the keyboard synth, so monitor speakers, a keyboard amplifier, or headphones need to be connected to the keyboard's audio output or headphone jack to hear it. With the

---

3. The output source could also be an audio interface being used. In this less common (more advanced) scenario, speakers or headphones would be connected to the audio interface itself to monitor sound.

later, the sound is actually coming from the computer, so monitor speakers or headphones need to be connected to the computer's sound out jack.[4]

MMP WEB APPLICATIONS

We are starting to see web applications that offer limited version of some of the features of conventional DAW software. These run via the Internet in the user's browser and therefore require a fast, broadband connection, a recent version of a supported browser, and updated multimedia plug-ins (such as Adobe Flash and QuickTime). Even still, recording audio remotely to a distant server will seem sluggish compared to doing the same thing "locally" using a program running on your computer. Another drawback of these web programs is the limited number of loops available to use, versus the thousands at your disposal with a program such as GarageBand. Even still, web music production applications can provide a free solution for multitrack music production for students.

At this time, Myna (by Aviary.com) seems to be offering the most reliable online multitrack recording application. Although this particular web app may not always be available, it is worth discussing its features for the purpose of comparing it to others. Myna allows for audio recording, uploading prerecorded audio, and looping—all in online tracks. Some of the loops provided with Myna are like soundtracks themselves, but the number and scope are limited. Project files are saved to the application's server, so users can work on their music wherever they can get online. I am sure we will be seeing more web applications like this; they are definitely worth investigating.

EXAMPLE LESSONS

On the pages that follow are several lessons that feature the use of MMP software in creative sound and music activities. One is a creative lesson *about* music ("My Favorite Things Podcast"), one is a tutorial to introduce and rehearse program features in a creative way ("Cut, Copy, Paste, Split, Move"), one is a timbre and movement game ("Identify and Move to Instruments à la Freeze Dance"), one introduces a vital arranging and composing principle ("Loops and Layering"), and others are more comprehensive, aimed at producing fully developed creative products ("New Clothes for an Old Tune" or "Winter/Holiday Tune Setting"). Also note that the chapter 13 lesson "Electronic Art Music Sound Collage" would be very effective using MMP software as well.

Unless otherwise indicated, all the lessons are ones I have developed and used in my own teaching at various levels.

---

4. In a more advanced setup where both external keyboard synth sounds and internal software instrument sounds are used together, there must be some sort of system to mix the two. For instance, a small mixer can receive audio signals from both the keyboard synth and the computer, mix the two, and send the output to monitor speakers. Some monitor speakers allow for multiple inputs and therefore can serve, essentially, as a mixer. A lab controller system, such as the Korg GEC (General Education Controller), will do the trick as well.

LESSON TITLE: MY FAVORITE THINGS PODCAST

Audience: Grades 5–12, all music courses.

Objective: Students will produce a podcast episode featuring several prepared sound clips and a recorded narration from a brief, original script. Although podcasts such as this may be used for research on a composer, musician, instrument, or any other music topic, this particular lesson is aimed at allowing students to briefly share something musically special to them.

Materials/Equipment: Any entry-level MMP program, such as GarageBand. You also need a means to record voice (such as internal microphone, USB microphone, microphone with an audio interface, or handheld recording device with the ability to "dump" audio into the multitrack audio program).

Duration: 180 minutes (or approximately four class periods).

Prior Knowledge and Skills: Experience using a computer mouse and keyboard and minimal facility importing, recording, and editing waveform audio; experience with an entry-level DAW is helpful but not necessary.

Procedure:

183

1. Introduction: Listen to one or more examples of a past "My Favorite Things Podcast," such as Julian S.'s "A Tribute to the Newmans" (see **Web Ex. 3.1**) or Megan A.'s "It Wouldn't Be Christmas Without" (**Web Ex. 14.1**). Discuss with students what makes these podcasts effective at conveying the creator's interest in the topic.

2. Selecting a Podcast Topic and Title: Podcast topics could be the music of a favorite artist, band, composer, ensemble, genre of music, instrument, and much more. Have students submit their topic for approval to be sure they can carry it out successfully. If the student chooses an obscure artist, confirm that they can locate audio examples. If students choose a broad or general topic (such as film soundtrack music), help them focus in on a favorite aspect and select representative examples. Also, students may unknowingly choose a vocalist or rapper whose lyrics are not in keeping with your school's or community's standards. When submitting their topic for approval, students should include an episode title. Examples of "My Favorite Things Podcast" titles/themes include "Guitar Heroes," "Danny Elfman: From Oingo-Boingo to the Silver Screen," "Favorite Beatles Covers," "Best of Coldplay," and "Icelandic Pop Music."

3. Crafting a Script: Finished podcasts will be between 1:30 and 2:00 in length, so scripts need only be 100 to 300 words (300 words is about two minutes of nonstop narration). The script should be built around three brief (30-second) sound clips of the music students will share (see below). Students should do some research on their topic using websites such as allmusic.com or Wikipedia, typing their script with a text editor. Caution students not to get bogged down with a lengthy,

detailed report—that is not the purpose of this project. The goal is to tell a story that communicates their enthusiasm for the topic. After hearing the podcast, the class should share one another's appreciation for each student's "favorite" musical thing. Students may use the following outline for their script but may vary this structure to suit their topic.

    a. Introduction: Why should your audience be interested in this topic? For what is your subject best-known?

    b. Background/description: How did he/she/they/it get his/her/their/its start? What defines his/her/their/its achievement in music? Describe the premise of your topic.

    c. Representative work: Tell us about some good examples that tell the story of your topic. Tell us why you like the music of your subject.

    d. Wrap-up/conclusion: Find an interesting and satisfying way to conclude, for example, what was your subject's contribution to music? What is your subject doing now? It there a musical or life lesson that emerges?

4. Prepare sound clips: Use the procedure described in the lesson "Creating a Sound Clip to Share" in chapter 13. There should be exactly three sound clips, approximately 30 seconds in length. Finding the best 30 seconds of each example is important, but caution students about spending too long choosing their sound clips. The sound clips can be placed in a single audio track set aside for sound clips, or two or more audio tracks if desired. Using more than one audio track for sound clips allows for cross-fading, where one clip fades out while another clip fades in.

5. Record voice narration: Students should record themselves reading the script, using the following steps.

    a. Decide the microphone/recording scheme (internal or USB mic recording in class; handheld recorder used in hallway, then imported to program; mic with audio interface recorded in isolation booth, etc.).

    b. Add a voice narration audio track in the software. Set input volume levels using the program's or track's VU (volume units) meter and consider using a pop filter to minimize vocal "plosives" if one is available.

    c. Rehearse the script a few times, deciding where to pause between thoughts.

    d. Record the narration in "chunks" (one paragraphs, or other such sections of the script, at a time). The chunks approach helps if you make a mistake when recording the voice since you will have to re-record only that chunk. It also allows you to easily move narration regions where they belong, before and after sound clips. If instead you record your voice narration in one long "take," that's okay, too; you will just have to "slice-and-dice" the waveform into separate "regions" to place before and after sound clips.

6. Arrange narration and sound clips: Move voice narration regions and sound clips, in their respective tracks, to create a narrative flow between commentary and musical examples. Use software features to add appropriate fade-ins and fade-outs to the clips. Normally, these automated volume changes are programmed graphically by clicking and dragging "break points" along an automation line in the track. For example, the podcast might start with the first sound clip at a strong level that then gradually fades until the level is low enough for the voice narration to begin. At this point the sound clip might continue at a low level or fade out altogether.

7. (Optional) Podcast extras: If time permits, consider adding podcast elements such as intro/theme music, closing music, and sound effects (applause, comic zingers, etc.). Free sound effects (SFX) may be found on the Internet, but software such as GarageBand includes these and a modest library of theme and "bumper" music to use.

8. Export and share: Have students export their podcasts to disk or a player such as iTunes. Ask several students who finish early to share their podcast and discuss. This will allow others to know if they are on the right track. At the conclusion of the project, share all podcasts as a class, leaving time for student reactions, praise, and criticism.

185

Adaptation: I have found that some students would rather record their narration apart from the class, keeping their script private until it is unveiled as part of a fully produced podcast. To do this, I have (1) used a special computer set up in a practice room (like a studio "isolation booth") for students to take turns recording narrations, and (2) given students handheld recorders to take turns recording their narrations in the hallway.

This particular podcast assignment works best when done individually. If it is necessary to have students work in pairs rather than alone, consider having students prepare podcasts on more neutral topics to support some area of your curriculum. These may be composer reports or brief tours of a musical style period (Baroque, Classical, Romantic, etc.).

Feedback/Evaluation: For formal assessment, use a rubric such as the one shown in chapter 11 (see **Fig. 11.2**), which you can download from the companion website (**Web Ex. 14.2**). Students will receive valuable feedback during the classroom discussion, reactions, and criticisms following playback of the podcasts as well.

Extensions/Follow-up: Export the project as an audio file to share by posting on the Internet (website, wiki, blog), including in a class podcast or on a CD of class projects, or playing as part of a school announcements program.

If possible, have students post comments and reactions online for one another.

Some MMP applications allow for graphic images to be dropped in a video track. If this feature is available, students (or just certain students) can create slides in PowerPoint, export them as JPEG images, and drop them into the video track. Slides might include titles of songs, pictures of their artist(s), or other graphic support for the script. If correctly exported (see software instructions), the audio and graphic elements will be saved as a video podcast in some multimedia format (such as QuickTime or MPEG). These can be posted on the web as well.

National Standards Addressed: Each of the following standards is addressed to some degree in this lesson:

- **Standard 4** (optional), Composing and arranging music within specified guidelines.
- **Standard 6,** Listening to, analyzing, and describing music.
- **Standard 7,** Evaluating music and music performances.
- **Standard 8,** Understanding relationships between music, the other arts, and disciplines outside the arts.
- **Standard 9,** Understanding music in relation to history and culture.

LESSON TITLE: BULLY RAP

Audience: Grades 4–6, general music classes.[5]

Objective: Students will write a rhyming, rhythmic rap based on specific bullying prevention guidelines adopted by your school/district.[6] Students will choose appropriate loops to accompany their rap, record in groups, and then finish the production by applying vocal and other effects.

Materials/Equipment: Any entry-level MMP program, such as GarageBand. You also need a means to record voice (such as internal microphone, USB microphone, microphone with an audio interface, or handheld recording device with the ability to "dump" audio into the multitrack program). Paper and pencil are needed for documenting lyrics. Optionally, slide presentation software (such as PowerPoint, Keynote) and/or a digital camera may be used to extend the lesson (see below).

Duration: Depending on the number of students, this should take between 60 and 120 minutes (or about two to four class periods).

Prior Knowledge and Skills: No prior knowledge is necessary, but student helpers may be employed who have experience with either MMP or slide presentation software.

Procedure:

1. Write and rehearse rhythmic/rhyming lyrics. Students work in groups to create a rhythmic chant addressing the topic (such as preventing bullying in your school, or any other curricular content you would like to reinforce). Students should create and rehearse their rhythms naturally and intuitively, writing out their lyrics but learning the associated rhythms by rote. Rapping may include sung phrases as well if the students are so moved.

2. Upon completion of the chant, each group chooses two complementary loops (ostinato patterns) from GarageBand that are appropriate for the rap genre. These loops are placed in new tracks of the MMP software. Ideally, students are given an opportunity to rehearse their rap along with the loops they have chosen.

3. Students are then recorded chanting the rap at the correct tempo. Set up an audio track, and be sure the microphone scheme being used is correctly configured. The trick here is having the students hear a reference tempo from either the playback of the loops or a metronome "click," so that their rhythmic rapping is in tempo with the loops they have chosen. The problem is that we want the microphone to pick up

---

5. This lesson contributed by Jill Crissy-Kemmerer, music teacher at Fogelsville Elementary School, Parkland School District (Allentown, PA).

6. The example posted to the companion website for this lesson is based is the Olweus Bullying Prevention Program (www.olweus.org) guidelines.

(record) only the students' voices, and not the sound of the loops or click sounding as they rap. Here are several strategies for recording the students chanting their raps for this lesson.

   a. Most practical: After practicing with the loops sounding, record the students without the loops or click, *but with a conductor* (teacher or capable student) beating the correct tempo. If the tempo is off (a bit too slow/fast), most entry-level DAW software allows the tempo of the loops to be adjusted accordingly.

   b. Good compromise: After practicing with the loops sounding, record the students with a metronome (or other) click playing back at a low level. Unfortunately, the soft click does become part of the vocal track but should not be very evident when the loops are mixed in.

   c. More sophisticated. If each student in the group can monitor loop playback in headphones as they record their rap, their voices would be perfectly synced to the loops but the microphone would pickup only their voices (and not the loops). This can be achieved by routing the computer's audio output to a "headphone splitter," which allows multiple headphones to monitor the sound.[7]

4. Attend to the following items in postrecording production:

   a. Volume levels for each track (vocals and loops) are adjusted to create a good balance. Automate the volume levels (vocals and loops), increasing and decreasing in order to hear the students' voices best. Add fade-ins and fade-outs to the loops where desired for additional interest.

   b. Add DSP[8] vocal and other effects as desired to the vocal/rap track.

5. Listen to and discuss with each group their preliminary results. Make adjustments (mix levels, etc.) as time allows.

6. Export and share: Export student rap productions to disk or a player such as iTunes.

7. (Optional) A slide presentation (such as Power, Point, or Keynote) can then be created, showing/animating the lyrics composed by the students. Embed the audio into the slide show and time the slides to correspond with the students voices. For fun, consider including pictures of the students in fun or tough, "rapper" poses at the end. View the example bully rap video at the companion website (**Web Ex. 14.3**).

Adaptations: The topic of the rap can really be anything in the general classroom or music curriculum, or of interest to students.

---

7. Headphone splitters can be as simple as a two-headphone "Y" adapter (less than $5), a multijack plug/cable (less than $20), or better quality, four-headphone boxes with separate level controls for each channel and possibly an amplifier to boost the signal ($50–200).

8. Digital signal processing (DSP) effects include reverb, echo, compression, equalization (EQ), chorus, flange, and so forth. See the discussion in chapter 13.

The above plan is based on the teacher facilitating the activity using a single computer music workstation at the front of the class. If available, each group could be assigned to their own workstation in a cluster or lab.

Feedback/Evaluation: Students will be assessed based upon the success of their composition project. Success is based upon the following criteria:

1. Did their lyrics make sense?
2. Was the content accurate and correct?
3. Did their chant rhyme?
4. Were two complementary loops used?
5. Was their chant rhythmic and performed at the correct tempo?
6. (Optional) Was at least one DSP effect applied to the vocal track?

Extensions/Follow-up: Share the exported audio file on the Internet (website, wiki, blog, as part of a class podcast), on a CD of class projects, or as part of a school announcements program. The slide presentation of the rap, which includes the audio track, could be exported as a movie and presented live at a school assembly or concert (projected to a large screen) or on a schoolwide TV program or posted on the Internet.

National Standards Addressed: Each of the following standards is addressed to some degree in this lesson:

- **Standard 1,** Singing, alone and with others, a varied repertoire of music.
- **Standard 3** (optional), Improvising melodies, harmonies, and accompaniments.
- **Standard 4,** Composing and arranging music within specified guidelines.
- **Standard 6,** Listening to, analyzing, and describing music.
- **Standard 7,** Evaluating music and music performances.
- **Standard 8,** Understanding relationships between music, the other arts, and disciplines outside the arts.
- **Standard 9** (optional), Understanding music in relation to history and culture.

189

LESSON TITLE: HANDS-ON TIMBRE

Audience: Grades 4–12, general and elective music classes.

Objective: Students will gain an applied understanding of timbre (instrumental tone color) by reorchestrating a prepared MIDI file of a familiar tune.

Materials/Equipment: Any entry-level MMP program, such as GarageBand. Also needed is a prepared MIDI file arrangement of any brief, familiar tune.

▶ **FIG. 14.2**

This simple arrangement of "Amazing Grace" works well with the "Hands On Timbre" lesson. Created by Scott Watson.

Amazing Grace

Traditional
arr. Scott Watson

For the best experience, acquire or create one that contains melody, accompaniment, and a bassline (percussion is optional). The arrangement of "Amazing Grace" shown in **Fig. 14.2** is an example music that would work well. For schools with GarageBand, download the file Amazing_grace.zip file (**Web Ex. 14.4**) to use with this lesson. Others may import the file Amazing_Grace .mid (**Web Ex. 14.5**) into any multitrack MIDI program to use.

Duration: 40–80 minutes (or about one to two class periods).

Prior Knowledge and Skills: Experience using a computer mouse and keyboard. Some familiarity with the basic features of the software is helpful but not necessary.

Procedure:

1. Introduce song arrangement: Open and playback the prepared MIDI file in the MMP software. Discuss the textural elements of the arrangement (melody, accompaniment, bassline, drums, etc.) and the track in which each resides. Allow students a moment to open the file in the MMP application being used and to test playback.

2. Demonstrate: Next, demonstrate for students how to change the instrument sound of each track.

3. Timbre changes: Discuss the plan for reorchestrating the file you want each student (or group) to follow. For instance, students (or groups) might be assigned an instrument family (such as woodwinds, brass, strings, percussion) or a style/genre (popular, classical, electronica, etc.). Working within the parameters for timbre choice that you decide and present, give students time to choose new timbres for their version of the arrangement.

4. Set levels: Different instrument sounds normally differ in volume level. Discuss the concepts of balance and blend, demonstrate how to set track volume levels, and give students time to make these adjustments to their version of the arrangement. Be sure the melody is present and the accompaniment and bassline are supportive.

5. (Optional) If time, or for students that finish early, encourage experimentation with adding rhythmic loops, applying DSP effects (reverb, chorus, etc.), or creating tempo changes (such as *ritardando* near end).

Adaptations: The entire lesson could be done from a single, teacher workstation projected to a screen or interactive whiteboard. The teacher would serve as the facilitator, with students offering suggestions for instrument sound changes and track volume settings. Students can come to the teacher workstation to perform various tasks.

Feedback/Evaluation: Use a rubric or task list that credits students with successfully changing instrument sounds for each track (within the choices allowed) and for adjusting track volume to create a balanced, well-blended playback.

Extensions/Follow-up: In a follow-up lesson, allow students to apply any of the optional elements suggested in step 5 above.

National Standards Addressed: Each of the following standards is addressed to some degree in this lesson:

- **Standard 4,** Composing and arranging music within specified guidelines.
- **Standard 6,** Listening to, analyzing, and describing music.
- **Standard 7,** Evaluating music and music performances.

LESSON TITLE: CUT, COPY, PASTE, SPLIT, MOVE

Audience: Grades 5–12, general and elective music classes.

Objective: Some of the most useful tools in any MMP software are the editing features. They can be used to great effect both practically (in terms of working efficiently) and artistically (in terms of employing good principals of composing, arranging, and song writing). In this lesson, students will use features such as cut, copy, paste, split, and move to re-create a model arrangement of a familiar tune (such as "Yankee Doodle"). Student arrangements should include these formal sections: introduction, verse, chorus, verse, chorus, tag ending.

Materials/Equipment: Any entry-level MMP program, such as GarageBand. The teacher must create a file that includes a MIDI track, assigned to any instrument sound, with the melody to a familiar tune such as "Yankee Doodle." Consider including an optional chordal accompaniment track and bassline track. For schools with GarageBand, download the file yankee _doodle_edit.zip (**Web Ex. 14.6**) to use with this lesson. Others may import the file yankee_doodle_edit.mid (**Web Ex. 14.7**) into any multitrack MIDI program to use.

Duration: 90 minutes (or about two class periods).

Prior Knowledge and Skills: Experience using a computer mouse and keyboard. Some familiarity with the basic features of the software is helpful.

Procedure:

1. Demonstrate: Briefly demonstrate for students the following editing features: cut, copy, paste, split. Also demonstrate how to move regions of waveform audio to different locations in the same or different tracks. The goal is for students to understand the power they have at their disposal in crafting an arrangement. Show students how easy it is to copy verse 1 material into verse 2, and so on. Also demonstrate how to change the instrument sound assigned to a track.

2. Example: Play an example of a model arrangement that follows the form (intro, verse, chorus, verse, chorus, tag) and exhibits some interesting instrument sound choices ("orchestration").

3. Arrange: Give students time to work on their arrangement. Depending on students' proficiency with the software, consider performing one operation with the students as a group. For instance, copy the last four bars of the chorus into measures 1–4 to create an introduction. Part of the arrangement should include percussion looping for rhythmic accompaniment. Students may place these wherever they like, perhaps to highlight the form (such as beginning a drum loop at the chorus). Students should change the instrument sound of at least one

193

track. Students may copy and paste MIDI data into new MIDI tracks to double existing parts.

4. Coaching and peer critique: During the "arranging" phase, have students play their works-in-progress for you and their classmates. Employ coaching methods and peer feedback to offer ideas for refining works.

5. Performance: Choose several strong projects to play in finished form for the class.

Adaptations: The entire lesson could be done from a single, teacher workstation projected to a screen or interactive whiteboard. The teacher would serve as the facilitator, with students offering suggestions for creating a class arrangement. Students can come to the teacher workstation to perform various tasks.

This lesson uses a prepared file with MIDI tracks to deliver experience with editing and arranging concepts. If no multitrack MIDI program is available, students could have a similar experience using a prepared Audacity (or other audio program) file with audio tracks. Unfortunately, students would not be able to change instrument sounds as they could with MIDI tracks.

Feedback/Evaluation: Use a rubric that credits students with creating each of the formal sections, at least one instrument sound change to a track, and maintaining good timing when assembling edits.

Extensions/Follow-up: Student who finish early may add more percussion loops where desired, adjust track volume and pan, and/or employ various DSP effects (reverb, etc.). If time, students might also add their own sections to the song, such as a percussion break (interlude).

National Standards Addressed: Each of the following standards is addressed to some degree in this lesson:

- **Standard 2** (optional), Performing on instruments, alone and with others, a varied repertoire of music.
- **Standard 3** (optional), Improvising melodies, harmonies, and accompaniments.
- **Standard 4,** Composing and arranging music within specified guidelines.
- **Standard 5** (optional), Reading and notating music.
- **Standard 6,** Listening to, analyzing, and describing music.
- **Standard 7,** Evaluating music and music performances.
- **Standard 8,** Understanding relationships between music, the other arts, and disciplines outside the arts.

LESSON TITLE: SCORING A CHILDREN'S POEM

Audience: Grades 5–12, general and elective music classes.

Objective: Students, working alone or in groups, will create a sound score to accompany a brief children's poem. Using at least four tracks, the score should include the following elements: (1) spoken word (one or more students reading the story), (2) tonal elements (drones, pads, loops, performance by electronic and acoustic instruments, etc.), (3) sound effects (such as newly recorded "Foley" sounds, prerecorded SFX found in the program or online), and (4) DSP effects (reverb, echo, pitch shift, etc.).

Materials/Equipment: Any entry-level MMP program, such as GarageBand. You will need to have books of children's poems, or Internet sites of children's poems, available for students to use. Poems could be children's classics, holiday themed (Halloween poems often have lots of aural imagery), witty (such as Shel Silverstein's *Where the Sidewalk Ends*, *Falling Up*, or *A Light in the Attic*, or for older students, Tim Burton's *The Melancholy Death of Oyster Boy*), or even those written by students. You also need a means to record voice (such as internal microphone, USB microphone, microphone with an audio interface, or handheld recording device with the ability to "dump" audio into the multitrack audio program).

Duration: 120–200 minutes (or three to five class periods).

Prior Knowledge and Skills: Some experience working with loops and with live audio recording.

Procedure:

1. Introduction: Discuss with students the way sound, including music, can enhance words and drama. Describe the project and play exemplary works by students in previous sections of the course.

2. Select poems: Have students, working alone or in teams, examine a variety of children's poems in books or online. Each should select a brief poem of approximately 4 to 12 lines. As students search, ask them to think of aural cues that the words suggest. Once selected, type or write out the poem on a paper, leaving much space between lines to jot down indications for sound or musical events. This will be the written "score."

3. Record the poem into a voice track: Use separate "takes" so each phrase or section of the poem is in a separate audio region. This way, each voice region can be moved to fit the music and sound effects if needed. If the recording is done in one continuous take, use the program's editing tools to separate phrases into separate audio regions where necessary.

4. Strategize, experiment, and improvise: Give students time to "spot" the poem, discussing the kinds of music, sound effects, or other sonic events suggested by the words. The sound score may be traditional (in

195

tempo, with measures) or more like a collage (free, perhaps with synthesized sound and lots of DSP effects). Ways to experiment and improvise include the following:

a. Audition the types of loops desired, placing potentially useful ones into the score to hear how they work with the words.

b. Ostinato rhythms and pedal point (drone, repeated note) are two easy, yet effective ways to generate background musical material. Most loops, by definition, are ideal for creating ostinati rhythms. Some loops, however, are more dronelike. Alternatively, students may create tracks for instruments they feel are appealing and improvise a "cue" using ostinato and/or pedal point.

c. Spot the poem for sound effects. Students may use prerecorded SFX that come with the program, those they find online, or those they record (real or MIDI).

d. Students that would like to record a vocal or instrumental performance as part of their sound score might sing a familiar tune or something original (brief melodic phrase, ostinato, etc.).

5. Record cues. As a result of step 4, students will have a good start on their sound score. Give them time to record any cues they still need to finish.

6. Refine levels, and so forth: Automate volume changes to balance the spoken word and music/SFX tracks. Encourage students to consider other settings and effects as they have time, including pan position and reverb.

7. Perform: Have students share (playback) their finished products in class. Encourage discussion, praise, and criticism.

Adaptations: For younger students, narrow the focus of this project by limiting the texts to a handful of preselected, shorter poems; limiting the musical cues to percussion improvisations (real instruments recorded with a microphone or MIDI drum kit sounds), MIDI drones (pedal point), and one- or two-note ostinati; and limiting the SFX to those you acquire and provide (place in a folder on student's computers, etc.).

Feedback/Evaluation: Create a rubric or other grading sheet that awards credit for the following project components: length; quality of voice recording; use of music, sound effects, and DSP effects in the score; appropriate volume levels; and effectiveness of the sound score in enhancing the text (**Web Ex. 14.8** provides an example rubric, available at the companion website).

Extensions/Follow-up: Export the project as an audio file to share by posting on the Internet (website, wiki, blog), including in a class podcast or on a CD of class projects, or playing as part of a school announcements program.

National Standards Addressed: Each of the following standards is addressed to some degree in this lesson:

- **Standard 1** (optional), Singing, alone and with others, a varied repertoire of music.
- **Standard 2,** Performing on instruments, alone and with others, a varied repertoire of music.
- **Standard 3,** Improvising melodies, harmonies, and accompaniments.
- **Standard 4,** Composing and arranging music within specified guidelines.
- **Standard 5** (optional), Reading and notating music.
- **Standard 6,** Listening to, analyzing, and describing music.
- **Standard 7,** Evaluating music and music performances.
- **Standard 8,** Understanding relationships between music, the other arts, and disciplines outside the arts.
- **Standard 9,** Understanding music in relation to history and culture.

LESSON TITLE: LOOPS AND LAYERING

Audience: Grades 6–12, general and elective music classes.

Objective: At the conclusion of this lesson, students will demonstrate an understanding of the arranging/composing principle of *layering* through the creation of a brief, musically satisfying loop-based composition. There is no restriction to style, but it must be at least a minute in length. Another arranging principle, the *100% rule*, may be introduced for more sophistication a well.

Layering, a device employed often by composers and arrangers, is essentially changing musical texture to create a compelling narrative for the listener. The narrative involves adding or subtracting vertical components, building up or tearing down the texture. The device is very apparent in popular music but is often a feature of concert art ("classical") music as well. Musical ideas (melodies, accompaniment grooves, rhythms, etc.) and/or instrumentation may be layered. Often the concept of *ostinato* is at work as well.

The ***100% rule*** is related and is concerned with not overusing an ensemble's performing forces. Rather, good arranging differentiates elements of an ensemble by giving each distinct moments in the form and distinct ranges within which to play, or by giving them distinct parts in a texture, and so on. If the sound of such a theoretical, ideal arrangement is "100%," too many amateur groups oversaturate by featuring everyone playing all the time, in the same register, and on the same basic part. This "200%" or "300%" (or more) sound is uninteresting—and sometimes confusing—for the listener.

Both concepts are explained fully in the tutorial movie *Layering and the 100% Rule* (**Web Ex. 14.9**).

Materials/Equipment: Entry-level DAW, such as GarageBand. Consider using the tutorial movie *Layering and the 100% Rule* (**Web Ex. 14.9**) to explain the musical concepts of this activity. You will also need pencil and paper for notating the formal plan for their project.

Duration: 80–120 minutes (or about two to three class periods).

Prior Knowledge and Skills: Some experience with the basic features of the software is helpful.

Procedure:

1. Listening: Share three or four examples of good music of all styles in which the concept of layering is evident. Help students see the prevalence of this principle in classical and popular music. If desired, point out application of the 100% rule as well. Use the movie *Layering and the 100% Rule* (**Web Ex. 14.9**), or your own listening examples with corresponding listening charts, to help students follow layering events. Examples of stylistically diverse music that clearly exhibit the use of layering (and the 100% rule) include *Canon in D*, by Johann Pachelbel,

"Saturday in the Park," by Robert Lamm (performed by the band Chicago), "Seasons of Love," by Jonathan Larsen (from the musical *Rent*), "Mars, Bringer of War," by Gustav Holst (from the orchestral suite *The Planets*).

2. Demonstrate, or review with students, how to create tracks and add loops with the software being used. If time, demonstrate/review how to automate volume in a track.

3. Play one or two excellent "Loops and Layering" project examples for students (such as **Web Ex. 14.10,** "Space Jam"). Discuss with students the effective elements of these examples.

4. Allow students to work alone or in pairs creating their own "Loops and Layering" projects, using the following guidelines:

   a. Begin by auditioning the available loops. Try to find loops that complement one another in terms of instruments and style. If loops in your library come in "families" (acoustic strum 1, acoustic strum 2, acoustic strum 3, etc.), exploit the way they repeat but with subtle variation. Some loops are percussive, and some are tonal; some loops are more sustained, and some are more disjunct. Exploit pairing loops with both similar and contrasting qualities.

   b. Urge and coach students to develop a plan for how the texture will change throughout in interesting ways. Here are just two of the many ways texture might be developed:

      i. Introduce loops one at a time until all loops are sounding. Then cut the texture back drastically to just one or two new loops. Gradually build the texture back up.

      ii. Begin with many loops sounding together and then cut back texture drastically to one or two of the existing loops. Return to the combined loops texture and then cut back to a different one or two loops. Repeat this process as desired, perhaps until the start of a new section.

   c. As an alternative to having loops suddenly appear or leave, have students automate the volume for tracks to create fade-ins and/or fade-outs.

   d. Have students devise their own mode of written notation for the texture/form of their project.

5. Have students play their works-in-progress for you and one another. Allow time for students to implement changes as a result of your comments/coaching and student criticism.

6. Play finished "Loops and Layering" projects for one another. Encourage feedback/criticism.

Adaptations: To simplify and narrow the task of auditioning/selecting loops, consider limiting the number of loops from which students may choose, or

LOOPS & LAYERING (and 100% RULE) Grading Grid

Name: _____

Project: _____

Category					Score
Timing [20 Points]:	15–29 Seconds [11–13 Points]	30–59 Seconds [14–16 Points]	45–60 Seconds [17–19 Points]	60+ Seconds [20 Points]	
USE OF LAYERING PRINCIPAL [10 POINTS]: Layering creates interest and a narrative for the listener. 					
ARTISTIC/APPROPRIATE LOOP CHOICE [10 POINTS]: Artistic chemistry created by pairing compatible loops. 					
AESTHETIC STATEMENT [10 POINTS]: This is our subjective reaction to your artistic statement. Does it sound like a piece, or just an "introduction"? 					
Total Score [50 possible]					

Comments:

▶ **FIG. 14.3**

Sample grading grid for the "Loops & Layering" project. Created by Scott Watson.

reducing the length (in seconds) of the project. Another limitation that can focus the project is to prescribe a form for the texture to follow, such as A–B–A (arch) or A–B–A–C–A–B–A (rondo).

This lesson could be accomplished with a single, "teacher" computer at the front of a classroom. The teacher or a strong student could facilitate, auditioning loops for the class to choose as a group, and changing texture on suggestions from students. Alternatively, if there is a cluster or pod of computers in the room, students can be rotated back to these computers to work in small groups once the teacher has demonstrated the project for the entire class.

Feedback/Evaluation: For formal assessment, use the rubric shown in **Fig. 14.3** (see also **Web Ex. 14.11**).

Extensions/Follow-up: Stronger students may add a real-time recording element if desired. Export the project as an audio file to share by posting on the Internet (website, wiki, blog), including in a class podcast or on a CD of class projects, or playing as part of a school announcements program (perhaps as theme or "bumper" music).

National Standards Addressed: Each of the following standards is addressed to some degree in this lesson:

- **Standard 2** (optional), Performing on instruments, alone and with others, a varied repertoire of music.
- **Standard 3** (optional), Improvising melodies, harmonies, and accompaniments.
- **Standard 4,** Composing and arranging music within specified guidelines.
- **Standard 5,** Reading and notating music.
- **Standard 6,** Listening to, analyzing, and describing music.
- **Standard 7,** Evaluating music and music performances.

LESSON TITLE: IDENTIFY AND MOVE TO INSTRUMENTS À LA FREEZE DANCE

Audience: Grades 1–4, general music classes.[9]

Objective: Students will aurally (and possibly visually) identify instrument sounds in a multitrack arrangement, create movements for these sounds, and then perform their movements on cue while music is playing. Freeze Dance is a game in which children improvise movement to music as it plays, but "freeze" in place when the music stops; those who do not are eliminated. Here, students perform agreed-upon movements when they hear specific instrument sounds (associated with percussion loops); students who move to the wrong instrument sound are eliminated.

Materials/Equipment: Entry-level DAW, such as GarageBand, and percussion instruments used in GarageBand percussion loops (or pictures of same) placed around the room. The teacher must prepare a GarageBand (or other DAW) file (1) with multiple tracks of solo percussion instrument loops that complement one another, creating an interesting composite groove, and 2) that is, as a whole, set to repeat (i.e. loop or cycle) again and again (such as **Web Ex. 14.12,** freeze_dance.zip prepared for GarageBand). In creating the file, use loops for percussion instruments you have in class (claves, cowbell, bongos, tambourine, shaker or maracas, guiro, etc.). Include a few tracks with bass or other loops just for fun.

Duration: 30–40 minutes (or approximately one class period).

Prior Knowledge and Skills: Some familiarity with a variety of percussion instruments is helpful.

Procedure:

1. MMP software allows the user to "solo" a track. Using this feature, play for students the solo percussion loops on each track, one at a time. Can they identify the instrument sound they hear? Can they see this instrument in the room? While playing the file again, randomly solo various tracks and quiz the students to see if they can identify the solo instruments they hear.

2. As a group, create dance (or otherwise) movements for each solo instrument (loop) used in the arrangement. Practice the movement/dance created, as a class, to the solo percussion loop with which it is associated.

---

9. This lesson was created by Mrs. Vietta Taylor, music teacher at Springhurst Elementary School, Dobbs Ferry School District (Dobbs Ferry, NY). About the success of the lesson with her students, Taylor shared, "They absolutely loved it! They do love to dance and move and they also love freeze dance, so it was perfect. They easily identified the instruments. In the initial introductory lesson, we identified the instruments and did 'the freeze' when those instruments were playing. In a follow up lesson we picked movements to accompany the percussion instruments and divided into groups for each instrument. The kids were so actively involved. The ones that were eliminated played a steady beat on rhythm instruments to the full track portion. It was fun and positive for all while reinforcing their listening skills."

3. Ask students to do any movement they want when they hear the entire arrangement as it is played once more, but this time when a solo instrument is isolated by soloing a track, they should perform the movement that goes with that instrument.

4. Divide the class into groups and assign each group to a solo instrument. Play the entire arrangement. This time, have only the group assigned to each solo instrument move/dance when that instrument solos, while the rest of the class freezes. If someone moves/dances to the wrong instrument, they are eliminated from play. The teacher may have those eliminated either (1) help the teacher monitor those remaining for correct movement (simpler) or (2) play a steady beat on a rhythm instrument when they hear the combined tracks playing all instrument loops (more sophisticated). Next, challenge kids to listen harder by soloing two or more distinct percussion sounds at a time, so that two or more groups dance uniquely at a time.

Adaptations: To add another layer of creativity, have students help choose the loops to be used in the multitrack arrangement. As the teacher (or chosen student) auditions loops on a teacher workstation, students can view on a projection screen or interactive whiteboard the process of adding loops and replicating them. In this case, students will have to discern if the loops are for solo percussion instruments or not.

Feedback/Evaluation: Informal authentic assessment: Who can quickly aurally identify the instrument and match the correct movement? Consider using a laminated seating chart where a check mark is placed by the name of students as they respond correctly.

Extensions/Follow-up: Once learned by students, use this fun activity when there is extra time at the end of a class. Students will have fun while sharpening their listening skills. Change the solo instruments, yourself or with student input, as students learn the sounds of more instruments (both percussion and tonal).

National Standards Addressed: Each of the following standards is addressed to some degree in this lesson:

- **Standard 2** (optional), Performing on instruments, alone and with others, a varied repertoire of music.
- **Standard 4,** Composing and arranging music within specified guidelines.
- **Standard 6,** Listening to, analyzing, and describing music.
- **Standard 7,** Evaluating music and music performances.
- **Standard 8,** Understanding relationships between music, the other arts, and disciplines outside the arts.

LESSON TITLE: NEW CLOTHES FOR AN OLD TUNE

Audience: Grades 6–12, general and elective music classes.[10]

Objective: In this lesson, students will make their own fresh, popular music style arrangement of a public domain baroque or classical period keyboard piece (or section of a piece). A successful project will exhibit elements of thoughtful *arranging* and orchestration, as well as an understanding of the concept of *musical fusion*.

Materials/Equipment: Any entry-level MMP program, such as GarageBand, and a standard MIDI file of a short Baroque- or Classical-era keyboard work (or section of a work). Optionally, some students may also want to use a keyboard (synth or controller) to enter their notes manually (real-time or step recording) or to program notes in addition to those in the MIDI file. A tutorial video, about 11 minutes in length, is available from the companion website that demonstrates the main features of this project (**Web Ex. 14.13,** MIDI_import.mov).

Duration: Depending on the number of students, this should take between 120 and 200 minutes (or about three to five class periods).

Prior Knowledge and Skills: Experience using basic features of DAW software and an understanding of some principles of arranging and orchestrating music such as layering and the 100% rule (see the "Loops and Layering" lesson above).

Procedure:

1. General listening: Share two or three excellent examples in which there is an evident musical fusion of traditional "classical" music and some popular style (rock, jazz, contemporary pop, etc.). There are many examples of classical-pop fusion that feature synthesizer sounds, the model for this project. I suggest the following listening examples:

   a. *Switched-On Bach*, by Wendy Carlos. When it comes to performing older music on new instruments, the granddaddy of them all is the seminal album *Switched-On Bach*, in which keyboardist Wendy Carlos performs music by Johan Sebastian Bach on an instrument that had only recently been invented by New York engineer Robert Moog, making the name Moog almost synonymous with the term synthesizer. A perfect track to share with kids is "Sinfonia" from Bach's *Cantata No. 29* from this album.

   b. "Baroque Hoedown," by Jean-Jacques Perrey and Gershon Kingsley. This neo-Baroque, synthesizer-based composition was created in 1967 and could be heard as the theme music for the Electric Light

10. I have had a lot of fun naming this lesson over the years. Past titles include "Switched-On Knock-Off" and "Extreme Makeover: Classical Music Edition."

Parade at Disneyland and Disney World for many years. The eclectically influenced indie-pop band They Might Be Giants produced a wonderfully quirky "cover" of this music as part of a tribute album for Robert Moog.

c. *Christmas*, by Mannheim Steamroller. Mannheim Steamroller creator Chip Davis has created album after album that fuses traditional and popular music elements along with prominently used synthesizer sounds. I would especially recommend sharing with students a track such as "Deck the Halls" from this album.

Discuss the benefits of fusing two musical styles together. Consider allowing students to bring in examples that fuse old and new styles to share.

2. Specific listening: Play one or two exemplary "New Clothes for an Old Tune" projects by students in previous sections of the course. Alison H.'s arrangement of Beethoven's "Solfeggietto" (**Web Ex. 4.1**) and Connor T.'s setting of Bach's "Invention No. 1" (**Web Ex. 14.14**) are two such examples.

3. Select music: Students will be using an existing MIDI file of a Baroque- or Classical-era keyboard pieces as the starting point for their arrangement. Depending on its length, they may use the entire file/piece or a section that stands on its own. The following are some ways students can locate and choose appropriate MIDI files for this project:

a. Screen and select a half dozen or so good MIDI files from which students may choose and place these in a computer or network folder to which students have access or post them to a course website or wiki.

b. Post links on a course website or wiki to preselected websites rich with appropriate MIDI files.[11] Students visit the sites to preview MIDI files and download one they like.

c. Decide ahead of time on an appropriate length of time (or measures) for the arrangement. This will depend on the level of each student and the number of periods you devote to the project. I usually aim for a project that is 44 to 75 seconds in length, or 16–24 measures of common time. J.S. Bach's "Musette in D major" (Fig. 14.4) is an example of a keyboard piece that works well for this assignment. Stronger students may want to create longer arrangements, but caution them about trying to tackle too much. The danger is that they will run out of time and their arrangement will be too shallow.

205

11. Examples of websites at this time that host MIDI files appropriate for this project include www .bachcentral.com, www.classicalarchives.com, www.mutopiaproject.org, www.kunstderfuge.com, www.mfiles .co.uk, www.classicalmusicmidipage.com, www.free-scores.com, and www.hymntime.com.

MUSETTE

J. S. Bach

Moderato

▶ **FIG. 14.4**
Brief keyboard pieces, such as Bach's Musette in D Major, work well for the "New Clothes for an Old Tune" arranging project. Typeset by Scott Watson.

4. Import the MIDI file: Open the MIDI file in whatever MMP software you are using.[12] This will give students the performance data (notes, rhythms, perhaps instrument sounds) for their piece usually in one or two tracks. In some cases, the instrument sounds will be assigned in the process. If not, students should set the instrument sound for each

12. With GarageBand, you can simply drag-and-drop the file into the Track Window. GarageBand will automatically import the MIDI data (notes, rhythms, and most instrument assignments).

track. This procedure is demonstrated in a tutorial video on the companion website (**Web Ex. 14.13**). If students will be using only a portion of the MIDI file (a stand-alone section), they can delete/cut unwanted measures in the MMP software.

5. Arrange: This is the artistic/creative stage of the activity and involves students making creative decisions and additions in several interrelated areas.

   a. Timbre: Students can choose their own instrument sounds for the tracks in their arrangement. Some programs only allow for a track's instrument sound to be set once at the beginning; others allow for instrument sound changes (sometimes called "patch" or "program" changes) throughout the track.

   b. Texture: To add depth to an arrangement, entire tracks, or track regions (portions of a track), can be copied and pasted into new tracks and then manipulated. The copied material may be transposed up or down an octave to add resonance and/or assigned to a different instrument sound to add timbral variety. The volume levels of the tracks can be set via a track's volume slider, by automating a track's volume, or by using the program's mixer (if it has one).

   c. Loops: The pop fusion that is a central feature of this project mainly comes from the addition of rhythm instrument loops. Students create a "groove" for their arrangement as they employ loops for drums, bass, guitar, keyboard, and more. Encourage students to use the principle of layering, presented in the "Loops and Layering" project.

   d. (Optional) Tempo: Sometimes an arrangement can take on a whole new feel or groove by altering the tempo for the entire piece. Students may use the software's tempo slider or setting to change the tempo if they like. A common, isolated tempo alteration for students to consider is slowing down just before the end of their arrangement (executing a *ritardando*). This can be programmed by automating the tempo in the software's "conductor" or "master" track.

   e. (Optional) Alter form: Students who have time may add formal sections such as an introduction (intro) and/or ending (outro) to enhance the arrangement.

   Help students to analyze the form of their source keyboard music and then encourage them to highlight phrases and sections using changes in timbre, texture, and rhythm section elements. This is essentially the idea of *layering* and the 100% rule.

6. Have selected (or all) students share their works-in-progress with the class for feedback (praise, criticism and suggestions). Use the remaining time to allow students to make adjustments and finish up.

7. Play the finished arrangements as part of an in-class recital.

207

Adaptations: For younger grades, limit the scope of the project, in any/all of the following ways:

1. Preselect four or five MIDI files from which students may choose. Place these in a computer or network folder, or on a class website or wiki, from which students may audition and choose them.
2. Designate the number of loop tracks that may be added (such as four tracks of loops: two percussion, one bass, and one additional of their choice).

If students work in cooperative learning groups, allow them to decide upon a good division of labor. The "producer" moderates discussions and decisions (which MIDI file will be used, which loops should be added, etc.) as different "sound engineers" take turns operating the software at each stage of the arranging process.

Stronger students may record their own MIDI or audio tracks (MIDI drum kit, live vocals, sound effects, etc.) to add to the imported MIDI file, if desired.

Feedback/Evaluation: Award credit for key elements of the project, including locating a MIDI file for a keyboard piece (or section of a piece) of suitable length, importing the MIDI file into the MMP software, assigning new instrument sounds, adding rhythm section loops, and evidence of layering and/or other creative approaches to arranging. Consider using a rubric such as the one shown in chapter 11 (see **Fig. 11.4,** available for download at the companion website [**Web Ex. 14.15**]).

Extensions/Follow-up: Export the project as an audio file to share by posting on the Internet (website, wiki, blog) or including in a class podcast or CD of class projects.

National Standards Addressed: Each of the following standards is addressed to some degree in this lesson:

- **Standard 1** (optional), Singing, alone and with others, a varied repertoire of music.
- **Standard 2** (optional), Performing on instruments, alone and with others, a varied repertoire of music.
- **Standard 3** (optional), Improvising melodies, harmonies, and accompaniments.
- **Standard 4,** Composing and arranging music within specified guidelines.
- **Standard 6,** Listening to, analyzing, and describing music.
- **Standard 7,** Evaluating music and music performances.
- **Standard 8,** Understanding relationships between music, the other arts, and disciplines outside the arts.

LESSON TITLE: WINTER/HOLIDAY TUNE SETTING

Audience: Grades 9–12, elective music technology/production class.

Objective: Students will arrange and produce a setting of a public domain or original winter/holiday tune using multitrack software and principals of good songwriting.

Materials/Equipment: Any entry-level MMP program, such as GarageBand, and either a standard MIDI file or sheet music of a public domain winter/holiday song. Alternatively, more experienced students may craft their own original winter/holiday track. Either way, the selection may be instrumental or with voice(s). Students using live vocal and/or instrumental performance as part of their song will need a means for recording various signals (such as USB microphone, XLR microphone[s] and/or electric guitar/bass and an audio interface).

Duration: 400–600 minutes, or 10–15 class periods.

Prior Knowledge and Skills: Experience using the basic features of an entry-level DAW. Understanding of song form (intro, verse, chorus, bridge, outro, etc.). Facility on some instrument (piano, guitar, bass, flute, etc.) is helpful.

Procedure:

1. Listening: Listen to commercial recordings, arranged in a variety of styles, of traditional winter/holiday music. Explain the basic premise for the project and listen to two to four exemplary projects by past students (such as Daniel I.'s setting of "Carol of the Bells," **Web Ex. 14.16**). Discuss what gives each of these arrangements its stylistic characteristics (instrumentation, rhythm section groove, changes to rhythm or meter, etc.).

2. Search for source tune: Give students access to a variety of source tunes to preview via websites that host free holiday/winter "sheet music" (PDF files), lyrics sheets with chords, and MIDI files.[13] Other sources for tunes include church hymnals, guitar and piano books, and guitar tablature music. Students may work with their source tune in whatever mode of notation they are most comfortable. If you or students are unsure whether a song is in the public domain, consult an Internet public domain song search site such as www.pdinfo.com.

3. Audition and select source tune: The process of "auditioning" a possible source tune to use will be different for each student. Some will acquire sheet music, or a lyrics/chord sheet, or guitar tablature, and then begin improvising with the tune on the instrument with which they are most comfortable (keyboard, guitar, etc.). Others will open a

---

13. Examples of websites that host free holiday/winter music include www.classicalmidiconnection.com, www.christmas-carol-music.org, and www.hymnsandcarolsofchristmas.com.

MIDI file in MMP software (similar to the "New Clothes for an Old Tune" project) and begin experimenting with different loops and instrument sound assignments. Even these should try to locate a lyrics/chord sheet or a "lead sheet" (with melody and chords) for ideas about how the tune might be harmonized. Through improvisation, students may discover new ways to harmonize their tune. The goal of this stage is to develop a *rhythmic and/or harmonic groove* that works well with the source tune and which will drive the arrangement. A good way to convey the idea of marrying a source tune with a groove is to demonstrate how a common tune such as "Jingle Bells" (or "Silent Night," "Good King Wenceslas," etc.) can be arranged in various musical styles. Students should select their source tune by a specified deadline.

4. Decide performing forces: An important part of music production is finding the right artists. In any given elective music class you may have students who feel comfortable playing or singing—reading conventional notation, chord symbols, or performing "by ear"—instruments such as keyboard, guitar, bass, various wind instruments, drums and other percussion, and voice. Students may work alone on this project, but should be encouraged to collaborate, especially where they need help. For example, one student might employ several tracks of drum loops, play the melody for his tune on keyboard himself in another track, ask a classmate to strum accompanying guitar chords in another track, and program (sequence) a bassline in another track. There are many possibilities and combinations, including exporting as a MIDI file accompaniment parts for combo instruments generated by intelligent accompaniment software such as Band-in-a-Box.

5. Thinking about the arrangement: Based on the experimenting and improvising done thus far with the tune and a groove, have students set up tracks in the MMP software for the instruments they plan—at least initially—to use. Those that feel comfortable with written music may want to develop a "lead sheet" or even a simple score. Those that just want chord changes over lyrics may use that, adding notes about formal sections. Others will work exclusively in the software, playing or programming notes, but not worrying about notation. A chord sheet, tablature, or conventionally notated part, however, may need to be developed for a classmate that will play a part. In this case, the collaborating student or a teacher may need to lend a hand.

Coach/discuss ideas for song form that lend themselves to the tune and the style/groove each student is using. Students should have an initial plan. For example, a student chooses the tune "Angels We Have Heard On High" and notices that there are basically two sections to the song: the verse ("Angels we have heard on high . . .") and the chorus ("Glo-ria, in excelsis deo . . ."). She decides to use some drums and

210

background chords (her groove) for a brief introduction, followed by the verse and the chorus. After the chorus, she decides to use the introduction material as an interlude, followed by another verse and chorus. After this second chorus, she decides to repeat the chorus one more time and then return to the introduction material, this time as the outro.

Remember, formal articulations (the beginnings of new sections) are great times to change texture by adding or subtracting instruments (layering). As per the 100% rule, sometimes "less is more." Encourage students to consider using very transparent texture at times and then building from there. Once the texture is built up to very full, consider having the "floor drop out" by cutting back to very little (for example, just drums).

6. Filling in the arrangement: Adding music to some tracks of the arrangement will be as simple as inserting loops. Other tracks may be MIDI or audio recordings done in real time, as well as MIDI programming (step recording). Here are some tips for recording.

   a. Real-time MIDI recording: Record-enable a track, click the "record" button, and use a MIDI keyboard (synth or controller) to record the notes desired. The program's tempo slider can be set to a much slower speed while recording and then increased later. One very important suggestion is to always real-time record along with a drum loop (not just the metronome "click"). This "temp track" will keep the timing true and help prevent rhythmic "tears" (phasing); the temp rhythm track can be deleted later if desired.

   b. Real-time audio recording: Students more comfortable expressing themselves with a live instrument or voice can record into tracks via a USB microphone or an XLR microphone or electronic instrument (such as guitar or bass) routed through an audio interface. I recommend that students record to a drum loop to keep the timing true. When using a microphone, be sure students monitor all accompanying tracks with headphones as they play/sing.

   c. Step recording:[14] Parts for which a student cannot find a performer can be programmed note by note. Most DAW software allows the user to draw or paint notes into a graphic editor view with a pencil tool or something similar. If the student is already familiar with entering notes in another MIDI application (such as Finale, Sibelius,

211

14. *Step recording* is the process of programming performance data (notes, rhythms) into a MIDI program one event at a time, without a click track or other means of maintaining a steady beat. Normally, the user would choose a rhythm from a palette or keyboard shortcut (the number 4 equals a quarter note, etc.) and the note(s) from a MIDI keyboard or by clicking them in with a mouse on a staff (notation software) or graphic editor (sequencing software). Once step recorded, the music can be played back in real time to sound as if a live player had performed it.

or Noteflight), the student could use that program to enter the notes, export it as a MIDI file, then import the MIDI file into the DAW.

7. (Optional) Replace synth tracks with live players: If students have the time and a willing player, some of the synthesized or looped tracks may be replaced by recording live players. Nonetheless, the initially synthesized tracks serve as a great temp track to give the live performer some idea of what is required. I have seen many an arrangement transform from sterile to inspired by adding a live player in place of a synthesized temp track. For example, a student with some keyboard facility plays in a simple accompaniment track, consisting of mostly quarter notes. Later a classmate uses a chord change sheet and records the part with more idiomatic, pop keyboard gestures. On the other hand, sometimes a temp track turns out to be far better than a live player. Often this is the case with drum loops versus recording a live drum kit (due to the difficulty in recording an acoustic drum kit).

8. Coaching/feedback: From time to time, have students play their works-in-progress for one another in class. Provide coaching and have students offer feedback, criticism, and suggestions. Sometimes hearing the cool things that others are doing motivates students who have been underperforming to "step up." Help each student make a "task checklist" of items you and they have identified as needing to be accomplished (see sidebar, "Sample Task Checklist"). Use this list to shepherd them forward.

Sample Task Checklist

The following are selected examples of items that might appear on a "task checklist" for student's works-in-progress:

Liam (song: "O Christmas Tree")

- Add string background parts to last chorus of "O Tannenbaum."
- Develop a lead sheet for sax solo, indicating where player plays.
- Book tracking session with sax soloist.
- Dr. W. would like to review your piano part.

Sam (song: original Hanukkah song)

- Type out lyrics and have your rabbi review them. Mention your idea of including sung/rapped Hebrew prayer. Get his okay.
- Consider adding a "bridge" (contrasting material that takes us back to main theme).
- Record vocals.

Steve (song: "Deck the Halls")

- Record keyboard part (slash/chord changes) to click track or drum loops.
- Remove current drum loops and replace with other loop(s) or programmed drum parts.
- Record live guitar and bass.
- Record MIDI "B3" organ.

Kevin (song: "Hark the Herald Angels Sing")

- Finish brass arrangement in Finale, show to Dr. W.
- Find agreeable, talented brass players. Extract parts (trumpet 1, trumpet 2, etc.) for them to practice.
- Book tracking session to record brass.

Taylor (song: "Silent Night")

- Finish bassline and drum tracks.
- Record (real) or program (MIDI) other instruments.
- Get help from Dr. W. with writing horn parts.
- Record real horns (if enough lead time) or MIDI (if last minute).

Nich (song: "Hark the Herald Angels Sing")

- Spend time with guitar learning melody from manuscript; decide chord changes you will use.
- Create drum track with loops to use as temp track for timing.
- Record chord changes in with actual guitar (mic and interface).
- Add MIDI bass track.
- Record melody track over drums/chord changes.
- Add intro and/or outro, and perhaps a guitar solo.

Lisa (song: original ballad)

- Decide who your vocalist will be.
- Rerecord sloppy keyboard parts.
- Write string parts. Record string "temp track" using softsynths. Once you have recorded "live" strings, decide if you want to omit the synth strings, or perhaps mix them in.
- Consider writing/improvising background vocals parts if time.

Chris (song: "O Holy Night")

- Record live guitar using microphone/interface.
- Double-check guitar harmonization throughout; some chords sound wrong.

213

- Live flute for intro and interludes?
- Add background string parts?
- Schedule vocal recording session for yourself.

Katie (song: "God Bless Ye Merry Gentlemen")

- Check levels for distortion and dropout.
- Consider adding tag ending to soften blow of song ending suddenly.
- Rerecord section with timing problems (phasing with drum loops).
  . . . did you record this against a loop, or alone?

9. When song arrangements are finished, students should export their music as a stereo audio file (sometimes called "bounce to disk") to burn onto a class "holiday CD."

Adaptations: This project, more than perhaps any other in this book, calls for flexibility and adaptation with the varied talents and strengths of a class. Some will be eager to arrange music, some love to jam and play, some love configuring microphones and setting levels, others can make up beautiful vocal harmonies on the fly, some want to write thoughtful lyrics, others have a gift for finding chords that fit, and still others enjoy finding unique DSP effects to spice up the sound of a track. Students may work alone or in groups on this project. Most likely, some students will participate in several projects due to their particular talents. This project can be carried out by individual students using computer music workstations in a music technology lab, or by groups of students taking turns using the resources of even a small school recording studio.

Some stronger students may express a desire to write and produce their own winter/holiday song. This is a judgment call best made by the teacher, who will know if the student has what it takes to pull this off. For the few (if any) students who pursue this, I recommend the following:

1. Search for good lyrics to use while other students are searching for a source tune. Lyrics may be from an existing poem, hymn, Christmas carol, and so on, or newly created by a peer. Good lyrics can elevate the music; bad ones can sink a song. The best student lyrics I have come across are on topics about which the students had a heart-felt interest. I require students to have original lyrics approved by me if they want to go this route.

2. Experiment with ways to set the lyrics while other students experiment and improvise with potential source tunes. A student that wants

WINTER/HOLIDAY TUNE SETTING

Name: _____

Tune: _____

Element	Considerations/Comments	Score
Length [20]	0:00–0:59 [0–12] 1:00–1:15 [13–14] 1:16–1:30 [15–16] 1:31–1:45 [17–18] 1:46–2:00 [19–20]	
Depth of Production [30]	Number of tracks, layers, independent parts. 7 or more parts [25–30] 5 parts [18–25] 4 parts [11–18] 1–3 parts [0–10]	
Arrangement [50]	Well thought-out form/structure, use of layering and "100% Rule" Deployment of form shows artistry/creativity [45–50] Clear, effective form [40–44] Some evidence of formal thought [35–39] Lacks coherent form [30–34] No effort at establishing form [0–29]	
Production Creativity [30]	This is subjective (welcome to the arts!) but depends on your ability to convey your "take" on the tune in a compelling way.	
Production Quality [50]	Clear/strong signals, mix levels appropriate, DSP processing adds to arrangement, clean transitions, absence of distortion.	
Music Deadline [20]	On time [20] Day late [15] Two days late [10] Three days late [5] Forget about it! [0]	
Total [200]		

Comments:

▶ **FIG. 14.5**
Grading rubric for use with the "Winter/ Holiday Tune Setting" project. Created by Scott Watson.

to write an original song should be able to explore ideas by improvising with guitar or keyboard. Students choosing this path will need some time to merge lyrics with music but are likely to require additional time out of school as well.

Excellent examples of *original* student winter/holiday songs include Sam P.'s "This CD Needed a Hanukkah Song" mentioned in chapter 5 (see **Web Ex. 5.3**) and Katie S.'s "Christmas Is So Much More" in which the songwriter reflects thoughtfully on all the peripheral, unimportant things that are unfortunately emphasized during the holidays. The lyrics and music to Katie's song are quite well done; I hope you will check out her recording at the companion website (**Web Ex. 14.17**).

Another student, Rich L., took an altogether unique approach to this project by writing original blues music as underscoring to the seasonal Clement Moore poem "'Twas the Night Before Christmas." Rich is a fine blues guitarist, and his playing on the track adds so much. He initially recorded himself as the narrator, but after receiving feedback from the class he recruited an English teacher, Timothy Schwarz, to read. Listen to Rich's track at the companion website (**Web Ex. 14.18**) and you will hear how perfect a choice Mr. Schwarz turned out to be.

216

Evaluation: Use a rubric like the one shown in **Fig. 14.5,** posted for download at the companion website (**Web Ex. 14.19**).

Extensions/Follow-up: Share the finished holiday CD by setting aside a period (or other time) for a "release" or "launch" party. At this event, students introduce their tracks before they are played. If possible, have live (perhaps "unplugged") performances. Consider inviting guests (administrators, other faculty and students, parents, local press, etc.) and having students, parents, or a club prepare special food to make the event really special!

National Standards Addressed: Each of the following standards is addressed to some degree in this lesson:

- **Standard 1** (optional), Singing, alone and with others, a varied repertoire of music.
- **Standard 2,** Performing on instruments, alone and with others, a varied repertoire of music.
- **Standard 3,** Improvising melodies, harmonies, and accompaniments.
- **Standard 4,** Composing and arranging music within specified guidelines.
- **Standard 5,** Reading and notating music.
- **Standard 6,** Listening to, analyzing, and describing music.
- **Standard 7,** Evaluating music and music performances.
- **Standard 8,** Understanding relationships between music, the other arts, and disciplines outside the arts.
- **Standard 9** (optional), Understanding music in relation to history and culture.

LESSON TITLE: SCORING A VIDEO

Audience: Grades 6–12, general and elective music classes.

Objective: Gain an understanding of the relationship between visual and musical expression by creating a musical score for a brief video.

Materials/Equipment: Any MMP program, such as GarageBand, that allows for syncing to digital video. Students will also need one or more brief digital videos that have no existing musical score (or from which the soundtrack has been removed). Scenes from older cartoons and silent films work well for this project, as do older commercials. Such digital video can be downloaded free at websites such as the Internet Archive (www.archive.org). To create a brief excerpt of a longer video, use software such as QuickTime Pro. I have found 30 seconds to be a good length for this type of activity. Place the video(s) to be used in a folder on a hard drive students can access, or post (or link) to an Internet wiki, blog, or website.

Duration: 200–280 minutes (or about five to seven class periods).

Prior Knowledge and Skills: Students should have a working knowledge of basic features of MMP software.

Procedure:

1. Acquire video: Older students may search for video online, or even create their own digital video.[15] I recommend a limited number of videos from which to choose be supplied to younger students. Students copy the video to be used to their computer hard drive.

2. Import the video: With some DAW software, videos can be imported into a video track alongside of (concurrent with) audio and MIDI tracks. Other DAW software opens the video in a separate, but synced, video window. In either case, the video runs in tandem as the multi-track file plays.

3. Spot the video and add markers: Have students view the video, noting key visual events. Do one of the following to keep track of visual "cues":
   a. Many DAW programs allow the user to add labels (sometimes called "markers" or "bookmarks") in the timeline. Use these to indicate visual events that may influence the musical score ("start of scene," boy starts running," "rocket launches," etc.).
   b. Create a separate "cue sheet" with entries that provide a brief label for the event. Consider creating a blank cue sheet ahead of time for students to use.

15. As evidenced by the numerous videos posted to YouTube, many high-school-age students are familiar with the procedure for creating their own digital movies. This involves shooting the movie with a digital video camera (with built-in mic). The video can then be transferred to a computer, then possibly edited and saved in various formats (MPEG, QuickTime, etc.) using a digital movie application such as iMovie or Movie Maker.

218

Also, discuss musical characteristics suggested by the tone and pacing of the scene. What tempo would make sense? Can one tempo work throughout, or is a tempo change suggested? What style or mood of music would work well?

4. Audition and then select a key loop: After students consider the character of the music they would like to create for their score, have them audition loops from those available for a specified amount of time. They should select one *key loop* that most represents the character they want for their score. Add that loop to a track and replicate (loop) as many times as they like.

5. Create other score elements: Building on the key loop, and being mindful of the markers ("cues") already indicated, students should add other musical content. The following are experience-appropriate suggestions.

    a. Loops: Students with limited experience can simply add more loops to create thicker textures, and/or different loops to change the mood/character.

    b. Background elements: Students with somewhat more musical experience may employ simple musical gestures such as pedal point "drones" and/or simple chord progressions that vamp (repeat). The purpose of a musical score is to support the video, not steal attention from it, so uncomplicated background elements such as these are entirely appropriate.

    c. Themes: Students with more sophisticated musical experience may write one or more *themes*—brief melodic gestures, or structured melodies—to go with visual activity. Themes may be monophonic, or accompanied by loops and/or recorded material.

    Student composers may use a combination of all three of these methods. Regardless, students should try to align musical events (formal articulations, dynamic climaxes, notable changes in texture or tempo, etc.) with the cue markers. Students will need to set track volume levels, or use the program's mixer window, to create a good mix.

6. Peer feedback: Give students the opportunity to react to each other's works-in-progress, making observations about the appropriateness and effectiveness of the music added to the videos, and sharing compliments and suggestions. Allow time for students to make adjustments based on peer feedback.

7. Export: Export the video and all tracks to a single multimedia file. Some DAW programs do not allow the video and audio to be merged, but rather combine all the audio tracks into a single, stereo audio file (such as MP3) in a process called by various programs "share," "export," "bounce to disk," or "mixdown." This mixdown of the score may be merged with the video using digital movie software.

Adaptations: If your school does not have DAW software that allows for syncing to digital video, the project can still be accomplished by creating a timeline ("cue sheet") for the video (including timings for key events) and producing music using those time parameters. The video and created scores can be combined using presentation software (such as PowerPoint) or entry-level movie software (iMovie, Movie Maker, etc.).

If each student (or group) is scoring the same video, consider "spotting" the video together as a class. The teacher can project the video to a large screen as students (or groups) complete a cue sheet. The class can discuss ideas for the score before setting about creating it individually (or in groups).

Right now, web applications are emerging that allow for multitrack recording and may be adapted for a project such as this. Those I have used allow for audio recording, uploading of audio files, and looping.[16] All of these elements can be used to produce a multitrack score that supports a video (using a separate "cue sheet"). The score can be "mixed down" to a single audio file (such as MP3) and then combined with the video using movie software.

Feedback/Evaluation: Formal evaluation of student's video scoring should take into consideration the following.

1. Timing: Specify the length of music (and other sound elements) students need to produce and award credit based on the percentage of this goal students achieve.

2. Texture/depth of production: Provide a baseline number of tracks, or a range thereof, for scores created for videos. Specify how many tracks may be used for loops, sound effects, imported MIDI files, real-time recorded MIDI data, audio samples, audio recordings, and so on. Considering that it is easy to use several tracks of loops, I suggest requiring at least four tracks. Award credit based on meeting your criteria for the type and number of tracks.

3. Creativity/appropriateness: Award credit for creating a score that supports, or even heightens, the video. How well does their scoring suit the video? How interesting is it to watch and listen to (do we laugh, say "wow!," or just yawn)? Award a small percentage of the grade for this artistic element.

Extensions/Follow-up: Post projects using nonprotected video on the Internet to a course wiki or video hosting site.[17]

National Standards Addressed: Each of the following standards is addressed to some degree in this lesson:

---

16. For example, the web application Myna, by Aviary (aviary.com).

17. YouTube.com and TeacherTube.com, for instance. Check to be sure you are in compliance with your school district's Internet policy.

- **Standard 1** (optional), Singing, alone and with others, a varied repertoire of music.
- **Standard 2** (optional), Performing on instruments, alone and with others, a varied repertoire of music.
- **Standard 3,** Improvising melodies, harmonies, and accompaniments.
- **Standard 4,** Composing and arranging music within specified guidelines.
- **Standard 5** (optional), Reading and notating music.
- **Standard 6,** Listening to, analyzing, and describing music.
- **Standard 7,** Evaluating music and music performances.
- **Standard 8,** Understanding relationships between music, the other arts, and disciplines outside the arts.

LESSON TITLE: GARAGEBAND KEY SOUNDS

Audience: Grades 6–12, general and elective music classes.

Objective: Students will learn how to store recorded sounds in GarageBand, to be triggered by keys on the QWERTY keyboard. Using these sounds, students will create a pop-style drum beat.

Materials/Equipment: GarageBand, the computer's QWERTY keyboard, and a microphone (built-in mic, USB microphone, etc.).

Duration: This lesson should take between 40 and 80 minutes (or about one to two class periods).

Prior Knowledge and Skills: Students should have some familiarity setting up audio ("real") and software instrument ("synth") tracks in GarageBand and with recording using a microphone.

Procedure:

1. Create a new GarageBand document with one "synth" instrument track and one "real" audio track. Set the synth track to one of the sound effects (SFX) "instruments" ("Comedy Noises," "Radio Sounds," etc.). Configure the real (audio) track to use the microphone you will use.

2. Record a short, percussive sound into the real track. I recommend things like a hand clap, a vocal exclamation (such as "Doh!"), clapping two textbooks together, or stomping feet.

3. Select the synth (sound effect) track. Open the Musical Typing window (Window menu → Musical Typing)—an emulation of the computer's QWERTY keyboard—and click on the "Details" tab to reveal which sounds are assigned to each QWERTY key (**Fig. 14.6**). As an option, in the Musical Typing window you may want to click the "Octave +" key (the letter "x") to move the range of the keyboard up an octave to "empty" keys. This way, none of the current sound assignments will be changed.

4. Now drag the region containing the recorded sound from the audio track and drop it onto one of the keys on the Musical Typing keyboard. This will store the sound there, to be triggered by the chosen key. Press the key to confirm the sound is there.

5. Using the procedure described above, give students time to store two or three sounds to be triggered by keys of the Musical Typing keyboard.

6. Students should next create a pop-style beat pattern using the sounds they have created and stored. When they have refined their beat pattern, they can record it to the synth (sound effects) track.

7. Finally, have students share their pop-style beat pattern with one another.

221

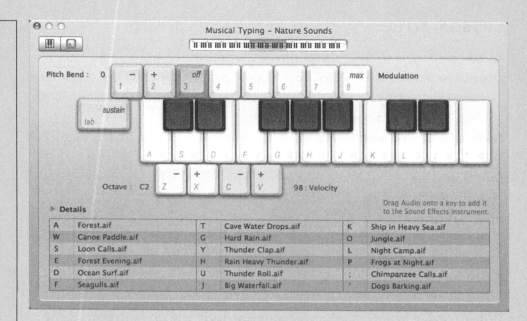

▶ **FIG. 14.6**
GarageBand's Musical Typing window can be used to assign various sounds to the computer's QWERTY keys. Created by Scott Watson.

Adaptations: If needed, two or three students can share a workstation, each participating in the recording and storing of sounds, and each "playing" a QWERTY key to trigger these sounds in a collaborative effort.

Feedback/Evaluation: Select students to share critical reactions to the beat patterns as they are performed in class. Award participation credit to students for successfully recording two or three sounds and arranging them into a pop-style beat pattern.

Extensions/Follow-up: When you note that any of the hundreds of existing GarageBand loops or sound effects can be loaded onto the Musical Typing keyboard in the manner shown above, the uses for the skill presented in this lesson activity are many. Custom loaded loops and sound effects could be triggered to score a poem or story.

Imagine a collaborative activity in which an entire class chooses various loops and sounds to be loaded onto laptops. Groups of students working together could form "laptop ensembles" with one loading/triggering percussion loops, another synth loops, another bass loops, and another keyboard or guitar loops. The laptop's built-in speakers are loud enough for a small group to interact, but routing the sound output through a lab controller system (such as Korg GEC) or multichannel mixer offers more possibilities.

National Standards Addressed: Each of the following standards is addressed to some degree in this lesson:

- **Standard 1** (optional), Singing, alone and with others, a varied repertoire of music.
- **Standard 2,** Performing on instruments, alone and with others, a varied repertoire of music.

- **Standard 3** (optional), Improvising melodies, harmonies, and accompaniments.
- **Standard 4** (optional), Composing and arranging music within specified guidelines.

223

REFLECTION ACTIVITY

MMP software can do so many things! With the addition of common peripherals such as microphones and audio interfaces, you have some powerful tools for carrying out creative projects with students. The lessons in this chapter, while varied, only begin to scratch the surface of what is possible. Consider how MMP (or DAW) software might be put to use by you and your students in creative projects in your teaching assignment.

1. In-service teachers: Describe a lesson/project presented in this chapter that you think would work well in your teaching assignment. Alternatively, describe a lesson/activity you already do that incorporates ideas presented in this chapter.

2. Preservice teachers: Describe how you could use or adapt a lesson/project idea presented in this chapter in the type of music teaching assignment you hope to do.

3. Describe a lesson/project idea not in this chapter but that comes to mind after examining the ideas presented in this chapter. How might the Eight Principles for Unlocking Musical Creativity enhance the activity? Which of the MENC National Standards for Music Education would be addressed?

CHAPTER 15
CREATIVITY WITH COMPUTER MUSIC NOTATION APPLICATIONS

A POWERFUL TOOL FOR MUSIC EDUCATION

COMPUTER MUSIC NOTATION (CMN) APPLICATIONS are often the first and most used area of music technology by music educators, perhaps because they can do so much for them and their students. Music notation software (such as Finale and Sibelius) and web applications (such as Noteflight) are invaluable tools in this digital age, not only for composing and arranging but also for myriad other tasks such as creating worksheets, drill and exercise sheets, warm-ups, tests and quizzes, musical figures (for use in print and multimedia presentations), playing MIDI files, creating MIDI files to export and use with other applications, creating rehearsal and/or performance accompaniment tracks, and much more. For this reason, I frequently share in the university courses I teach and in the workshops I present that if you only have time to learn to use one technology tool, you will get the most from your investment by choosing music notation software.

Learning Basic and Continuing CMN Skills

Today CMN applications are necessary for undergraduate and graduate music study and are either necessary or very useful in K–12 music teaching. As a result, I have observed each year that more and more university music students and in-service music teachers have a working knowledge of some CMN application. A basic skill set for a CMN application includes tasks such as

1. setting up a score (number of staves, instruments used, key and time signature, etc.)
2. entering and editing notes (using both QWERTY and MIDI keyboard input)
3. adding score expressions (tempo and dynamic markings, indications for technique, etc.) and articulations
4. adding text elements (title, composer and/or arranger, page numbers, etc.)

5. basic score layout (number of measures-per-system, distance between staves in a system, distance between systems, etc.)
6. changing key and time signature

A second tier of CMN tasks useful for music educators, not hard to learn as needed, includes things such as

1. layering two independent parts on a single staff (for instance, soprano/alto in a vocal score or trumpet 1/trumpet 2 in an instrumental score)
2. entering lyrics for vocal scores
3. adding lead sheet style chord symbols and guitar fretboards
4. effecting a scheme for numbering measures (shown at the start of each system, every measure, rehearsal numbers at formal articulations, etc.)
5. formatting and extracting parts from a score
6. making playback more realistic (tempo, dynamics, and articulation indications "performed," use of quality software instruments, etc.)
7. exporting music created with CMN software as a graphic image (to use in a word processing document, multimedia slide show, web page, etc.)

In some cases, pre- and in-service music educators are learning these CMN features as part of a required or elective course. In other cases, especially for younger, tech-savvy individuals, these skills are learned informally, self-taught or picked up piecemeal from instructors or friends.

Indeed, I have found that high school students with some music experience (band, chorus, orchestra, guitar or piano lessons, etc.)—when sufficiently motivated—can figure out all of the features listed in the first tier above. By "sufficiently motivated," I mean that they have an intrinsic desire to accomplish a CMN task. With a bare minimum of formal instruction on using Finale and Noteflight, my elective music students routinely figure out how to create lead sheets and small scores (piano, solo instrument and piano, SATB chorus, SATB chorus and piano, etc.) on their own. And that brings us back to the topic of musical creativity. This chapter, setting aside many of the great ways CMN applications can serve in music education, focuses on using these tools to foster and realize student creativity.

A SEQUENCE FOR INTRODUCING CMN APPLICATIONS WITH STUDENTS

At first blush, it might seem as if CMN applications might be profitable only for working with students that already have a good grasp of the conventions of traditional written music notation. Instead, I encourage you to think of them as tools to develop an understanding of how music works—even for very inexperienced students. Imagine an analogous scenario in instrumental music. In most cases when fourth or fifth graders begin music instruction in the school band program, they have no experience with music notation, producing a characteristic tone, or the fingerings for the dozens of possible notes. Yet, one note at a time, via explanations, demonstrations, rote experience, trial-and-error, and repetition (practice), the students learn many things about how their instruments, and music in general, work.

This practical, applied style of learning offers an excellent model for working with students using CMN applications. Michele Kaschub and Janice Smith do warn that it is "important not to push the use of standard notation too soon, but to concentrate on the sounds and add the use of written notation as another tool." They recommend that the "sounds and the techniques of organizing sounds should precede any work on the means of preserving sounds."[1] Concurrently, these elementary-age students are learning to read and perform from traditional music notation in general classes and possibly instrumental lessons. First attempts at documenting creative efforts might involve invented notation systems or some hybrid form of traditional notation done in the student's own hand. The latter could involve writing note letter names or drawing simple noteheads on a staff, in melodic order; rhythm is left to the student's memory. Progressing to the next stage, students could first use pencil and manuscript paper,[2] and then CMN software, to notate existing familiar melodies (such as "Frère Jacques" or Beethoven's "Ode to Joy") as a means of reinforcing their understanding of music reading and performance skills. The move from handwritten manuscript to music typeset with CMN software does not need to take long; it could happen in the same activity or unit. Shortly after that, the CMN application students have used to document the music of others can be used to record their own musical expression.

BENEFITS OF CMN APPLICATIONS FOR CREATIVE WORK

Below are several aspects of working with CMN applications that make them ideal for unlocking the musical creativity of students in music classes. Note how each involves an advantage CMN applications have over handwritten traditional notation.

CMN Applications Eliminate Distracting Chores

When you write music by hand, with a pencil on manuscript paper, many peripheral tasks threaten to sidetrack the creative process for students: setting

---

1. Kaschub and Smith, *Minds on Music*, 165–166. CMN software is a "means of preserving sounds."

2. I agree with Kaschub and Smith that writing music by hand is a valuable precursor to typesetting music with CMN software.

up staves with clefs, and time and key signatures; drawing in (straight) bar lines; placing correctly shaped noteheads precisely on a line or a space; making stems straight and parallel with one another; making beams straight; aligning concurrent musical events in a duet, trio, piano grand staff, or score; making sure that measures contain the number of beats allowed by the time signature; and more. CMN software, however, handles these items automatically, allowing students to turn their energy toward creative tasks defined by the teacher.

CMN Applications Allow for Immediate Aural Feedback

As mentioned in chapter 6, playback of CMN files allows students to hear the *sound* of the music they have composed or arranged. This sound-based auditioning process allows students to make a critical evaluation of their works-in-progress in a way that—for most—is more meaningful than other types of feedback (visual examination of the score, teacher comments/suggestions, etc.). As a result, students can make adjustments and revisions until the music on the page matches *the music in their imagination.*

CMN Applications Facilitate Tasks Essential to Creating

One of the most-used devices of composers of music of lasting worth is repetition. Think of the opening bars of Mozart's Symphony no. 40 in G minor, K. 550 (**Fig. 15.1**). Note how many times the opening three eighth notes are reused in some way throughout the passage. The opening three-note motive (eighth-eighth-quarter) is first repeated exactly, then with the addition of a leap (a minor sixth), making a half phrase. Next, to complete the (antecedent) phrase, Mozart descends using the three-note motive rhythm. The second (consequent)

▶ **FIG. 15.1**

A three note motive pervades the opening theme of Mozart's Symphony No. 40 in G Minor. Created by Scott Watson.

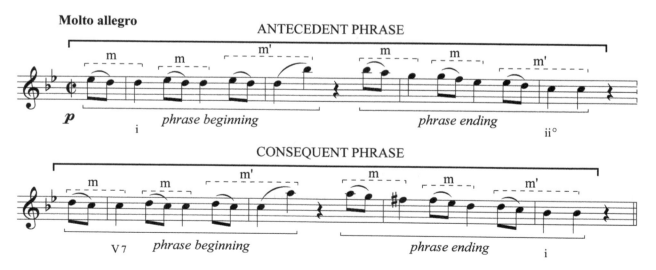

phrase is similar, only down a step.[3] We saw exactly this same economy of musical material in **Fig. 8.3,** an example from Copland's Third Symphony.

One way to ensure that students' works are musically intelligible is to stress the use of *repetition.* There is no easier way to do this than having them copy and paste a measure or phrase using CMN software. The complement of repetition is *variation*, which is also easily effected with CMN software by copying and pasting a passage and then *editing* the copy. Changing selected notes and rhythms to create a variation is a snap using the intuitive tools of today's CMN applications.

A while back I challenged students in my high school AP music theory class to enter a student choral music competition being sponsored by a professional choir in our region. One student, Ryan M., took up the challenge with an original setting of portions of Psalm 12. Ryan has had no formal piano or composition lessons but is an excellent high school baritone in the school chorus. Sketching at home and using class time for coaching and revising over the course of about a month, Ryan developed a fine composition that was selected as one of three winning works. The opening bars of Ryan's *Psalm 12* appear in **Fig. 15.2;** a recording of a longer excerpt (**Web Ex. 15.1**) can be heard at the companion website. In discussing the impact of using CMN software[4] during the composition process, Ryan pointed to the immense value of having immediate aural feedback for auditioning notes, harmonies, and so forth, and the ability to apply editing features such as copy/paste to build the form of the composition.

CMN Applications Provide a Fixed Record of a Student's Creative Work

There are several layers, if you will, to this idea. While it may be hard to quantify, anyone who has composed or arranged music knows that the hard copy printout is a beautifully affirming record of what has been achieved. It feels good to have this for one's self, or to share with others (such as parents and friends). Something more tangible is the value for assessment that the printed score brings. The idea of a "fixed record" also includes the audio realization of the work. I mentioned above the value of playback for revising and editing. Here I am referring to playback as a performance *of sorts*, though admittedly an electronic realization, that allows the creator and others to appreciate the complete musical statement.

During our school district's elementary summer band and strings camp, students have the chance to take an exploratory composing and arranging elective.

---

3. Mozart's melody, with its similar antecedent and consequent phrases, is a *parallel period.*

4. Ryan used Finale music notation software.

Psalm 12

Ryan McCarty

▶ **FIG. 15.2**

The opening measures of Ryan M.'s *Psalm 12*. Used with permission.

One of the most rewarding things about using Noteflight, a web-based music notation application, as the centerpiece of the elective is that students can go home, log on, then show and play for their parents what they have been doing. Throughout the fall I hear from parents whose children are continuing to use Noteflight to compose at home.

I like the way Matt Barr, music teacher at Kennard-Dale High School in Pennsylvania, puts it when he says that music technology such as CMN software lets students "hold onto their music" from one session to the next.

PROJECT PROFILE: ELEMENTARY BAND STUDENTS COMPOSING A MARCH

Elementary band students in the Ladue School District (St. Louis, MO) used CMN software in a year-long project to write melodies that became the basis for marches, one of which was selected to be performed in an annual spring concert. Spearheading the project was then-band director Rick Dammers. Dr. Dammers, now Assistant Professor of Music Education at Rowan University (Glassboro, NJ), provides the following account of the stages of the activity.[5]

Overview

For the last four years that I taught in the Ladue School District, we had each of the four elementary school bands embark on a project to compose their own school march.

About the Program

The Ladue Elementary Band Program began in fifth grade with 130 students from four elementary schools. Classes met twice weekly for 45 minutes in woodwind and brass class groupings.[6] The classes were team taught by myself and another band director in the district.

The project was divided into three phases:

Phase I, Foundations (Sept.–Oct.), involved learning songs by ear and creating invented notations for these songs.

Phase II, Standard Notation (Nov.–Jan.), involved students translating their invented notation to standard notation. This phase culminated in the first concert.

5. The project was related to the author by, and used with the permission of, Dr. Rick Dammers.

6. Percussion instruments were started in sixth grade in the Ladue School District.

Phase III, Melody (Feb.–May), focused on an exploration of melody. Students imitated and improvised on the I, IV and V chords as well as composing and evaluating their own melodies.

Goals

Through this project, I sought to develop the students' musical cognition by providing an opportunity for divergent musical thought and for them to develop independent musicianship. In addition to having the students experience the compositional process, I also hoped to strengthen their note reading abilities and to develop a stronger sense of tonality and phrasing. Ancillary goals included increasing student practicing by increasing their sense of ownership.

Composition Project

The project began with a group listening lesson. After announcing to the students that we were going to compose our own school march, we suggested that it might be a good idea to listen to a few marches as models. We found that the students were very engaged in these listening lessons because they had a need to figure out just what makes a march a "march." The students described the attributes of the model marches, with a particular focus on how the melodic themes defined the form, and how dynamics offered contrast between sections.

In the next lesson, we met in the lab. In some schools, the classroom teachers were kind enough to give us additional contact time with the students. In others, the lab days replaced rehearsal times. In most of the schools, these sessions took place in traditional desktop labs, but in a few schools, we utilized laptop carts.[7]

The session began with a basic introduction to using NotePad, listening and revising, and saving files. We also modeled how to set up a chord progression (the students were already familiar with I, IV, and V in the key of B-flat). This introduction was generally complete in 10 minutes. Students then began to work on creating an 8- or 12-measure melody, using whole through eighth notes in a playable range. We encouraged them to listen often and to make revisions that made sense to their ear.

Over two composing sessions, all of the students completed at least one melody, and many students completed multiple melodies. A few even

---

7. After the first year of the project, Finale NotePad was included on every elementary computer in the district, leading to even more compositional activity.

downloaded NotePad at home and emailed in additional melodies. The level of coaching and guidance varied by class and individual needs.

All of the compositions were collected (from a dropbox folder on the server) after the second session. The melodies were compiled, transposed and edited if needed for range, and distributed to the students. The students were then given a week to play the melodies at home. Next the melodies were performed in class, accompanied by a discussion of what makes a good melody. At the end of the class, students voted for their favorite four melodies. The melodies had been assigned an anonymous ID number so students would not be temped to vote for their friends' compositions regardless of merit.

From Melody to March

After the votes were tallied, the band members made suggestions for the formal construction of the piece on a "Build Your Own March" worksheet developed for the project. The directors then arranged the melodies following their suggestions, writing accompaniment parts that followed the implied harmonic content of the melodies (not always an easy task!).

Performance

The project culminated in the performance of these pieces at a year-end, all-district concert. While it was daunting to start a concert cycle thinking, "One of our pieces is not written yet," the students were enthusiastic about the project. The marches generally turned out well, plus the students practiced their marches perhaps more than "off the shelf" published music. Students presented their school's march, appreciated so much by parents and administrators, with pride and enthusiasm.

Dammers's account highlights several aspects of engaging students in a project such as this. First is the presence of collegiality and teamwork both among the elementary band directors and between them and the classroom teachers. When the entire learning community "owns" an endeavor, everything works better. Second, note how the project began with listening examples, models to imitate. Third, note that there is a good balance of parameters and freedom in the actual composition process. This keeps students moving forward with their work but allows them to be expressive without an undue, stifling concern about what is right or wrong artistically. Fourth, note the prevalence and importance of coaching throughout the project. Coaching guidance, if even only a minute or two per student, allows for differentiated instruction and makes all students' end results stronger. Fifth, note the key role that an end-of-project performance —both of each student's melody in class and of the selected melody (converted to a full band march) in a public concert—had on the entire arc of the project. I believe the knowledge of others hearing their music affects how students write. Finally, Dammers's statement that "it was daunting to start a concert cycle thinking, 'One of our pieces is not written yet'" sums up how a certain amount of risk taking accompanies doing (especially larger scale) creative projects with students. The fact that Dammers and his colleagues kept repeating this activity year after year, however, reveals the accompanying reward as well.

EXAMPLE LESSONS

On the pages that follow are several lessons that feature the use of CMN applications in composing and arranging activities. Each lesson can be accomplished with an entry-level CMN application (such as Finale NotePad or the web application Noteflight). Unless otherwise indicated, all the lessons are ones I have developed and used in my own teaching at various levels.

LESSON TITLE: MELODY JUMBLE

Grade Level: Grades 4–8, general and elective music classes.

Objective: At the conclusion of this lesson, students will copy measures of a simple melody to recreate the tune and then reorder the measures to create their own "rearrangement."

Materials/Equipment: Any CMN application (Finale NotePad, Noteflight, Finale, Sibelius, etc.). Also, prepare ahead of time a starter file with measures of a familiar tune in a "notes bank" and blank measures equal to the number of measures in the familiar tune. Copy the starter file to all student computers ahead of time. If using Noteflight, bookmark the URL to the starter file in students' web browsers, or include a hypertext link on a course web page or wiki. A sample starter file, using the tune "Frère Jacques" (**Web Ex. 15.2**), can be downloaded from the companion website.[8]

Duration: 40–80 minutes, or approximately one to two class periods.

Prior Knowledge and Skills: Some experience using basic editing features (such as copy, paste) and file playback is helpful.

Procedure:

1. Recreate: Have students copy and paste measures from the notes bank into the blank measures so that the familiar tune is recreated. In the example shown in **Fig. 15.3,** students would copy each measure exactly two times to recreate the familiar melody "Frère Jacques." Students should use the program's playback controls to audition the results until they are satisfied they have the measures in the correct order, copied the correct number of times.

2. Rearrange: Next, have students clear (erase) the measures and start all over again with a clean slate. This time, allow students to experiment with a different order for the measures of the familiar tune. Again, students should use the program's playback controls to audition the results until they find a satisfying arrangement. Suggest that students close their rearrangement with a measure that ends on the first scale degree (the syllable "Do").

3. Have selected, or all, students play back their new melody for the class.

4. Discuss with the class the use of repetition in the original tune (repeated motives, measures, phrases, etc.) and various qualities of student rearrangements they like the most.

5. (Optional) Have students perform their rearrangements on keyboard or classroom (Orff, etc.), band, or string instruments.

---

8. The sample starter file at the companion website is an XML file that can be imported into most CMN applications, including Finale, Sibelius, and Noteflight.

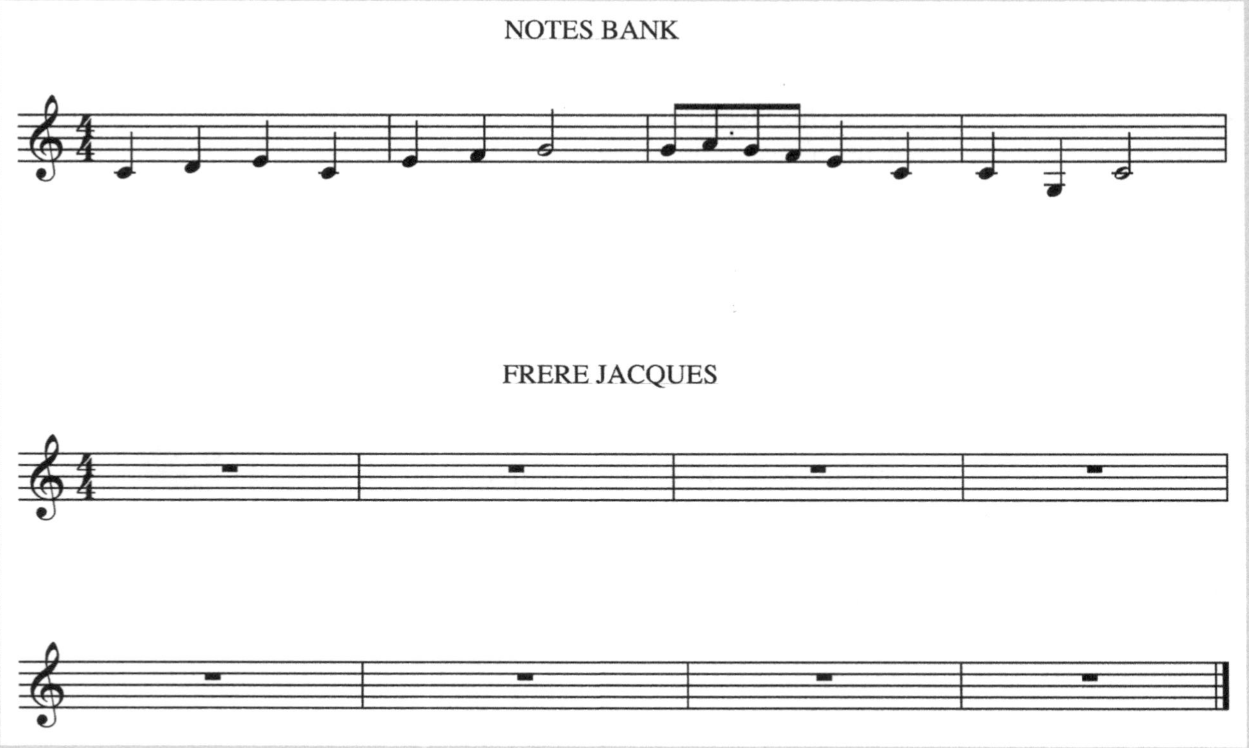

NOTES BANK

FRERE JACQUES

▶ **FIG. 15.3**

A "notes bank" with four different measures. Students copy these measures into the "empty" ones to recreate the tune, "Fréres Jacques." Created by Scott Watson.

Adaptations: In a classroom with one or two computers, consider having students—working alone or in small groups of two or three—begin with a hard copy of the starter file on which they can pencil in (by hand) the notes of the familiar tune. Students would then use a second hard copy of the starter file to experiment with rearranging measures of the tune. As all students work this way, individuals or small groups take turns entering their rearrangements into the computer(s).

This lesson works well in a general-purpose computer lab or with a laptop cart. If computers are connected to the Internet, consider using Noteflight, which allows for students to work on their rearrangements from home if desired.

Feedback/Evaluation: Award credit for correctly recreating the familiar tune, and for rearranged measures of the familiar tune in a new way, leaving none empty.

Extensions/Follow-up: Students that finish early should add dynamics, articulations, and tempo markings.

For a follow-up lesson, have students start from scratch entering the notes of the familiar tune (to provide review of note entry skills) and then make a *variation* of the melody (see the "Theme and Variation" lesson below). Some ideas for varying the tune include

1. altering the rhythm (changing some/all quarter notes to eighth note pairs, changing pairs of quarter notes into sets of dotted quarter and eighth notes, etc.)
2. altering the melodic contour (maintain the rhythm but rework the shape of the melody); inversion (reversing the melodic direction) is one example of this
3. decorating the original melody with extra notes
4. changing mode—some notation programs make it very easy to change the key to that of the parallel minor or major

National Standards Addressed: Each of the following standards is addressed to some degree in this lesson:

- **Standard 2** (optional), Performing on instruments, alone and with others, a varied repertoire of music.
- **Standard 4,** Composing and arranging music within specified guidelines.
- **Standard 5,** Reading and notating music.
- **Standard 6,** Listening to, analyzing, and describing music.
- **Standard 7,** Evaluating music and music performances.

LESSON TITLE: COMPOSING A MELODY IN PERIOD FORM

Grade Level: Grades 5–8, general and elective music classes.

Objective: Students will demonstrate their understanding of period form by composing a melody that adheres to the traits of a parallel or contrasting period.

Materials/Equipment: Any CMN application (Finale NotePad, Noteflight, Finale, Sibelius, etc.). You will also need a specially prepared demonstration file, consisting of four versions of the opening of Stephen Foster's "Camptown Races," created with CMN software (**Web Ex. 15.3,** available as an XML file[9] at the companion website). The four versions, to be used when explaining period form, are as follows:

1. Measures 1–4 of the tune, with measures 5–8 empty (**Fig. 15.4**). No formal period is apparent yet.
2. Measures 1–4 of the tune, with measures 5–8 an exact copy of measures 1–4 (**Fig. 15.5**). This creates the most literal type of parallel formal period, though the unresolved ending makes it unsatisfying.
3. Measures 1–4 of the tune, with measures 5 and 6 an exact copy of measures 1 and 2 but measures 7 and 8 altered to create a satisfying phrase ending (**Fig. 15.6**). Since the opening of each phrase is similar (in fact, identical), this creates a *parallel* period, but now with a more satisfying ending.
4. Measures 1–4 of the tune, with measures 5–8 fashioned from new, *contrasting* melodic material (**Fig. 15.7**). This creates a satisfying contrasting period.

Duration: 80–120 minutes, or approximately two to three class periods.

238

▶ **FIG. 15.4**
The first phrase (mm. 1–4) of "Camptown Races," with the second phrase incomplete. Created by Scott Watson.

9. Many CMN applications open XML files.

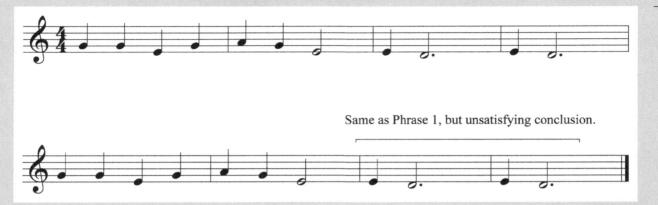

Same as Phrase 1, but unsatisfying conclusion.

Prior Knowledge and Skills: Experience using basic features of the software, including copy/paste.

Procedure:

1. Study period form: Using the prepared CMN file with four versions of Foster's "Camptown Races," preferably projected to a large screen, explain parallel and contrasting period form as changes are made to the file. Alternatively, work through the following on a whiteboard or chalkboard in front of the class.

   a. Begin with version 1 (**Fig. 15.4**), which consists of a *single phrase*.[10]

   b. Copy that phrase into measures 5–8 to create a *parallel period*. Play this for the students and discuss how/why the exact repetition is somewhat unsatisfying (**Fig. 15.5**).

   c. Now alter measures 7 and 8 so that they match **Fig. 15.6** (the way Foster actually closed the phrase). Discuss how/why this is still a *parallel period*, but yet it is more pleasing.

   d. Finally, compose new, contrasting material in measures 5–8 to create a satisfying *contrasting* period (**Fig. 15.7**).

▶ **FIG. 15.5**

A version of "Camptown Races" in which the second phrase is an exact repetition of the first, making it a *parallel period*. Created by Scott Watson.

239

▶ **FIG. 15.6**

"Camptown Races" in its normal state. The second phrase begins like the first, but departs to end differently. It is still considered a parallel period. Created by Scott Watson.

Satisfying departure from Phrase 1.

10. Use the terms "antecedent" and "consequent" phrases with older (high school) students.

Phrase 2 uses material that contrasts with Phrase 1.

▶ **FIG. 15.7**

The first phrase of "Camptown Races" (mm. 1–4) followed by a second phrase comprised of all new material. This is a *contrasting period*. Created by Scott Watson.

240

2. Score setup: Using CMN software, have students set up a single-staff score. At first, except for the most experienced students, keep this simple: use the key of C major or A (pure) minor, and use common time. If necessary, demonstrate things such as how to set up a score, basic note/rest entering, and how to make edits (delete or change notes/rests, delete measures, etc.).

3. Generate melodic motive: Give students time to improvise melodic motives using synth keyboards or to experiment and audition short melodic ideas by entering them into the CMN software, playing them back, and then revising as desired. Circulate and coach students, helping less experienced students with rhythmic or melodic notation chores. Each student (or group) should arrive at a melodic idea they like.

4. Complete phrase 1: Have students compose an opening phrase (four measures for older students, two measures for younger students) based on their melodic motive.

5. Copy into phrase 2: Understanding that phrase 2 will be largely based upon material in phrase 1, use the software's editing functions to copy/paste measures 1–4 into measures 5–8.

6. Make adjustments to phrase 2: Have students play back the newly created parallel period to decide where, if at all, they need to alter the second phrase to create a satisfying ending ("satisfying" often involves the phrase ending on the first scale degree, which is C in this key).

7. (Optional) Have students write lyrics to their parallel period melodies. Just as the first phrase is melodically related to the second phrase, insist that they recycle the opening words of phrase 1 at the start of phrase 2.

8. (Optional) Invite students who finish early to create a contrasting period by composing a new, differing melodic idea in phrase 2.

9. Perform: Have students play back (using CMN application) or sing (along with CMN playback) their parallel periods for one another, offering praise, criticism, or other appropriate reactions.

Adaptations: This lesson works well in a general-purpose computer lab or with a laptop cart. If computers are connected to the Internet, consider using Noteflight. This allows students to work on their period melodies from home if desired. Student in groups might also take turns using computers in a cluster on the periphery of a classroom or large ensemble (band, chorus, orchestra) rehearsal room. Explain the project guidelines to everyone first, as a group.

Consider doing this lesson as a complementary activity with instrumental music (band, strings) students. In this case, include a final step in which the students transpose their melody to a key that works well for each instrument if necessary. Help students check for out of range notes, making alterations where needed.

Feedback/Evaluation: Award credit for (1) creating an opening, four-measure phrase that exhibits a melodic motive and (2) creating a second, four-measure phrase that mirrors the first, and which has a satisfying ending.

Extensions/Follow-up: Consider having students create an accompaniment for their single-line, period form melodies using multitrack music production software. In the CMN software, export their melodies as MIDI files. Then, import the MIDI files into an entry-level DAW application such as GarageBand. Use loops and real-time recorded material to fashion an accompaniment.

National Standards Addressed: Each of the following standards is addressed to some degree in this lesson:

- **Standard 1** (optional), Singing, alone and with others, a varied repertoire of music.
- **Standard 2** (optional), Performing on instruments, alone and with others, a varied repertoire of music.
- **Standard 3,** Improvising melodies, harmonies, and accompaniments.
- **Standard 4,** Composing and arranging music within specified guidelines.
- **Standard 5,** Reading and notating music.
- **Standard 6,** Listening to, analyzing, and describing music.

LESSON TITLE: PEDAL POINT DUET

Grade Level: Grades 4–12, general, elective, and instrumental music classes.

Objective: Students will incorporate the idea of pedal point in an original duet composition that they or their peers can perform.

Materials/Equipment: Any CMN application (Finale NotePad, Noteflight, Finale, Sibelius, etc.). Optional: A printout showing the key signature and first note for both parts of the duet for band and string instruments. Use this with younger instrumentalists.

Duration: 90 minutes, or approximately two class periods.

Prior Knowledge and Skills: Minimal experience using basic note entry and editing features of the software is helpful; however, this project could be used to introduce these skills.

Procedure:

1. Listening: Share recordings of classical and other music that prominently features the use of pedal point. Optional: View the video *Pedal Point Duet* on the companion website (**Web Ex. 15.4**), which explains pedal point technique and outlines this duet project. Also consider sharing recordings of past students' Pedal Point Duet projects. Rebecca L.'s "A Day in the Park" (see **Fig. 5.1** and **Web Ex. 5.1**) or Noam F.'s "asdfjkl;" (see **Fig. 5.2** and **Web Ex. 5.2**)—both mentioned in chapter 5—are two examples.

2. Score setup: Each student's (or group of students') pedal point duet will be written for two of the same instrument. General/elective students may write their duet for recorder or playback by the CMN application. Instrumental students should write their duet for the instrument they play (consider using the "Starting Keys for Various Instruments" handout, **Web Ex. 15.5**). Use the CMN application to set up a duet score.

3. Composing the pedal point (lower) part: The bottom part of the pedal point duet will remain on one note—the first scale degree, or "Do"—throughout. Target length for the duet is eight measures of common time. The rhythm for this part should be based on a rhythmic motive. Have students follow these steps to compose the pedal point part:

   a. Instrumental students should only write music they can play themselves.

   b. Using clapping, improvise a one- or two-measure rhythm pattern of interest to student, and then share with the teacher. Discuss the tempo and character of this rhythmic motive.

   c. Notate this rhythm on the first scale degree in the opening measure (or two) of the bottom part of the duet. (See **Web Ex. 15.5**, the "Starting Keys for Various Instruments" handout, which shows the first scale degree for all instrument transpositions.) The teacher may need to help transcribe the rhythm. Students should add an expressive tempo indication (allegro, andante, etc.).

  d. Using the software's editing features, copy/paste the opening statement of the rhythmic motive for the remainder of the eight measures of the duet.

  e. Students who accomplish this quickly should be encouraged to look at the possibility of varying the rhythmic motive later in the duet using the software's editing and note entry features.

4. Composing the melody (top) part: The student has much more freedom in writing the top part of the duet. However, it should adhere to these basic guidelines:

  a. Instrumental students should only write music they can play themselves.

  b. Like the lower part, it should start and end on the first scale degree ("Do") but can follow any melodic contour in between. For instance, many popular songs (such as "Happy Birthday," each phrase of Beethoven's "Ode to Joy," and "Deck the Halls") exhibit an "arch" melodic contour that ascends to a high point and then proceeds down.

  c. Its rhythm should be based on, or even identical to, the rhythmic motive used in the lower part.

  d. An easy way to get started writing is to copy the bottom part into the top part and then alter the notes to create a contour.

5. Ongoing coaching: At every stage, from the score setup to creating a rhythmic motive, to composing the pedal (lower) part of the duet, to composing the melodic (top) part of the duet, you should be actively engaged in coaching students. Coaching should consist of suggesting, challenging, modeling, and questioning students to get the most out of them and move them forward in the creative process. Topics/suggestions that yield good musical decisions include the following:

  a. The eight-measure length of the project lends itself to a balanced form consisting of two, four-measure phrases (which can be broken down further into two-measure units). Examine the relationship between form and repetition.

  b. Consider the rhythm relationship between the top and lower parts. Are they going to be identical? Sometimes the same, sometimes different? If so, where would it be effective for their rhythms to be the same? Or might the lower (pedal) part always differ from the top part, but with a complementary (accompanying, interlocking, etc.) rhythm?

  c. Good writing employs repetition; use copy/paste to recycle recognizable components of the top part. Variation is easy, too; just copy/paste and then alter a musical passage.

d. Occasional rests might help the piece breathe (sometimes "less is more") or—if placed in a way that creates syncopation—create rhythmic energy.

e. Consider a back-and-forth dialog between the top part and the lower part. In this case the pedal point would be interrupted as the lower part rests.

f. If students have not used expressive elements such as dynamic and articulation indications thus far, have them apply some of each.

6. Audition and revision: Use the CMN application's playback controls to audition the duet as it develops.

7. Have general/elective students play back their duets for the class. Have instrumental students (or general students composing for recorder) print out, rehearse, and mount a performance of the duet in class or elsewhere (concert, etc.).

Adaptations: This project can be completed by students working alone, or in pairs. Students collaborating in a computer lab or cluster should have a headphone splitter so they can monitor the sound of their work-in-progress together. Students using a web CMN application such as Noteflight can set up their duet file so that each can make changes remotely from home.

Instrumental students might engage in this project during small-group lessons or even during ensemble rehearsal by rotating onto available computers equipped with headphones. This is a great "elective" activity for a summer instrumental music camp.

For the younger students with little or no CMN experience, the teacher can streamline this activity by choosing a common eight-measure pedal point part for all students to use (see **Fig. 15.8**). In this case, the project will be divided into two phases: (1) music notation activity, during which the students will learn how to set up the score and enter/edit the notes to the bottom (pedal) part, and (2) music composition activity, during which students create the top (melodic) part to the duet.

To adapt this activity for vocal students, have students write lyrics to the melody (top) part of the duet and then sing their projects.

Feedback/Evaluation: Try to find at least one point during the writing process to play back, and discuss/critique each work-in-progress. What do students find compelling and successful? What might improve the work?

If assigning a formal grade, award credit for the following elements: eight-measure (or whatever you decide) length, tempo indication at start, use of rhythmic motive in pedal (lower), lower part that remains on the first scale degree, melody (top) part that exhibits melodic contour but starts/ends on the first scale degree, and use of some dynamic and articulation markings. An example rubric for the "Pedal Point Duet" project can be downloaded at the companion website (**Web Ex. 15.6**).

244

FIG. 15.8

Template for the Pedal Point Duet. Created by Scott Watson.

Follow-up: Have students write a contrasting "B" section to their pedal point duet, in which the top part takes on the pedal point (possibly on the dominant or other scale degree) and the bottom part assumes the melody. Use da capo form to return to the opening material to close the extended duet (for example, *D.C. al fine*).

National Standards Addressed: Each of the following standards is addressed to some degree in this lesson:

- **Standard 1** (optional), Singing, alone and with others, a varied repertoire of music.
- **Standard 2,** Performing on instruments, alone and with others, a varied repertoire of music.
- **Standard 3,** Improvising melodies, harmonies, and accompaniments.
- **Standard 4,** Composing and arranging music within specified guidelines.
- **Standard 5,** Reading and notating music.
- **Standard 6,** Listening to, analyzing, and describing music.
- **Standard 7,** Evaluating music and music performances.

LESSON TITLE: THEME AND VARIATION

Grade Level: Grades 4–8, general and elective music classes.

Objective: Students will learn or review basic CMN application skills for setting up a document and entering notes/rests, and create at least one variation to a given simple melody.

Materials/Equipment: Any CMN application (Finale NotePad, Noteflight, Finale, Sibelius, etc.) and printouts of the simple, familiar tune you will use for the project. Melodies that work well for this activity include, "Frère Jacques," "Ode to Joy," "Mary Had a Little Lamb," "Old MacDonald," and "Jingle Bells" (chorus only).

Duration: 80–120 minutes, or approximately two to three class periods.

Prior Knowledge and Skills: Experience using basic features of the software, including copy/paste.

Procedure:

1. Hand out printout copies of the simple, familiar melody for use in the project. Discuss the features of the melody: How many measures? What is the key signature? What is the time signature? What kinds of note and rest rhythms do you see (quarter notes, eighth notes, half rests, etc.)? Is there any use of repetition?

2. If necessary, demonstrate how to set up a notation file (instrument choice/clef, key and time signature, etc.), basic note/rest entering, and how to make edits (delete or change notes/rests, delete measures, etc.).

3. Have students typeset the melody for themselves. This will be their "theme."

4. Discuss the idea of *variation*. Listen to an example from the literature that incorporates theme and variation such as the third movement of Mozart's Piano Sonata in D major ("Theme With Variations," K. 284), Morton Gould's "American Salute" for concert band, or Benjamin Britten's *Young Persons' Guide to the Orchestra* ("Variations and Fugue on a Theme by Purcell," op. 34). Important point: a good variation of a theme possesses both (a) enough salient traits from the original to be recognizable as that tune and (b) enough variation so that it constitutes a new version of the tune.

5. (Optional) Show students examples in which the concept of theme and variation is at work in visual art, dance (via video), architecture, or another related art.

6. Discuss ways to vary a tune, including
   a. altering the rhythm (changing some/all quarter notes to eighth note pairs, changing pairs of quarter notes into sets of dotted quarter and eighth notes, etc.)

b. altering the melodic contour (maintain the rhythm but rework the shape of the melody); inversion (reversing the melodic direction) is one example of this

c. decorate the original melody with extra notes

d. Change mode: Some notation programs make it very easy to change the key to that of the parallel minor or major.

7. Have students choose one variation technique and apply it to their tune using a CMN application, creating their own variation.

Adaptations: This lesson works well in a general-purpose computer lab or with a laptop cart. If computers are connected to the Internet, consider using Noteflight. This allows for students to work on their rearrangements from home if desired. Students in groups might also take turns using computers in a cluster on the periphery of a classroom or large ensemble (band, chorus, orchestra) rehearsal room. Explain the project guidelines to everyone first, as a group. Consider doing this lesson as a complementary activity with in-strumental music (band, strings) students as well.

Feedback/Evaluation: Award credit for successfully typesetting the sim-ple, familiar source tune, and for creating a variation that possesses both (1) enough salient traits from the original to be recognizable as that tune and (2) enough variation so that it constitutes a new version of the tune.

Extensions/Follow-up: Compile the tune and all the class variations of that tune in an order that makes dramatic sense and hold a performance in class, recital, concert, or elsewhere (software playback, recording, or live) of the entire theme with variations.

Also consider having students create an accompaniment for their single-line, melodic theme with variations. One way would be to add a piano grand staff to the score and then add a chord-based accompaniment (block chords, an "oom-pah" march pattern of left-hand bass note alternating with right hand chords, or arpeggiated "rolling" chords, etc.). Another, conceptually easier method would be to export the theme with variation as a MIDI file, import the MIDI file into a multitrack music production application such as GarageBand, and then use loops and real-time recorded material to fashion an accompaniment.

National Standards Addressed: Each of the following standards is addressed to some degree in this lesson:

- **Standard 2** (optional), Performing on instruments, alone and with others, a varied repertoire of music.
- **Standard 3** (optional), Improvising melodies, harmonies, and accom-paniments.
- **Standard 4,** Composing and arranging music within specified guide-lines.

247

- **Standard 5,** Reading and notating music.
- **Standard 6,** Listening to, analyzing, and describing music.
- **Standard 7,** Evaluating music and music performances.
- **Standard 8** (optional), Understanding relationships between music, the other arts, and disciplines outside the arts.

LESSON TITLE: FOLK SONG SETTING

Grade Level: Grades 9–12, music theory classes.

Objective: Students will demonstrate their understanding of harmonic rhythm by arranging a folk song setting for voice or melodic instrument, and piano accompaniment.

Materials/Equipment: Any CMN application (Finale NotePad, Noteflight, Finale, Sibelius, etc.). You may want to provide a list or collection of folk songs that work well for this project.

Duration: 135 minutes, or approximately three class periods.

Prior Knowledge and Skills: Experience using basic features of the software and an understanding of the concepts of implied harmony (harmonizations suggested by notes of a melody) and harmonic rhythm (the rate at which chords change).

Procedure:

1. Select source tune: Allow students time to find a folk song they find attractive for use in their setting. Many theory texts, specialized anthologies, and websites contain notation for appropriate tunes. The sidebar lists many examples of songs that work well for this project.

The following are examples of folk songs that work well for the "Folk Song Setting" activity: "Amazing Grace," "America," "Arkansas Traveler," "(The) Ash Grove," "Aura Lee," "Barbara Allen," "Battle Hymn of the Republic," "Billy Boy," "Camptown Races," "Clementine," "Danny Boy," "Dixie," "Drink to Me Only With Thine Eyes," "Greensleeves," "I've Been Workin' On the Railroad," "I Wonder As I Wander," "Long, Long Ago," "(The) Marine's Hymn," "Red River Valley," "(The) Three Ravens," "Turkey in the Straw," "Scarborough Fair," "Simple Gifts," "Streets of Laredo," "Sweet Betsey from Pike," "(The) Water Is Wide (O Waly, Waly)," "When Irish Eyes Are Smiling," "When Johnnie Comes Marching Home," "Yankee Doodle," and "(The) Yellow Rose of Texas."

Once selected, have students print out (or typeset and then print out) the tune so they have a hard copy.

2. Harmonic analysis: Considering the possible harmonies implied by the notes of the melody, have students select chords to accompany the folk song, jotting their choices onto the hard copy. Some improvisation/experimentation at the keyboard (or guitar) may be helpful here.

3. Choose an accompaniment scheme: While there are an infinite number of ways to accompany a folk song, students should choose one of the following four basic accompaniment styles for their folk song setting (**Fig. 15.9**).

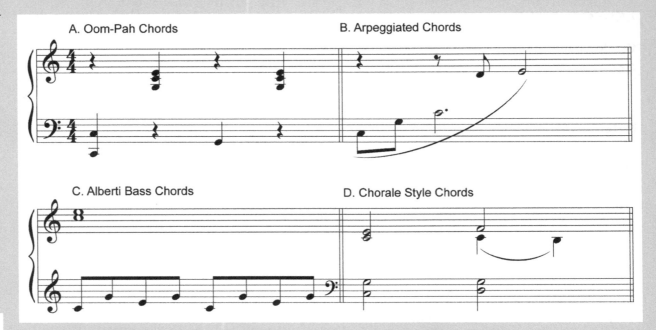

A. Oom-Pah Chords   B. Arpeggiated Chords

C. Alberti Bass Chords   D. Chorale Style Chords

▶ **FIG. 15.9**

Four accompaniment styles to use with the Folk Song Setting project. Created by Scott Watson.

a. Oom-pah chords: This is the typical background chording for a march or waltz, where a chord root (or sometimes another chord member) is played on strong beats (beats 1 and 3 in 4/4 time, beat 1 in 2/4 or 3/4 time) while full chords are played on the weak beats.

b. Arpeggiated chords: This style, in which chord tones are rolled out in a flowing manner (often in the piano left hand), is typically used in moderate to slow ballads.

c. Alberti bass chords: This is the typical Mozart-esque accompaniment created by presenting chords one note at a time with the piano left hand fingering of 1–5–3–5, 1–5–3–5, and so forth.

d. Chorale style chords: This is the homophonic texture, hymn-like, "block-chord" accompaniment in which chords share the same vertical rhythm.

Andrew K.'s setting of "I've Been Workin' on the Railroad" uses both oom-pah and chorale style chordal accompaniment to good effect (**Fig. 15.10** and **Web Ex. 15.7**).

Once an accompaniment scheme has been chosen, students should apply it to the harmonization previously fashioned, typesetting their folk song setting in a three-staff score. The top staff is for the tune, to be played or sung, and the bottom two staves (grand staff) are for the piano accompaniment. If possible, have students write the melodic part for an instrument they (or a classmate) play.

4. Revision/extension: Students may preview their work via playback and consider altering harmonies and/or employing a second accompaniment scheme if desired. Changing accompaniment styles at phrase

I've Been Working on the Railroad

Andrew K.

articulations (for instance, from arpeggiated chords to chorale style chords) can be an attractive way to achieve variety. Also, brief formal extensions such as an introduction or codetta (that is, "tag" ending) may be added easily by copying and pasting material.

▶ **FIG. 15.10**

Folk Song Setting: "I've Been Workin' On the Railroad," arranged by Andrew K. Used by permission.

All of these refinements can be facilitated with teacher coaching. It can be very helpful and rewarding to do some of this coaching on a large screen in front of the class.

5. Perform: Mount in-class performances by class members and/or guest performers (from band, orchestra, chorus, etc.) of student folk song settings. Solicit critical reactions from students regarding the effectiveness of each setting.

Adaptations: This lesson works well in a general-purpose computer lab or with a laptop cart. If computers are connected to the Internet, consider using Noteflight. This allows for students to work on stages of their setting from home.

Feedback/Evaluation: For a formal assessment, use a rubric like the one shown in **Fig. 15.11** (**Web Ex. 15.8,** available for download from the companion website).

Extensions/Follow-up: Record live performances of student folk song settings using digital audio recording software or a handheld recorder. Post recordings to a course wiki.

Folk Song Setting　　　　　　　　　Date: _____

Name: _____　　Score for Piano and: _____

Folk Song: _____

	(20 thru 16)	(15 thru 11)	(10 thru 6)	(5 thru 1)	Scores
Harmony & Harmonic Rhythm	Chords fit notes of melody	Chords fit with minor exception	Chords fit with few exceptions	Chords inconsistently follow melody	
Folk Song	At least one iteration of tune, transposed if necessary for solo instrument	Tune transcribed for solo voice or instrument, but with some error	Tune transcribed or transposed with errors	Less than one iteration of tune, or transcribed sloppily	
Effectiveness of Accompaniment	Accompaniment style(s) deployed clearly and with artistry	Accompaniment style(s) executed well	Accompaniment style(s) moderately convincing, some awkwardness	Accompaniment style(s) not clear, minimally evident	
Deductions (late, etc.)					
Total Score (60)					

Comments: _____

253

▶ **FIG. 15.11**

Sample grading rubric for the Folk Song Setting. Created by Scott Watson.

National Standards Addressed: Each of the following standards is addressed to some degree in this lesson:

- **Standard 1** (optional), Singing, alone and with others, a varied repertoire of music.
- **Standard 2** (optional), Performing on instruments, alone and with others, a varied repertoire of music.
- **Standard 3,** Improvising melodies, harmonies, and accompaniments.
- **Standard 4,** Composing and arranging music within specified guidelines.
- **Standard 5,** Reading and notating music.
- **Standard 6,** Listening to, analyzing, and describing music.
- **Standard 7,** Evaluating music and music performances.

REFLECTION ACTIVITY

When one thinks of composing and arranging, CMN software is the first kind of technology that comes to mind. After reading this chapter, consider how CMN applications might be put to use by you and students in creative projects.

1. In-service teachers: Describe a lesson/project presented in this chapter that you think would work well in your teaching assignment. Alternatively, describe a lesson/activity you already do that incorporates ideas presented in this chapter.

2. Preservice teachers: Describe how you could use or adapt a lesson/project idea presented in this chapter in the type of music teaching assignment you hope to do.

3. Describe a lesson/project idea not in this chapter but that comes to mind after examining the ideas presented. How might the Eight Principles for Unlocking Musical Creativity enhance the activity? Which of the MENC National Standards for Music Education would be addressed?

4. Do you think the clean, polished look of typeset music notation affects the way student composers and performers approach music generated with it? If so, how?

CHAPTER 16
CREATIVITY WITH INSTRUCTIONAL SOFTWARE AND OTHER MUSIC APPLICATIONS

OVERVIEW

THIS CHAPTER EXAMINES SEVERAL TYPES of music applications not covered thus far in part II of this book. Many have diverse components that can be used with music students to accomplish a variety of educational goals. While this versatility makes these applications appealing for music teachers, it certainly makes it daunting to try to categorize them. A further distinction can be made between conventional software programs that run locally on a particular computer and web applications that run in the browser of anyone with access to the Internet. I divide our examination of these varied music programs into three broad groups: (1) instructional software, (2) creativity applications, and (3) web applications. The common thread in all three groups is their potential to be used with students in producing creative musical content.

I do not attempt to provide a comprehensive catalog of useful, available music creativity applications here. Why? First, I do not want to give the impression that the approach presented in this book depends on any *particular* software (or hardware). Second, technology is changing all the time, so any listing could not help but be dated. Recently I presented on the topic of this book at a large music educator conference. During the several days of the conference I learned of two great, new programs that could be used to this end. One was a traditional computer software program, and the other a newer web application. I ended up making last-minute changes to my presentation to include them both. Literally dozens of such programs have come to my attention just during the time I have been working on this book!

INSTRUCTIONAL SOFTWARE

The main focus of music instruction software is to introduce and reinforce musical concepts using tutorials, drill and practice activities, and even fun review games. However, some instructional programs also include components that allow students to put the concepts presented to use in appealing creative activities. The following are examples of instructional software that have a creative component. My criterion for including each here, instead of in the section on creativity applications, is simply that they possess a thorough, well-thought-out sequence of instruction about music topics.

Music Ace (Harmonic Vision)

Music Ace content is divided into two main areas. In the Lessons area, an amusing, German-accented maestro leads kids through 24 sequential lessons on the fundamentals of music ("Introduction to the Staff," "Basic Rhythm Notation," etc.). In the Doodle Pad area (see **Fig. 16.1**), students can create their own music by dragging colored "note bubbles" of different widths (representing various rhythms) and colors onto a grand staff. The different colors represent available timbres (piano, oboe, marimba, trumpet, jazz guitar, and clarinet), all of which may be used polyphonically. Two sliders, one "slow/fast" and one "quiet/loud," allow students to adjust tempo and dynamics. A "Play" button allows students to audition the results. It is fun to watch the animated note bubbles actually "sing" their notes as Doodle Pad creations play back (**Web Ex. 16.1**). There are basic editing features so kids can make revisions. Songs created by students in the Doodle Pad may be saved for later use. As a bonus, a small library of mostly classical repertoire can be played back using the Doddle Pad's "Jukebox" feature.

The Doodle Pad allows younger composers to work with pitch, duration, timbre, tempo, dynamics, and more via a kid-friendly, unintimidating interface.

▶ **FIG. 16.1**

The Doodle Pad area of Music Ace, a popular music instruction program. Created by Scott Watson.

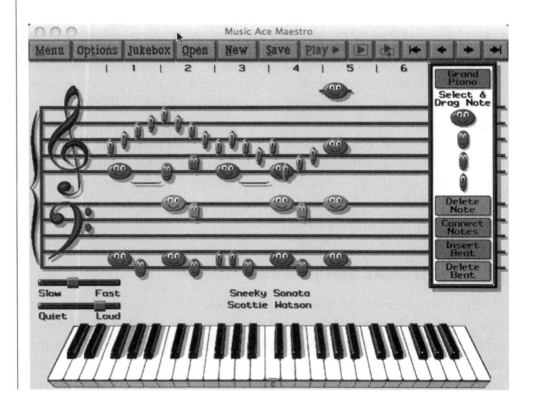

Groovy Music (Sibelius)

The Groovy Music series, described briefly in chapter 6, consists of three programs: Groovy Shapes (ages 5+), Groovy Jungle (ages 7+), and Groovy City (ages 9+). Each Groovy program is divided into two areas: Create and Explore. The fundamentals of music are presented in the Explore area of each, using increasingly more sophisticated terminology. Explore topics include such concepts as tone color, long and short (rhythm), fast and slow (tempo), loud and soft (dynamics), beat (and meter), and making melody.

The Create area works like an animated loop-based sequencer. Instead of tracks, a character walks along a path in a jungle or a street in a city. In Groovy Shapes, for instance, bright, colorful shapes that represent melodic, chord, bass, and other loops can be dragged onto the character's path. Trees (percussion loops), butterflies (melodic loops), cobwebs (chords), and insect swarms (arpeggios) replace the shapes in Groovy Jungle (see **Fig. 16.2**). These objects, regardless of the program, can be stacked vertically for higher pitch levels and more complex textures. They can be arranged and repeated horizontally to build form into a piece (**Web Ex. 16.2**). There are many other options made accessible by the attractive interface, including swapping instrument sounds for loops and using a pencil tool to create custom loops. Kids using any of the Groovy Music series will feel more like they are playing a video game than doing school work.

257

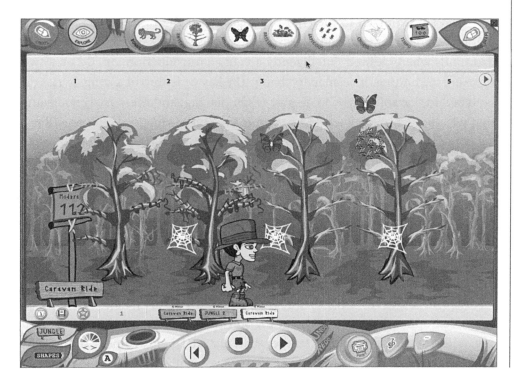

▶ **FIG. 16.2**

Groovy Jungle: trees signal rhythms, butterflies are melodic gestures, tufts of grass are bass lines, insect swarms signal arpeggios, and spider webs trigger various chords. Created by Scott Watson.

CREATIVITY APPLICATIONS

The programs in this group are primarily concerned with *creating* music. For this reason, they share certain elements with music recording and notation applications. Yet because each takes a quite unique approach to facilitating creative musical expression, it would be incorrect to lump them in with those more homogeneous, conventional categories. Each program's unique approach seems to be aimed at circumventing the traditional path to composing and arranging (which normally includes an understanding of music notation, harmony, and more) and bringing the process of musical creation within the reach of those with limited musical experience. This is the theme of removing "parameters and limitations that stifle creativity" presented in chapter 7. Generally, as a by-product of all of this, these programs are simply fun to use. The following are examples of creative applications.

Band-in-a-Box (PG Music)

Band-in-a-Box (BIAB), discussed somewhat in chapter 6, uses sophisticated programming to transform chord progressions into combo arrangements played in many styles as if by many different legendary performers. Type in a series of chords using commonly accepted nomenclature (C7, Dm, Asus, etc.), choose a style (jazz swing, bossa nova, pop ballad, etc.), hit the play button, and a small combo of piano, bass, drums, and a few other instruments plays the chords in the chosen style.

Many other refinements can be made easily. Record a melody with a MIDI keyboard and then let BIAB harmonize the notes of the melody you played. Record a solo yourself to the chord changes or let BIAB generate a solo automatically, mimicking a famous player you choose. You can ask BIAB to insert drum fills where desired, intelligently create an introduction, or add on a two-measure tag ending. It's a snap to change the key or tempo of a song. Lyrics can be typed in, karaoke-style, to display when playing, and there is even a feature that will suggest inventive titles for you to consider using for your song. Band-in-a-Box creations can be exported as MP3 files, or as MIDI files for those that want to continue working on their song in a multitrack music production environment instead.

The many uses for creative musical activities with students using BIAB should be apparent. Although the program has a notation view, most students never need to take advantage of that feature. Kids of all musical backgrounds can harmonize given melodies and develop unique arrangements, write their own 12-bar blues compositions, or fashion an accompaniment to an original rap.

Band-in-a-Box has been around for a long time, always being developed and improved upon. Recent versions of the software allow for more audio recording, and playback by sampled (rather than just MIDI) instrument sounds. The longer you use BIAB, the more neat features you will find. One of my favorites

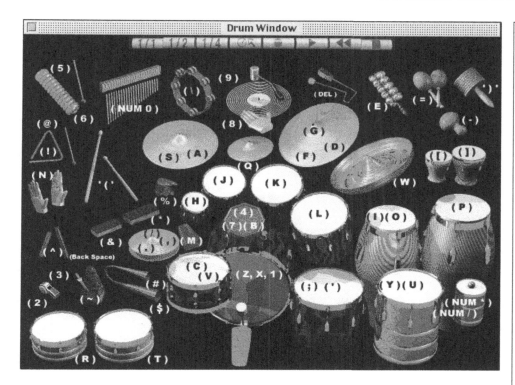

▶ **FIG. 16.3**

The percussion instruments in Band-in-a-Box's Drum Window can be triggered by the computer's QWERTY keys. Created by Scott Watson.

is the Drum Window, which allows students to see a large drum kit being played as the music plays back.[1] Students can trigger the various parts of the drum kit by pressing the corresponding QWERTY key (**Fig. 16.3**). By hitting the record button, students can record their own drum parts using this animated drum kit (**Web Ex. 16.3** is a brief movie that demonstrates recording Drum Window improvisations).

O-Generator (O-Music Ltd.)

O-Generator is built around a unique type of 16-step, circular pattern sequencer.[2] Dots trigger all sorts of percussion and tonal rhythm section instrument events (bass notes, guitar chords, etc.). Dots are arranged in four concentric rings of 16 dots each (**Fig. 16.4**). Each ring focuses on a particular category of events, selected by the user from many possibilities. The events of all four concentric rings are triggered concurrently in clockwise order when you click the play button, creating a multilayer loop pattern; one full circuit represents a measure of 4/4 time (**Web Ex. 16.4**). The tempo for the pattern can be adjusted. The volume level of each ring can be set independently as well. When users are

---

1. For details on how to open the Drum Window in BIAB, see the lesson "Band-in-a-Box Drum Window Improvisation" later in this chapter.

2. *Pattern sequencers* are programs or devices that trigger sounds in a chosen order, over and over again in a cycle. When a drum machine triggers a repeating measure with a bass drum on beats 1 and 3 and a snare drum on beats 2 and 4, it is performing a simple pattern sequence.

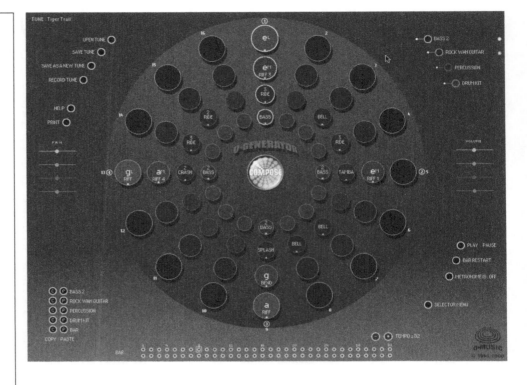

▶ **FIG. 16.4**

O-Generator's unique interface. Created by Scott Watson.

happy with one pattern, they can move on to create another in any of the 64 memory slots provided for each song file. Complex song arrangements can be fashioned by creating and selecting multiple patterns to be played back in order. These songs can be exported as audio files, to stand alone or be incorporated into other music productions (GarageBand, etc.).

Even though O-Generator limits the texture to just four types of sounds (tracks) and cannot be changed from its 16-step format (essentially 4/4 time), there are many timbre and rhythm possibilities to keep a student's aesthetic interest. O-Generator comes with an easy-to-follow on-screen tutorial ("O-Instructor Lessons") and "Teacher Lesson Guide" that makes integrating the program into a creative music course almost effortless.

Making Music and Making (More) Music (Viva Media)

As described in chapter 6, Morton Subotnik's two Making Music software programs are aimed at making the tools of composing accessible to children. Selected features of these programs, as well as Subotnik's other titles (Playing Music, World of Music Beginner, World of Music Intermediate, and Hearing Music), can be experienced for free at Subotnik's Creating Music website (creatingmusic .com).

I really love the object-oriented Musical Sketch Pad, incorporated into Subotnik's Making Music programs and on the Creating Music website. The Sketch Pad presents the tools of composition in a nontraditional, disarming way. Stu-

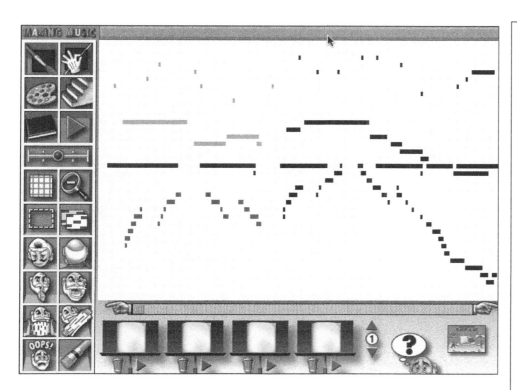

▶ **FIG. 16.5**
The Sketch Pad in Morton Subotnik's Making Music. Created by Scott Watson.

261

dents draw notes onto a canvas with a pencil tool. The vertical axis corresponds to pitch and the horizontal axis corresponds to duration/rhythm (**Fig. 16.5**). The color of the notes corresponds to one of several instruments that may be selected. A selection tool (each with a fun-looking icon) allows notes to be highlighted for a handful of compositional operations such as copy, invert, reverse (retrograde), stretch (augment), and squeeze (diminish). A play button allows students to hear what they have created. In the software version students can save their work into "sketchbooks."

Interestingly, the Sketch Pad facilitates a more linear approach to composing. It is easy to jot melodic contours, or even contrapuntal lines, using the pencil tool. Chord structures, on the other hand, require deliberate, precise gestures with the pencil tool. Because students can limit their note choice by selecting from several modes (signified by different staircase icons), melodies drawn with the pencil tool can be cohesive; drawing a countermelody does not necessarily create random dissonance. Perhaps because of this, along with the tools provided for copy, inversion, retrograde, augmentation, and diminution, I find that students using the Sketch Pad often turn out music that falls into the tradition of contemporary concert art music.

The Music Interactive (www.themusicinteractive.com)

The Music Interactive (TMI) is an exciting website for music educators. Creators Marc Jacoby and Craig Gonci have developed a bunch of graphically appealing

▶ **FIG. 16.6**

MyJamz's simple, attractive interface facilitates young music students composing melodies. Created by Scott Watson.

and educationally useful music applications. Many can be downloaded for free from the site, while a handful cost a modest fee. All are meant to be used with an interactive whiteboard and many are perfect for general classroom use.

Most programs at TMI reinforce music reading skills or focus on a specific performance skill such as tuning. However, several focus on musical creativity. The program, SOund BOard, provides an easy way to load and trigger sound events and could be used for some of the sound effect and music scoring activities described in this book. Boom is a program that allows students to create boom whacker compositions graphically. MyJamz (**Fig. 16.6**) allows youngsters to compose melodies by choosing colorful creatures (in any order or timing) representing various notes. The creatures can play back notes using a handful of available instruments. Students can experiment and practice their melodies until they have refined them; then they can press record and perform them in real time. Recorded melodies can then be played back for review. Certainly as the site continues to develop, watch for even more great budget-conscious applications.

WEB APPLICATIONS

Terms such as Web 2.0 and "cloud computing" refer to the more interactive environment we are seeing on the Internet. Web pages are no longer simply static repositories of information, but increasingly more interactive and dynamic places for contributing content and accomplishing tasks. Web 2.0 is used to describe the online applications (programs)—such as web logs (blogs), wikis, and a variety of "social networking" tools—available to anyone with access to the Internet. The Internet offers free programs for word processing, creating spreadsheets, maintaining calendars, storing and editing photos, and much more. "Cloud" is a metaphor for the Internet, both in the way that users are connected by it and in the way they are increasingly able to work above (unaware of) its technological infrastructure. In other words, whereas a decade or so ago you needed knowledge of hypertext markup language, or at least an HTML editor, to design a web page, now elementary school children can contribute to a classroom wiki with no specialized knowledge. Another characteristic of the "new" web are the many mobile devices that allow users to access and use all of this functionality. Although terms such as Web 2.0 and cloud computing, as well as specific applications such as Google Docs and Facebook, are bound to transform or fade with time, I believe it is important to note the larger trend they represent. This new paradigm of *access* and *interactivity* has significant implications for education, including music education.

As mentioned in part I, web applications are being introduced all the time for music notation, music production, and a host of other creative tasks. One of the most visible and expertly developed of these, Noteflight, is mentioned in chapter 15. Several others were briefly described in chapter 6 in a section on technology items that remove students' musical limitations.

Web applications can provide a viable alternative to software running locally on individual computers as long as they prove to maintain a stable presence online and function well on a wide variety of platforms, operating systems, and browsers. Online music applications generally do not have as many (or as advanced) features as do their conventional software counterparts, but for the price —often free—they may be the best solution for many school districts. One concern, especially for younger students, is that most of these web applications require users to register in order to use them, or at least to save one's work. Registration usually entails choosing a user name and a unique password. Younger students may not even have an email address, and if they do, teachers should obtain parental consent to allow students to register for anything online (better yet, make it an assignment for the students to register with their parents at home). One "work-around" I have used with elementary-age students is to create a single, new website registration for an entire class to use. This only works if the web application allows for multiple instances of a single user to be logged in simultaneously (which some do).

The following are examples of fun and useful web applications for musical creativity. It probably goes without saying that, due to the nature of technology and the ever-changing web, some of these web applications will disappear in time. Nonetheless, I want to provide some examples of what is available.

Noteflight (noteflight.com)

Noteflight, first introduced in 2008, has proven itself a useful, reliable web music notation application, and it is getting better all the time. An indication of the respect this web application has garnered thus far, several prominent university music programs have adopted Noteflight for use by its music majors. In fact, its user interface and basic features are simple enough for elementary school children to use almost intuitively, yet the program boasts features powerful enough for accomplishing high school and college music theory music typesetting tasks. Noteflight has been mentioned and described in this book numerous times, especially in chapter 15 (dealing with notation applications), but I list it hear to signify its importance for twenty-first century music educators.

According to their website, Noteflight "is an online music writing application that lets you create, view, print and hear music notation with professional quality, right in your web browser. Work on a score from any computer on the Internet, share it with other users, and embed it in your own pages." While the basic Noteflight program is free, there are some limitations. Noteflight Crescendo is a premium service that extends the features for a yearly subscription fee with things such as guitar and bass tab and score templates. When I tell colleagues about Noteflight and show them all it can do, the most frequent question I hear is, "How long will it continue to be free?" I have spoken with Noteflight founder and president, Joe Berkovitz, who confirms this statement from their website: "Noteflight will continue to offer a basic level of service that is free. It's a fundamental aspect of our business."

Myna (aviary.com)

This online multitrack recording and looping application was described in chapter 14. Tracks can consist of audio recorded via a built-in microphone (or other audio input configured to a computer), prerecorded (imported) audio, and loops (selected from a built-in, free loop library). Students can use normal edit functions (cut, copy, paste, etc.) and a handful of basic, useful DSP effects. Unfortunately at this time Myna does not facilitate MIDI recording. Even still, all of the lessons described in chapter 12 could be accomplished using Myna.

The collaborative and cost-saving benefits of web-based music production applications are very exciting. However, without a very fast, broadband Internet connection, users will experience Internet audio processing delays that can frustrate creative work. The fact that other similar web applications are appearing all the time—such as Indaba Music (www.indabamusic.com) and Soundation Studio (www.soundation.com)—should give music educators comfort that even if a particular online music production application disappears, the genre is here to stay.

Audiotool (audiotool.com)

Audiotool is really a virtual electronic music studio, similar to the highly regarded software program Reason; of course, Audiotool is smaller in scope, but it is free and available to use anywhere you can get online. Components available for producing music include several drum machines, a synth pattern sequencer, a bassline generator, a nice variety of effect pedals (compressor, parametric EQ, reverb, flanger, etc.), a 16-channel mixer, and an amplifier. The graphic user interface is very realistic: components look like their real-world counterpart and can be dragged and dropped into the studio setup, or deleted if not needed (**Fig. 16.7**). In a high school audio recording or music production class, one or more class meetings could be dedicated to learning each component. Some components, such as the pattern sequencer, are very intuitive and can be learned in seconds. Others, such as the bassline generator (a pattern sequencer of sorts), can do a lot and are therefore somewhat complex.

What is both great and a little challenging about Audiotool is that users must add and configure the components of the studio with which they want to work. The virtual gear comes complete with "input" and "output" ports, and with the click of a mouse, virtual cables connect the devices. This online studio could be very valuable in teaching why and how these common music production tools are used in a studio, especially in terms of signal flow. For instance, a drum machine might be connected directly to channel 1 of the mixer, but the bassline generator might be routed first to an effect pedal of some sort (phaser, crusher, etc.), which is then connected to channel 2 of the mixer. If you want the bass to sound above the drums, set the volume for channel 2 on the mixer higher than

▶ **FIG. 16.7**

Audiotool, a virtual music studio online. Created by Scott Watson.

channel 1. The output of the mixer must then be connected to an amplifier so both these instruments can be heard. Fortunately, you do not have to start with a "blank slate" (though you can); Audiotool offers several start-up templates with appropriate components preconfigured and ready to use. Users can make recordings of up to five minutes, and these audio files may be saved to the user's account and posted at the audiotool.com website.

The synthesizer and pattern sequencer-based Audiotool studio tends to facilitate production of electronica, dance club, and trance-style music. Nonetheless, this web application offers so much. If you have a computer lab with a reliable, fast Internet connection, you could build an entire course—or at least an entire unit—around learning to use and create music with Audiotool.

iNudge (www.inudge.net)

iNudge is a multilayer, matrix pattern sequencer. This nifty little utility is very easy to use and is recommended for elementary-age students, although my high school students enjoy spending time creating with it as well. Students point and click their mouse on any of the squares on a 16×16 matrix, triggering a sound event. The higher the square is on the matrix, the higher its pitch; each matrix allows for 16 different pitches. The square's horizontal placement determines the time the sound event will trigger (see **Figs. 6.1** and **6.2** for examples of matrix pattern sequencer grids). The 16 squares along the horizontal axis correspond to 16th notes in a measure of 4/4 time. When playback of a matrix is initiated, that "measure" repeats, cycling its pattern over and over in an ostinato (**Web Ex. 6.1**). iNudge provides for eight different matrixes, each with a different timbre. Seven of the matrixes are various electronic instrument sounds (synthesizer sounds, organ, Rhodes bass, harp, etc.), but the eighth matrix is a drum pattern sequencer. One, several, or all eight matrixes can sound at a time; the user can create or clear matrixes independently to develop changes in texture. The overall tempo can be adjusted, and the volume level and pan position can be set for each matrix independently.

Use this great web application and I guarantee your students will be making music in under a minute. Be sure everyone has headphones; the repeated, hypnotic nature of pattern sequencer music can wear on one's ears after a while. iNudge makes it easy for students to share their creations via social networking (links, embed, email), but unfortunately at this time it does not allow for export "as audio." A resourceful, tech-savvy music educator, however, could capture iNudge playback using various recording software.[3]

---

3. For instance, route the audio output of the computer back into the audio input (line in) and use Audacity to record the iNudge playback in real time. The program WireTap Studio (Ambrosia Software) captures whatever is sounding on a computer without having to connect cables.

EXAMPLE LESSONS

I think there are benefits to allowing students time to freely explore and create with the kinds of applications mentioned in this chapter. Especially after learning the basics of an application in a more structured activity, students given the opportunity to experiment and explore are bound to intuitively figure out the tools and operations they need to create limited, but meaningful, musical expressions.

On the pages that follow are several lessons that use instructional and creativity applications to accomplish creative music activities with students. The first lesson could be done with any of the web-based pattern sequencers I have come across. The others call for specific software and therefore include some product-specific details. All the lessons are offered as examples of creative music activities that can be fashioned for students using the kinds of music programs discussed in this chapter. Maybe you already use some of these programs. If so, I encourage you to look at them anew with a vision for their creative possibilities.

267

LESSON TITLE: THE SOUND OF MY NAME

Audience: Grades 3–12, general and elective music classes.

Objective: Students will deepen their appreciation for the musical concepts of pitch, rhythm, timbre, and texture by composing a "pattern" (or patterns) based on the letters in their name using a matrix pattern sequencer (such as iNudge). At the same time, students will gain a basic understanding of the way a pattern sequencer works.

Materials/Equipment: Computer, with headphones, running a software or web-based matrix pattern sequencer.

Duration: 30 minutes, or approximately one class period.

Prior Knowledge and Skills: An introductory knowledge of the musical concepts listed above (pitch, rhythm, timbre, texture) is helpful. Other than experience using a PC, no prior technical skills are required.

Procedure:

1. Demonstrate for students, preferably on a large screen at the front of the class, how a matrix pattern sequencer works. Click high and low squares and discuss how pitch is implemented. Click squares on a horizontal plane (x-axis) that correspond to simple rhythms (such as quarter notes on the beat), and then some randomly selected squares, and discuss how rhythm is implemented. Show how thicker, more complex textures can be programmed by choosing simultaneous sound events. If instrument sounds can be chosen, audition them and discuss timbre.

2. Continue demonstrating, by presenting the premise of the activity. Click squares in the matrix that form the letters of either your (or a student's) initials or first name (or nickname). Discuss the shape/contour of the repeating pattern that results (**Web Ex. 16.1**).

3. (Optional) If the matrix pattern sequencer being used allows for multiple matrixes, with different timbres, click first name (or initial) in one matrix and last name (or initial) in another. Try clicking other characters (such as a student's age) or shapes (circle, heart, smiley face, etc.) in additional matrixes.

4. Share: Ask students to share the sound of their name by playing for the class the patterns they have created. When possible, discuss the correspondence of the letters or other characters used to the melodic contour or rhythm of the pattern created.

Adaptations: When using a single teacher workstation at the front of a class, the teacher can first demonstrate the activity and then call students up individually to create patterns based on their names.

Feedback/Evaluation: For this simple activity, I would award participation credit for successfully entering one's name (or initials) and verbally being able to talk about at least two musical elements (pitch, rhythm, etc.) in the resulting pattern.

Extensions/Follow-up: If students have the opportunity to work further with the matrix pattern sequencer, have them create patterns based on more musical considerations than letters in their name. For instance, encourage them to create a pattern whose melodic contour mimics some familiar tune, or create a pattern that employs melodic sequence.

Additionally, if the software or web application allows, students could export their pattern(s) as audio (such as MP3) to be combined with other patterns, loops, or additional material in an entry-level DAW (such as Garage-Band) or digital audio recording program (such as Audacity) to create a larger work.

National Standards Addressed: Each of the following standards is addressed to some degree in this lesson:

- **Standard 4,** Composing and arranging music within specified guidelines.
- **Standard 5,** Reading and notating music.
- **Standard 6,** Listening to, analyzing, and describing music.
- **Standard 7,** Evaluating music and music performances.

LESSON TITLE: MELODIC FORM WITH GROOVY MUSIC

Audience: Grades 2–5, general music classes.

Objective: Students will demonstrate an understanding of repetition and contrast in melodic form by creating a melodic phrase with one of the Groovy Music programs (Shapes, Jungle, City).

Materials/Equipment: Groovy Shapes, Groovy Jungle, or Groovy City, whichever is most age appropriate.

Duration: This activity should take between 30 and 40 minutes (about one class period).

Prior Knowledge and Skills: Any prior experience with one of the Groovy Music programs is helpful but not necessary.

Procedure:

1. Demonstrate the basics of creating music with the Groovy program, especially the following:
   a. The difference between shapes (melody, rhythm, etc.) in the menu
   b. How to drag and drop shapes onto the Play Space
   c. How to move and delete shapes
2. Rhythm: Have student choose a rhythm shape from the menu. Drag it into measures 1–4.
3. Melody: Have students choose an opening melodic shape, dragging that into measures 1, 2, and 4. Next have students choose a contrasting melodic shape, dragging that into measure 3 (**Fig. 16.8**).

▶ **FIG. 16.8**
Using Groovy Shapes to create music with AABA form. Created by Scott Watson.

4. Edit. Using the program's playback feature, have students audition the sound of their A–A–B–A creations. Allow time for making the following edits, with the help of coaching, as desired.

   a. Change the tempo: Click on the Tempo icon (speed limit sign to the right of menu) and choose from the available speeds.

   b. Change the pitch level of any of the melodic shapes.

   c. Substitute different melodic shapes, as long as the overall form remains A–A–B–A.

   d. Change the instrument sound assigned to one or all of the melodic shapes: Click on the "Instruments and Dynamics" icon (circle with color wedges on lower left) and then drag one of the available instruments onto the melodic shape in the Play Space.

5. Share: Ask for student volunteers to play their melodic phrases for others to enjoy. Ask students to raise their hands when they hear the contrasting (B) melodic shape and/or describe which instrument(s) played each section of the melody.

Adaptations: The best scenario for this lesson is students working on their own with headphones; however, the activity could be done as a class with a teacher facilitating from a teacher workstation projected to a large screen or interactive whiteboard.

Feedback/Evaluation: Award credit to students for accomplishing the essential elements of this activity: (1) adding rhythm shapes to provide a percussion background, and (2) arranging two melodic shapes to create an A–A–B–A phrase.

Extensions/Follow-up: Certainly allow students who finish early to add shapes from the basslines, arpeggios, or chords categories to animate the texture of their creations.

Also, the teacher may want to assist students in exporting their music as MIDI files to post to a class blog or wiki. To export/save Groovy Music files as MIDI files, press the following key combination while clicking on the Groovy Save button: Windows, alt + shift; Mac, shift + option or option + command.

National Standards Addressed: Each of the following standards is addressed to some degree in this lesson:

- **Standard 4,** Composing and arranging music within specified guidelines.
- **Standard 6,** Listening to, analyzing, and describing music.

271

LESSON TITLE: BAND-IN-A-BOX DRUM WINDOW IMPROVISATION

Audience: Grades 4–12, general and elective music classes.

Objective: Students will explore the many percussive instruments incorporated into BIAB's Drum Window drum kit, choose several of their favorites, and then create their own rhythmic ostinato pattern.

Materials/Equipment: Band-in-a-Box and the computer's QWERTY keyboard. Also helpful is the BIAB Drum Window sound worksheet shown in **Fig. 16.9,** available as a download from the companion website (**Web Ex. 16.5**).

Duration: Depending on the number of students, this should take between 30 and 45 minutes (or about one class period).

Prior Knowledge and Skills: Experience using BIAB is helpful but not necessary.

Procedure:

1. Discovery: Launch BIAB and open the Drum Window. Demonstrate how each of the instruments that are graphically represented in the Drum window can be triggered by hitting a corresponding QWERTY key (Fig. 16.3).[4] Allow students (working individually or in pairs) to

▶ **FIG. 16.9**
Worksheet to use with students when exploring sounds in the Band-in-a-Box's Drum Window. Created by Scott Watson.

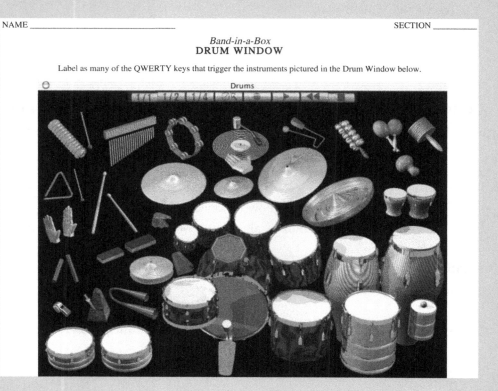

4. To see the QWERTY key that corresponds to each instrument pictured, click on the Settings dialog-box button at the top center of the Drum Window controls. A Drum Window Settings dialog box opens, in which you select "Display Qwerty Chars on Drums."

explore the drum sounds; use the BIAB Drum Window sound worksheet to identify sounds as they are found.

2. Improvisation: Have students each select two contrasting sounds (high vs. low, wood vs. metal, etc.) they like best. Give students time to create an ostinato pattern. They should use one finger per hand. Students working in pairs should create an interactive pattern using all four sounds (two sounds per student). The pattern should repeat/cycle in a recognizable way (such as every four or eight beats).

3. Share: After working in pairs with headphones for a while, have students perform their creations. Encourage group discussion that includes praise and helpful critique. Allow them to talk about the challenges of creating collaboratively.

Adaptations: You can manage these activities in a variety of settings. With a larger lab (say, 12 or more computers), seat the kids one or two to a workstation. In smaller labs, rotate the kids on the computers and have those who are observing participate by clapping or keeping time with small percussion instruments such as hand drums and tambourines. If you have only one workstation, teach your activity using a pair of students in front of the class, and then allow pairs to rotate onto the computer to work independently while you continue with something else.

Feedback/Evaluation: For this activity, I recommend awarding full participation credit to students that successfully create and perform an ostinato using two drum sounds.

Extensions/Follow-up: Depending on the amount of time you have in the lab or the level of comfort you have with BIAB, you may want to have the kids save their creations as BIAB files. Use the Record button in the Drum Window.[5]

National Standards Addressed: Each of the following standards is addressed to some degree in this lesson:

- **Standard 2,** Performing on instruments, alone and with others, a varied repertoire of music.
- **Standard 3,** Improvising melodies, harmonies, and accompaniments.
- **Standard 4,** Composing and arranging music within specified guidelines.
- **Standard 7** (optional), Evaluating music and music performances.

273

---

5. To record the percussion alone, without any of BIAB's combo ensemble instruments, you may need to create your own "empty" BIAB style to use. From the User menu, choose Make a New Style. When the Style Maker dialog box opens, leave everything blank (as is), click the Save button, and name the new style. Now choose "Load Style from Disk" from the User menu, and select the empty style you just created. All of this, once configured, can be saved in a BIAB document that you can use as a template. Configured and saved correctly, all your students need to do is launch the template and go.

LESSON TITLE: BLUES COMPOSITION

Audience: Grades 5–12, general and elective music classes.

Objective: Students will demonstrate their understanding of blues structure—the 12-bar blues chord progression, and the poetic A–A–B form of some blues lyrics—by creating an original blues composition.

Materials/Equipment: Ideally, a music workstation running Band-in-a-Box. Alternatively, any entry-level multitrack music production program that uses looping (such as GarageBand) will do. You will also need a worksheet, such as the one shown in **Fig. 16.10** (which may be downloaded from the companion website, **Web Ex. 16.6**), and a blues listening example that exhibits A–A–B lyric form, such as Bessie Smith's "Lost Your Head Blues" (**sidebar** and **Web Ex. 16.7**) or B.B. King's "Three O'Clock Blues."

Duration: 120–160 minutes, or approximately three to four class periods.

Prior Knowledge and Skills: Some experience using the basic features of the software.

- BIAB: Choosing key, tempo, entering and editing chords, choosing a style, and playback.
- Multitrack software: Choosing key, tempo, setting up instrument tracks, choosing appropriate tonal accompaniment loops, transposing loops for the IV (+5 semitones) and V (+7 semitones) chords, editing loops, and playback.
- (Optional) Either program: Setting volume levels for various instrument tracks.

Procedure:

1. Listening: Play for the students a recording of a blues composition whose lyrics follow an A–A–B form (see example in sidebar). Point out how the first and second lines are the same (or similar), presenting a statement (perhaps a problem), but the third line is a reaction or solution to the first two lines.

"Lost Your Head Blues" by Bessie Smith

LINE 1 (A): I was with you baby when you didn't have a dime.

LINE 2 (A): I was with you baby when you didn't have a dime.

LINE 3 (B): Now, since you've got plenty of money, you have throwed [sic] your good gal down.[6]

---

6. From "Lost Your Head Blues" (1926, Frank Music Corp.) by Bessie Smith.

Blues Composition Project

Group Members: _____   Section: _____
                 _____   Date: _____
                 _____
                 _____
                 _____

> **Blues Lyric:** A typical "blues" lyric has three lines. Line 1 is a *statement of some problem.* Line 2 is the same as Line 1; you just repeat it. Line 3 might briefly restate the problem, but speaks to the *solution* or *outcome* of the problem.

LINES 1 & 2: _____

_____

LINE 3: _____

_____

SELECT KEY: [　]   CHORDS: I = [　]   IV= [　]   V= [　]

Choose from key of C, G, or D. Then fill in the traditional chords for the 12-bar blues, or your own variation. Regardless, be sure to start/end with the I chord.

C7
F7
G7
D7
A7

	1	2	3	4
LINE 1: (I-I-I-I)	[　]	[　]	[　]	[　]

	5	6	7	8
LINE 2: (IV-IV-I-I)	[　]	[　]	[　]	[　]

	9	10	11	12
LINE 3: (V-IV-I-I)	[　]	[　]	[　]	[　]

▶ **FIG. 16.10**
Worksheet to use with the "Blues Composition" activity. Created by Scott Watson.

Discuss and diagram the A–A–B form of the lyrics on a board or screen. As an option, you can project or hand out the lyrics to the example song and sing it as a class with the recording.

2. Briefly explain/review the harmonic form of the traditional 12-bar blues chord progressions. Consider the following method:

   a. Practice singing the first five notes of a major scale; use solfège syllables (Do, Ro, Mi, Fa, Sol) or numbers (1, 2, 3, 4, 5).

   b. On a staff, notate the first five notes of the C-major scale. Explain, "Chords are groups of notes that form a harmony associated with a particular scale step. You can have a chord on the first scale degree (I), the fourth scale degree (IV), and the fifth scale degree (V). These are the primary chords used with a typical blues progression." Circle the first, fourth, and fifth scale steps, and then perform the chords (on keyboard, guitar, etc.) for students.

   c. Practice figuring out the I, IV, and V chords in other keys (such as G and D) using the above method.

   d. (Optional) For older students, explain how chord tones are the scale degree itself, called the "root," and certain intervals above the root (such as third, fifth, and seventh). Listen to the difference between triads and seventh chords (C7, G7, etc.).

3. In groups or individually, have students complete the two tasks associated with the "Blues Composition" project worksheet (**Fig. 16.10,** and **Web Ex. 16.6**):

   a. Write original A–A–B lyrics. Encourage students to make their blues lyrics about topics relevant to them (homework, chores, sports, food, etc.).

   b. Select a key and notate the appropriate chords for the blues progression.

4. Software setup: Create a new document using your software; select key and tempo. If using BIAB, also choose a style (blues shuffle, jazz swing, etc.). If you are using DAW software, set up at least three instrument tracks: keyboard, bass, and a drum loop track. The kind of drum loop used ("Lounge Jazz Drums," "80s Pop Beat," "Classic Rock Beat," etc.) will suggest the style for the arrangement.

5. Enter chords: Use the chord names sketched on the "Blues Composition" project worksheet to enter the chords.

   a. BIAB: Click a measure; type the chord symbol. Use the forward arrow to advance to the next measure; use the space bar to erase.[7]

   b. DAW: For each new chord in the blues progression, add appropriate tonal loops into the keyboard and bass tracks. Transpose as neces-

---

7. Check with the BIAB manual for other operations.

sary (with GarageBand, select a loop's region and move the pitch slider in the Track Edit window the desired number of half-steps):

    i. I—No transposition.

    ii IV—Transpose the loop up five half-steps.

    iii. V—Transpose the loop up seven half-steps.

  c. (Optional) DAW: Students comfortable doing so may play/record their keyboard and/or bass parts in real time. Record full chords in the piano track, as if accompanying. For the bass track, consider these two ideas.

    i. Simple: Play the roots of all the chords, using any rhythm, as your bassline.

    ii. Intermediate: Play the typical 1–3–5–6–7–6–5–3 blues bassline, and variants, using any rhythm as your bassline.

6. Compose "blues lead": Allow groups time to find—via improvisation—a melody or rap for their blues lyrics, following the A–A–B form. Students will read the lyrics from the "Blues Composition" project worksheet, memorizing the melody and/or rhythms they compose.

7. Perform: There are two options for student performance of their blues compositions:

  a. Groups (or individuals) may perform their blues composition live for the class, singing or rapping to the software accompaniment they have created.

  b. Groups (or individuals) may record their blues lead (melody or rap) and then play back their entire production for the class.

    i. BIAB: Record melody or rap into the Melody track (Melody menu → Record melody).

    ii. DAW: Set up an audio track to record voice, using one of the microphone schemes described earlier in this book in chapter 13.

Adaptations: If using a pod or cluster of computers instead of a lab or laptop cart, students must work in groups. I actually think this project works best with groups of three or four anyway, so this is not a problem. Consider assigning cooperative learning roles for leading the group in choosing key and chords, writing the blues lyric, operating the software (entering chords, etc.), and composing/rehearsing the lead melody or rap.

Feedback/Evaluation: During student work time, while coaching, stop periodically to share with the class the work of any group that has done something exemplary or is on the right track. Following each in-class performance, discuss with students the effectiveness of various elements of each group's composition (style, tempo, blues lead, anything unique added, etc.).

For a formal assessment, award credit for key features of the project: (1) correctly filling out the worksheet, (2) choosing a key and tempo, (3) correctly programming the chord progression, (4) selecting a style (BIAB) or adding a drum loop (DAW), and (5) performing the blues lyric lead (melody or rap).

Extension/Follow-up: Students/groups with extra time may add to their compositions by using any of the following.

DAW: Add more percussion and other loops.

BIAB: Using various features of the software (consult manual), add an introduction, tag ending, or additional chorus.

Add a solo chorus for a student improvisation (vocal scat, MIDI keyboard, acoustic instrument, etc.).

In a substitute or follow-up lesson, consider allowing students to use the blues chords in any order, as long as their progression begins and ends with the I (tonic) chord. In this case, you may also want to be flexible with the song length (such as 8, 12, or 16 measures).

National Standards Addressed: Each of the following standards is addressed to some degree in this lesson:

- **Standard 1,** Singing, alone and with others, a varied repertoire of music.
- **Standard 2** (optional), Performing on instruments, alone and with others, a varied repertoire of music.
- **Standard 3,** Improvising melodies, harmonies, and accompaniments.
- **Standard 4,** Composing and arranging music within specified guidelines.
- **Standard 6,** Listening to, analyzing, and describing music.
- **Standard 7,** Evaluating music and music performances.
- **Standard 8,** Understanding relationships between music, the other arts, and disciplines outside the arts.

REFLECTION ACTIVITY

Instructional software and other music applications, both traditional and web based, have potential for leading your students in creative musical activities. The creative components of these programs often allow students to explore, improvise, and create using an intuitive interface that avoids conventional music reading skills. After reading this chapter, consider how such applications might be put to use by you and students in creative projects.

1. In-service teachers: Describe a lesson/project presented in this chapter that you think would work well in your teaching assignment. Alternatively, describe a lesson/activity you already do that incorporates ideas presented in this chapter.

2. Preservice teachers: Describe how you could use or adapt a lesson/project idea presented in this chapter in the type of music teaching assignment you hope to do.

3. What are some creative music web applications that you have found on the Internet?[8] Which do you think hold the most potential for use in school music programs? Why?

4. Describe a creative music activity you might be able to use with music students that employs the web application(s) mentioned above. How might the Eight Principles for Unlocking Musical Creativity enhance the activity? Which of the MENC National Standards for Music Education would be addressed?

---

8. You may be able to find a website, blog, or wiki that highlights or even reviews such Web applications.

CHAPTER 17
CURRICULUM INTEGRATION

THREE APPROACHES

A HEALTHY MUSIC CURRICULUM employs several modes of teaching and learning. Creative music activities can be used to reinforce, augment, or even deliver portions of K–12 music courses. Other worthy components such as delivering information and performing music are fundamental and, at times, may be more appropriate. Music educators wishing to tap the appeal and potency of creative music projects that employ technology to support and enhance their music curriculum have many options, summed up broadly in three approaches: independent lesson or activity, creative project or unit, and creativity-based curriculum.

Independent Lesson or Activity

One teacher may decide to begin modestly by augmenting a normal instructional unit or two with a brief creative music lesson or activity. Elementary classroom music students might use loops to create rhythmic ostinato accompaniments for a song or Orff arrangement they have learned. Middle school general music students might explore sounds on keyboard synthesizers as part of a unit on timbre. High school students in jazz band or an elective keyboard class might work on blues improvisation concepts with Band-in-a-Box software. Lessons such as these might take one to three class periods.

In each of these, the creative music activity is a welcome "add-on" to more conventional learning activities. The creative lesson reinforces the curriculum, which remains basically unchanged; however, a window of time must be found to accomplish the creative task. Teachers may need to devote additional time to learning, or refamiliarizing students with, certain music technology tools when engaging in these isolated activities.

This approach is great for metaphorically "dipping one's toe in the pool" to get a feel for employing a technology-based, creative activity with students. It may also be the best plan for certain music educators, such as the instrumental teacher whose schedule is packed with lessons, rehearsals, and performances but who finds he or she has a few "down times" during the year.

Creative Project or Unit

Another teacher, perhaps with more comfort using technology and experience coaching creative endeavors, might use the technology at his or her disposal in one or more comprehensive creative music projects or units over the course of the year. Older elementary classroom students might wrap up their unit on the blues by working in groups to create a blues composition. Middle school general music students might produce an end-of-semester composer report podcast. High school instrumental students could pair up to compose a duet for their instrument. Projects/units such as these might take one to three weeks.

To make room for these worthwhile, but larger, undertakings in what is no doubt already a full curriculum, other learning activities must be curtailed. As they say, "You can't pour a gallon of water into a quart container." The goal is to accomplish the same learning and reinforcement with the creative project that might have been accomplished with more conventional means. Although work on a creative unit might take place on successive class meetings, it does not have to be so. Instead, students may put in work at intervals that make sense to the educator, such as once a week when the computer lab is available, or several times a grading period.

This approach is best for music educators who have experienced the benefits of using creative music projects and who are comfortable with the different style of classroom management (and risks) that accompany technology-centered creative work. This approach could positively animate many elementary and middle school general music units. I believe secondary elective music courses, such as music theory (written and aural) or guitar class—traditionally viewed as fact based and/or performance based—can be enhanced by using creative projects to give application to the core knowledge and skills presented. The same students who have learned to solfège and harmonize a melody would benefit by creating their own lead sheet (computer music notation, or CMN) or multi-track music production (DAW) arrangement of the tune.

Creativity-Based Curriculum

The most comprehensive application of the creativity-based approach to music learning presented here is for courses that *feature* creative music tasks using technology tools as their primary mode of learning. In such a course, other modes of learning are employed as needed, but the curriculum is predominantly delivered via a series of creative activities and projects. Obvious examples of such courses are middle school and high school elective courses that go by names such as "Electronic Music" (or "Music Technology"), "Music Production," or "Audio Recording."[1] As has been mentioned, these sorts of courses can

---

1. This is not to say that a largely creativity-based curriculum could not be fashioned for elementary general music classes, but it is far less common.

offer positive, meaningful music learning to nontraditional music students.[2] Much of the learning is applied, "hands on," and experiential.

SAMPLE CREATIVITY-BASED CURRICULUM: MUSIC PRODUCTION

To put some flesh on the bones of what I have described above, let me present a sample creativity-based curriculum. It is my hope that music educators at all levels will find in this sample curriculum a model for developing their own courses. As you will see from the course description below, it is a high school music production elective aimed at an eclectic mix of students with diverse musical backgrounds and talents.

While there are many other ways to tackle a course such as this, what follows is a curricular outline I have used with great success. You will notice that the sample curriculum is assembled mainly by arranging various lessons from this book to suit the arc of the course. One feature of the course that contributes to its effectiveness, and therefore worth imitating, is the way the activities sequentially build in the number of creative elements and the amount of freedom given to students—students "walk" before they "run." Also remember that, though not explicitly stated, most of the Eight Principles for Unlocking Musical Creativity are applied during each course activity.

Music Production Course Description

This semester-long course will introduce students to the theory and fundamentals of using software and hardware tools for commercial music production (computer, multitrack recording software, waveform editor, signal processing plug-ins, synthesizer keyboard, CMN software, and microphone technique). The class will stress application and creative content, using a series of creative activities and projects that expose student to improvising and performing with electronic and other instruments, multitrack recording (both MIDI sequencing and live instruments), music arranging, generating performance materials for others (typesetting music), and equipment configuration.

Prerequisites for this course are some experience performing any style of music (vocalist, pop guitar or keyboards, jazz bass, classical trumpet, etc.) and some facility reading any common form of popular or classical "art" music notation (traditional staff notation, tab, lead sheet, rhythm chart, etc.).

This is a hands-on course, delivering to class members an experience with software applications for music playback, mastering, and burning, waveform

---

2. Nontraditional music students are drawn from a school's general population as opposed to the more conventionally trained musicians in band, chorus, and orchestra.

audio editing, multitrack music production, and basic music notation. These programs represent a large portion of the types of things musicians are doing under the umbrella of "music production." While most of the course work will be applied, some theory will be presented in order to explain terms and operations in which we engage.

Introduction: Two Preliminary Activities

To open the course, the teacher should lead students in the following two class activities.

Introduction 1: What Is a Music Producer?

In this first part of the introduction to the course, students discuss—based on their preconceived ideas—the role of a music producer. Two activities that can aid in this discussion are the following:

1. Share with students background information on legendary music producers. For instance, Jerry Wexler (Ray Charles, Wilson Pickett, Aretha Franklin) worked very differently than Quincy Jones (Michael Jackson, Miles Davis, film scores). Both were music producers with vision but brought different gifts/talents to their role; Wexler's strengths, for instance, were in music business, whereas Jones's strengths were as a composer/arranger.
2. Listen critically, side by side, to two different "covers" of the same song. Discuss the differences and how the role of the music producer might have shaped each version.[3]

In the end of this introduction, the class should generate a listing of all the "hats" a music producer—depending on his or her gifts/talents—might wear, such as

- Recording engineer
- Musical arranger (traditional notation and pop/folk nomenclature)
- Music director (rehearse and conduct sessions)
- Performing artist
- Composer and lyricist
- Artist development (spotting, pairing, and grooming talent)

---

3. Two examples I like to compare with my students are Wilson Pickett's 1965 original "In the Midnight Hour" and the 1991 cover version from the film *The Commitments*, and the Beatles 1966 (released 1976) original "Got to Get You Into My Life" and the 1977/78 cover version by Earth, Wind and Fire (see **Web Ex. 13.3**).

- Business person (financing, paying bills, copyright, etc.)
- Marketer, promoter, publicist
- Concert tour manager
- Artist manager

Introduction 2: What Is GarageBand?

In this second part of the introduction to the course, the teacher should briefly demonstrate the features and functions of GarageBand. Note that although GarageBand is mentioned here, this music production course could be taught with any entry-level DAW program. I have found that some students already have some experience with GarageBand or another multitrack music production application; others that do not are aware of the idea of multitrack recording and are very interested to see what GarageBand can do. Features include waveform audio recording and editing, MIDI file playback, MIDI recording ("sequencing") and editing, application of digital signal processing (DSP) effects, podcast production, video and still image scoring, basic CMN, and more.

Especially worth highlighting are the different types of track *regions* in GarageBand, each with their own color:

1. Green: MIDI data (MIDI loops and recordings)
2. Blue: digital audio loops
3. Purple: digital audio recorded with GarageBand
4. Amber: imported digital audio, prepared apart from GarageBand

To see if students comprehend, discuss with (or quiz) students on the following questions:

1. How is audio represented in GarageBand?
2. What is MIDI (or MIDI data)?
3. How is MIDI data shown in GarageBand?
4. What's the difference between the audio represented in the purple and the amber regions?
5. When a GarageBand file plays back, what is the vertical line that indicates the current position in the song called?
6. What is a loop? What is the difference between *audio* loops and *MIDI* loops?

Creative Activities and Projects With GarageBand

The following is an annotated listing of GarageBand activities that lead students from exploring basic features of the program with minor creative expression, to using the program at a high level with creative independence. Most of the activities mentioned here are presented earlier in part II.

Lesson: "Cut, Copy, Paste, Split, Move" (chapter 14)

This activity gives students a chance to perform common, basic editing operations on track regions. Since the lesson uses a prepared file, with all note material entered, students at any level can jump right in and fully participate. Students get a taste for arranging as they use the editing operations to build a basic tune ("Yankee Doodle") into song form, along with options such as altering instrument sounds and adding drum loops.

Recording an Audio Signal Into GarageBand

In this activity students learn how to use one or more microphone schemes to record voice into an audio track of GarageBand. The lesson "Do-Re-Mi (or 1–2–3) Editing: Cut, Copy, and Paste" (chapter 13) allows students to do just this, while reviewing editing operations as well. For a quicker approach, walk students through the steps for microphone recording presented in the "Capturing Student Performances, and Recording in General" section of chapter 13.

Lesson: "Favorite Sounds" (chapter 12)

At the end of the "Favorite Sounds" lesson (chapter 12), an adaptation is described for using a keyboard controller triggering GarageBand sounds. This activity allows students to get to know the software instruments available to them via exploration and improvisation.

Lesson: "My Favorite Things Podcast" (chapter 14)

Still early in the course, students use what they have been learning to produce a podcast that shares some of their favorite music. Music production tasks for this activity include audio recording a "voice-over" narration, preparing sound clips, automating volume levels for fade-ins and fade-outs, creating a stereo mixdown, and other optional elements (adding SFX, theme music, using loops for underscoring, etc.).

Lesson: "Loops and Layering" (chapter 14)

Students pick up the theme of musical arranging again, this time using the modular approach of arranging loops to create music with an interesting musical narrative. Using loops allows students at any level to have an experience creating an interesting progression of musical ideas and complementary textures.

Lesson: "Introduction to Digital Signal Processing" (chapter 13)

Digital signal processing (DSP) effects will be valuable tools for adding luster, sonic interest, and uniqueness to GarageBand productions. This brief lesson from chapter 13 is fun and informative for students as they explore various DSP "plug-ins" such as reverb, echo, compression, flange, filters, distortion, pitch and time shifting, and much more.

Lesson: "New Clothes for an Old Tune" (chapter 14)

This lesson from chapter 14 builds even further on the concepts of editing, arranging, and producing music. Students start by importing a MIDI file of a brief Baroque- or Classical-era keyboard work; only students with keyboard proficiency and the desire to MIDI record their own tracks need to do so. Therefore, students at any level can enjoy a valuable aesthetic experience creating a fresh, contemporary arrangement of the source music by (1) using editing operations to create the form, (2) selecting instrument sounds, (3) employing loops to create a characteristic rhythmic groove, (4) creating a good mix by automating volume and pan settings, (5) applying DSP effects to enhance the production, and (6) employing the principles of *layering* and the *100% rule* (described in chapter 14) throughout to craft a compelling musical narrative.

Creating a Lead Sheet With Computer Music Notation (or Chord Sheet With a Text Editor)

Somewhere before the "Winter/Holiday Tune Setting" project (see below), the teacher should demonstrate a simple, straightforward plan for creating a lead sheet (melody with chord symbols, using a CMN program) or a chord sheet (words with chord symbols, using a text editor). The free, Web-based music notation application Noteflight is fine for the former; so are most computer-based CMN programs. Any word processing program will work for the later. I usually assign a simple folk song to typeset (lead or chord sheet) as practice.

Some students will finish previous projects early and can begin to learn basic note entry and editing features for whichever CMN software you use. This is one area where teachers can employ differentiated instruction, allowing more proficient students to work independently typesetting or composing music with CMN software.

Lesson: "Winter/Holiday Tune Setting" (chapter 14)

In the "New Clothes for an Old Tune" project, students crafted an original, contemporary setting of a brief keyboard work. In this project, students bring all the production skills they have been learning to bear as they produce an original arrangement of a public domain winter/holiday tune. While students have the option of "programming" all or most tracks for playback by software instruments and loops, as "producers" they do not necessarily have to. Student producers can "employ" a keyboardist to MIDI record lead melodies, chordal accompaniment, basslines, and so on. Revisiting the idea of microphone recording, students can record classmates or friends performing a vocal track, acoustic rhythm guitar track, or wind instrument solo. Electric guitar and bass can be recorded through an audio interface if available.

This project represents the culmination of the technical and artistic skills presented in the Music Production course.

Final Weeks of Music Production

Normally there will be one to two weeks of the semester left following the "Winter/Holiday Tune Setting" project. During this time, teachers may want to allow students to explore some related topic not touched upon during the course, either independently or together as a class. Suggested activities for winding down the class, which may or may not be graded, include the following:

1. "Blues Keyboard Improvisation" (chapter 12)
2. "Electronic Art Music Sound Collage" (chapter 13)
3. "Scoring a Video" (chapter 14)
4. "The Sound of My Name" (chapter 16)

Sample Curriculum Final Thoughts

The potential for technology-centered creative musical activities is vast and may result in an educator developing more worthy projects than course time permits. If the above music production course were longer, for instance, it could have appropriately included activities to give students more practice recording with various microphone techniques, more arranging techniques, or an experience with electronic art music.

The activities associated with creative work—listening to examples, improvising, coaching, revising, performing—take time. It is better to do fewer things with depth than more things in a shallow manner. In light of this, and remembering Murphy's law,[4] I advocate building a margin of time into any curriculum dependent on technology and concerned with developing creative ideas. Then occasionally, for variety (or perhaps to replace activities that did not live up to my expectations), attractive new lessons can be rotated into a course.

THE META-PROJECT: PUTTING IT ALL TOGETHER

Students generally use a higher level of learning when they work through a creative project than they might for traditional assignments. Consider Benjamin Bloom's six levels of cognitive learning outlined in his "taxonomy," or classification, of levels of intellectual behavior. They are, from lowest to highest: knowledge (remembering), comprehension (understanding), application (applying), analysis (analyzing), evaluation (evaluating), and synthesis (creating).[5] Note that

---

4. Murphy's law, part of American folk parlance, states, "Anything that can go wrong, will go wrong."

5. Benjamin Bloom, *Taxonomy of Educational Objectives, Handbook I: The Cognitive Domain* (New York: Longman, 1956) and Lorin Anderson and David Krathwohl, editors, *A Taxonomy for Learning, Teaching, and Assessing: A Revision of Bloom's Taxonomy of Educational Objectives* (New York: Longman, 2001). Bloom's original taxonomy of 1956 was revised during the 1990s by a group led by a former Bloom student, Lorin Anderson. The new model uses verbs rather than nouns to describe the levels (such as "remembering" vs. "knowledge"). The new version also swaps the top two levels (evaluation/evaluating moves down and synthesis/creating moves up).

Bloom's taxonomy moves from the basics of receiving information to ways of working with and thinking about this information, to more sophisticated levels that involve criticism, synthesis, and creativity. When composing a melody, it is not enough to know about pitch, or even to be able to recognize or build various scales. Instead, composers make decisions about note groupings, combined with rhythmic gestures, and other elements (dynamics, instrument choice, etc.).

Opera (and its more recent relative, the Broadway musical) is an artistic endeavor that synthesizes and integrates many artistic disciplines. Literature (the libretto) is fused with vocal and instrumental music (the score). But there are also visual art (scenery), costumes and make-up, sound and lighting design, choreography and dance, and more. In the sense that all of these are combined in an aesthetically satisfying, unified whole, opera is a *meta-art form*.

Likewise, when we undertake with our students creative projects that integrate multiple artistic components, we are engaging them in a *meta-project* that constitutes a very high level of artistic activity. Meta-projects might incorporate **musical elements** such as composition/arranging, improvisation, and vocal and instrumental performance; **nonmusical creativity** such as lyric writing and visual art; and various **applied technologies** such as multitrack music production (audio, sequencing, looping, etc.), CMN typesetting, video recording and editing, Web content creation, and computer graphics.

The style of teaching and learning that takes place when students are engaged in a meta-project reminds me of what Jackie Wiggins calls a "cognitive apprenticeship."[6] This approach emerges from research that supports a constructivist view of learning and seeks to "make school learning more like 'life' learning." According to Wiggins, characteristics of a cognitive apprenticeship are as follows:

1. Learners engage in real-life problem-solving situations.
2. Learning situations are holistic in nature.
3. Learners have opportunities to interact directly with subject matter.
4. Learners take an active role in their own learning.
5. Learners have opportunities to work on their own, with peers, and with teacher support, when needed.
6. Learners are cognizant of the goals of the learning situation and their own progress toward goals.

No doubt many implications for meta-projects are suggested by this listing, even without further explanation of the six traits.

Meta-projects do take lots of shepherding on the part of the teacher. They also depend on organization and planning by participating students and involve

---

6. Wiggins, *Teaching for Musical Understanding*, 18–19.

risks all around, but the results are very rewarding. The more sophisticated the stage of learning, the more appropriate and useful are these longer term creative projects. Most courses that do employ such projects will employ them sparingly, likely only once or twice per year due to their far-reaching scope and time demands. Because of their broad scope, meta-projects always involve collaboration and interaction in some way. Only through the synergy of students working together can these creative feats be accomplished.

What follows are descriptions of two meta-projects I have employed with high school elective music classes. I do not mean to suggest that meta-projects work only at the high school level, or for such electives. There are as many ideas for meta-projects as there are creative music teachers. I offer these two examples in order to convey the type of structure, components, and schedule that might be employed.

Meta-project Example 1: Holiday CD Project

The "Winter/Holiday Tune Setting" project from chapter 14 serves as the core of a very rewarding meta-project for my high school music production class.[7] In essence, we transform the class into a music production company, called "Music4Good," to produce an entire holiday CD that we sell to the school community as a fund-raiser for a worthy charity selected by the class. The CD, called *Parkland: A Season for Giving*, has become an annual event with much school and community support (**Fig. 17.1**). Please take a moment to visit the companion website to download and listen to an eleven minute podcast that gives an overview of the 2010 edition of this project (**Web Ex 2.5**). The idea of a student-produced CD was far from new when I initiated it as a meta-project with my students. I was able to follow the successful example of others, most notably Ken Simpson (Brookwood High School, GA) and Joe Cantafa (Howell High School, NJ), adapting and refining to suit my program.

Important Choices

There is no "right" or "wrong" way to proceed with a project such as this, but certain choices will lead to certain emphases, taking the project in one direction or another. For instance, selecting what kind of, and which particular, tracks to include is significant. Some teachers may want to include every student-generated track on the CD, regardless of quality. Others might want to use a review process to certify that students' tracks meet a standard in order to be included. It will also need to be decided whether or not to include individuals or school ensembles performing published, protected music. This leads into the whole area of copyright, forcing the class to either seek a waiver of, or pay for, mechanical

---

7. Note that this meta-project could be built around a nonholiday variation of that lesson and involve *any* public-domain tune or original song.

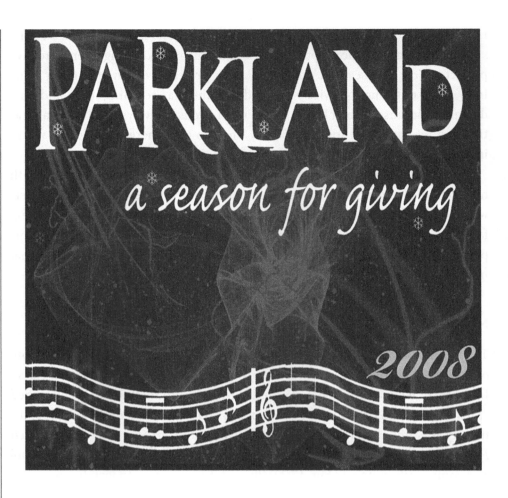

▶ **FIG. 17.1**

Cover art for Parkland High School's *Parkland: A Season for Giving (2008)* holiday CD. Designed by Emily N. Cover art by Emily N. Used with permission.

rights through the copyright holder (usually the publisher) or a service such as Harry Fox Agency (www.harryfox.com). It certainly is simpler to limit CD tracks to arrangements of public domain tunes and original songs. Licensing published music, however, allows students to see an important aspect of the music business while offering positive exposure to school ensembles. Issues of copyright are discussed more fully in the next chapter.

I am in favor of having students do as much nonmusical work as possible, but teachers may want to handle some administrative chores themselves. Another choice involves whether or not to sell the CD for profit. Your school district may prohibit such a practice, but I know of schools that sell student-produced CDs to raise funds for new equipment. In my school, we donate the proceeds from CD sales to a charity chosen by the students. Another important decision, with important consequences, involves employing human resources outside the class. Student performers from outside the class can participate as "session players." Students in an art or computer graphics class can generate the CD cover art, others in creative writing classes can contribute lyrics, while students in a business or marketing class can help with advertising and selling the CD. Once the CD tracks are produced and assembled onto a master, you will need to choose a plan for duplicating them. The class could duplicate the CDs themselves (one at a time with computer CD burners, or several at a time with a duplication machine). The master could also be sent to a duplication service, which often either designs the CD art or incorporates art you send.

A CD release event allows students to share their final product with others, by playing back tracks from the CD or performing them live. This can be a modest, in-class affair or a schoolwide event with decorations, invited VIP guests and press, and a master of ceremonies introducing artists as their tracks are played or performed.

Student Roles

If you include the students in the organizational tasks, consider assigning or awarding them jobs such as producer, assistant-producer, marketing director, public relations director, permissions director, sound engineer, treasurer (or business manager), director of artist development, charity liaison, social networker (blogging, etc.), and so forth. You probably know your students well enough to assign these jobs; some teachers find a benefit in having the students go through an interview process to "apply" for the jobs. When I begin the holiday CD project with students, I hand out thumbnail descriptions of the production team jobs (see **sidebar,** "Holiday CD Project Jobs") and ask students to take a few days to think about where they see themselves fitting in.

Holiday CD Project Jobs

Producer (leadership, organizer with artistic vision): Lead class meetings as needed to coordinate efforts of all areas. Develop a timeline for the project and a track list reflecting selections to include on the CD. Check in with individuals to see if they're on track (as per project timeline). Facilitate their efforts if needed. Lend your "vision" to the entire CD (for example, do you see collaborations that might work within the class? Is there a song or type of music that should be included on the CD which we have overlooked? Is there enough music to fill out the CD?).

Associate Producer(s): Help with all of the above, especially two important, organizing items: (1) Caring for the track list. The CD should be representative of the talents in our class and the school. It should include a variety of styles and moods to give interest to the diverse listeners in our school community. Work with the producer and class members to attain an ideal track list. Work with the design/layout person to be sure they have the track list copy ready for whoever is preparing the CD graphic design. (2) Posting the timeline. Work with course teacher and project producer to create a timeline for completing the project. Post this visibly (large calendar, etc.) in the music room or tech lab during the duration of the project.

Permissions Director (enjoys the legal side of things): Check public domain Web sites to confirm fair use for most tunes that will be on the CD. Contact the permissions department of any copyright holders to clear the few (if any) protected pieces we decide to use.

Artist Development (connected, aware of building talent): Investigate, flush out, and develop talent (musicians, singers, narrators, etc.) to consider for tracks of the CD. As needed, help members of the class find appropriate talent for use on their tracks. Talk to student, teacher, and administrator "artists" about becoming involved, especially to increase the appeal of the CD to consumers.

Marketing Director (strong business sense): Someone with an affinity for creative marketing is needed to develop a plan for getting the CD into the hands of consumers, by answering this question: Where and how can the CD best be advertised and sold?

Design/Graphics Coordinator (eye for layout): If you can enlist a computer graphics class at your school to design the cover art, even better. If not, a student interested in cover art who is good with computer graphics can do this. **Fig. 17.1** shows the CD cover art designed by a high school computer graphics student for a holiday CD.

Public Relations Director (articulate speech and writing, comfortable speaking to adults): This student is the class's liaison with school district/outside press. This person should be taking pictures of the process for possible use promoting the project. At the appropriate time, the PR director will write and distribute a press release. Once the project is under way, this person should post news and updates, as well as other content to promote the CD, on a project blog or Web site. An assistant to the PR Director may be responsible for all social networking to generate online interest in the project.

Charity Liaison (heart for community need): Gather ideas for potential charities to support, and facilitate the class in choosing one. Continue to serve as go-between with a representative from the charity. Perhaps they can help us with advertising or selling the CD, come share with our class about their mission, join us and say a few words at a CD release event, and so forth.

Treasurer/Business Manager (ethical servant with decent math skills): Managing a project account (school activity account, etc.), handle reimbursements for items we may need, keep track of expenses, collect/count money from CD sales, and record deposits, and so on.

Sound Engineer(s) (technical, good with multitrack recording gear, microphones): Assist class members and producer with technical/recording tasks (these students may even have their own recording gear). Interview artists ahead of time and set up sessions; strategize microphone schemes. Some engineer(s) might specialize in operating the multitrack software; others could specialize in microphones techniques.

After a few days I meet with students individually, discuss their interests and talents, and assign roles. Lots of decisions need to be made with a project such as this, all of which the teacher should oversee. The more choices left in the hands of students, however, the more students will sense ownership and put forth the effort required.

Timeline

The following general timeline is based on Parkland High School's holiday CD project and gives an idea how a class might proceed. This corresponds to the detailed "Winter/Holiday Tune Setting" lesson in chapter 14.

- **Days 1–3:** Listen to examples of winter/holiday song settings. Explain project and ask kids to begin thinking of ideas for an original arrangement or song. Demonstrate how to pair a tune with a pop groove, and build song form (intro, verse, refrain, bridge, tag, etc.). If kids come in with an idea, develop it publically (such as begin arranging/producing it in GarageBand, projecting work to a large screen, to show the process). Students search for their public domain tunes to produce. Teacher, or possibly selected student, visits computer graphics class to explain the project.
- **Days 4–8:** Students select public domain tune to arrange/produce, or pitch idea for original song to teacher for approval. Some students may want to pursue recording a school ensemble (such as band, chorus, orchestra), with the cooperation of the ensemble director. Begin improvising and sketching ideas for song. Determine which tracks will be programmed (sequenced), which will use loops, and which will use live players (recorded); set up the multitrack music production software each. Share sketches with class/teacher for feedback. Develop preliminary track list.
- **Days 9–13:** Assign students jobs/roles for project. Continue to share works-in-progress with class/teacher for input. Begin setting up free period and after school "tracking sessions" to record vocalists and other live talent (guitar, bass, etc.) as needed. Select charity and choose CD release event. Review CD art submitted by computer graphics class; select design to use for CD. Continue to hone track list.

- **Days 14–17:** Final mixing and DSP. Export multitrack file as uncompressed stereo audio file.[8] Confirm track list. Send press release to school district and media outlets. Create a master CD and send to duplication service, along with CD art.
- **Days 18–22:** Now that the tracks are complete, the class can turn fully to other (mainly business) matters, including planning the CD launch event, setting up sales points (concerts, cafeteria, etc.) and signing up for sales shifts, creating and distributing flyers and posters, rehearsing tracks to be performed live at release event, and creating karaoke versions of selected tracks for singers to use at release event. Carry out marketing, advertising, and public relations plan. Other curricular elements, such as creating a podcast, may be put in service of public relations for the holiday CD.
- **Days 23–25:** CDs arrive from the duplicator. Sales officially begin with a release event. Continue to sell CDs as per marketing plan; however, the class moves on to other lessons/units since most of these tasks occur outside class time.

Example of Holiday CD Project Tracks

To hear examples of tracks from a holiday CD meta-project (*Parkland: A Season for Giving*) visit the companion Web site. Songs included as examples are

1. "This CD Needed a Hanukkah Song," original words and lyrics by Sam P. (**Web Ex. 5.3**).
2. "Spend All Night," original words and lyrics by Ed B. (**Web Ex. 8.2**).
3. "Carol of the Bells," arranged by Daniel I. (**Web Ex. 14.16**).
4. "Christmas Is So Much More," original words and music by Katie S. (**Web Ex. 14.17**).
5. "'Twas the Night Before Christmas," words by Clark Clement Moore and original music by Rich L. (**Web Ex. 14.18**).

Meta-project Example 1: Final Thoughts

At the end of the holiday CD project, each class member has contributed to at least one track on a CD purchased, and listened to, by hundreds in our school community. At the risk of sounding too saccharine, students also have the satisfaction of using their talents to contribute to making their community and world a better place.

Meta-project Example 2: Class Musical

In the final weeks of my AP music theory class, I charge my students with conceiving a self-directed final project. We begin by having a class meeting to dis-

---

8. The technical description of "Red Book" (Phillips/Sony) Compact Disc audio is stereo (two-channel), 16-bit sample resolution, and 44.1 kHz sampling rate.

cuss the options; I share examples of past years' final projects. After some preliminary brainstorming, one class hit upon the idea of writing a miniature musical drama, an operetta, based on something they had learned in science class: the parts of the digestive system! It was decided that they would compose for vocalists and instrumentalists drawn from their class as well as the music theory 2 class that met the following period.

The Libretto

A libretto for a class operetta, musical, and so on, may be original or borrowed. The spark that catapulted these students' work forward in a big way was hitting on the idea of having an original libretto written from the point of view of selected parts of the digestive system. Although I gave them much freedom, I still served as overseer and editor to help avoid major pitfalls, making sure things moved forward. I insisted that the text for each movement be compact, confined to a handful of lines. I knew with our time limitations that the only way for their musical settings to be colorful and expressive was to keep the text brief.

With such a fertile topic, the students were crafting fun, witty poetry for their assigned movements in no time. In the first movement, the Mouth urges, "Brush your teeth and keep me clean; floss and rinse with Listerine."[9] In the second movement, the Esophagus warns, "I'm the esophagus. I hope you chew your food because I don't want to suffocate. You will start to cough, your airway's blocked; can't yell for help, can't even talk, unconscious upon your plate!"[10] The Stomach growls hungrily in the third movement, "I am the Stomach, don't you forget. You'd better have that table set!"[11] In the fourth and final movement, both the Small and Large Intestines argue over who is more important:

Small Intestine: "I am the Small Intestine, I think there is no question. I am the best, at your behest, absorbing all the food you give me, 'till the Large Intestine pulls it down."

Large Intestine: "Small Intestine thinks she's best? I will put her to the test. Load the canons, drop the anchor! I will make it so much ranker now!"[12]

Setting the Text to Music

Because these students had lots of experience writing projects small and large, all they really needed was time: time to improvise, time to experiment and

---

9. "The Mouth," by Rachael H., from the operetta *The Digestive System* (Parkland High School AP Music Theory class project, spring 2009).

10. "Eh Soffa Guess," by Sam P., from the operetta *The Digestive System*.

11. "The Stomach," by Michael T., from the operetta *The Digestive System*.

12. "The Intestines," by Tyler S., from the operetta *The Digestive System*. Note the clever, though somewhat bawdy, euphemisms for what happens at the end of the digestive system!

295

develop ideas, time to meet with me for coaching, and time to rework and revise. The Web-based music notation application Noteflight allowed students to work in class and at home (**Web Ex 17.1** shows playback of the movement, "The Mouth," in Noteflight).[13] I was very impressed with the way students appropriately implemented many compositional devices. "The Mouth," written in an ebullient, quasi-Baroque manner, used a brief orchestral ritornello to begin and end. The three vocal parts (soprano, baritone, bass) employed imitative counterpoint. Both "Eh Soffa Guess" and "The Stomach" (for sopranos) made extensive but effective use of pedal point. Also, when the Stomach is recounting all the food he likes to eat, there is a clever quote of Rogers and Hammerstein's "My Favorite Things." "The Intestines" is a partner song: first we hear from the Small Intestine (a soprano), then the Large Intestine (a bass), and then the two complementary parts combine in a duet.

Rehearsal and Performance

After writing the four movements, performance parts were generated for the singers and members of the small orchestra. For two class periods the AP music theory and music theory 2 classes rehearsed. I directed while our student composers listened and reacted with suggestions. Finally, an in-class concert performance–videotaped and audio recorded[14] before a live audience of invited guests—capped off the project. I imported the video and audio into a digital movie application (iMovie), added titles and transitions, and produced a movie/DVD of the project, used to reflect on in class and sent home with each student.

You can view video of all four movements of *The Digestive System* at the companion Web site (**Web Exs. 2.1–2.4**).

Meta-project Example 2: Adaptations

Students with a less sophisticated command of conventional notation, such as those in the elementary grades, can still generate expressive music for a project like this. Michele Kaschub and Janice Smith suggest a scenario in which a teacher, "Mrs. McRae," helps her young elementary-age students invent melodic ideas for a song. The students improvise ideas; the teacher coaches them, records their intentions, and then refines and assembles the music:

> Slowly at first, children begin to sing ideas. After each idea is sung, Mrs. McRae echoes it in a strong voice and asks the class to repeat it, too. She jots each idea in solfège in her notebook. She is also recording the class

---

13. In the end, students imported their Noteflight files (as XML files) into Finale so they could do more with dynamics, articulations, lyrics, and especially part extraction.

14. A small, handheld digital video camera was operated by a student videographer. The audio recording was made by a student sound engineer with several microphones routed through an audio interface into a laptop running GarageBand.

so that she can focus on what the students are singing. . . . The children are encouraged to consider when ideas should repeat and when new ideas should be used to create interest. After about ten minutes of work, Mrs. McRae says, "Boys and girls, very nice work making up our song melody today. I will take all of your ideas and polish them up into one song for us to work on next week."[15]

Older elementary students might develop their own melodies, documenting their efforts to recall using alternate notation or audio recording.

Students might generate their own accompaniments using diverse means: clapping and stomping, hand percussion, Orff instruments, drum machine or pattern sequencer, DAW software using loops, creative music software (such as Band-in-a-Box or Groovy Music), strumming a guitar, or improvising on a keyboard synthesizer.

An adaptation to consider for students of any age is performance of their music by older, experienced musicians. Benefits of such an arrangement include allowing the young composers to write more demanding material, saving time in rehearsal of the works, and providing the opportunity for older players to offer helpful feedback (criticism, suggestions, etc.).

REFLECTION ACTIVITY

Consider the curricular models for integrating technology-centered creative activities in the music curriculum presented in this chapter.

1. Do you have experience using any of the three curricular approaches presented at the start of this chapter (independent lesson or activity, creative project or unit, or a more comprehensive creativity-based curriculum)? Describe a music course and grade level that you think is well suited for each.

2. Discuss the pros and cons of engaging music students in a meta-project. Try to think of a meta-project idea not mentioned in this chapter and describe.

3. The examples in this chapter involved creative musical activities for older students. What are some specific ways the second meta-project (class musical) might be adapted for use with younger students?

15. Kaschub and Smith, *Minds on Music*, 153.

CHAPTER 18
VARIOUS IMPLICATIONS

IN THIS FINAL CHAPTER I address several important implications presented by the idea of using technology to facilitate creative work in music education. They are (1) copyright considerations, (2) the creative output of teachers themselves, and (3) a discussion of common reservations teachers have about integrating technology.

COPYRIGHT CONSIDERATIONS

Teachers whose students engage in creative music projects need to be mindful of copyright implications. Those who have grown up accustomed to freely downloading and sharing digital media (music, movies, pictures, etc.) may have a hazy idea of what is appropriate when it comes to using protected material. Aside from the need to comply with copyright law to protect teachers and their school district, dealing with these issues as they arise provides a great opportunity for teaching students some valuable lessons regarding intellectual property. When a project involves arranging, recording, or disseminating existing musical material, some important criteria need to be addressed.

Fair Use

Fair use allows persons to employ protected material in a very limited way without a fee. Many educators incorrectly assume that they and their students may use protected music without restriction because it is education related and not for profit. However, for the use to be "fair," at least *three criteria* must be met. **First, the use should not be a substitute for or discourage normal sales of the material.** If the use you have in mind circumvents you or your students having to make a purchase, it probably is not fair use. Let's say you have personally purchased a great collection of drum and bass loops. It would not be right to copy those loops onto all the computers in your music tech lab at school so the kids could enjoy using them, even if they would be using them for a class project. Instead, you should have your school or district purchase the appropriate number of loop collections.[1]

Second, the use should be limited. If you are appropriating protected music for use in an educational project, it should be a very brief excerpt, not a complete work or movement. For instance, imagine a group of students is doing a composer podcast on the music of Beethoven. They want to include several audio examples of important works, including Beethoven's Fifth Symphony. Although the work is in the public domain, pretty much any good recording they are likely to find is not. If the students include the complete 1975 Deutsche Grammophon recording by Carlos Kleiber and the Vienna Philharmonic Orchestra in their podcast, anyone who downloads the podcast would have that recording without having paid for it. Even including the entire first movement crosses the line. Copyright law allows for educational use of up to 10%, but generally not more than 30 seconds, from a single work or stand-alone portion of the work (such as a movement). Including a 30-second sound clip from the opening movement of the Beethoven symphony would be okay and should be enough for students to make their point.

Third, the use should be noncommercial in nature. If students use Garage-Band to produce their own arrangement of Tito Puente's "Oye Como Va," which is then included on a CD of student work sold to parents as a fund-raiser for new equipment, a mechanical license must be secured. A mechanical license "is the right to record and distribute (without visual images) a song on a phonorecord for private use. Mechanical rights or a mechanical license must be obtained in order to lawfully make and distribute records, CD's and tapes."[2] Right now the statutory mechanical royalty rate is about 9 cents per song for songs up to five minutes in length. A mechanical license can be obtained by contacting the copyright holder (usually the music publisher) directly. Music teachers, however, often use the services of the Harry Fox Agency (www.harryfox.com) when they need to secure a mechanical license. Harry Fox adds a nominal charge for their services, but many busy educators find the administrative chores they are spared well worth the fee.

Let's say your middle school music recording club will be producing a CD to sell as a fund-raiser. There will be nine tracks: six original songs, and three "covers" of songs that are protected by copyright law. Assuming the three cover songs are each about four minutes long, and that you expect to sell 250 CDs, it would cost the club about $68 to license the music (9 cents × 3 songs × 250 units = $67.50), or about $115 if using the Harry Fox Agency (whose fee is

299

---

1. I do know of certain instances where software manufacturers have granted permission to educators to make limited copies, so it never hurts to ask.

2. "Customer Licensees: Common Music Licensing Terms," Website of the American Society of Composers, Authors and Publishers (www.ascap.com/licensing/termsdefined.html).

about $15 per song). If the club sold the CD for only $5.00, their gross sales would be $1,250 (250 units × $5 = $1250). Even with the Harry Fox Agency fee and a few miscellaneous expenses, the club would realize a net profit of about $1,000 ($1250 – $115 = $1,135).[3]

Sometimes, as they say, "money speaks louder than words." Conducting a recording project such as the one described above delivers a potent message: doing things the right way can still be a very profitable way.

Public Domain

There is a huge treasure trove of musical and other content that your students can use for free: works in the public domain. *Public domain* describes music that has been around so long that it is now fair game for anyone to use it without a fee. In general, under the U.S. Copyright Act of 1976, music enters the public domain 70 years after the death of the composer.[4] Whether or not a work is in the public domain depends on when it was created, whether its copyright was renewed, and whether its creator has passed away. One good rule of thumb is as follows: **anything written in the United States before 1923 is in the public domain.**

Students looking to incorporate public domain content—audio files, MIDI files, sound effects, still pictures, or videos—in class projects can find much from which to choose at websites like the Internet Archive (www.archive.org).

Learning More

Copyright law as it pertains to music education in general, and specifically with regard to content used and created by students in music courses, has many variables and implications. *The Teacher's Guide to Music, Media, and Copyright Law*, by James Frankel (2009) is the best resource I have seen devoted to the topic of copyright considerations for twenty-first-century music teachers. I have it on my shelf at school and have found it a valuable reference for practical situations I encounter each year. As Frankel says in the introduction to his book, "As we move forward into the 21st century, and as technology causes the law to adapt, we as educators must be informed digital citizens. Perhaps more important, the students we teach will have to be informed consumers of copyrighted materials."[5]

---

3. More if the teacher or a student contacts the copyright holder (publisher, etc.) and gets them to waive the mechanical fee.

4. Note that recently published *arrangements* of music that would otherwise be public domain (Bach, Beethoven, Brahms, etc.) are protected.

5. James Frankel, *The Teacher's Guide to Music, Media, and Copyright Law* (Milwaukee: Hal Leonard, 2009), xxi.

TECHNOLOGY UNLOCKING CREATIVITY IN MUSIC TEACHERS

Another wonderful implication of the way technology unlocks creativity can be seen in twenty-first-century music teachers themselves. Facility with technology has led many music educators, reveling in these new tools, to a burgeoning of artistic and pedagogical creative activity. I have experienced this personally and witnessed it in the work of colleagues. For many music teachers, notation software kick-starts composing and arranging; skill with multimedia elements, text editors, and slide show programs yields great-looking desktop publications and presentations; easy-to-use sequencing and recording software—and the associated hardware (synthesizers, microphones, etc.)—motivates music production; and tools for web content and multimedia creation have released a floodgate of blogs, wikis, and podcasts. This is the power that technology has to unlock musical creativity.

Custom Arranging, Composing, and Producing

Examples of music teachers behaving creatively with technology include the custom arrangements and original compositions many are undertaking with computer music notation (CMN) software. Others are producing attractive accompaniment tracks using multitrack music production (MMP) software.

A fourth-grade band director wanting to include in her spring concert third graders who have been learning recorder spawns a unique band and recorder feature created with CMN software. The limited rehearsal time she has is not a problem as her composition only uses the B–A–G notes and simple rhythms she knows the kids have been taught. The recorders will practice to an accompaniment track made by saving the CMN file as audio. A fifth-grade chorus teacher uses MMP software to create a rehearsal accompaniment that frees her from the piano so she can work on choreography. Sequencing each voice part in a different track helps the kids gain confidence; when they are ready, those tracks can be muted. The MIDI sequence allows her to slow down the tempo when working on tough passages, and to motivate her students; she's even added electric bass and drum set tracks. A high school chorus director uses CMN software to put together a lovely, lush arrangement of a favorite folk song to use in both his upcoming concert and as an audition piece for next year's select chorus. The arrangement is posted on the chorus website or wiki—both in PDF format to download and print, and as a MIDI or MP3 file to hear—for students to learn.

Example: Elementary Band and Strings Concert Finale

Where I teach, fifth-grade (second-year) instrumentalists from our eight elementary schools assemble on our high school stage for a districtwide band and

301

strings concert. After performing separately, both groups combine for a finale to close the concert. Since there is very little repertoire for combined band and strings, we usually put CMN software to work, either writing our own combined finale or adapting an existing arrangement to include parts for the missing band or string parts. This year we adapted a published patriotic band arrangement by creating parts for strings. A few years back we adapted a published full orchestra arrangement by creating parts for the missing winds (such as tenor sax and baritone) and percussion we desired. Last year I wrote a Dixieland jazz piece for our finale that featured as soloists each of our secondary instrumental directors: our high school band director on snare (with brushes), one of our middle school band directors on clarinet, the other middle school director on trumpet, and our middle school strings director on violin. All four instrument families (percussion, woodwind, brass, and strings) are represented by the soloists. The piece, called "In the Cool Department,"[6] was designed to help our elementary players transition to the intermediate level by introducing them to their future directors. A few years before that, I wrote a combined finale for band, strings, and basketball team! Our basketball team—composed of district physical education and music teachers—functioned as a featured percussion unit, dribbling and slapping rhythmic patterns along the front of the stage. You can see an excerpt of a performance of the piece, called "Slam Jam!,"[7] at the companion website (**Web Ex. 18.1**).

Multimedia Presentations

Multimedia includes podcasts, PowerPoint-type slide presentations, movies, interactive websites and wikis, and more. An elementary general music teacher creates a popular blog to share her successes and challenges with colleagues around the world. An elementary band director produces his own series of videos explaining the basics of instrument repair to post on his band program website for students and parents. A middle school general music teacher produces weekly podcasts with GarageBand to share with families what his class has been doing. Many (mostly secondary) music teachers organize curricular and extracurricular content on creatively designed course or program websites and wikis.

Example: In Concert Video Conference With Composers

One of the most innovative, creative uses of technology I have witnessed was during a concert in May 2008 by the Mercer Middle-Senior High School Bands (Mercer High School, PA) and their director, Travis Weller. Weller had arranged

---

6. "In the Cool Department," by Scott Watson, is published by Wingert-Jones.

7. "Slam Jam!," by Scott Watson, is published by Alfred Publishing.

to have three composers of works he had programmed on hand during the concert to introduce their music via videoconferencing technology.[8] A gifted music technology specialist, Dr. Joseph Pisano (Grove City College, PA), helped Weller with the technical arrangements: the free Internet phone/videoconferencing program Skype was used on a laptop setup in the hall; the Skype audio was amplified for the audience, while video was projected to a large screen to the left of the stage. You can see a video excerpt from the concert, in which Weller interviews composer Brian Balmages about his work "Summer Dances," at the companion website (**Web Ex. 18.2**).

MAKING A WAY

In conversations with colleagues all over, I sense an increase in interest in using technology tools for creative music projects with students. Despite this, music educators voice several reservations about moving in this direction. These reservations—focusing on funding, technical know-how, and time—constitute a third area of implication.

Money for Hardware and Software

Some schools have very tight budgets for purchasing new equipment and software whether the economy is up or down. However, most schools today—even in economically depressed areas—have computers, if not in every classroom then at least in a computer lab or library. Using freeware applications such as Audacity (audio recording and editing), students can do a lot. If the computers are connected to the Internet, and in most cases they are, teachers and their students can use some of the exciting and increasingly functional web-based music applications.[9]

If your school does need technology hardware or software, I encourage you to get Tom Rudolph's book *Finding Funds for Music Technology*,[10] an excellent resource providing ideas for locating money for music technology purchases. Over the years, I have learned that one of the greatest ways to get assistance is to simply ask—reach out to school district administrators, local businesses, and national corporations to ask for funds to support music technology initiatives. You will not always get the answer you want, but sometimes you will be pleasantly surprised by the responses . . . responses you would never have gotten if you did not ask.

8. Participating composers were Brian Balmages (*Summer Dances*), Andrew Boysen (Symphony No. 4), and Scott Watson (*The Siege of Badon Hill*).

9. Such as Noteflight, iNudge, Audiotool, and Myna (see chapter 16).

10. Thomas E. Rudolph, *Finding Funds for Music Technology* (Melville, NY: SoundTree, 1999).

A resource for generating technology funding you might not have considered is your own students. The holiday CD meta-project described in chapter 17 raises money each year, most of which is donated to a deserving charity chosen by the students. When we first started the project, I asked my superintendent for permission to hold onto a few hundred dollars as "seed money" for the next year's project. Over the years, this has allowed us to purchase a microphone, handheld recorder, and other items used by the students during the course.

In addition, I have found that a handful of high-school-age students own their own laptops, microphones, multitrack music production software, audio interfaces, and more. Sometimes, with parent's permission, these can be incorporated into school projects.

Technical Ability and Training

It is true that it takes an incredible amount of training and practice to use programs such as Finale, Sibelius, Reason, or ProTools at their highest level. On the other hand, most kids can figure out what GarageBand is all about *intuitively*, with no formal instruction at all. Most new users of such programs as Audacity and Noteflight need only a few, basic instructions before they can set out on their own producing and creating. Software and web-based pattern sequencers such as O-Generator or iNudge, which produce such interesting musical figurations, can be learned literally in a few minutes. The trend in creative software and hardware is to hide the technical side of technology below the surface, so that users can work freely and intuitively above it all.

Technology for Music Education (TI:ME)

Nonetheless, formal training can be of great value. More and more undergraduate music education programs are including at least one "technology for music education" elective. As one who has participated in interviews for hiring new music staff for my school district, I strongly endorse taking such a course.

Music technology workshops and summer courses afford busy in-service music teachers the sort of concentrated interaction sometimes necessary for learning to stick. In many states, participation in such training helps educators meet professional development requirements. Technology for Music Education, known as TI:ME (www.ti-me.org), is the foremost organization focused on K–12 music education technology. Universities and other educational institutions in many states offer courses developed by TI:ME, taught by TI:ME-certified instructors, for using technology in music education. TI:ME's national, regional, and state conferences offer useful, level-appropriate clinics and workshops, and their website and newsletters are full of helpful articles. Especially as many states increase teacher professional development and continuing education requirements, consider attending a TI:ME conference or participating in a training course.

Time

This is the biggie—there never seems to be enough time. The idea of adding more content to an already crammed curriculum is unthinkable. That is why I advocate *using creative activities and projects to accomplish elements of your music curriculum that you must teach anyway*, replacing or updating traditional lessons with ones like those described throughout this book. Remember the three curricular approaches described in chapter 17: (1) independent lesson or activity, (2) creative project or unit, and (3) a more comprehensive creativity-based curriculum. Consider which approach is right for the music courses you will teach (both in terms of content and schedule) and your comfort level with music-related technology.

About one thing I am certain: Whether you use technology to augment your music teaching with one creative activity or build an entire course around technology-centered creative music projects, your students will be glad you did! I think you will be too.

REFLECTION ACTIVITY

This chapter examined three implications for using technology in creativity-based music learning: copyright considerations, the creative output of teachers, and ideas for getting past several areas of reservation.

1. Take a moment to reflect on how you or your music program use music protected by U.S. copyright law. Do you arrange, record, copy, broadcast, post to the Internet, or repurpose in any way music that is not in the public domain? Does this use meet the guidelines for "fair use"? If not, what adjustments need to be made to bring this use into compliance?

2. Can you describe any creative output (either pedagogical and/or artistic) of your own or a music educator colleague you know that was facilitated by technology?

3. What, if any, are your greatest reservations to engaging in creative activities with your students? How might you get past these reservations to make way for a shift toward that goal?

APPENDIX 1
COMPUTER MUSIC WORKSTATION

A BASIC COMPUTER MUSIC WORKSTATION typically consists of (1) a computer to run music software, (2) a keyboard controller or synthesizer for inputting or triggering musical events or data, (3) an interface for relaying and translating musical data between the keyboard and the computer (and visa versa), (4) an instrument source for realizing musical data triggered by the software (such as keyboard synth sounds or software instruments), and (5) a means of monitoring the sound output from components of the workstation (such as headphones or monitor speakers). Additional add-ons include a sustain pedal for the keyboard, a USB microphone for recording audio, and/or an audio interface with inputs for recording electronic instruments. While this may seem a bit complicated, it's really not. The trend over the years with computers and peripherals has been toward standardization and "plug-and-play" simplification.

COMPONENTS

Fig. A1.1 shows the components and configuration of a basic computer music workstation. Let's examine the components in the diagram first.

1. Computer: The desktop or laptop computer is the central hub of the workstation. Not only does it run software applications (music and otherwise) and web applications (in a browser), but it also has an on-board audio system (sound card) and various ports (USB, FireWire, etc.) and jacks (1/8-inch stereo in and out). It may have a built-in microphone, video camera, and/or built-in speakers, and its QWERTY keyboard can be used as an input device by many music applications.

2. MIDI keyboard: As described in chapter 12, MIDI keyboards have become the predominant input device for entering musical data (notes, durations, intensities, etc.) either in real time or step time. A MIDI keyboard may have on-board instrument sounds or just serve as a controller for entering or triggering musical events. If the former, some means of hearing the audio output of the keyboard must be employed (headphones, amplifier, etc.). The latter, using software instrument sounds involves only the audio output of the computer that "hosts" them.

3. Headphones: Stereo headphones allow a single user to monitor the audio output of the computer and/or a keyboard synthesizer. In most music education scenarios, with multiple workstations, this is preferred. A headphone splitter, which turns a single headphone jack into two, allows students to work in pairs.

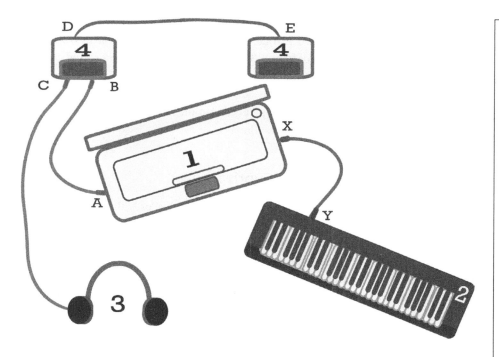

▶ **FIG. A1.1**

A typical computer music workstation. Illustration by Andrea Hegedus and Scott Watson. Used with permission.

4. Monitor speakers: When you want the sound from a workstation to be heard by the class, the audio may be routed to a pair of powered monitor speakers. Monitor speakers, which are essentially a pair of small amplifiers, can be very basic or quite sophisticated. At the least, they will have a volume control knob and a jack for plugging in an input source. For maximum flexibility, I always look for monitor speakers that include a headphone jack (in case you or students want to work alone) and multiple audio inputs (1/8-inch stereo plug, stereo pair of RCA plugs, etc.). Sometimes the amplifier for a pair of monitor speakers resides in just one of them, called the "head." In this case, an audio cable (shown from D to E in **Fig. A1.1**) connects the second speaker to the head.

CONNECTIONS

Now let's look at the several useful ways to connect components in a computer music workstation.

As Shown, with Keyboard Controller

The workstation configuration shown in **Fig. A1.1** allows for the user to work with MIDI applications such as GarageBand and Finale (1) using a keyboard controller as an input device, (2) relying on software instrument sounds, and (3) monitoring playback either privately with headphones or publically with monitor speakers. The laptop computer (**1**) is connected to the MIDI keyboard controller (**2**) via a USB cable (**X to Y**).[1] Note that the

---

1. The *USB* (Universal Serial Bus) cable is the most common used for MIDI. These are bidirectional, meaning data can pass back and forth between keyboard and computer on the same cable. Most keyboard controllers and synths these days have a built-in USB MIDI interface.

actual MIDI interface is built into the keyboard.[2] Sound emanating from audio and MIDI software running on the computer is routed to the monitor speakers via an 1/8-inch stereo cable (**A to B**). Without the headphones (**3**) plugged in, the computer's sound comes from the monitor speakers. However, to monitor the sound privately, plug the headphones into the headphone jack (**C**) on the monitor head.

I also prefer to have a sustain pedal plugged into the keyboard (not shown) to provide more expressivity when recording in real time.

As Shown, with Keyboard Synth

If the user is working with basically the same setup as above, only there is a keyboard synthesizer instead of a controller, a slight modification needs to be made. To be able to hear the on-board sounds emanating from the synth, an audio cable (not shown) needs to be connected from the keyboard to the monitor speakers. A *simple* way to do this is to connect an 1/8-inch phone plug from the keyboard's headphone jack to a second audio input jack (usually on the rear) of the monitor head. In this way, all sound coming from the computer and the keyboard synth will be mixed in the monitor speakers.

Basic Setup, Without Monitor Speakers

A more modest, and simpler, computer music workstation can be created with just the computer (**1**) and keyboard controller (**2**). In this case, all the connections would be as they are above except that the headphones (**3**) would be plugged directly into the computer's audio OUT jack (**A**). The only public playback in this scenario would be via the computer's built-in speakers when the headphones are not plugged in.

Microphones and Other Audio Input

Although not shown, it is easy to add a microphone to a basic computer music workstation. USB microphones can be plugged into an available USB port on the computer. XLR microphones and electronic instruments that use cables with 1/4-inch plugs (such as guitar, bass) can be routed through a USB audio interface box that also plugs into an available USB port.[3] Also, some keyboard controllers double as audio interfaces complete with built-in XLR and 1/4-inch phone jacks (usually on the back). The same USB cable that connects these keyboards to the computer relays MIDI and audio data.

2. For older keyboard synths without a built-in USB MIDI interface, a separate (external) USB MIDI interface box is necessary. These keyboards have ports for two 5-pin MIDI cables (MIDI IN and MIDI OUT). MIDI cables allow data to pass in one direction only (that is, either from keyboard to computer, or from computer to keyboard). One MIDI cable is connected from the keyboard's OUT port to the interface's IN port; a second MIDI cable is connected from the interface's OUT port to the keyboard's IN port. Note the pattern: OUT-to-IN and IN-to-OUT. On the other side of the MIDI interface box, a standard USB cable goes between the box and the computer.

3. If a USB port is not available, an inexpensive USB port *hub* can be used to multiply a single USB port.

APPENDIX 2
HOW DIGITAL AUDIO WORKS

BASICS OF SOUND RECORDING

HUMANS PERCEIVE SOUND WHEN THINGS VIBRATE at a frequency and amplitude that is detectable to them. *Frequency* is the rate at which things vibrate and corresponds to pitch. It is expressed in *hertz*, or cycles per second. Pitched (or harmonic) sounds vibrate at a regular, periodic rate. Nonpitched sounds, such as noise, have more random vibrations. The frequency of the A above middle C on the piano is approximately 440 hertz, for instance. If anything—whether it is a guitar string or a rubber band—vibrates consistently at that rate, you will sense you are hearing the A above middle C. *Amplitude* is the strength of the sound and corresponds to volume. Sometimes the term *decibel* is used to describe amplitude. A zero-decibel sound is undetectable; a 100-decibel sound—like that you would hear standing near a jet engine—causes pain to one's ears!

The physical vibrations of an object (such as a guitar string or a singer's vocal chords) cause quick fluctuations in the air molecules around them, producing waves of *compressions* (molecules bunching up) and *rarefactions* (molecules expanding) that move through the air. The quicker the vibration, the higher the frequency (or pitch). The stronger the vibration, the greater the swing or fluctuation, and therefore the greater the amplitude or volume.

ANALOG VERSUS DIGITAL

We often hear the term "analog" with reference to older recording technology, yet it is very relevant to digital recording. *Analog* is, in one sense, the opposite of digital and refers to continuously changing values (as opposed to the discretely changing ones—ones that change in steps—in the digital realm). For instance, imagine you are turning up a volume dial on a sound producing device. Let's say this dial is labeled 1 (softest setting), 2, 3, 4, 5, 6, 7, 8, 9, and 10 (loudest setting), but you can sweep the dial to any position on or in between these numbers. Theoretically, there are an infinite number of settings for the dial in between 1 and 2, or 2 and 3, and so forth. Now imagine a dial that "clicks" or locks into place only at the numbers 1, 2, 3, and so on, instead of sweeping continuously—you can set the volume to 1, 2, 3, and so forth, but nowhere in between. On this dial there are only 10 discrete settings. This is digital, and from this example it does not seem as good as analog, does it? But let's get back to our vibrating object.

Analog Recording

Perhaps the waves emanating from the vibrating object (or objects) are on their way to a listener's ear, or a microphone that will record them. Either way, some membrane such as an ear drum or a microphone ribbon will intercept the waves and begin vibrating too, swaying back and forth at a rate and strength *analogous* to the original sound. The nerve endings connected to the ear drum (and other parts of the ear) process this sound in a way similar to the wires, magnet, and other electronics connected to a microphone ribbon. As the microphone's membrane swings quickly back and forth in response to the sound waves coming at it, the attached electronics produce a varying-voltage electronic signal *analogous* to the original sound.

In an analog recording scenario, the fluctuating voltage sent from the microphone can be recorded on magnetic tape (or some other medium). The voltage fluctuation is documented *continuously* for every moment of the recording onto the magnetic tape; there is never a time for which the signal strength is not recorded. Also, the strength (amplitude) of the voltage fluctuation is precisely documented regardless of level; there is no level that is not described.

Digital Sampling

In a digital recording scenario, the fluctuating voltage sent from the microphone is sent to an analog-to-digital converter, or ADC. This device, perhaps housed in an audio interface box, takes "snapshots," or *samples*, of the continuously changing amplitude levels at frequent, regular time intervals. The number of amplitude levels to which a sample can be assigned is called the *sample resolution*. The rate at which samples are taken is called the *sampling rate*. The sampling rate for commercial compact disks (CDs) is 44,100 hertz (44.1 kHz). This means the ADC samples the signal from the microphone 44,100 times every second, each time assigning and storing in memory a particular amplitude level. That's a lot of amplitude records (or samples) in just one second!

Sample Resolution

Remember, the job of the ADC is to convert an audio signal from the analog to the digital realm. Every 1/44,100th of a second, when the ADC records and stores the amplitude levels, it stores them *as numbers*. These numbers are stored digitally in a computer's (or recording device's) hardware memory as bits.[1] It turns out that with n bits you can store 2^n values. A single bit (2^1) offers just two values—a 1 or 0—to which to assign an amplitude sample from a signal. This means that it records the voltage all the way on (1) or all the way off (0). Obviously, one-bit amplitude resolution is pretty course! Even four bits (2^4), offering 16 different levels to which the voltage may be assigned, is far too crude a resolution to describe with any detail an audio signal. **Fig. A2.1** shows a continuous (analog) sine wave and the same wave sampled digitally in four-bit resolution. The dynamic range (loudest to softest sound in a system) is reflected in the vertical aspect of the graph, which is divided into the 16 levels available with four bits. The way actual amplitudes along the original sine wave are forced to the nearest of the 16 levels is called quantizing (rounding). The difference between any of

---

1. *Bit* is short for binary digit. Eight bits form a *byte*.

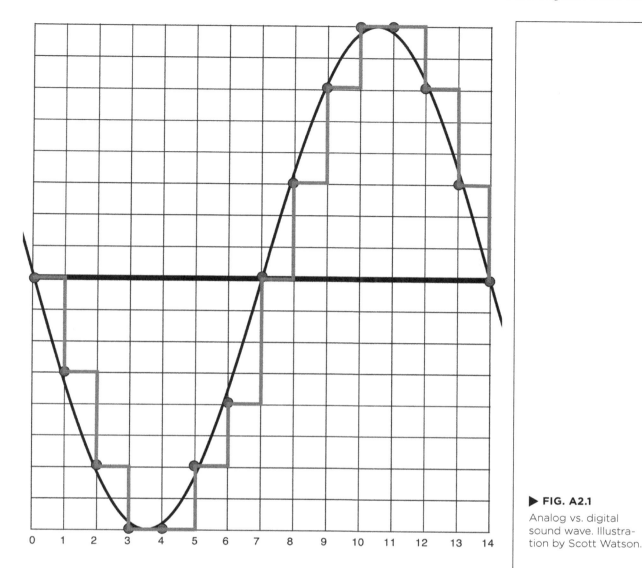

▶ **FIG. A2.1**

Analog vs. digital sound wave. Illustration by Scott Watson.

these quantized amplitude values and the actual amplitude of the sine wave at that time is digital noise (sometimes called quantizing noise). Obviously, the more bits a device can devote to describing amplitudes of samples, the truer the sound and the less digital noise.[2]

Commercial CDs allow for 16-bit resolution (2^{16}), meaning that each amplitude sampled and stored can be assigned to one of 65,536 levels. All this to say that the ADC samples the analog audio signal coming into it at time intervals and stores them as a string of numbers representing amplitude values. This string of numbers describes the waveform, and although it is still an approximation in discrete steps of the continuous analog sound wave, the average listener cannot tell the difference when the sample resolution is great enough (as with CDs).

2. Without going into the gory details, it turns out that for every bit used to store amplitude sample values in a digital system, you reduce the digital (quantizing) noise by 6 dB (decibels). An eight-bit recording device has a dynamic range of 48 dB; the ratio of the loudest sound it can represent to the noise floor (barely audible) is 48 dB (8 bits × 6 dB). For a 16-bit system, the loudest sound is 96 dB above the noise floor. With 16-bit resolution, noise created by quantizing (96 dB softer than the signal) is basically unnoticeable.

Memory

Memory is a factor that directly affects the cost of all sorts of digital devices, from computers, to synth keyboards, to storage media. Take the example of a synth keyboard which stores its on-board sounds as samples in built-in memory. While longer, higher resolution samples sound much better, they also require more memory to store.

A fairly straightforward formula can be used to calculate digital memory:

$$\text{Time} \times \text{Sample Rate} \times \text{Resolution} \times \text{Channels} = \text{Memory}$$

Notes:

1. Time, the length of the digital recording, is in *seconds*.

2. Sample rate, the number of amplitude readings taken per second, is a frequency (in *hertz*).

3. Resolution, how accurately an amplitude level can be recorded, depends on the number of *bytes* (8 bits) allotted to each sample. With n bits, an amplitude can be recorded on any of 2^n levels.

4. Channels, usually one (monaural) or two (stereo).

As an example, let's figure out how much memory it takes to record a minute of audio at conventional CD-quality specifications. The time, at one minute, is 60 seconds. The sampling rate for CDs is 44,100 hertz. The sample resolution is two bytes since the specification for CDs samples is 16 bits. Finally, since CDs are in stereo, they use two channels. Here is the memory calculation using the formula:

$$60 \text{ seconds} \times 44,100 \text{ hertz} \times 2 \text{ bytes} \times 2 \text{ channels} = 10,584,000 \text{ bytes}.$$

As you can see, one minute of CD-quality audio requires about 10.5 megabytes of memory storage.

APPENDIX 3
MUSIC EDUCATION TECHNOLOGY GLOSSARY

This glossary includes terms used throughout the book and those you will likely encounter when working with the various kinds of music technology employed for the lessons, activities, and projects described. I have tried to keep the definitions and explanations straightforward, using as little technical jargon as possible.

AIFF   Audio Interchange File Format: Format for storing sampled sound developed by Apple and used on Macintosh computers. AIFF is uncompressed audio; fidelity is high. File size is large, about 10 MB (megabyte) for every minute of recorded audio. These files have the extension .aif or .aiff.

Amplitude   The strength of a (sound) signal.

Analog   In electronic recording, a system that allows the voltage of the signal to vary (up and down) continuously with the sound pressure (from the microphone or going to a speaker) or an electronic musical signal from an electric instrument (guitar, bass, keyboard, etc.).

Application   Also "software application": Software designed for a specific task.

Audio interface   Using an analog-to-digital converter (ADC), an audio interface allows a signal recorded with a microphone or from an electronic instrument to be sent to recording software on a personal computer.

Audio range   For humans, about 20 through 20,000 hertz (Hz).

Auto-Tune   Popular audio processing software (by Antares Audio Technologies) and DAW plug-in that can tune recorded vocal and instrumental pitches to the nearest semitone. It is also used to distort human vocals, making them sound "metallic" or "robotic." The term *auto-tune* has come to be used as a verb when referring to its application to recordings ("Her voice has been auto-tuned").

Blog   Short for web log: Basically, an online journal that allows users to make posts incorporating text, images, audio, video, web links, and more. The Web 2.0 interface makes it easy to create and manage a blog with no knowledge of specialized code (such as HTML). Subscribers to the blog are notified when new posts are added and can comment on them.

Break point   With audio recording software, a point of articulation entered along a track's automation line. Each breakpoint allows for an automated change of direction in volume, pan position, or some other parameter during playback.

CD-R   "Compact disk–recordable": A recordable compact disk. Audio or other files can be copied onto the CD-R from a computer, after which the disk is finalized, making its content permanent. This process is known as "burning" the CD. A CD-RW ("compact disk–rewritable") can be unfinalized after burning.

Chorus   An electronic effect that modifies a signal to emulate a section sound (string section, choral voices, etc.) by replicating/detuning and more.

Clipping   When a device cannot accommodate a signal's maximum voltage or current requirements (such as when the amplifier output is overloaded or its input is overdriven), so named because the waveform appears to have a flat top.

'Comping   Short for "accompanying": Chordal accompaniment within a stylistically appropriate rhythmic groove played from a chord chart (as opposed to traditional notation). Used primarily by keyboardists and guitarists in jazz and popular music.

Compression   Squashing the high peaks of an audio signal, reducing the overall dynamic range. Compression is often used in combination with gain to raise the strength of the overall signal.

Controller   A device that allows music performance data to be entered into a MIDI program but that (in the strictest sense) does not have any sound-producing components. The controller depends on sounds coming from either some software or other hardware device. The most common controller sold and used is a keyboard controller. Keyboard controllers may be full sized (88-keys), mid-sized (61-, or 76 keys) or smaller (49- or 25- keys). Any MIDI-capable synthesizer, however, is a controller since its keys can be used to enter notes.

There are MIDI controllers available for string players (both violin family and guitars), wind players, and percussionists that allow for recording performance data into MIDI programs, but they are not very prevalent in K–12 music due to their expense and the time required to become fluent with the technology. A MIDI wind controller, for instance, looks like a space-age, high-tech recorder and allows the player to use a fingering system similar to that of a flute or saxophone to play MIDI data into tracks of programs such as GarageBand.

Decibel   Commonly used as a measure of sound intensity, it is technically a *ratio* representing the comparison of two power values. Zero decibels is at the threshold of hearing. Comparatively, a quiet whisper is around 30 dB, normal speech around 60 dB, a loud rock concert about 100 dB, and a jet airplane taking off is about 120 dB (and painful). The decibel scale is logarithmic rather than linear. A sound that is 10 times more intense represents a 10 dB change, 100 times more intense is 20 dB, 1,000 times more intense is 30 dB, and so on. Of course, distance and frequency (since we are not equally sensitive in every frequency range) greatly affect human perception of loudness.

Digital audio   Representing sound in discrete (steps, rather than continuously as in "analog") values.

Digital Audio Workstation (DAW)   A single software application that allows for many aspects of multipart music production, including, most notably, audio and MIDI recording, editing, and mixing; applying digital signal processing effects; and use of audio and MIDI loops. It is assumed that a DAW system has accompanying hardware for translating an audio signal from the analog domain (voice sung into a microphone, guitar output from a patch cord, etc.) into the digital domain. This sort of analog-to-digital converter might be as uncomplicated as a simple USB ("plug-and-play") microphone or as sophisticated as a Firewire audio interface with inputs for multiple XLR (typical microphone) and 1/4-inch phone (typical guitar, synth keyboard) plugs. The most ubiquitous DAW application in music studios around the world is indisputably ProTools, but there are many other professional (Mac OSX: Logic, Digital Performer;

Windows: SONAR) and entry-level (Mac OSX: GarageBand; Windows: Mixcraft) programs that serve school programs well.

Digital signal processing (DSP)   The manipulation and modification of signals in the digital domain. Today's DSP enhancements are a carry-over from analog features. A distinction is made between effects and processors. *Effects* are added to the original signal, while a *processor* changes the original signal. Examples of effects include reverb, echo, delay, chorus, phasing, flanging, and pitch shifting. Examples of processors include equalizers (EQ), gates, and compressors. In the digital realm, the distinction between effects and processors is blurred since these alterations can be made "nondestructively." A digital audio stream is in essence a series of numeric values representing the amplitudes of successive samples. Applying digital effects to the signal consists of running the series of numbers through an equation (as opposed to an analog effects processor unit).

Dynamic range   Comparison of the softest to the loudest sound of a system. A full orchestra may have a dynamic range of 90 dB.

Envelope   The shape of a sound, usually described in stages: attach, decay, sustain, release (ADSR). Better synthesizer keyboards allow the user to edit the stages of the envelope to alter the sound.

Equalizer (EQ)   Allows the user to amplify or attenuate various frequency regions, sometimes called "bands" (say, 100 through 1,000 Hz). Multiband EQ allows the user to set the levels for each of the defined bands. For example, a thin vocal sound can be filled out by boosting the bass frequency bands and pulling back a bit the extreme high frequencies.

Feedback   Unwanted, self-referencing loop between a microphone and a speaker in the same system. Either the volume for the amplifier is set too high, or the microphone is placed too close to the amp. Also called *regeneration*.

Filter   In digital recording, a process that rejects or attenuates certain frequency components of a signal. By eliminating some of the spectral content, you can alter the timbre subtly or greatly. Filters may be low pass (allows only frequencies below a threshold), high pass (allows frequencies above a threshold), or band pass (allows frequencies between a low and high limit). Depending on the software, you may be able to control parameters such as the filter's center frequency and the range of the area to be attenuated (bandwidth).

Firewire   Apple Computer's name for the "IEEE 1394" serial interface cable/connection, used for high-speed serial communications and real-time data transfer with many computers. At about 800 megabits per second, Firewire 800 transfers data at roughly twice the speed of Firewire 400. Each have a unique connector, but Firewire 800 is backward compatible. An adapter cable can be employed when using Firewire 400 equipment with a computer that has a Firewire 800 jack.

Flange   This effect produces a swooshing sound, originally accomplished by splitting the signal into two identical versions; applying a constantly varying, short delay (usually 2 to 15 milliseconds) to the signal; and mixing the altered signal with the original. The name comes from the act of pressing a finger against the flange of a reel-to-reel tape deck's supply reel to slow it down, causing the delayed signal to be out of phase with the original.

Freeware   Free software application available for downloaded from the Internet.

Frequency   Measure of the rate of a periodic (regular rate) vibration, in hertz (cycles per second). The frequency of a sound is inversely proportional to its *period* (the time it takes to complete a single cycle of the sound wave; see below). That is, $F = 1/P$, where F is frequency and P is period. For example, if it takes 0.01 seconds (1/100th of

315

a second) for one complete cycle of the waveform to occur, then the frequency is 100 hertz (1/0.01).

Frequency response Description of the way the gain of a system responds to a frequency stimulus. For instance, various microphones have differing frequency responses, causing them to color the sound differently according to the frequency spectrum they allow.

Fundamental The lowest, and with acoustic sounds the dominant, frequency heard in the spectrum of a particular sound.

Gain The amount of increase in the power of a signal by an amplifier.

Harmonic series The fundamental and all overtones of a sound. All the members of this series are called *partials*.

Hertz Cycles per second, abbreviated "Hz."

Interactive whiteboard Device that projects an enlarged image of a computer display onto a whiteboard but allows the user to interact with the image, just as he or she would with a mouse on a computer, by touching the board. A popular interactive whiteboard is the SMART Board.

Keyboard controller MIDI-capable keyboard without on-board sounds that allows note data to be played or entered into MIDI programs (such as GarageBand and Finale). Typically, controllers depend on the software being used to produce the instrument sounds desired. Keyboard controllers come in different sizes (25-key, 49-key, etc.) and with various other features (limited on-board sounds, built-in audio interface, tap pads for triggering drum sounds, etc.) which affect cost.

LED Light-emitting diode: An electronic light source technology used for text and video displays on many electronic devices, including synth keyboards.

Loops Short, musical gestures whose repetition is facilitated by music production software. Most loops involve recordings (audio) or sequences (programmed MIDI) of rhythm instruments (percussion, bass, guitar, etc.) performing some groove element. The tempo and pitch (if applicable) of loops may be easily adjusted, independent of one another, using the host music production software.

Matrix pattern sequencer *See* Pattern sequencer.

Microphone An electro-acoustical device that delivers an electric signal when actuated by, and analogous to, a sound. A microphone consists of an acoustic system which supplies mechanical energy to a transducer, which is then converted into electrical energy.

There are many types/variables of microphones: dynamic (close range), compressor (more detail, farther away), omnidirectional (equal signal from any angle), unidirectional (cardioid and super cardioid, long range), those requiring phantom power (some extra preamplification, usually initiated in mixer or audio interface) and those not. Other parameters such as frequency response and dynamic range have practical recording applications.

MIDI Musical Instrument Digital Interface: The hardware and software standard protocol developed in 1984 that allows musical instruments, personal computers, and music software to interact with one another.

MIDI drum kit Refers to a mapping of different percussion sounds to each of the keys of the keyboard. Press a low C and get a bass drum, a D above that triggers a snare drum, the F-sharp above that is a hi-hat, and so on.

MIDI file more formally, standard MIDI file (SMF): Record of certain performance data including key number (such as key 60—middle C), note on and off timing (when in a measure a note starts and how long it lasts) and velocity (how hard a key was hit), channel number (different instrument sounds play back on different channels), program number ("patch," that is, a specific sound on a synthesizer), and much more. MIDI files may be saved and opened interchangeably by most MIDI applications, but a MIDI program's proprietary data (information specific to that software) will not be included. MIDI files require an instrument (hardware or software) to play them back and are not the same as audio files.

MIDI interface   For many years an external interface box that translates performance data flowing back and forth between a synth keyboard and a computer running music software. A serial cable connects the box to the computer; specialized MIDI cables go between the box and the keyboard's MIDI IN and OUT ports. While the benefits of MIDI are wonderful, many found negotiating this configuration daunting. Thankfully at this time it is far more prevalent for the MIDI interface to be built into the keyboard (synthesizer or controller), requiring only a USB cable to connect it to a computer.

Millisecond   One thousandth of a second (0.001 seconds).

Mixer   A device that allows several signals to be combined into one signal. Each source signal (such as 1/4-inch phone or XLR mic plugs) is assigned a channel (or channels), usually with independent control for volume level, pan position, and effects levels. The output, a stereo mix, is usually sent to monitor speakers, headphones, and/or a recording device.

Monaural (mono)   Recording to a single channel.

MP3   Short for "MPEG-1 Audio Layer 3" (where MPEG is the Moving Picture Experts Group): A sophisticated compression scheme for digital audio. Audio converted to MP3 remains very faithful to the original sound at about a tenth of the file size, about 1 MB (megabyte) for every minute of recorded stereo audio.

Noise   Sounds that cause random vibratory motion of molecules.

Normalize   This procedure raises the level of the highest peak to 0 dB and then raises all other parts of the signal by the same proportion. Normalizing is useful when a signal has been recorded at too low a level or when the volume is inconsistent throughout.

Onset   The beginning of a sound.

Overtones   Integer multiples of the frequency of the fundamental. For example, a sound with a fundamental frequency of 100 hz. has overtones at 200 hz., 300 hz., 400 hz., and so on.

Pan   Left-right position of the stereo image.

Partials   The members of a harmonic series; numbered in ascending order from the fundamental (1) on up through the overtone series.

Pattern sequencer   Software application or hardware device that triggers playback of sounds stored in any one of a series of equally spaced steps, called a *course*. Pattern sequencers provide a course for each sound (kick drum, snare drum, hi-hat, suspended cymbal, tom, etc.). Often the number of steps in a course can be set by the user, but 16—where each step is 1/16th of the course—is common. Rhythmic patterns are formed by selecting various steps. For instance, in a 16-step kick drum course, selecting the first, fifth, ninth, and thirteenth steps will play back as a steady beat. More sophisticated pattern sequencers also include settings for volume or intensity for each step in a course, allowing for accents. A *matrix pattern sequencer* is normally limited to a single timbre but offers both horizontal and vertical steps on an x-y grid, adding the dimension of pitch.

PDF   Portable Document Format: A ubiquitous file type created by Adobe for electronic exchange of documents. PDF files incorporate text, fonts, images, and layout independent of specific applications, operating systems, and platforms.

317

Period   Time it takes for one complete cycle of a periodic (regular rate) vibration. The period is inversely proportional to the frequency. That is, P = 1/F, where P is period and F is frequency. For example, take a sound with a frequency of 100 Hz. It takes 1/100 seconds (0.01 seconds) for one complete cycle of the waveform to occur.

Phone jack   The straight plug found at the end of guitar cables but also used to connect computer audio components. Phone jacks may be mono (one black insulator band on the plug) or stereo (two black insulator bands on the plug) and come in 1/4-inch or 1/8-inch sizes.

Pitch   The way humans perceive a regular, vibratory repetition that is faster than approximately 30 times per second. We say this sound is musical.

Pitch correction   Applied to a signal to correct the pitch of out-of-tune notes performed by vocalists. The most popular pitch correction plug-in, called Auto-Tune, was created by software manufacturer Antares. Its use by recording engineers is widespread.

Pitch shifting   Operation applied to an audio signal that raises or lowers the pitch (frequency) without affecting durations of recorded events (that is, rhythm or length of file). Likewise, you can shorten or lengthen audio without changing its frequency. Normally this process leaves certain timbral artifacts (altered spectral content).

Pop filter (or pop screen)   A screen, usually attached to a microphone stand, that stands between the microphone and a singer's mouth to eliminate the "popping" that results from spoken or sung "plosives" such as the hard "p" at the beginning of the word "pop."

Quantization error   Also called digital noise: The wide band noise resulting from the rounding of sample values in digital recording. When the sample resolution is high (such as 16-bit), the rounding is slight and quantizing noise is virtually imperceptible.

Quantizing (digital audio recording)   In digital recording, rounding the actual value (analog) of an amplitude measure to the nearest value represented by the digital system (due to its bit resolution).

Quantizing (rhythm with MIDI software)   When applied to MIDI performance data, quantizing is the rounding of rhythms played to the lowest subdivision of the beat or measure chosen. For instance, if you choose for a recording a quantizing value of a 16th note, any rhythm played into the software that is smaller will be rounded to the nearest 16th note. In other words, play a 32nd note ahead of the beat and the software will "fix it" so it sounds as if you did not enter early.

Ramp   A linear (straight-line) change in volume applied to automated fades (fade in, fade out).

Ratio   A comparison of two values, often expressed as "1:2," or as a fraction (such as "1/2"), or even as a decimal (such as "0.5").

RCA jack   Found on the end of many cables used with stereo equipment, usually red and white for stereo left and right. The "male" connector is a plug with a sleeve and connects to the "female" port, a knob with a hole.

Remixes, bootlegs, mashups   Creative arrangements that reassemble sectional elements (called *stems*) of commercial music recordings, usually combined with new rhythmic material (such as loops).

Resolution   In digital recording, the number of bits (or bytes) allocated to store each sample. One bit (2^1) allows for only two amplitude positions (on or off), two bits (2^2) allows for four different amplitude positions, eight-bit systems (2^8) allow for 256 different amplitude values, and so on. The higher the sample resolution, the less digital noise (quantizing).

Reverb   Short for "reverberation": The decaying residual sound that remains after a sound occurs, created by the sound's multiple reflections off of surfaces in an acoustical space. The time of reverberation is defined as the time it takes for the sound pressure level to decay to 1/1,000,000th (one millionth) of its former value. This is a 60 dB reduction. Adding digital reverb can liven up samples and alter the virtual acoustics of the space within which your digital audio exists, creating anything from subtle room ambience to the rich echo of a large stadium. Echo is a DSP effect similar to reverb.

Sample   In the strictest sense of the word, a sample is a digital record of the amplitude (strength) of a sound signal at a discrete point in time. Some use the term to mean a series of many consecutive samples, which constitutes a short digital recording of a note or musical phrase.

Sampling   Short, note-length recording of an instrument or other sound captured and played back in various ways by electronic instruments (keyboards, etc.) and sound modules. Often the middle of a sample (after the attack, but before the release) is looped or cycled to vary the playback duration and save on memory.

Sampling rate   In digital recording, the time interval between recording amplitude readings (samples). For compact discs, the sampling rate is 44.1 kHz.

Sequencer   MIDI software that records and plays back performance data for realization by a connected MIDI instrument. Basic performance data includes things such as program number (the sound), key number (the note), onset time, duration, note on velocity (intensity of attack), and volume. *Sequencing* is the act of programming this data, often in step time (as opposed to real time). More expressive data for things such as reverb level, pan position, and pitch bend can also be encoded and realized. Most MIDI recording and editing (sequencing) software is part of a multitrack environment that also allows for audio recording and editing.

Shareware   Low-cost software application available for download from the Internet.

Sibilance   Excessive loudness of vocal sibilants (such as the "sss" and "sh" sound). A de-esser is used to reduce this unwanted effect.

Signal-to-noise (S/N) ratio   Comparison (expressed in decibels) of the level of a signal to the level of inherent noise in the system. If a signal is 50 dB above the low-level noise, we say its S/N ratio is 50 dB.

Sound   Our subjective impression of the episodic perturbation (compression and rarefaction) of air molecules.

Spectrum   The sum of all the frequencies heard simultaneously in a (usually musical) sound. These composite frequencies are one of the major factors responsible for a sound's tone color (timbre).

Step recording   The process of programming performance data (notes, rhythms) into a MIDI program one event at a time, without a click track or other means of maintaining a steady beat. Normally, the user would choose a rhythm from a palette or keyboard shortcut (the number 4 equals a quarter note, etc.) and the note(s) from a MIDI keyboard or by clicking them in with a mouse on a staff (notation software) or graphic editor (sequencing software). Once step recorded, the music can be played back in real time to sound as if a live player had performed it.

Stereo   Two-channel (left and right) recording.

Synth   Common truncation of the term *synthesizer*. Keyboard synthesizers employ various sound synthesis (frequency modulation, pulse code modulation, etc.) and sampling technologies.

Timbre   The term used for the tone color, or quality, of an instrument's sound.

Time expansion/compression   Operation applied to an audio signal that shortens or lengthens it without changing its pitch content (frequency). Normally this process leaves certain timbral artifacts (altered spectral content).

Track   A separate, isolated, concurrent space for any recorded component of a multitrack audio/MIDI recording environment. Separate tracks may be used for separate instruments (piano, bass, guitar, etc.), but multiple tracks may also be used for the same instrument (for example, one track for recording the piano's right hand, one track for recording the piano's left hand, and one track for recording the piano's sustain pedal). "Track" is also used to refer to separate songs on a CD.

USB   Universal Series Bus: A cable/protocol for sending information via a cable serially. The current, USB 2.0, data transfer rate is about 400 megabits per second (roughly equal to Firewire 400). USB 2.0 is backward compatible to USB 1.0 (12 megabits per second, same jack).

Velocity   The time it takes for a key on a MIDI keyboard to go from the up to the down position when depressed; corresponds with dynamic level.

VGA   Video Graphics Array: Hardware and software protocol for video transmission and display used on many computers and computer projectors.

Video projector   Also Computer Video Projector or VGA Projector: Projects the video signal from a computer to a large presentation screen. Some video projectors have a built-in monitor speaker (and an audio-in jack), but much better sound can be achieved by connecting to a sound system or external, powered speakers.

WAV   Waveform audio file format, the format for storing (usually) uncompressed, digital audio on Windows/PC computers but is very similar to AIFF audio files.

Waveform   A graphic representation (picture) of a musical sound, consisting of a graph of amplitude (strength) over time.

Waveform editor   Digital audio software that allows the user to graphically view and manipulate an audio signal.

Web 2.0   Web 2.0 and the term "cloud computing" refer to the increasingly more interactive and dynamic places on the Internet for contributing content and accomplishing tasks. Web 2.0 is used to describe the online applications (programs)—such as web logs (blogs), wikis, and a variety of "social networking" tools—available to anyone with access to the Internet..Web 2.0 tools also include programs for word processing, creating spreadsheets, maintaining calendars, storing and editing photos, and even music notation and recording. Whereas a decade or so ago you needed technical knowledge to create a website, now even elementary school children can post to a wiki. Another characteristic of the "new" web are the many mobile devices that allow users to access and use all of this functionality.

Wiki   A website that allows multiple users/members to easily create pages, contribute and update content (text, images, audio, video, web links, and more), and participate in threaded discussions. The Web 2.0 interface makes it easy to create and manage a wiki with no knowledge of specialized code (such as HTML). The wiki administrator determines which other members can contribute content and at what level. Members of the wiki are notified when new content is added.

XLR cable   The most common connectors for connecting microphones to other sound equipment. XLR cables are balanced (reduces interference often introduced with longer lengths) and have a three-pin male plug on one end and a female plug on the other.

SELECTED REFERENCES

BOOKS/ARTICLES

Anderson, Lorin, and Krathwohl, David, eds., *A Taxonomy for Learning, Teaching, and Assessing: A Revision of Bloom's Taxonomy of Educational Objectives*. New York: Longman, 2001.

Bloom, Benjamin. S. *Taxonomy of Educational Objectives, Handbook I: The Cognitive Domain*. New York: Longman, 1956.

Burns, Amy. *Technology Integration in the Elementary Music Classroom*. Milwaukee: Hal Leonard, 2008.

Frankel, James. *The Teacher's Guide to Music, Media, and Copyright Law*. Milwaukee: Hal Leonard, 2009.

Franken, Robert E. *Human Motivation*, 3rd edition. Belmont, CA: Brooks/Cole Publishing, 1994.

Hodson, Robin, Frankel, James, Fein, Michael, and McReady, Richard. *Making Music with GarageBand and Mixcraft*. Florence, KY: Cengage Learning, 2011.

Kaschub, Michele, and Smith, Janice. *Minds on Music: Composition for Creative and Critical Thinking*. Lanham, MD: Rowman and Littlefield Education in partnership with MENC, 2009.

Langol, Stefani, Whitmore, Lee, Rudolph, Tom, and Richmond, Floyd. *Sequencing and Music Production*, Book 1 (Alfred's Music Tech Series). Van Nuys, CA: Alfred Publishing, 2007.

Levitin, Daniel J. *This Is Your Brain on Music*. New York: Penguin Group, 2006.

Levitin, Daniel J. *The World in Six Songs*. New York: Penguin Group, 2008.

Pink, Daniel H. *A Whole New Mind: Why Right-Brainers Will Rule the Future*. New York: Penguin Group, 2005.

Reese, Sam, McCord, Kimberly, and Walls, Kimberly, eds. *Strategies for Teaching: Technology* (MENC's Strategies for Teaching Series). Reston, VA: National Association for Music Education, 2001.

Richmond, Floyd, Rudolph, Tom, Whitmore, Lee, and Langol, Stefani. *Composing Music With Notation*, Book 1 (Alfred's Music Tech Series). Van Nuys, CA: Alfred Publishing, 2007.

Rinehart, Carroll, ed. *Composing and Arranging: Standard 4 Benchmarks*. Reston, VA: National Association for Music Education, 2002.

Robinson, Ken. *Out of Our Minds: Learning to Be Creative*. Oxford: Capstone, 2001.

Rudolph, Thomas E. *Finding Funds for Music Technology*. Melville, NY: SoundTree, 1999.

Rudolph, Tom, and Whitmore, Lee, Langol, Stefani, and Richmond, Floyd. *Playing Keyboard*, Book 1 (Alfred's Music Tech Series). Van Nuys, CA: Alfred Publishing, 2007.

Rudolph, Thomas E. *Teaching Music With Technology*, 2nd edition. Chicago: GIA Publications, 2004.

Rudolph, Tom, Richmond, Floyd, Mash, David, Webster, Peter, Bauer, William, and Walls, Kim. *Technology Strategies for Music Education*, 2nd edition, edited by Floyd Richmond. Wyncote, PA: TI:ME—Technology for Music Educators, 2005.

Ruthmann, Alex. "The Composers' Workshop: An Approach to Composing in the Classroom," *Music Educators Journal*, Vol. 93, No. 4 (March 2007): 38–43.

Sternberg, Robert J., and Williams, Wendy M. *How to Develop Student Creativity*. Alexandria, VA: Association for Supervision and Curriculum Development, 1996.

Stravinsky, Igor. *Poetics of Music in the Form of Six Lessons*. Cambridge, MA: Harvard University Press, 1970.

Vandervelde, Janika. *Music by Kids for Kids: Blueprints for Creativity: A Composing Curriculum*. Saint Paul, MN: American Composers Forum, 2007.

Varèse, Edgard, and Wen-chung, Chou. "The Liberation of Sound," *Perspectives of New Music*, Vol. 5, No. 1 (Autumn–Winter 1966): 11–19.

Watson, Scott, ed. *Technology Guide for Music Educators*. Boston: Thomson Course Technology, 2006.

Wiggins, Jackie. *Teaching for Musical Understanding*. New York: McGraw-Hill, 2001.

INTERNET

Dammers, Rick, and Williams, David B. *Music Creativity Through Technology*. Available: www.musiccreativity.org. June 1, 2010.

322

INDEX

323

329

Lightning Source UK Ltd.
Milton Keynes UK
UKOW07f0956130116

266322UK00014B/222/P